SCREENING NEOLIBERALISM

Screening Neoliberalism

Transforming Mexican Cinema, 1988–2012

Ignacio M. Sánchez Prado

Vanderbilt University Press
Nashville

© 2014 by Vanderbilt University Press
Nashville, Tennessee 37235
All rights reserved
First printing 2014
First paperback printing 2015
Fourth printing 2016

This book is printed on acid-free paper.

Library of Congress Cataloging-in-Publication Data on file
LC control number   2013034449
LC classification number   PN1993.5.M4S28 2014
Dewey class number   791.430972--dc23

ISBN 978-0-8265-1965-8 (hardcover)
ISBN 978-0-8265-1966-5 (paperback)
ISBN 978-0-8265-1967-2 (ebook)

Contents

Acknowledgments vii

Introduction: The Reinvention of Mexican Cinema 1

1. Nationalism Eroded: Mexican Cinema in Times of Crisis. 15

2. Publicists in Love: Romantic Comedy, Cinema Privatization, and the Aesthetics of the Middle Class 62

3. The Neoliberal Gaze: Reframing Politics in the "Democratic Transition" 105

4. The Three Amigos and the Lone Ranger: Mexican "Global Auteurs" on the National Stage 155

Conclusion: Mexican Cinema after Neoliberalism. 209

Notes 227

Bibliography 249

Index. 281

Acknowledgments

Writing a book about Mexican cinema means being in a state of dialogue and exchange with two wonderful scholarly communities: Mexicanists and Latin American film specialists. This book has benefited from constant conversations with members of both groups. At the expense of possibly forgetting someone, and realizing that very many colleagues touch one's work during a long-term project, I want to thank the following people (in strict alphabetical order) for the dialogues and debates, as well as for the invitations to present my work and for helping me work through some ideas and materials: Susan Antebi, Ericka Beckman, Steve Bunker, Irma Cantú, Cristina Carrasco, Gabriela Copertari, Rosana Díaz Zambrana, Linda Egan, Craig Epplin, Oswaldo Estrada, Sebastiaan Faber, Manuel Gutiérrez, Anne Hardcastle, Hermann Herlinghaus, Emily Hind, Robert McKee Irwin, Horacio Legrás, Ilana Luna, Joshua Lund, Misha MacLaird, Kathleen Newman, Dianna Niebylski, Anna Nogar, Joanna Page, Pedro Ángel Palou, Andrew Paxman, Ana Peluffo, Adela Pineda, Juan Poblete, Sarah Pollack, Sara Poot-Herrera, Brian Price, Carolina Rocha, Eva Karene Romero, Anne Rubenstein, Victoria Ruétalo, José Ramón Ruisánchez, Fernando Fabio Sánchez, Jacobo Sefamí, Georgia Seminet, Helena Simonett, Carolina Sinitsky-Cole, Nohemy Solórzano-Tompson, Sam Steinberg, Juana Suárez, Dolores Tierney, Patricia Tomé, José del Valle, John V. Waldron, Tamara Williams, Edward Wright-Ríos, and Oswaldo Zavala.

The research underlying this book was conducted at Washington University in Saint Louis, which has been a great source of institutional support. Two faculty research grants and a grant from the International and Area Studies Program funded parts of my research project. The support from the Offices of the Dean of Arts and Sciences and the Dean of the Graduate School, as well as the Office of the Provost, was invaluable. I want to thank my department chairs in Romance Languages (Elzbieta Sklodowska and Harriet Stone) and International and Area Studies (James V. Wertsch and Timothy Parsons) for their continuing support. A special mention is reserved for Mabel Moraña, my mentor and the director of Latin American Studies. She is always there for me, and my work has been personally, intellectually, and professionally influenced by her. My colleagues and the staff in Romance Languages and Literatures, International and Area Studies, and other areas of Washington University in Saint Louis provide an enviable academic context for any scholar. I deeply thank all of them.

The ideas in this book have been road-tested by a wonderful group of students, both graduate and undergraduate. I want to thank all the students in my Mexican Film in the Age of NAFTA seminar, who heard most of the arguments in this book and helped me make them better and more accessible. I also want to thank three students—Nadia Mann, Alyse Rooks, and Ania Wojtowicz—who helped me find archival materials as my volunteer research assistants. Another student, Olivia Cosentino, read parts of this book from the perspective of an undergraduate student and was instrumental in helping me make the book accessible. Four graduate students—Britta Anderson, Megan Havard, Sara Potter, and José Montelongo—helped at different stages of research and revision too. Finally, I want to thank Anna Eggemeyer's clinical eye for helping me catch those pesky language issues that I miss as a second-language speaker.

The ability to research Mexican cinema is tied to the wonderful work performed by many people in the country's cultural institutions. I need to recognize the Instituto Mexicano de Cinematografía (IMCINE), the Cineteca Nacional, and the Filmoteca de la UNAM, because their combined efforts make Mexican cinema available for scholarly inquiry. My mother, María del Carmen Prado, helped me find and secure many films and books when I was unable to conduct research on site, and she has become at times more apt in finding materials than myself. I also want to thank Vanderbilt University Press in general and Eli Bortz in particular for believing in this project and for being stellar and professional people to work with. The two readers of the manuscript were very generous in their endorsement and useful in their comments. Joell Smith-Borne was very helpful during the production process, and Peg Duthie did an exceptional job as a copyeditor. And of course, I want to thank my wife, Abby Hathaway, without whose love, personal support, and company I would have never been able to complete this book with success and sanity.

INTRODUCTION

The Reinvention of Mexican Cinema

Going to the movies in Mexico City in the mid-to-late-1980s was a unique—and uniquely surreal—experience. Most film theaters at the time were part of a State-owned conglomerate named Compañía Operadora de Teatros S. A. (COTSA), largely made up of huge single-screen venues scattered all over the city. Many of these sites had a long history. For instance, Cine Ópera, located in the working-class neighborhood of Santa María la Ribera, abandoned for many years afterwards, and now a concert venue, opened its doors as a cinema in 1949 with a seating capacity of about 3,500 spectators. Known as a jewel of Art Deco style, Cine Ópera premiered with a showing of *Una familia de tantas,* Alejandro Galindo's melodrama about the clash between traditional Mexican family values and the Americanized modernity of the time. From its inception, Cine Ópera was part of an important transformation in the practice of cinema that took place in the late 1940s and early 1950s, thanks to the tidal wave of modernization during the administration of President Miguel Alemán. Andrea Noble recalls this period: "Prompted by the formation of an emergent middle class, whose values were imitative to some large degree of North American cultural models, these films focused on the disintegration of traditional family bonds in the wake of modern social mores, displaying in so doing varying degrees of anxiety about the process" (102). *Una familia de tantas,* Noble argues, was peculiar because it offered "a more progressive narrative that endorses the positive benefits that modernity is implied to bring to the family and society more generally" (103). The fact that Cine Ópera opened with such a movie was telling: it was part of a wave of renewal in Mexican cinematic production and consumption made possible by an increasingly urbanized middle class.

By the late 1980s, the iconic status of Cine Ópera, as well as the memory of the cultural significance invested in its foundations, had disappeared. I personally remember going frequently to Cine Ópera as a child, mostly to see Hollywood movies of the day, thanks to the fact that the theater manager was an old friend of the family who allowed us to watch them for free. The experience of watching a movie there was both exciting and unpleasant. On the one hand, the theater presented the films on a magnificently large screen, which gave a larger-than-life sense to the already spectacular movies of the era. On the other, the theater was full of small and large inconveniences that, for many people, became reason enough not to spend their money there. The floor was consistently sticky, thanks to layers upon layers of spilled soda and food residue. The popcorn from the concession stands was so unbelievably stale that I sometimes wondered why my mother kept purchasing it (perhaps she was compensating for not paying admission). Most incredible of all, the theater had a cat running around the seats: its function was to chase mice enticed by the same food that made the floor sticky. It is thus not surprising that the 3,500 seats of the theater—at least those that were not broken—were for the most part empty. The advent of video and the possibility of watching movies on the emergent cable systems had allowed the middle class to avoid theaters like Cine Ópera altogether. Tomás Pérez Turrent documents that, between 1989 and 1991, "992 movie theaters were closed and 10,082 video clubs had opened" in the country and, perhaps more importantly, most of the closed cinemas "had exhibited primarily Mexican films" (111). The issue here is that this transition took place mostly because of lackluster film attendance, which undercut exhibitors' financial viability, even when the showings were financed by the State. The fact that the shut-down screens had been showing primarily Mexican films was not, as Pérez Turrent seems to imply, a cause but rather a consequence: a clear sign that audiences were simply not going to see Mexican movies.

    Nonetheless, the late 1980s revealed the remnants of a fading cultural geography of cinema. One could still find double features of classic Hollywood movies playing every week at Cine Bella Época, a theater located in the middle-class neighborhood of Condesa. Originally called Cine Lido, Bella Época was another Art Deco venue originally built in the mid-1940s, following a design from the American architect Charlie Lee. In the 1970s, the theater changed its name and, taking advantage of its central location in the now trendy Condesa neighborhood, it became one of the central venues for the distribution of Hollywood film in the city. By the late 1980s, though, it had turned into an altogether different business, one mostly devoted to showing old movies from its collection. If memory does not betray me, the last time I went, around 1988, I saw a marathon-length double feature: David Lean's 1962 epic *Lawrence of Arabia* and William Wyler's 1959 classic *Ben-Hur*. My mother and I sat in the back of the theater, and the fact that there were people in attendance was so remarkable that the projectionist came out of the screening room to personally greet us.

Another popular theater at the time was Cine Continental, located in the northern part of an old middle-class neighborhood, the Colonia del Valle. The venue was so well attended because it was the major distribution space for Disney and other children's films at the time. It also offered a somewhat better viewing experience: it was cleaner, and its design, rather than following the anachronistic Art Deco style of other theaters, provided a decent replica of the Disney castle. Also, a group of vendors sold toys and candy outside, thus making it a very attractive destination for children. That theater, however, did not last long either. Along with Bella Época, Ópera, and other iconic COTSA cinemas, like Cine Latino or Metropolitan, Cine Continental shut its doors in the early 1990s. The ruins of the beloved Disney castle replica stand abandoned on a busy avenue, after a failed attempt to turn it into a multiplex. Many moviegoers who developed their taste for cinema in these theaters mourned the loss of this traditional film culture. Film critic Rafael Aviña, one of the leading reviewers in Mexican media, offers a telling take: "By the eighties, movie theaters had become smaller and many of them started to disappear. The movie palaces died out and were replaced by dim and small multiplexes, some of them in spaces that had been occupied in the past by single screens, like the Latino, the Palacio Chino, or the Real Cinema, until the arrival of the new concept of computerized, functional, and technically well-equipped but ultimately impersonal theaters" (237–38; my translation).

A major transformation in the economics and politics of cinema distribution in Mexico defined the experiences of Mexico City's moviegoers in the late 1980s. In 1989, the administration of President Carlos Salinas de Gortari started a large-scale privatization program. In this context, the Secretaría de Hacienda y Crédito Público (SHCP), the Mexican equivalent of the U.S. Treasury Department, surveyed a project of *desincorporación*—that is, of extricating COTSA and film exhibition from the umbrella of government funding and management. According to research conducted by Isis Saavedra Luna, the closure of hundreds of screens and a very messy process of privatization that lasted well into 1994 defined a period that started in 1989 (132–39). As David Maciel points out, the proceeds from the sale of COTSA were not used for the improvement of the production industry (216). Screens for national distribution became unprecedentedly scarce and Mexican filmmakers had to look elsewhere for the creation of a viable film industry. Interestingly, the shockwaves brought about by the dismantling of COTSA were contemporary to the shooting of some of the most influential films in contemporary Mexico. *Como agua para chocolate, Danzón,* and *Cronos* were among the landmark movies entangled in this crisis of distribution.

The long decline of the Mexican film industry, which reached its nadir because of the undoing of the State's distribution and exhibition networks, is an ideal point of departure toward understanding the Mexican cinema's radical transformations in the period surrounding neoliberalism and NAFTA. As some critics have noted (D'Lugo "Authorship"; Noble 93), these closures were part of a general continental trend, a distance between film production and public imaginaries that resulted in a reduction of Latin American film audiences by half. In the specific case of Mexico, this issue has to be examined as two related but distinct problems, which I will analyze respectively in Chapters 1 and 2. First, the cultural economy of so-called national cinema had faded away. I understand "national cinema" as a cultural genre that acts around the idea of "national culture," as a repository of those signs that define the polity, and as a site of contestation for definitions of national sensibilities.[1] Film historian Carl Mora attributes the decline of Mexican cinema to the fact that the country did not have a cultural experience as traumatic as the Argentine "Dirty War" or Spanish *franquismo*, thus keeping Mexico from the development of a bolder and more political cinema capable of leading an artistic and ideological renovation (186). In fact, continental readings of the cinema of the period show the ways in which Mexican filmmakers fell short in the wave of political and aesthetic renovation identified with trends such as "Third Cinema." In Zuzana Pick's *The New Latin American Cinema*, the landmark book about regional filmmaking in the 1970s and 1980s, only one Mexican film, Paul Leduc's *Frida*, deserves mention, in contrast with a groundbreaking wave of South American films by transformational directors such as Fernando Solanas, María Luisa Bemberg, Jorge Sanjinés, and Glauber Rocha.

In view of this, I argue that the central problem at the level of production was the fact that the ideologies of the Mexican self—or *Mexicanidad*—that were instrumental in the emergence of national cinema and national culture at large in the 1930s and 1940s no longer carried the same social significance, particularly with middle-class movie audiences.[2] This rendered meaningless the political potential of Mexican film at the time, since it worked within outdated notions of political engagement and directors did not face any political or social shock comparable to the brutality and violence of the Southern Cone dictatorial regimes. In short, while Mexico as a country was fortunate enough to be spared such an atrocious historical fate, Mexican cinema did not have any reason to move beyond inherited models of representation. In fact, Jorge Ayala Blanco devoted substantial parts of his 1986 work *La condición del cine mexicano*, perhaps the best and most influential Mexican book on cinema of the decade, to a careful yet vitriolic denunciation of the stereotypes of poverty (the "jodidismo" [miserabilism] of filmmakers like Luis Alcoriza), gender, and history that plagued supposedly political films of the time. Thus, as I will discuss in Chapter 1, there was a fundamental disconnect between the still-nationalist ideology of 1980s and early-1990s film and the increasingly neoliberal and Americanized frameworks of meaning that would define Mexico after 1988. In other words, the problem was not merely that of a crumbling film infrastructure. It also involved the decline of the hegemonic codes of culture that still shaped Mexican cinema both aesthetically and ideologically, and the economic and intellectual exhaustion suffered by Mexican film at large.

The first step toward the commercial rebirth of Mexican cinema was freeing its production from the nationalist imperatives that had defined the industry since its inception in the post-revolutionary period, in order to reflect the experiences of new social groups that were emerging along with the process of cultural remodernization brought about by the neoliberal economic and political model. Cine Ópera opened its doors with *Una familia de tantas,* a film that aptly represented the conflicts, aspirations, and cultural repertoires of a new urban middle class that would evolve into a steady moviegoing audience. Similarly, the new Mexican cinema of the late 1980s and early 1990s had to break with the inherited languages of film nationalism in order to provide a comparably significant experience for a new generation of potential moviegoers—a generation defined by the collapse of the Partido Revolucionario Institucional (PRI) regime and of the Mexican post-revolutionary system at large, as well as by the mirage of prosperity brought about by NAFTA and its surrounding socioeconomic models and practices. Chapter 1 will explore the ways in which nationalism reinvented itself in films, with varying degrees of success, as a response to the social changes in the imagined community caused by NAFTA and neoliberalism.

The second point, which I will develop in Chapter 2, is that Mexican cinema at the time was decisively focused on a specific social class that lacked the economic power to sustain a viable film industry. Noble argues that post-1950s cinema, unlike that of the so-called Golden Age that spanned the years between 1939 and 1950, failed to unite all of Mexico's social classes and groups into a single audience, and ended up targeting urban popular classes through genres such as masked wrestler films and risqué cabaret melodramas based on Mexico City's working-class nightlife (91–94). To be sure, these genres have a cultural iconicity of their own and they are essential instruments for understanding Mexico City's marginalized urban populations. However, one of the things that allowed Mexican cinema to thrive commercially was its capacity to produce films like *Una familia de tantas,* constructed on the basis of a cultural language and a system of values that appealed to moviegoers who could afford to purchase tickets at a profitable level. Thus, in order to survive as an industry, Mexican filmmakers needed to bring the middle class back into the theaters. As the collapse of theaters like Cine Ópera or Bella Época clearly showed, the fundamental problem faced by the industry was its deep disconnect with middle-class national audiences, which rarely, if ever, saw Mexican movies. Thus, as I will attempt to show, film producers and directors gradually and unwittingly engineered a class displacement of audiences, making the growing urban middle class the main target of their movies.

Screening Neoliberalism is about the radical change in the regimes of production and consumption of Mexican cinema in the wake of the neoliberal economic reforms implemented from the mid-1980s onward. My arguments and analyses revolve around two claims. First, the neoliberal experience meant for culture in general, and for cinema in particular, a vast privatization of production which led to major changes in the communities of spectatorship and in the social function of film. Cine Ópera was part of a nationalist cultural paradigm that regarded cinema as an essential instrument for the education of the citizenry and for the construction and preservation of political and social values in postrevolutionary Mexico. Renowned cultural critic Carlos Monsiváis has shown that "in Mexico, the idea of cinema as art does not even get a look in. It is a mass entertainment, offering an immediate link to the metropolis, a subliminal modernization of rural and urban groups" ("All the People" 146). In more practical terms, this view of cinema created a sprawling State-centered infrastructure, sustained by a network of government-owned theaters, strict controls on ticket prices, mandated percentages of screen time for Mexican films, and vast subsidies for film production.[3] This book is concerned with the cinema that emerges when this longstanding model collapses and gives way to a semi-private model that gradually but decidedly overtakes Mexican cinema at all levels: production (thanks to the transition from State sponsorship to mixed public-private and fully private schemes), exhibition (thanks to the decline of State-owned theaters and the corresponding surge in privately owned multiplexes, which today account for nearly 90 percent of total screens in the country), and consumption (from the urban popular sectors who largely benefited from the pre-1992 model to the middle and upper classes who could afford to attend the private multiplexes in the wake of price liberalization). My study will argue that the true relevance of these structural transformations is in the major displacements in the ideologies and aesthetics of cinema brought about by the economic changes in production and distribution, and by the demographic changes in spectatorship. In other words, the first central claim of this book is that the paradigms of filmmaking that radically altered Mexican cinema after 1988 are the consequences of deep transformations in the material practices of producing and consuming cinema, triggered by changes in the very idea of the role of culture in society developed under neoliberalism.

This last issue, the role of culture under neoliberalism, leads to the second claim in this book. The depth of the transformation in film at all levels—economic, symbolic, ideological, aesthetic, social—as a result of neoliberal reform makes cinema a uniquely apt site for studying the social and cultural impact of neoliberalism in Mexico. While "neoliberalism" is not a term widely used in the United States to describe the brand of free-market reforms designed after the economic ideas of Milton Friedman and others, and implemented on a global scale since at least the 1970s, the word is employed as common currency in Mexico to refer to these reforms, both among their proponents and their critics.[4] Thus, I use the word "neoliberalism" in this book not merely as a technical term, but as a representation of its presence in everyday Mexican political and social discourse. In this, I follow David Harvey, who has shown that "neoliberalism" has evolved from its definition as a "theory of political economic practices that proposes that human well-being can be advanced by liberating individual entrepreneurial freedoms and skills" to a "hegemonic mode of discourse" that "has become incorporated into the common-sense way many of us interpret, live in and understand the world" (3). The point here is that, in this book, the transformation in cinema is not a mere superstructural reflection of reform at the structural level of economics. Rather, I understand neoliberalism as a cultural signifier that constitutes social and cultural fields beyond the mere economy. Paraphrasing Pierre Bourdieu's idea of the "social structures of the economy," my study of Mexican film can be framed as part of a paradigm in which private enterprise engages in "competition for power over state power" (204). Insofar as the market is, as Bourdieu poses, "the totality of relations of exchange between competing agents" (204), culture can be an instrument that allows the interpretation both of the material economic processes and the system of ideology, belief, and aesthetics that emerge from it and make possible the reproduction and contestation of its premises. To say it in a more concrete way, I argue that Mexican cinema allows for the reading both of the process through which private enterprise competes with the State in the production of cultural commodities and the way in which actual films perform or resist the cultural values and implications of the neoliberal process.

Because of the complexity of this process, I have decided not to organize this book chronologically, as I find it crucial to discern and separately study some of the interwoven phenomena involved in the neoliberalization of post-1988 Mexican cinema. I have identified instead four major processes, all of which are central to the claims I've laid out. I will devote a chapter to each of the first three of these processes, tracing each process from a foundational film in the generation of films produced and released during the Salinas de Gortari presidency (1988–1994) to films that represent the peak of such processes in the 2000s. Chapter 1 engages in the decline of cinema as a cornerstone of "national culture" and as an entity devoted to the production of "national identity." In an arc that goes from Alfonso Arau's iconic film *Como agua para chocolate* (1992) to Carlos Carrera's *El crimen del padre Amaro* (2002), the highest-grossing film in the history of the Mexican domestic market, this chapter shows the ways in which the transformations brought about by neoliberalism undermined cinema's role as a vehicle for national identity, and how "Mexicanism" as a cultural ideology came under attack. Chapter 2 studies the correlation between emergence of middle-class audiences as a result of the privatization of exhibition with the deep transformation of cinema as a language of affect and emotion. The chapter explores the parallel between the gradual privatization of exhibition and production and the increasing centrality of the romantic comedy as the major narrative device in Mexican commercial cinema, from the release of Alfonso Cuarón's *Sólo con tu pareja* (1991) to Jorge Colón's *Cansada de besar sapos* (2006). Chapter 3 engages with the transformation of political cinema from the leftist-activist paradigms inherited from the 1960s to a paradigm engaged with the political concerns of middle-class Mexico. The chapter will thus show how the need to intersect with a market defined by middle- and upper-class tastes and aspirations ultimately resulted in a gradual shift from traditional *engagé* filmmaking to the use of ideology as a commodity.

While Chapters 1 through 3 are mostly concerned with the dynamics of the Mexican domestic film market, Chapter 4 extends the analysis to the internationalization enjoyed by Mexican cinema during the past twenty years. This chapter is not structured as a single temporal arc, but rather analyzes four individual directors: Guillermo del Toro, Alfonso Cuarón, Alejandro González Iñarritu, and Carlos Reygadas. Given that these four figures have had unique trajectories of internationalization, focusing on them individually allows me to show how the perceived global success of Mexican cinema rests on distinct articulations of the processes analyzed in the first three chapters. With this structure, I seek to overcome the study of Mexican cinema as a "Nouvelle Vague," as Jeff Menne calls it, and point instead to the fact that the crucial transformation that allows for the globalization of Mexican cinema happens in the domestic market. In doing so, I claim that each director belongs to a distinct process within the paradigmatic transformation of cinema, which in turn shows why the division of the present book into processes will provide a better understanding of Mexican cinema than a straightforward chronological retelling of the period.

The Question of "Mexican Film Studies"

Before embarking on the analysis proposed by this book, it is important to briefly account for the status of Mexican film vis-á-vis the disciplines that constitute so-called film studies. The systematic study of Mexican cinema presents a disciplinary and methodological challenge, in large part because "film studies" as such does not exist in Mexican academic contexts. Most major scholars dedicated to the study of film are based in social science programs: sociology, communication sciences, and even law and education. This means that most studies of Mexican cinema produced in Mexico are concerned with the social practice of cinema, and with the sociological study of audiences. Another issue to consider here is the precarious state of film criticism in Mexico. Film criticism lacks an institutional research base in Mexico, given that the major academic film programs (such as the Centro Universitario de Estudios Cinematográficos [CUEC], run by the National University, and the Centro de Capacitación Cinematográfica [CCC], run by the Mexican State) are geared toward the production of cinema rather than to its study and interpretation. In fact, most recognized Mexican film critics are journalists and reviewers for newspapers and magazines.

Given these adverse conditions, it is not surprising that academic work on Mexican film has been produced more extensively in the American and British academies, where scholars of cinema are able to find institutional homes in programs of Spanish language and literature or Latin American studies. It is important to note that even though film studies is a growing part of the humanities, many programs still lack a Latin Americanist on their core faculty. The result of this situation is that many scholars of Latin American and Mexican cinema, including myself, are based in literature and culture programs and are trained in PhD programs in Latin American or comparative literature. In my view, this has created some disciplinary limitations for the study of cinema in the United States and Britain, such as an excessive focus on auteur cinema at the expense of commercial film, given the translation of the aesthetic values of literature to movies. Furthermore, given that most of the publications coming out of Mexico are sociological in nature, one can find a deep disconnect between Spanish-language and English-language bibliographies, not only because of the usual disconnect between academies, but also because of the inability or unwillingness of literary scholars to read work by quantitative social scientists.[5]

In light of this landscape, *Screening Neoliberalism* aims to be a systematic study of post-1988 Mexican cinema at the structural level. To achieve this goal, the book makes an attempt to work out some of the limitations faced by scholarship on Mexican film. Thus, this book bridges—across its pages—the divide between the social science literature produced in Mexico, the work of Mexican film critics, and the literature produced in the English-language academy. I believe that by putting together the still-disconnected knowledge produced by these three spaces, my analysis can show some aspects of Mexican film that remain unstudied, as well as provide an account of contemporary film production that is wider in range and more rigorous than most of the scholarship produced so far. In addition, by cross-referencing work on the social practice of cinema with the interpretation of actual films, I will attempt to overcome both the hermeneutic limitations of the social-science approach and the aesthetic prejudices of the interpretive tools inherited from literary studies. And, by placing Mexico's most famous directors in the final chapter of the book, I intend to demonstrate the importance and relevance of considering Mexican cinema at large, along with its practices and its most commercial angles, even when one's primary interest is one of the "three amigos." In sum, this book's goal is to serve as the most wide-ranging study of contemporary Mexican film to date, by considering both the largest corpus of films analyzed by any work on the subject and by encompassing the most diverse body of academic literature in the field, ultimately providing what I hope will be the most complete account of post-1988 Mexican cinema on social, ideological, and aesthetic levels.

Beyond the "Cinema of Solitude": National Cinema Reconsidered

It is important to understand the starting point of the processes I will describe in the following chapters. In his landmark 1992 study *Cinema of Solitude,* Charles Ramírez Berg offered a systematic account of Mexican film from 1967 to 1983. Ramírez Berg's study, besides being one of the best books ever written on Mexican cinema, is for my purposes a very symptomatic example of the formal and aesthetic constraints faced by filmmakers in the late 1980s. Ramírez Berg uses the notion of *Mexicanidad* as the structuring principle of his study, strongly following Octavio Paz and his 1950 book *The Labyrinth of Solitude* as a guide.[6] *Cinema of Solitude*'s aim is described in the following terms: "By illuminating certain 'signs of identity' imbedded within Mexican films of *la crisis,* I hope to give North American readers a sensitivity to and an appreciation of Mexicans' deepest cultural concerns" (11). Beyond the obvious fact that such an objective would by definition privilege identity as a mode of analysis, the analysis actually works in the specific corpus addressed by Ramírez Berg. By structuring his work around the construction of gender and social communities in Mexican cinema, Ramírez Berg shows a compelling landscape in which filmmakers struggle to go beyond the legacies of nationalist Golden Age cinema but ultimately remain in a strongly identitarian cultural framework. Ramírez Berg thus concludes: "Based on the cinematic evidence, Mexicans are a nation of estranged survivors" (210). The book clearly identifies a relationship between film and the consistent sense of political and economic crisis that defined post-1968 Mexico. Given the political nature of this, it is quite puzzling that Ramírez Berg ultimately replicates Octavio Paz's diagnosis of the Mexican self: "Sadly, my own conclusion is that there is no end . . . to Mexicans' solitude. . . . In the final years of the twentieth century, Mexicans may be just as lost in solitude . . . as they were before the Mexican Revolution" (218).

The issue that stands out, though, is the fact that Charles Ramírez Berg himself seems somewhat trapped by the *Mexicanidad* paradigm, and his work takes at face value the identitarian statements put forward not only by the films but also by the 1950s tradition of Mexican identity studies in literature and philosophy.[7] Post-1988 Mexican film would start making strong dents in the cultural edifice of Mexican identity as constructed in previous years. Accordingly, I contend that an assessment of the early films of the neoliberal period and subsequent films within the same aesthetic vein requires a perspective that steps outside both cultural concepts of the Mexican self and, more crucially, the idea that film is a "representation" of any kind of "Mexican culture." Still, some distinctions between the 1970s and the 1990s are necessary, so in Chapter 1 I will use the term "neo-Mexicanist" to speak of a particular form of Mexican cinema in the age of NAFTA, engaged in the recovery or reconstruction of national identity and/or the cultural symbols and practices that constitute that identity. A critical work on neo-Mexicanist film in the context of neoliberal culture requires a reformulation of the idea of "Mexican national cinema" that goes beyond the mere representation of the imagined community I've laid out here. In fact, against the backdrop of the institutional crisis surrounding film exhibition and distribution, the central transformation of Mexican cinema in the early 1990s—the one that will ultimately define contemporary cinema in Mexico—lies in the much wider understanding of national cinema achieved both by neo-Mexicanist filmmakers such as José Luis García Agraz, María Novaro, and Alfonso Arau, and by those who would ultimately break the molds of national identity, such as Alfonso Cuarón and Guillermo del Toro.

A good language for understanding how cultural productions in the 1988–1994 period in Mexico (the Salinas de Gortari administration years) transcend the cultural language described by Ramírez Berg may be found in Roger Bartra's book *The Cage of Melancholy* (*La jaula de la melancolia*, 1987). Bartra's work is a scathing critique of the long tradition of studies on *Mexicanidad* and the Mexican self and the way in which they are entwined in political power. Bartra argues: "Studies on Mexicanness constitute an expression of the dominant political culture. This hegemonic political culture is bound by the set of imaginary power-networks that define socially accepted *forms of subjectivity* and that are customarily considered as the fullest expression of national culture. . . . These images of Mexicanness are not a reflection of popular consciousness. . . . I intend to tackle them not as mere expressions of ideologies, but rather as myths produced by the hegemonic culture" (*Cage* 2; emphasis in the original). Bartra's strong words bring up two important points regarding the study of contemporary Mexican cinema. First of all, the idea of *Mexicanidad* present in film must be read neither as a "true" representation of Mexican culture nor as an ideology to be denounced and deconstructed. Rather, Bartra understands identity as a cultural construct produced by the elite (such as filmmakers and writers), which in turn reproduces itself at the social level. Therefore, insofar as cultural artifacts connected to Mexican identity sometimes result in cultural practices by the audiences that consume them, the role of cultural critique lies in the understanding of both the formal structure of the "myths" that constitute Mexican identity and the way in which they become "socially accepted forms of subjectivity." Ultimately, the meaningful issue here is that *Mexicanidad*, for Bartra, is a function of what he calls, in an Althusserian vein, the "imaginary networks of political power"—namely, the ways in which political power reproduces itself as meaningful social practice. Or, to use Michel Foucault's vocabulary, Bartra highlights the ways in which cultural production and cultural critique around Mexican identity become part of the "microphysics of power" (173–84). A critical method stemming from these insights must read films at two levels: first, it must observe the ways in which they construct, reconstruct, and deconstruct the cultural myths of Mexican nationalism in relation to the considerable archive of nationalist film and literature they draw upon; second, it must ponder the ways in which each film links itself with the imaginary networks of political power that sustain the political system in Mexico at a given time. In fact, one of the contentions of this book is that film is a particularly apt genre for studying cultural transformation in Mexico precisely because it follows the transformation of hegemonic political and social ideologies in a very organic way. In other words, while Mexican film struggles at the content level with the heavy legacies of *Mexicanidad* and other cultural imperatives of identity and politics, at the sociocultural and formal levels it tends to reproduce the ideologies about Mexico developed in the many transitions of the neoliberal period.

The aesthetic paradigm behind the "cinema of solitude"—as well as the critical languages deployed by Ramírez Berg to study it—was considerably out of step with contemporary critiques of Mexican nationalism. In the mid-1980s, for instance, the work of chronicler and critic Carlos Monsiváis explored the deep relationship between identity and power in a large set of popular practices, such as State-sponsored beauty contests for indigenous women. Books like *Entrada libre* (1987) and *Escenas de pudor y liviandad* (1988) show the ways in which Monsiváis constructed a distinction between "national culture" as a set of practices produced within the symbolic space of the nation and "nationalist culture" as a top-to-bottom imposition of symbols and values with the purpose of reproducing hegemony (Mudrovcic; Sánchez Prado, "Carlos Monsiváis"; Egan 179–211). Monsiváis and Bartra were part of an emerging paradigm in which the gradual erosion of the PRI regime resulted in forms of thinking and performing Mexican culture beyond the imperatives of *Mexicanidad*. Many films produced after 1989 were, at heart, attempts to undertake this critical mandate: they sought either to reinvent Mexican identity (like the neo-Mexicanist films I will engage in Chapter 1) or to turn it upside down or sidestep it altogether (like Alfonso Cuarón's *Sólo con tu pareja* or Guillermo del Toro's *Cronos*).[8] These engagements with identity should be read in relation to the role that *Mexicanidad* played both at the level of cultural institutions at the time and as part of the larger ideologies of political power in the transitional processes lived by Mexico in the past twenty years.

To be sure, the era of the "cinema of solitude" was itself a period when cinema production depended largely on the swings and vacillations of State cultural ideology and had become, quite literally, a family affair: President Luis Echeverría (1970–1976) placed his brother Rodolfo in charge of the renovation of the film industry in 1971, while President José López Portillo (1976–1982) put his sister Margarita in command not only of cinema, but also of television and radio. The so-called New Age of the early 1970s, which yielded works by directors such as Alcoriza, Arturo Ripstein, and Felipe Cazals, resulted from the government's interest and investment in what were conceived as "socially relevant productions," but was ultimately subject to forms of self-censorship that, according to Maciel, limited the discussion of religion, the military, and the sitting government (203). Still, the drive to create a cinema of social significance, combined with the regime's uneasiness about direct censorship (due to the fresh memory of the 1968 Tlatelolco massacre in the national consciousness), allowed filmmakers to produce a highly disillusioned cinema that exercised politics through (sometimes questionable) class representation. This phenomenon is iconically represented in Luis Alcoriza's highly successful film *Mecánica nacional* (1971), the largest box office hit of the time, which, in the words of Carl Mora, held a "Buñuelian distaste for bourgeois society in general" and an interpretation of Mexico as "materialistic, uncultured, irrational, while responding in a semiconscious way to certain half-remembered folkways" (127). The key point in this description lies in the fact that Alcoriza remained ultimately tied to inherited codes of cinematic representation: a *lumpenproletariat* already canonized visually by Luis Buñuel's 1950 film *Los olvidados* (Ramírez Berg, *Cinema* 183), along with a telling distaste for urban popular classes that was a departure from their idealization by Golden Age films.[9] Ramírez Berg characterizes Alcoriza's work as a "primitive world" whose ideological standpoint is "divided between progressive and reactionary tendencies"—that is, between the revival of the "urban neighborhood film" as a genre of social critique and a moralistic portrayal of the poor based on the assumption that morality is "highly situational and always secondary to survival" (182–86).

As I move on in the next section to the analysis of films such as *Como agua para chocolate* and *Danzón,* the important issue here rests on two facts. First, Mora and Ramírez Berg's analyses, as emphatic as they are in discussing Alcoriza's achievements, ultimately show how derivative his movies are in relation to the film languages of the 1940s and 1950s. Buñuel's looming shadow has to do, at least in part, with the fact that *echeverrista* cinema had a very hard time finding languages of social and political engagement of its own: the notion of "socially significant cinema" was heavily defined by the same agendas that defined nationalist cinema in the mid-1940s' wave of modernization: the decay of the middle class and the plight of urban popular classes. Second, and more crucially, it is clear that Alcoriza's images and ideas of *Mexicanidad,* regardless of their departure from popular class idealization, were clearly inscribed into the processes critiqued by Bartra and Monsiváis a decade later. It was ultimately the work of a State-protected (and even State-generated) elite whose framing of Mexico accompanied Echeverría's populist but authoritarian regime. Alcoriza's attack on the depoliticized working class that failed to rise up in the aftermath of Tlatelolco moved the focus of political critique away from Echeverría, the very man accused of ordering the massacre (Mora 128).

What we can see up to this point is that the "cinema of solitude" ultimately represents both the aesthetic stalemate and the institutional and political entanglements in post-1968 Mexican cinema. Still, this brief analysis, both of the period and of the scholarship on the period, illustrates important methodological lessons for those engaging with neo-Mexicanist cinema. First, I would insist that it is crucial to resist the temptation to draw any conclusions regarding Mexican identity from the movies. If anything, the limitations of Ramírez Berg's method of analysis surface mostly in those moments when he extracts definitions of Mexican culture from the films. Second, the ideological context that makes films meaningful is essential here. Insofar as the Salinas de Gortari presidency frames a Mexico radically different from that of Echeverría's administration, it is important to identify the aesthetic codes of cinema that still reproduce themselves while acknowledging the new roles they play in relation to the "imaginary networks of political power." Finally, it is important to engage, whenever possible, with the critical traditions developed around specific films to show how certain studies of interpretation and reception are themselves entangled in the same cultural logic deployed by those movies.[10] From the perspective constructed on the basis of these lessons, neo-Mexicanist cinema emerges as a pivotal component in the reconfiguration of cultural discourse and practice during the early years of the neoliberal program. This will be the subject of Chapter 1.

1

NATIONALISM ERODED

Mexican Cinema in Times of Crisis

When one considers both the economic crisis in cinematic production and distribution and the heavy constraints suffered by Mexican film language in the late 1980s, the commercial success of Alfonso Arau's 1992 film *Como agua para chocolate* is surprising, even more than twenty years later. Showing for the most part on only six screens, in a six-month run, the film grossed an unprecedented six million dollars at the box office in Mexico, and an additional twenty million in the United States. The film is based on an already very successful novel by Laura Esquivel, Arau's wife at the time, and, as Claudine Potvin pointed out in a 1995 article, it follows the book's plot very closely (55). Set between the latter part of the nineteenth century and the end of the Mexican Revolution, *Como agua para chocolate* tells the story of Tita (Lumi Cavazos), who is forbidden to marry her suitor Pedro (Marco Leonardi) because of a family tradition that forces her to take care of her mother (Regina Torné) throughout the mother's elderly years. Tita turns to cooking in order to express her feelings and the story, both in the film and the book, develops alongside a succession of recipes and around the evolution of the family at large.

Como agua's astounding success has been the subject of ample debate in Latin American film studies and the movie has elicited a highly negative backlash. Deborah Shaw and Brigitte Roller offer a compelling account of this commercial success:

> *Como agua para chocolate* is, then, a highly entertaining, colourful film with all the ingredients for an international box office hit: it is full of romance and characters who conform to Western Christian notions of good and evil, it has an old world rural location, it conforms to traditional

> notions of Mexicanness, it is set in a pre-sixties and pre-AIDS era and filled with old-fashioned family values, idealizing traditional notions of marriage, womanhood and maternity. More importantly, and more disturbingly ideologically, is the fact that the film works on the level of the emotions and carries the audience with it at all times so that no option is given but to identify with the heroine, a beautiful, wronged Mexican woman whose only aspiration is to reach the sacred position of wife, mother and cook. (91)

In other words, Shaw and Roller attribute the film's success to its apt use of the imaginary of melodrama, which works both within a Mexican cultural context where such narrative structures are highly familiar, and in relation to a conservative international audience that tends to seek a repository of authenticity and tradition in non-Western cinema. Beyond this, one must not overlook the one thing that distinguishes the film from basically every movie made in Mexico since the Golden Age: superior production values. Unlike the gritty palette that characterizes the films of Alcoriza and Ripstein, or the impoverished worlds of post-Buñuelian Mexican film, *Como agua para chocolate* offers unprecedentedly luscious imagery, focused on a highly beautified world portrayed, through the film's cinematography and art direction, in warm, earthy tones. It is a world suspended in time and space, where the social concerns that characterized the "cinema of solitude" give way to traditionalist worlds in which ideological engagement is supplanted by affect and sensuality.

Most academic critiques of *Como agua para chocolate* have come from scholars focused on women and gender studies. These scholars usually underscore the ideologically regressive nature of the movie's representation of women, by contending that the film ultimately upholds an idea of the feminine closely connected to the private space and the kitchen. In other words, most critics identify the movie's highly aestheticized appeal to the past as an ideological construction based on a feminine world that, regardless of its focus on women, ultimately sustains both patriarchal values and the ideals of the traditional wife and mother. Without contradicting the evident role of gender set forward by these readings, I would contend the movie is more significant because of the particular way in which it engages national identity. In an article entitled "Consuming Tacos and Enchiladas," Harmony Wu argues that, while the climactic scene in which Pedro and Tita finally make love "*should* be the foundational moment of the text: the final consummation of the new ideology of the nation," Pedro's death in the middle of the sexual act "frustrates" it (182; emphasis in the original). Furthermore, Wu points out that while the film relies on a feminine narrative voice for most of its story, it ultimately surrenders narrative control to a North American character, Dr. Brown (Mario Iván Martínez). In consequence, Wu argues, by avoiding the consummation of the forbidden love and surrendering the narration to a male voice, "the resolution promises that there is no danger of subversion to patriarchal order to come out of their union, making their story a cautionary tale rather than a liberating one" (182). Wu's analysis is quite accurate regarding the ideological aporias of the film.[1] It is surprising, nonetheless, that she ultimately reproaches the film for not creating a national narrative, directly invoking Doris Sommer's notion of "foundational fiction" as the basis for the political and allegorical appropriation of melodrama.[2] In view of this perspective, I would argue that the critical interest of *Como agua para chocolate* lies precisely in the surprising ways in which it prefigures the transformations of Mexican national cinema in the context of NAFTA.

In order to fully engage Arau's movie as a neo-Mexicanist text, the question of gender has to be partially bracketed. To be sure, critics like Wu have done a good job in denouncing the reactionary gender views espoused by the film, a necessary response to the celebration of the movie as a "feminine" film. However, the focus on gender obscures the sociopolitical backdrop against which the film becomes meaningful. Instead, the importance of *Como agua para chocolate* lies in the ways in which it displaces the social and political functions of national cinema from the ideological to the commercial, while repositioning the site of national identity in film from urban popular classes to the middle class. In a perspicacious article on the book, Victoria Martínez argues that behind the "false feminist message" of the novel (28), one finds elements through which one can tie the book to neoliberal ideology. I would contend, on the basis of this, that the film plays a more crucial role than the book in connecting neoliberalism with its neo-Mexican aesthetic, because of its capacity to supplement Esquivel's narrative with a visual set of referents and with a space of circulation and distribution—that of cinema—much wider than the one available for a work of literature.

Before fully delving into this, it is important to emphasize an interesting fact that, surprisingly, critics have not fully discussed: that Alfonso Arau, of all people, would put forward this kind of aesthetic. Before *Como agua para chocolate,* Arau was essentially a director of comedies that used humor and parody as devices to counter the darker national world portrayed by the main directors of the "cinema of solitude." His rise to prominence in the Mexican film world came with his second feature, *Calzonzin Inspector* (1973), about an indigenous man who, after arriving at a small town, is confused with an inspector general, and ultimately uncovers the corruption of local officials. The movie departs from the political disappointment of Alcoriza and other directors of the 1970s and is based on the premise that political corruption is at the core of the problems of an otherwise "authentic" Mexican nation. In a 1979 article on the status of Mexican cinema, critic Jesús Salvador Treviño identifies "a clear and honest perception of Mexican hopes and aspirations while commenting bitterly on those who betray these ideas" (29), proving that this perspective had a degree of resonance with audiences. Furthermore, the nationalist devices in the film are quite obvious and, in some cases, are offshoots of the nationalist cinema of the Golden Age. The fact that the protagonist who embodies "true" national identity is an indigenous man comically recasts a very similar idea represented in Ismael Rodríguez's *Tizoc* (1957), a Pedro Infante vehicle in which the protagonist is a hard-working Indian who ultimately embodies the values of the nation. Arau's cinema evolved in the late 1970s and 1980s with two films that followed analogous paths of comedic populism: *Mojado Power* (1979), a picaresque movie about an undocumented worker, which has been identified with a subgenre of border films that use humor and satire to idealize the travails and the survival skills of the immigrant working class (Herrera-Sobek 63; Fojas 10), and *Chido Guan: El tacos de oro* (1985), a soccer movie that follows the structure of rags-to-riches sports movies.

Arau's *Como agua para chocolate* is a major departure from the directorial aesthetics of his previous work and even the comedic line he had pursued both as director and actor. In fact, the distance between his 1992 film and everything else he did up to that point suggested to some that the movie could be read as a parody of Mexican national discourse (Niebylski).[3] One could also argue that Arau channeled the aesthetics of his wife's book rather than his own, but such an argument is problematic if one considers that Laura Esquivel also wrote the script for *Chido Guan*. The fact that Arau would direct such a different cinematic product is, I would contend, symptomatic of the key displacement represented by *Como agua para chocolate*. First and foremost, this displacement is only possible when considering the disjointed relationship between the ideas of the nation put forward by Mexican cinema in the two prior decades vis-à-vis the culture and practices of the intended audiences. As Carlos Monsiváis famously argued, Mexican Golden Age cinema was successful in making "great use of what is stored in the cultural memory of the people" ("All the People" 150), thus contributing to an idea of the nation that "mediated between the shock of industrialization and the rural and popular urban experience which has not been prepared in any way for this giant change, a process that from the 40s on modifies the idea of the nation" (151). In a way, cinema from the period was capable of creating a social contract in which the affective identification with figures such as Pedro Infante worked across class and geographic lines, giving film a strong relationship with a "broad spectrum of Mexican society," which turned moviegoing into "an everyday social practice" (Noble 74). From the 1960s on, this social contract started to erode, partly because of the emergence of competing media (like television) and genres (like *telenovelas*), and partly because of the nature of the work of people such as Alcoriza, whose highly critical representations of the Mexican poor preempted any affective identification with the audience. Arau's work could therefore be read as a succession of attempts to reengage audiences with ideal representations of the Mexican self: his depiction of the noble but betrayed people of *Calzonzin Inspector* is in stark contrast to Alcoriza's view of popular classes, and the sports-based populism of *Chido Guan* can be viewed as an effort to galvanize national identity on the eve of the 1986 World Cup, which was organized by Mexico. *Como agua para chocolate* shares this ethos with all of Arau's early oeuvre: it is an attempt to repair the broken relationship between national cinema and the imagined community, and to restore film as a privileged genre for the articulation of the national.

The cultural conservatism perceived by the film's critics results from Arau's attempt to reengage national discourse. If one considers the fact that the film came out in the middle of the distribution crisis described in the Introduction, it is clear that looking for an audience amid the urban popular classes at the time was a futile pursuit. First, the theaters were simply not there, and many of the venues where the working classes had accessed Mexican films had either shut down or become privatized by 1992. Besides, Arau's own experience in the 1970s and 1980s showed that even when his films had achieved a certain degree of commercial success among the working classes, the films' identification with a nationalist ideology was questionable, especially in a landscape where most commercial films in Mexico came from exploitation genres, like *fichera*, a popular type of movie named after women who danced for tokens in working-class bars. There were also films that combined the tropes of the *ficheras* with the emerging culture of *narcotráfico*, like Raúl Fernández's three-film series *Lola la trailera* (1983, 1985, 1991), the last installment premiering with some success just a year before *Como agua para chocolate*. In fact, if one looks in a catalog, like *The Mexican Filmography, 1916 through 2001* by David E. Wilt, for movies produced between 1989 and 1992, one will see that the vast majority of the films that attained commercial notoriety were in fact quite lowbrow: music star vehicles like Pedro Galindo's *Pelo suelto* (1991), starring raunchy pop singer Gloria Trevi; candid-camera comedies like René Cardona's eight-film series *La risa en vacaciones* (1990–1996); or comedies starring TV and cabaret actors, based on sexualized humor that found its only outlet in cinema, such as Óscar Fentanes's Juan Camaney films (such as *Picoso pero sabroso*), vehicles for the popular comedian Luis de Alba. A brief glance at this period makes it sufficiently clear that popular audiences were decidedly opting for a cinema that carried no didactic pursuits, and clearly resisting attempts by political filmmakers like Cazals or even Arau to use film for a radical or nationalist message.

Arau's innovative solution was to construct a nationalism that clearly engaged with the values and expectations of a conservative middle class whose cultural ideologies remained in place regardless of the process of modernization brought about in the early years of the neoliberal project. This is, in fact, manifested in many of the ideologies that constitute the film's plot. Victoria Martínez, for instance, has shown that the book "sandwiches the revolution between the *Porfiriato* [the presidency of Porfirio Díaz against which the Revolution took place] and the neo-liberal possibilities offered in the 90's, and I believe that [Esquivel's] text serves to redirect Mexico toward a new appreciation and recognition of its need of American interests" (39). Moreover, Martínez argues that "because the ensuing Revolution called for social and land reforms and turned decidedly anti-American Esquivel's novel cannot approve of the Revolution" (39). One can supplement this reading by saying that a critical element in the film is the presence of a contemporary Tita (Arcelia Ramírez) whose narration is based on the premise that the values embodied in her family's history remain alive in her. The fact that, in the 1990s, Ramírez's character ultimately claims the history of a landowning family that retained its bourgeois status regardless of the revolution is very telling.

Most classical films on the revolution focused on the value and virtue of the revolutionaries and strongly antagonized the landowning elite. Arau turns this narrative around by treating the revolution as an integral part of bourgeois family history. The best example here is Tita's older sister Gertrudis (Claudette Maillé). Unlike Tita, Gertrudis resists her mother's iron fist. In one of the film's magical realist moments, one of Tita's home cooked meals awakens in Gertrudis a highly sexual scent that attracts a revolutionary who spirits her away and becomes her partner. Gertrudis becomes a *soldadera,* a woman who fights in the Revolution; as a social type, the *soldadera* has evolved to embody ideas of women's liberation and political agency.[4] Up to this point, one could claim Gertrudis as a symbol of female independence, and as a successful escapee of the oppressive feminine world constructed by Mamá Elena. However, the character makes a crucial return at the end of both the book and the movie: she shows up at Esperanza's wedding in a Model T (a symbol of social status in the 1930s) and married to the former revolutionary. While there is a minor debate as to whether this marriage shows a previously strong, feminist figure capitulating to the patriarchal order (Martínez 37; Sinnigen 122), the point here is that this revolutionary woman not only returns to the life of her powerful family, but also has powerful connections and a social status of her own, as a member of the ruling elite of revolutionary officers turned postrevolutionary government officials. Gertrudis's example puts forward the main ideological device behind Arau's movie: an attempt to inscribe national history in the very body of the middle class, via sexual relations, food practices, and genetic inheritance. The casting of Claudette Maillé as Gertrudis is significant here, given that the protagonist of the movie (as portrayed by Lumi Cavazos) is a dark-haired, brownish-skinned heroine, whereas Maillé, the actress playing the woman who becomes a revolutionary soldier (and was raised as the protagonist's sister) is white and blonde, and in fact of French origin. Visually, this gesture seems calculated to elicit melodramatic identification from women of the conservative middle class, who would be reluctant to identify with a darker-skinned character.

By creating a vision of national identity clearly focused on the middle class and the elite, Arau seeks to cater to what he perceives as the new audience of Mexican cinema, an educated and well-to-do social group that can afford to go to the movies in a privatized distribution system but still holds affective ties to the national past. The economic success of the film in Mexico can be misleading in terms of the movie's cultural appeal, given that it was shown on very few screens during most of its exhibition time. This fact can be interpreted as an indication of the film's capacity to attract an audience who would actually seek out the film, and who would be aware of it in the midst of Hollywood's dominance of Mexican screens and the film industry's state of disarray. It is hard to believe that an urban popular audience, whose film tastes were closer to the *sexycomedias* and TV star vehicles of the 1980s than to a stylized view of the Mexican past, would go out of its way to see the film. Thus, the film's Mexican success can be credited to a middle class that had the economic means to pay for increasingly expensive movie ticket and the curiosity to watch a movie validated by its success in the United States. In fact, at the level of national ideology, the film is essentially a way to suggest to the elite that it remains at the core of the cultural signifiers of Mexican identity, after decades of State-fueled cultural populism. In this sense, Deborah Shaw remarks, "the film thus reassures the middle and upper classes that there is no ethical problem with having servants, provided that they treat those servants well" (*Contemporary Cinema* 42). The revolution in Arau's movie is never an issue of class inequality, but rather a guarantee that social change in Mexico, like the one brought about in the 1920s or the one taking place in the late 1980s, never threatens the status of the privileged.

At this point, it is important to revise Harmony Wu's previously cited claim that *Como agua para chocolate* does not create a foundational fiction. Wu is right in that Pedro and Tita's romance ultimately fails to constitute one, but another more telling foundational fiction does take shape in the movie: the marriage of Esperanza, the youngest representative of the De la Garza family, to Alex Brown, a Harvard-bound American, identified as such by Victoria Martínez. Martínez also points out that Esquivel and Arau's focus on the American characters like John Brown and Alex as scientists and as educated men "suggests an emphasis on the superiority of United States empirical thinking" (39n). "John Brown" and "Alex Brown" are purposefully generic American names, which underscores Arau and Esquivel's intention to mark these characters as such.[5] However, this U.S. reference has its traditionalist tilt, since John Brown is partly Native American. The not-so-veiled allegory here is that the future of the family, and of the traditional national elite represented by the De la Garza, lies in espousing the visions of American modernity brought about by a close relationship with the United States. The very configuration of gender in the movie points toward this idea. In one of the most lucid readings of the film, Sergio de la Mora contends that "Mexico in this film is gendered female while the United States is gendered male, although both non-threatening and hardly virile, thereby foregrounding a 'natural' pairing of U.S.-Mexican intercultural relations" (*Cinemachismo* 148). Consequently, I argue that Arau's movie ultimately holds a schizophrenic view of the role of Mexican cinema within neo-Mexicanist frameworks. On the one hand, Arau breaks with the entrenched nationalism that characterized most Mexican films in the post-revolutionary and *echeverrista* periods by incorporating the United States as an organic element in the historical evolution of Mexico toward modernity and in the preservation of its elites and the social structure of inequality that sustains Mexican modernization. On the other, Arau's sugary visual palette, along with its affective engagement with an element as traditional as "authentic" cuisine, shows a clear reluctance to renounce the Mexicanist imagery that colonized Mexican visual culture for decades. The iconic status of *Como agua para chocolate,* beyond its commercial success, lies in the fact that it tried to resolve the core ideological conflict of Mexican culture in the early years of neoliberalism. At the level of its narrative construction, it succeeds in tying nation and modernization to the genealogical legacy of the elite. In this, the movie is unique: subsequent directors would actually attempt to either recover the lost signifiers of Mexicanism through films such as *Danzón* and others discussed in this chapter, or would altogether do away with nationalist imagery and wholeheartedly embrace the culture of an increasingly Americanized and increasingly wealthy urban middle class, in films like the romantic comedies discussed in Chapter 2.

Arau's claim on historical memory is grounded in the particular way in which film intervenes in historical narrative, a procedure that is essential to understanding the stakes of neo-Mexicanist cinema in the context of the early neoliberal transitions. Some film scholars inspired by Deleuze have explained this procedure as the tension between "official history" (as a discourse that exists in the "movement image" and in territorializing objects such as textbooks and family photos) and the "time image" that actualizes the potentiality of history into narratives that "shock" the spectator into an act of remembrance.[6] In these terms, neo-Mexicanist cinema is based on the deployment of both time-images and movement-images against the background of Mexican official history—and of the portrayals of that history against the populist background of national revolutionary ideology and cinema. *Como agua para chocolate* establishes its starting point in the present day and in the figure of a narrator who reactualizes Mexican history through her intimate rendition of her family history. However, the memory presented by the film is actually structured as a movement-image: it presents a chronological, historical narrative that begins with a "first cause" (Tita's inability to marry Pedro) and ultimately develops a teleological narrative that ends with the marriage of Esperanza and Alex. The crucial point of David Martin-Jones's analysis for this reading of *Como agua para chocolate*, is that

> a film does not have to be a time-image, or a hybrid image to critique the dominant ideology usually found in the movement-image. Many movement-images critique the dominant view of national identity in their narratives.... Although the demonstration of national deterritorialisation found in these films often turns out to be a lesson on how national identity is currently reterritorialising, it always contains the potential to enact a minor deterritorialising of the time of the nation. (38)

Como agua para chocolate creates a template for the study of neo-Mexicanist cinema precisely because it shows this constant tension between deterritorialization and reterritorialization in the neoliberal period. The act of memory exercised by the film's narrator allows for the critique of national history as portrayed by State ideologies. Or, to use Bartra's terms, it presents cinema as a way to deterritorialize national identity from its previously organic connections to the imaginary networks of political power. As the Mexican PRI regime evolves from the populist discourses of the 1970s and those who officially supported the New Wave movies of Cazals and Ripstein, and moves toward the ideologies of modernization that foreground NAFTA and the surrounding neoliberal project, movies like Arau's prove crucial to a reexamination of national history and national identity that breaks with the national revolutionary ideology of the past but ultimately results in a reterritorialization of national identity into a different configuration of hegemony. So, while *Como agua para chocolate* exercises a critique of official history by locating it in family memory and the private space of the kitchen, it reemerges as an official history of a different sort—as an allegory in which Mexico's symbolic marriage to the United States via NAFTA is narrated as the logical and chronological result of a historical saga (or a movement-image) that starts in the *Porfiriato*, traverses the revolution and, teleologically, concludes in a foundational fiction of Americanized modernization.

Two fundamental corollaries to the understanding of neo-Mexicanist cinema and the evolution of Mexican film into a cultural practice organic to the neoliberal period emerge here. First, the questioning of the official nationalism inherited by national revolutionary ideology and the PRI regime is not in itself a "progressive" act. If anything, *Como agua para chocolate* clearly shows that such revisions may result in an account of the nation that is not only more conservative, but also, and more importantly, one that produces a new official history that neatly ties the imaginaries of national identity to an emerging neoliberal hegemony. Second, as I will explore both in the rest of this chapter and in the following two, even when there is a substantial difference between the aesthetic procedures of neo-Mexicanist films and other movies, the underlying process of deterritorialization and reterritorialization may still operate along the same lines. My contention in the next chapter will be that urban romantic comedies such as Cuarón's *Sólo con tu pareja* operate within the same framework of neoliberalism and cultural hegemony.

Arau's movie remains unique because no other neo-Mexicanist film is as transparent in the relocation of national identity within the neoliberal framework. The fact that neither he nor his protagonists played a particularly significant role in the development of Mexican cinema after *Como agua para chocolate* further heightens the singularity of Arau's cinematic impact. Ultimately, the movie's success did not result in a true aesthetic transformation of Mexican film production. This may sound surprising given the film's importance, which may have resulted in part because of its capacity to present an "alternative" history of the nation while ultimately conforming to a hegemonic model of identity. However, its cultural location as a film for export shows why it failed to become an influential piece. *New York Times* critic Janet Maslin celebrates the movie because it "relies so enchantingly upon fate, magic and a taste for the supernatural that it suggests García Márquez in a cookbook-writing mode." It is precisely this reliance that ultimately dooms Arau's film as an aesthetic alternative to the "cinema of solitude," foregrounding its ultimate reterritorialization of a national identity in the symbolic space of the conservative middle class. The film was, in the end, a recognizably official film that played a role in the promotion of Mexico, to the point that Arau boasted that the Mexican tourism ministry was grateful to him because of the publicity that his movie created for the country (Shaw, *Contemporary Cinema* 39). In fact, one of the possible cultural fields of meaning for the film lies in the Mexican government's campaign to promote the country in the United States on the eve of NAFTA, in its attempt to change the prejudices of the American public.[7] While the movie's success in the United States would anticipate the strategies of promotion used by films in the latter part of the decade, this official use of nationalism was increasingly irrelevant in terms of actual cultural production, as cultural elites moved to what Roger Bartra, in *Blood, Ink and Culture,* calls the "post-Mexican condition." In fact, it is very telling that Arau, after a stint in Hollywood, never again directed a film with any kind of cultural impact in Mexico, while his main actors, Lumi Cavazos and Marco Leonardi, failed to become stars in the new Mexican film industry. To be sure, neo-Mexicanist aesthetics still played an important role in 1990s Mexican cinema, manifested in forms in which the tension between deterritorialization and reterritorialization, or between time-image and movement-image, happened in more subtle and complex ways. Where Alfonso Arau's film ultimately failed, however, another film succeeded. María Novaro's *Danzón* became the other foundational neo-Mexicanist film, one that ultimately enjoyed greater critical acclaim and a more significant cultural life.

A Not-So-Golden Age: The Aesthetics of Nostalgia in the Neo-Mexicanist Wave

While not as economically successful as *Como agua para chocolate,* María Novaro's *Danzón* (1991) remains another iconic example of the way in which filmmakers sought to reconfigure the connection between film and national culture as a way to reengage audiences. *Danzón* tells the story of Julia Solórzano (María Rojo), a phone operator and single mother whose main source of leisure comes from the *danzonera* culture in urban popular nightclubs in Mexico City. One day, Julia's dance partner, Carmelo, disappears from the *danzonera* scene for reasons that are never quite made clear. After receiving an ambiguous lead regarding his whereabouts, she decides to go to Veracruz to find him. In Veracruz, her search is ultimately futile, but in the process she befriends the owner of a hotel that happens to be the home of some prostitutes, and establishes a friendship with a group of transvestite performers. Julia also meets Rubén (Víctor Carpinteyro), a young port technician with whom she ends up having a romantic and sexual affair. In the end, in spite of her attraction to Rubén and the newly found albeit uncertain happiness she has found in Veracruz, she decides to go back to her life in Mexico City, where Carmelo reappears on the dance floor at the very end. The use of *danzón* as the cultural core of the movie is quite symptomatic. As Robert Buffington shows in his article on the *danzonera* culture, *danzón* is a musical and dance genre from the first half of the twentieth century, mostly practiced by working-class men and women in Veracruz and Mexico City. Novaro's movie, in Buffington's account, responds to a revival of this urban popular culture in the 1980s (88). In the next section, I will show that Novaro's choice of *danzón* as the central signifier for her movie focuses on nostalgia to reterritorialize national identity in a feminine space that exists not in the conservative middle classes, but rather within a fading urban popular class which, after the harsh portrayals of the 1970s, returns as a cultural alternative to the emergent neoliberal modernity. Before fully engaging with *Danzón,* though, a brief foray into the role of nostalgia in Mexican cinema of the early 1990s is necessary in order to understand the cultural location of the movie's neo-Mexicanist aesthetic in a larger landscape that includes not only *Como agua para chocolate,* but also various attempts at rethinking the nation in cinema.

The idea of restoring the relationship between cinema and audience was clearly in the air at the time, as shown by a strongly nostalgic drive in the films of the period. In fact, two of the most important films of the early part of the decade were remakes of successful classical films: *La mujer del puerto* and *Salón México.* Arturo Ripstein's *La mujer del Puerto* (1991) is a remake of Arcady Boytler's landmark 1934 film about a prostitute who falls in love with a man who happens to be her brother (neither she nor he is aware of the connection).[8] The return to this movie is not coincidental at all, considering the fact that many critics consider it the "first singular Mexican film" (Monsiváis, quoted in Mora 39). In fact, as Andrea Noble contends, Ripstein's remake shares a cultural preoccupation with the original, since both movies were made "at a time when debates around Mexico's status within the international geopolitical order were coursing through national cultural politics" (42). Ripstein was evidently facing the same questions as Arau: the need for a national cinema in the wake of a process of economic internationalization is strictly related to the filmmakers' attempts to claim a unified national self to be defended from the transnational threat. A similar idea lies behind José Luis García Agraz's 1996 remake of Emilio Fernández's 1949 film *Salón México.* By placing the story in a romanticized portrayal of cabaret life in the 1930s, García Agraz seeks to actualize the glory days of an iconic cultural space in the city that granted a particular cultural density to the cinema of the time. Still, just as Arau is trapped by a certain cultural conservatism in order to sustain his neo-Mexicanist aesthetic, these remakes bring back not only the popular films, but also the conservative ideologies espoused by them. Furthermore, one could even contend, invoking once more the previously cited ideas of David Martin-Jones, that these remakes do not even perform the reterritorializing operations of films like *Como agua para chocolate,* opting instead for a rebirth of previous configurations of culture.[9]

Still, these remakes question the role of nostalgia in the reformulation of Mexican cinema, precisely because neo-Mexicanist cultural ideologies in the early 1990s do not necessarily advocate the pedagogic identification of the citizenry with a fixed idea of the nation as exercised by Golden Age cinema. Neo-Mexicanist films are, first and foremost, cultural texts engaged with a crisis of the relationship between film and polity and in search of new forms of meaningful connection. Bartra has called this cultural attitude "melancholy," based on the idea that the intellectual class defines national identity through the yearning of a lost primordial unity that still wanders in some corners of the nation (*Cage* 29–38). However, I contend that nostalgia is a more appropriate term for the specific discussion of Neo-Mexicanist cinema, because its retrospective gesture does not point to the constitution of a certain configuration of identity, but rather to the ability of film to engage with popular imaginaries across Mexico's social spectrum.

In her book *The Future of Nostalgia*, Svetlana Boym offers a theoretical framework that may be used to illustrate neo-Mexicanist engagements with the past. Boym speaks of "two kinds of nostalgia" that "are not absolute types, but rather tendencies, ways of giving shape and meaning to longing." The first, "restorative nostalgia," seeks "to rebuild the lost home and patch up the memory gaps" and is defined by its engagement "in the antimodern mythmaking of history by means of a return to national symbols and myths," as well as "in total reconstruction of monuments of the past" (41). Unsurprisingly, Boym identifies restorative nostalgia with nationalist revivals. When extrapolated to the case of neoliberal Mexico, restorative nostalgia refers to an attempt to recuperate the lost plenitude of the (revolutionary) nation in the face of the radical disconnects at the level of politics and culture that emerged post-1968: the citizenry's broken relationship with the State, the gradual erosion of the post-revolutionary polity, and the threatening Americanization and modernization of neoliberal policy. Thus, remaking films like *La mujer del puerto* or *Salón México* in the middle of the first major neoliberal transition, the years leading to the implementation of NAFTA, is an attempt to recreate a cultural aura that supposedly comes from a moment when film had a more public role in social life. By reawakening the cinematic myths of a bygone world and its outmoded aesthetic, filmmakers like Ripstein and García Agraz are in fact resisting the need to engage with the historical defeat of the national revolutionary discourses of popular identity by establishing a visual space in which those memories emerge as an alternative imaginary to the increasingly modernized world of 1980s Mexico. Unlike Arau, whose nostalgic fantasy unreservedly embraces U.S. characters as integral parts of the national family saga and deterritorializes revolutionary popular images to fold them into an ode to the social elites, Ripstein and García Agraz would rather short-circuit both cultural modernization and the "cinema of solitude." After the exhaustion of the identity models of 1970s and 1980s cinema that Ripstein and García Agraz respectively pursue in films like *El lugar sin límites* (1978) and *Nocaut* (1984), the only way to bring back the lost densities of cinema is, literally, to fully reconstruct them. This reconstruction may be brought about via the practice of the remake, or even through the recourse to a somewhat uncritical current of historical film, as in Ernesto Medina's Independence saga *Gertrudis Bocanegra* (1992) or Eduardo Rossoff's conventional telling of Sor Juana's story in *Ave María* (1999).[10]

Of course, remakes are the most basic and obvious examples of restorative nostalgia. Another genre that found notoriety in the early and mid-1990s was the biopic, particularly the kind that recreated the lives of iconic figures of national culture. The best-known example is Alejandro Pelayo's *Miroslava* (1994), which narrates the life of Miroslava Stern, a Czech-born actress who was a celebrity in the Golden Age until her suicide in 1955. Nayibe Bermúdez Barrios shows that "Miroslava is the focus of the narration because the film concentrates on the chronological mapping of her life via a voice-over originating in a narrator and, through this filter, by flashbacks 'originating' in the character's conscience" (134). This structure is remarkably similar to the central narrative device of *Como agua para chocolate,* further unfolding the story into a time-image that elicits a double act of remembrance: that of a narrator and the memories of Miroslava herself. The interesting point here is that the movie suspends itself in time, rather than actualizing the narrative into any kind of allegorical project. Unlike Arau, who recovers Tita's story from the body and memory of his modern-day narrator, Pelayo begins and ends his movie with the day on which Miroslava died, simply presenting a fragmentary reconstruction of her suicide. Pelayo's reterritorializing gesture is thus not directed toward an ideological configuration of the present. Rather, it constructs a specifically cinematic space in which the memory of the past ultimately serves only the film itself.

It is important to note two facts about Pelayo here. First, most of his previous directorial work had been focused on documentaries about either the Golden Age or the "cinema of solitude." Second, Pelayo was director of IMCINE, the national institute of film, and of the Cineteca Nacional, the national film archive, in the late 1990s.[11] Thus, we can see in a very literal sense two instances of restorative nostalgia. First, Pelayo creates a cinema that consistently reflects upon itself and, more particularly, upon the history of its social role. Second, this restorative nostalgia takes place in a film industry that claims cultural nationalism because its capacity to build itself upon the cultural institutions of the State. In the end, biopics and remakes exercise a similar gesture; that is, they attempt to restore a lost form of film art in the face of increasing privatization and Americanization of film production. Not coincidentally, Ripstein was the director not only of a remake, but also of another important biopic, *La reina de la noche* (1994), about the life of Lucha Reyes, another actress of Mexican Golden Age cinema and a performer who debuted and made famous one of Mexico's most nationalistic songs, "Guadalajara."

Perhaps the most extreme example of restorative nostalgia in the first half of the 1990s is Juan Mora Catlett's 1991 *Retorno a Aztlán.* Filmed entirely in Náhuatl, the language of the Aztecs, this movie presents two overlapping stories. First, it depicts a fifteenth-century drought that coincided with the death of Emperor Moctezuma Ilhuicamina the Elder in 1469, ending the period of Aztec splendor and expansion. The movie also tells the mythical story of the birth of the Fifth Sun, which Moctezuma imagines on his deathbed. According to Carl Mora, the film makes quite an effort to be faithful to its source materials, following the visual and narrative structure of pre-Hispanic codices that documented indigenous myths and legends (215). The existence of this film attests to the impact of restorative nostalgia as an apparently viable aesthetic and cultural alternative: a movie in Náhuatl faithfully recreating a pre-Conquest period is an obvious attempt to recast national cinema as a return to the nation's alleged roots. One could certainly argue for the importance of recognizing indigenous cultures as a fundamental component of national culture and the symbolic importance of shooting what was, at the time, the first feature film in an indigenous Mexican language. The problem here is that this gesture is not an organic recognition of indigenous cultures in the context of contemporary Mexico. It is simply a nationalistic nod that, in its attempt to fully restore a cultural past, produces a movie that cannot lead to a substantial reconsideration of the connection between cinema and identity. Indeed, the film clearly shows the limitations of such a project: the acting is rather poor and unconvincing, because the director had to dub his actors' voices with those of actual speakers of Náhuatl in order to achieve the correct pronunciation of the language. Also, perhaps because of budgetary constraints, the setting is not historically accurate: the colorful and monumental cities of the Spanish chronicles are represented by short, gray pyramids that look neither like ruins nor the real thing. The film is more successful in other areas, particularly the soundtrack, which makes good use of Aztec musical instruments. In the end, the movie is important because it shows a clear aesthetic dead end: it is an example of the ultimate inability of restorative nostalgia to produce a viable contemporary cinema.[12]

Restorative nostalgia is a gesture that emerges as a radical reaction to a feeling of cultural loss and senselessness. Given the distribution crisis faced by Mexican cinema and the rapid social changes brought about during the Salinas de Gortari presidency, the drive to restore cinema's older nationalist glory is quite understandable. One should note, though, that the gesture of restorative nostalgia belongs mostly to the cinema produced during the first half of the 1990s, and that some of the directors involved in these trends often broke the ideological and aesthetic constraints posed by neo-Mexicanist imperatives. García Agraz provides an instructive case of the ways in which neo-Mexicanist aesthetics emerged from a cinematic identity crisis experienced by directors who were formed in the two preceding decades. Two years before *Salón México*, García Agraz shot a quite personal film, *Desiertos mares* (1992), which was unfairly overlooked by academic critics and which, in my view, constitutes a very telling narrative of the aesthetic crisis faced by directors in the early 1990s. In *Desiertos mares,* Arturo Ríos plays Juan Aguirre, a film director who faces a personal and creative crisis after his wife, Elena (Lisa Owen), leaves him. After this event, the film connects the main story (primarily located in contemporary Mexico City, with particular attention to the historic downtown area) with two subplots. The first consists of flashbacks to Juan's childhood, in which he remembers a family road trip through the Sonoran desert to the Gulf of California during the 1950s. The story unfolds when Juan's father has to return to work, creating an opportunity for his mother to have an affair with a local man. The other story depicts one of Juan's movie screenplays, about the story of a *conquistador* in the early days of the Conquest. Interestingly, the same actor, Juan Carlos Colombo, plays both Juan's father and the *conquistador,* creating a symbolic connection between his personal story and a foundational event of the nation. Another element of the story is that, in the contemporary storyline, Margarita (Verónica Merchant), a young aspiring director, becomes personally involved with Juan, since she wants Juan to help her with the production of a vampire film. The fact that Margarita is pursuing such a project is significant here, because it links Margarita with a tradition of "Mexploitation" cinema that Mexican directors like Juan were trying to overcome.[13]

Desiertos mares may be read as an allegory of a director who, faced with the creative crisis of cinema, ponders the different genres that may be used to tell his story. In fact, the four genres presented in the film were, at the time, viable aesthetic possibilities, each with major representatives in the movie scene of the early 1990s. Nicolás Echevarría brilliantly engaged the topic of the Conquest with the exceptional *Cabeza de Vaca* (1991), a movie that avoids the romantic idealization of *Retorno a Aztlán* by focusing on Álvar Núñez Cabeza de Vaca's failed expedition to Florida, presenting a brutal picture of the Conquest and its violence while questioning the idealistic narratives of the event produced on the eve of the 1992 Columbian quincentennial. I will discuss this movie further in the following section. The father story clearly points to the recreations of the mid-twentieth century in Mexico, as in the later part of *Como agua para chocolate* and even *Danzón*'s winks at the 1940s and 1950s. Cuarón's *Sólo con tu pareja* had already explored the contemporary urban story about the family and love issues of the urban middle class. Finally, the vampire film proposed by Margarita had already been shot by Guillermo del Toro in *Cronos.* By revisiting the recent spectrum of film aesthetics deployed by Mexican film, García Agraz shows the enormously creative space that the crisis had paradoxically generated and, in doing so, points to the fact that restorative nostalgia was perhaps the least interesting and culturally relevant of the available aesthetic devices. Furthermore, the films referred to by the genres presented in *Desiertos mares* were perhaps the most influential movies of the period, something I will show in this and in future chapters.[14] Still, it is telling that his choice for his next film was *Salón México*. In the middle of such aesthetic openness, the cinematic codes of the familiar were, perhaps, comforting.

Danzón and the Poetics of Reflective Nostalgia

Danzón departs from the codes of restorative nostalgia by focusing on a different type of engagement with the past. Boym's second category, "reflective nostalgia," dwells "in longing and loss, the imperfect process of remembrance" and "lingers on ruins, the patina of time and history, in the dreams of another place and another time" (41). If restorative nostalgia focuses on national memory, reflective nostalgia "is more about individual and cultural memory," an individual memory "that savors details and memorial signs, perpetually deferring homecoming itself" (49). Novaro's visual language exemplifies this second category of nostalgia. Rather than placing her story in the past, Novaro creates the image of a present-day Mexico City, where the ruins of the Golden Age linger in the outfits worn to the nightclubs and the music played there. Claudia Schaefer describes Novaro's Mexico City through some telling details:

> The setting of the 1991 film is fairly mundane: a vaguely insinuated urban neighborhood with neon signs along its dark streets; the beckoning strains of a yet-unseen local orchestra emanate from a dingy doorway set in an old-fashioned façade in the old part of the city. Both aspects establish an overall look of time without event, as if it could be either 1948 or 1991. There are no indications of anything having transpired since 1948 with the exception of the advent of color photography. The dance hall appears both dissociated from the flow of historical time—it remains standing, even if run-down and worn—and a confirmation of the impossibility of a cultural vestige surviving intact. (59)

This quote adequately transmits the aesthetics that Novaro sets forward in her film: a Mexico irrevocably marked by the persistently haunting specters of its popular culture.

Still, the world described by Schaefer corresponds more to the nightclubs than to the everyday life of the characters in the movie. Both Julia and her daughter are telephone operators, and significant scenes occur in their modern Mexico City apartment, in the phone center, and in the busy streets while waiting for public transportation. The importance of the juxtaposition of old and new rests on the fact that Novaro is neither recreating the past nor restoring a lost utopia. Rather, her film engages with the irreversible movement of time and posits nostalgic agency on Rojo's character. Julia literally embodies the past, not only through her passionate commitment to *danzón,* but also in the way she dresses to seduce men. One particular scene of the movie points this out clearly. One day in Veracruz, Julia receives a tip that Carmelo may be working as a cook on a Greek ship docked in the port. She wears a 1940s-style dress in an attempt to look attractive for Carmelo, attracting catcalls from the sailors. At the end of this scene, after failing to find Carmelo, Julia meets Rubén, who falls for her in part because of her outfit. The scene is significant for two reasons. First, while Novaro presents Julia in a beautiful yet anachronistic outfit, with an emotional *bolero* in the background, the port remains a contemporary space—a gray, industrialized, and dirty landscape that inevitably interrupts the dreamy semiotics of the nation lost. Second, it is important here that dress and music represent the core of the lost past, because the nation longed for by Novaro's aesthetic is not restored as a scene, but rather woven into Julia's body and affects. In a way, Julia is a deeply quixotic character, the believer in a sense of wonder that the harshness of the contemporary world has destroyed. Márgara Millán points out that Novaro's camera "likes to travel through space, portray objects, [and] suspend itself in the colors [of the film] as part of the emotional content—for example, in the planes that 'present' vital space, giving contextual information: who lives here, what are their tastes, what is their mood" (*Derivas* 176; my translation). Novaro's movie works in the consistent contrast between the rapid movement of modernity and the slow pace of culture and emotions: the camera contemplates Julia's world in all its glory as a way to resist the rapid pace of modernity.

In these terms, gender plays a radically different role here vis-à-vis the nation from the one in *Como agua para chocolate*. In Arau's movie, the feminine is by and large a mechanism of transmission of the nation, where family tradition, cuisine, and kin become the meaningful links between the present and the past. In *Danzón,* feminine spaces are not confined to the domestic arena, but instead colonize the entire space of the city and the night. In Mexico City, most of the action occurs either in Julia's house, where she lives with her daughter, or in the phone center, where all the employees are female. The only site of contact with the masculine lies in the nightclub, a highly self-contained and ritualized space. Similarly, in Veracruz, Julia stays in a hotel mostly inhabited by women, especially prostitutes, and frequents gay nightclubs, creating a separate gendered space that is ultimately presented as feminine: the gay characters are, in fact, transvestites. For Julia to meet Rubén, she has to venture to the only masculine space in the film, the docks, where she stands out in stark contrast to the background. Óscar Robles suggestively coins the term "maternational identity" to speak of Novaro's work and, in the particular case of *Danzón,* he argues that the plot "reincorporates the mother in other more free, vital and human *terrains* of feminine identity, altering the polarized hegemonic schemes" (119). Robles goes on to suggest that this new centrality of the mother in the film displaces the State, which is allegorized by the figure of the absent father. While this last allegory is somewhat problematic, since the presence of the State is not indicated in any way in the film itself, the notion of maternational identity is useful in explaining Novaro's constructed world. The nation here does not lie in the political or the historical, so Novaro does not need flashbacks to the revolution or the *Porfiriato,* as Arau does. Instead, the traditions of the nations are inscribed in the contemporary through gendered practices: dressing, dancing, and singing. It is significant that most of the soundtrack of the film is based on songs interpreted by a woman, Toña la Negra, an iconic singer from mid-century Veracruz.

In *Danzón,* gender is the site of reflective nostalgia, the place where the nation is simultaneously deterritorialized through the deliberately anachronistic cultural codes adopted by the movie and reterritorialized through the affective identification of Julia with the imaginaries of the past. Anachronism becomes a key issue here, because it is crucial to understanding Novaro's aesthetic objective. All the elements of modernity in the movie are fading. Julia's job as a phone operator is heavily charged with meaning in 1991, since one of the neoliberal regime's most important economic policies was the privatization of the telecommunications industry. Telmex, the national phone company, was privatized in 1990. This privatization sets forth not only a clear example of Mexico's rapid economic and social changes during the neoliberal period, but also an illustration of the changes in labor and economic relations of the time. Julia's job, in this context, was one of the things in peril, as privatization radically changed labor relations in Mexico, weakening unions and contributing to deeper social inequalities. In fact, historians and political scientists frequently point out the case of Telmex as one of the most paradoxical in the neoliberal modernization project, since it represents an industry that was privatized according to the economic vogue, but that ultimately became a monopoly and an example of crony capitalism (Haber et al. 89). That Julia works for a phone company—although it is unnamed in the film, it is obviously Telmex, the only operator at the time—in 1990–1991 clearly inscribes her everyday life into the heart of a key neoliberal transformation. Unlike *Como agua para chocolate,* in which the narrator sits in a kitchen, cutting onions and detached from history, in *Danzón* the contemporary exists as an inescapable backdrop that haunts the reterritorialized nation of reflective nostalgia. The ending is quite significant: rather than renouncing her contemporary life to stay in the idyllic spaces of Veracruz, where the past seems to linger a little more persistently, Julia decides to come back. The present is ultimately unavoidable.[15]

This foreshadowing presence of the contemporary must be underscored, since critics have surprisingly overlooked that fact, perhaps because of their fascination with the neo-Mexicanist codes deployed by the movie. Most works have either focused on the movie entirely as a representation of the feminine or its intersections with the homoerotic (Suárez, "Feminine Desire"; Valdés; Robles; Iglesias), or as a revival of a lost cultural scene (Schaefer; Arredondo; Buffington; Tierney, "Silver Sling-Backs").[16] Even the most intuitive readings of the movie have not fully acknowledged the subtle but all too real presence of neoliberalism in the film. For instance, Dolores Tierney argues that the film's structure is based on dance and its use "to shape and punctuate the narrative," and she ultimately interprets it as a purely gendered allegory: "The *danzón* at first represents Julia's old-fashioned view of the world . . . but it comes to represent her self-awareness and self-liberation" (369). In other words, Tierney ultimately digs out of the traditional culture a feminist reading that, in my view, contradicts in the most basic sense the premise of the movie: a woman leaving everything behind to chase a man she barely knows. Clearly, this is hardly a feminist premise. Therefore, the film's allegedly feminist stance can be easily criticized for not going far enough. In his essay on the film, Ayala Blanco argues that it is based on an "insipid femininity" that sacrifices the sensuality of the dance for a narrative that reestablishes "the Joy of Being a Woman" (*La eficacia* 388; my translation). *Danzón*'s limitations in portraying gender issues help show that the interesting dimensions of the film exist elsewhere.

Schaefer takes the notion of a popular culture that disconnects the movie from the contemporary even further: "Novaro locates Julia and the musical tradition within the cinematic frame but outside the narrative of history. In fact, the historical is extradiegetic, lurking somewhere just outside of our vision but never directly intruding upon the scene" (75). Schaefer does not ignore the fact that the middle of neoliberal turmoil has a role in the movie, since, following Tomás Pérez Turrent, she argues that the movie's success reflects the trend in which nationalist movies are particularly popular in moments of modernization and economic bonanza (79). Still, Schaefer mentions this issue mostly in passing, as an interruption of the romantic plot (62), thus giving Julia's working status a more anecdotal role in her analysis. Given the high profile of the Telmex privatization at the time, it is likely that such a reference would be familiar to spectators of the movie acquainted with Mexico's affairs at the time.

I would contend that the historical, and more particularly, the sociopolitical, are in plain sight, in a movie about a female employee of one of neoliberalism's crucial industries. In fact, the phone company is not the only sign in the movie of a fading history and a cruel present. Another significant moment comes from Julia's trip to Veracruz: she travels by train. This is noteworthy because, in 1990, trains were far from being a common form of transportation: most people would fly or take a bus, which made the trip considerably shorter. Train cars in some cases dated back to the *Porfiriato*, making rail an inefficient form of transportation. Still, the train Julia rides has quite a history: it belongs to the first railroad line in Mexico, dating back to the 1840s.

It played a very significant role in the revolution and in the massive railroad strikes of the 1950s. And, like Telmex, the project of privatizing it was in the air in 1991: it would ultimately go into private hands in 1995. Novaro also notes in the commentary section of the DVD that she chose the train over the bus to further highlight Julia's social class.[17] In this way, Novaro inscribes history in subtle but decisive ways in her movies, and her nostalgic world is not an attempt to escape: it holds on to the remnants of a world slowly but surely fading away. The true critical strength of the movie does not lie, then, in its cultural signifiers, which in themselves are less significant than they might seem, nor in Novaro's work on gender, which is not quite as interesting as that put forward in her other movies, including *Lola* (1989) and *El jardín del Edén* (1994). Rather, it turns out to be the most important neo-Mexicanist movie of the period, thanks to its use of its reterritorialized nation to fully and unequivocally engage with the destructive forces of neoliberal modernity.

Popular culture in Novaro's cinema is not a way to put the present or history under erasure, but rather to create a beautiful mirage that is ultimately haunted and defeated by time. Boym argues that "one becomes aware of the collective frameworks of memories when one distances oneself from one's community or when that community itself enters a moment of twilight" (54). The *danzonera* community takes this proposition even further, given that it is based in a culture already in decline, whose revival happens only in the clearly inscribed spaces of the urban popular class in Mexico City and of old working-class people in Veracruz (whose life experiences are still framed by this tradition). In fact, some of the movie's detractors attack Novaro precisely for the anachronistic nature of her cultural world. Writer and critic Enrique Serna, for instance, argues that her image of the urban popular class "has been falsified and sanitized [*adecentada*] with the purpose of exporting it. Danzón is already a lyrical music, but Novaro converted it into an emblem of a popular culture that exists only in her fantasy" (102; my translation). Ayala Blanco goes further in this line, and accuses the film of "offering the middle class an insipid femininity so it can discover a popular class with which to identify without staining itself, since, at the end of the day, [*Danzón*] is as stupid and shallow as the middle class itself" (*La eficacia* 388; my translation). Ayala Blanco's and Serna's virulent attacks are based on the premise that Novaro ultimately puts the "real" working class under erasure and substitutes it for an idealized version defined by its allegiances to a no longer current popular culture. While there is some merit to Serna's argument, and one could go so far as to argue that this is a problem of neo-Mexicanist aesthetics at large more than of Novaro herself, his critique misses an important point. The fact that this culture is lost is quite obvious to her and to her audiences and it is hard to imagine that anyone watching this movie in Mexico would see an accurate representation of nightlife or national identity in it. Critics favorable to Novaro also miss this point, and tend to argue that her style is "populist" and her work is an attempt to reinscribe these traditions back into the popular (Arredondo, "By Popular Demand" 195). As my description of the exhibition crisis of the early 1990s should make clear by this point, neo-Mexicanist films did not enjoy mass popular attendance, and any claim that popular identity was defined in them is a factually incorrect extrapolation of theories Mexican cinema designed around the films of the Golden Age.

Certainly, Novaro herself has contributed to these readings by emphasizing in interviews her desire to play with the forms of the Golden Age and her attempt to construct a narrative about a woman's path to emancipation (Arredondo, "María Novaro"). Nonetheless, I would argue that the movie is actually fully aware of the anachronistic nature of its sources. In fact, in one of the most intuitive readings of the film, Geeta Ramanathan has suggested that "the inadequacies of the melodrama in sustaining female desire are rendered apparent" (112), opening a space where working-class female characters are constructed by "auditory subjectivity" (112–19). While Ramanathan incorrectly connects the movie with magical realism (113), an aesthetic that is nowhere to be found in Novaro's film, her reading clearly shows that the uses of *danzón* in the movie are not about the constitution of a hegemonic national identity, which seems to be the object of Serna's critique. Rather, I would argue that Novaro's film attempts, with some degree of success, to use nostalgia as a form of subjective engagement for female characters clearly outside both the patriarchal structures of Mexican culture and, more importantly, of the structures of development brought about by the neoliberal model. However, Novaro's film fails at the end, as Carmelo's sudden return to the dance floor is quite dissonant with the process behind Julia's subjective development. The crucial moment, though, is Julia's homecoming to Mexico City and her ultimate rejection of the alternative life offered by Veracruz. Julia returns to the neoliberal time where her job and her culture are fading away, a temporal disjuncture in Mexico City's new neoliberal time. This misplaced temporality exists in tension with a contemporary world where the affects that move Julia and her colleagues are threatened not only by men—who, in fact, are not really that threatening in the movie—but by modernization itself. Hence, Novaro's anachronism attempts the constitution of a site of resistance to these particular processes of modernization, with an ultimate acceptance that, even if Julia really does manage to forge her own path, the neoliberal present is here to stay.

To use Boym's terms, by making us aware of the collective frameworks of memories activated by the movie's anachronism, *Danzón* ultimately exercises a work of mourning vis-à-vis the Golden Age and its cultural legacies. Rather than restoring them, Novaro hesitantly closes the door to this past and, through this mourning, ultimately accepts its loss. This is a crucial step for neo-Mexicanist cinema, because the codes and symbols of the national are in a process of clear erosion, and filmmakers would have to search for new languages to construct a national cinema. Perhaps the most salient feature in *Danzón*'s cultural engagements comes from its capacity to avoid the restitution of a conservative social order in its recovery of highly ritualized social practices of the past. As José Quiroga shows, "Nostalgia—for the particular order, for the universe of the danzón—reconfigures the characters of María Novaro's film, but nostalgia never obliterates the fact that these characters want to live within the safety of an order regulated by them and not necessarily by a return to heterosexual male dominance" ("(Queer)" 205). This break with the reterritorialization of conservative traditional values, present in movies such as *Como agua para chocolate* or *La mujer del puerto,* opened a creative space in the late 1990s and early 2000s, in which neo-Mexicanist aesthetics ultimately emerged as a highly critical cultural device, turning against the very hegemonic mechanisms it sustained for over seven decades. The last section of this chapter explores these transformations.

The Nation Otherwise: Transcultural Literary Adaptation and the New Languages of Neo-Mexicanism

While *Como agua para chocolate* and *Danzón* still occupy much of the attention devoted to early-1990s Mexican cinema, perhaps the most striking scene of the period comes from another movie, Nicolás Echevarría's *Cabeza de Vaca*. The film narrates the misadventures of sixteenth-century Spanish explorer Álvar Núñez Cabeza de Vaca (Juan Diego) and is based on his chronicles *Naufragios* and *Comentarios*. At the very end of the film, we see a considerable group of indigenous people carrying a large cross through the desert, following the drumbeat of a Spanish soldier. The scene is significant because of its elegance and its violence: we see the foundational moment of a new colonial town depicted as a decisive act of domination and subjection rather than the mythical encounter of two races. In fact, the absence of such an encounter is the leitmotif of the entire movie, constructed by Echevarría in a succession of slow scenes without dialogue to express the radical lack of communication between the *conquistadores* and the indigenous peoples. Echevarría's work is remarkable because of its exceptional quality, which led critic Ayala Blanco to a quite atypical recognition of its status as a "masterpiece" (*La eficacia* 278), something Mexican critics rarely confer to a Mexican movie. Perhaps more importantly, Echevarría's aesthetic was boldly constructed against the grain of inherited Mexicanist and neo-Mexicanist film codes, using traditional resources of historical film to deconstruct the official narratives of origin of Mexican *mestizaje*.[18] It is, in my view, the first major example of neo-Mexicanist cinema as a counterhegemonic political device in the context of neoliberalism.

Cabeza de Vaca was filmed and released in the same context that led to *Retorno a Aztlán,* around the 1992 quincentennial of the Columbian expedition. As Michel-Rolph Trouillot has shown, this particular commemoration of Columbus Day was underpinned by a strong transnational campaign by the Spanish government to celebrate the occasion, setting off an onslaught of films, books, and festivals designed to sustain a positive depiction of the event (136–40). Film, as an instrument of public history, became key to the development of this narrative, as demonstrated by the production of two transnational biopics about Columbus: Ridley Scott's *1492: The Conquest of Paradise* (1992), starring Gerard Depardieu, and John Glen's *Christopher Columbus: The Discovery* (1992), a less interesting film starring George Corraface and Marlon Brando.[19] Mexico was clearly part of this wave. In film, both *Retorno a Aztlán* and *Cabeza de Vaca* were funded with this purpose, while scholars across the social sciences and humanities produced a considerable body of scholarship and thought around the occasion.[20] In this context, *Cabeza de Vaca*'s ending proved to be quite a bold gesture, a decisive acknowledgement of the violence and despair behind the historical moment represented as a foundational and celebratory encounter by official historiography and culture. A good indication of the movie's incisive depiction of the foundations of transatlantic colonialism lies in the considerable amount of scholarship that, under frameworks such as postcolonial studies, devotes itself to questions of the body, otherness, and representation in the film, as well as to a discussion of the complex ideological devices of the Conquest deployed by the film. Krista Walter has argued that the film's ending leaves the spectators with "a heavy-handed sense of impending doom as we realize that the innocence of the New World can never be regained. And yet, such terrible knowledge does not prevent the postmodern conquistadors of consumer culture from persevering in their intrepid search for spiritual renewal and historical redemption through fetishized, mystified native others in whose image we wish to remake ourselves" (145). Other readings have emphasized the gendered nature of the native's naked body (Suárez, "Dominado"), the theoretical consequences of representing the encounter between self and other (Alvaray; Hershfield, "Assimilation"), or the presumably Orientalist and hagiographic structures behind the film's narrative (Barrueto 31–48). While these critiques underscore important issues, such as the film's somewhat exoticist depiction of indigenous cultures, the focus on theoretical questions of otherness has overlooked the importance of *Cabeza de Vaca* in the reconfiguration of ideas of national and historical film in Mexico.

The naturalized relationship between historical film and the imagined community has been an obstacle to fully understanding *Cabeza de Vaca* and its role in renewing Mexican cinema. For instance, in an otherwise brilliant article on the movie, Joanne Hershfield contends that, while "*Cabeza de Vaca* dramatizes a moment in the colonial process that forced a reconsideration between conqueror and conquered, between self and other," it ultimately results in "an effort to narrativize the production of a New World identity through the process of assimilation and identification with the Other" ("Assimilation" 9). Within the framework of postcolonial readings of the movie, this argument has strong merits and reflects a strong consensus among critics. However, when considering the movie as historical cinema, Hershfield's arguments rely a bit too heavily on the influential writings of Marcia Landy on the subject, contending that film's "focus on the relations among individual, history, and the nation provides a site for studying the complex web of social discourses that nations produce to define national identity," thus placing Echevarría within "a new generation of filmmakers" that "continues to search for a way to redefine Mexican identity cinematically while revising the narrative, stylistic and ideological models of the classic Mexican cinema" (11–12).

The problem lies in the assumption that revisiting historical scenes and stylistic models of classic cinema is naturally connected to an attempted definition of national identity.[21] This is the case in Arau's *Como agua para chocolate* and in the attempt to redeem pre-Columbian culture in *Retorno a Aztlán*. Both films clearly appeal to the viewer's codes of family and cultural identity, but it is hard to see how Echevarría's aesthetic of violence and noncommunication, as well as the visual harshness and slow tempo of his style, could lead spectators to an identity anagnorisis. This misreading of *Cabeza de Vaca* has two sources: the strong role, discussed before, of identity studies in Mexican studies, and the strong influence of European and Hollywood film in the definition of Mexican historical cinema. In fact, Hershfield specifically refers to *British Genres,* a work in which Landy famously contends that "the historical film is deeply intertwined with myths of the nation that are integral to most national film cultures" (53). This kind of film indeed exists in contemporary Mexico, as proven by the aforementioned *Retorno a Aztlán* and *Gertrudis Bocanegra,* as well as Felipe Cazals's biopic *Su alteza serenísima* (2000), which pedagogically reconstructs the life of nineteenth-century president Antonio López de Santa Anna from the perspective of his old age, or even in the many films produced for the bicentennial celebrations of 2010. These movies used visual languages that strove for "accurate" representations of the specific historical periods in question and that, alongside *telenovelas* like *El vuelo del águila,* about the life of Porfirio Díaz, created a widespread media practice that presented history in more or less the same visual and ideological terms accepted by the official history and by public consensus.[22] Still, Landy develops her argument within the context of British national cinema, where ideologies such as imperial nostalgia and global structures of mercantile and personal circulation create social functions of historical cinema that are absent from nonhegemonic cinematic traditions. In another book, *Cinematic Uses of the Past,* Landy recognizes that her theoretical approach is mostly useful for two particular forms of historical cinema, "melodramatic" and "operatic," without exhausting other forms of studying historical cinema (24). Insofar as *Cabeza de Vaca* does not fall into either category, I think that Landy's model provides an insufficient framework to understand Echevarría's work as national cinema.[23]

In order to explain the break represented by *Cabeza de Vaca,* I propose to read the movie outside the framework of historical films. In my view, the device that allows Echevarría to depart from the visual and ideological codes of nationalism, particularly in a context as charged as that of 1992, is not historical recreation, but rather literary adaptation.[24] As Mike Chopra-Gant has pointed out, a true understanding of historical film must crucially recognize the distance between academic history and media representation, as well as the fact that, as mediatic representations go, history remains in a constant process of making and remaking itself (95). In films that present a dissonant historical narrative that preempts an identity-constructing reading, this means that the critical focus must shift from issues of veracity and official history to the devices that allow filmmakers to be active producers of the historical narrative. In the case of *Cabeza de Vaca,* this potential lies both in the choice of Cabeza de Vaca's texts as source materials and in the ways in which Echevarría's film language uses them to configure a visual aesthetic that negotiates familiar historical signs with a semiotics that is highly critical of national discourses. It is quite telling that Echevarría did not opt for a more obvious figure, like Hernán Cortés, who more clearly corresponds to official narratives of the Conquest. In fact, Echevarría's idea to shoot a film about Cabeza de Vaca predated the quincentennial. As Carl Mora documents, Echevarría tried to shoot the movie in the mid-1980s but the film was denied funding by CONACINE, the precursor of IMCINE. Ultimately, Echevarría raised funds from the same sources that financed the quincentennial, including Televisión Española and Spain's Comisión del Quinto Centenario (Mora 196), probably on the premise that any recreation of the Conquest was acceptable for them. Still, as Mora also shows, the movie was criticized by Spanish reviewers, who considered it "far from satisfactory" (198). The fact that Echevarría got financing from such sources, then, is quite paradoxical. As Beatriz Pastor demonstrates in her authoritative study on Conquest literature, Cabeza de Vaca is a figure who creates tensions with imperial accounts of the encounter, and one whose relationships with the indigenous peoples undermined the mythical and heroic portrayals of the conquistador in other texts (246–86). Unlike the Columbus movies commissioned by the official institutions of the quincentennial, Echevarría stumbled into the financing opportunity, but his film did not belong organically or ideologically to the promotional machine of the event. In fact, beyond this context, the only other example of a Conquest film that may be categorized with *Cabeza de Vaca* is Werner Herzog's *Aguirre: The Wrath of God* (1972), which also focuses on a failed mission and whose discourse reflects the hubris of empire and the ultimate road to madness of the conquistador figure. Like Herzog, Echevarría presents neither a positive view of the encounter nor a nostalgic recreation of the lost world of pre-Columbian myth. Cabeza de Vaca's story does not reterritorialize national history, but rather leaves it suspended in an indeterminate space of violence and silence. Or, to extrapolate from Richard Gordon's suggestive analysis, it "exorcizes the nation" (this is Gordon's expression) via the critique of its colonial originalism (47).

Ultimately, *Cabeza de Vaca* resists the identity temptation, thanks to the particular way in which Echevarría adapted his source text. Unlike Mora Catlett, who conceived *Retorno a Aztlán* as a faithful recreation of pre-Columbian codices, Echevarría and screenwriter Guillermo Sheridan took many liberties with the original *crónica*. Mora has already pointed out that *Cabeza de Vaca* "is not an accurate historical reconstruction of Cabeza de Vaca's odyssey, nor is it meant to be. It is a symbolic, impressionistic, mystical interpretation" (195). The first consequence of this choice is that the film escapes both the operatic and melodramatic structures identified by Landy, as well as the pedagogic tone that plagues movies like *Retorno a Aztlán*. This is also the reason why *Cabeza de Vaca* has elicited so many theoretical readings detached from its specifically Mexican context: it contains an elegant aesthetic that sustains it beyond the constrictions of national cinema. In exercising a creative act of adaptation, Echevarría freed himself from the inherited discourses of national representation. Rather than opting for the idealized representation of indigenous people that runs from *Tizoc* to *Retorno a Aztlán*, *Cabeza de Vaca* presents the indigenous Other as engaged in a level of miscommunication that matches that of the conquistador and that shows the structures of violence and power prevalent in the colonized communities. Certainly one can find problems with the colonizing gaze of this approach, as the aforementioned critics have done, but the more important issue is that, in 1991, this depiction of indigenous people functioned as a major short circuit in the cultural semiotics of appropriations of pre-Columbian cultures on the eve of the quincentennial.[25] This achievement, which makes *Cabeza de Vaca* such a relevant film in the history of Mexican and Latin American cinema, is made possible by literary adaptation, insofar as it allows filmmakers to engage both with cultural narratives outside official national history and with the visual codes of national cinema inherited from Mexicanist and neo-Mexicanist films. Therefore, adaptation becomes a very prominent mechanism in the unlikely but fundamental transformation of the languages of Mexicanism into critical perspectives vis-à-vis neoliberal ideology and official discourse.

The true potential of literary adaptation as a way to gradually transcend the historical biases of neo-Mexicanist aesthetics resulted from a puzzling but crucial purchase of film rights. In the early 1990s, legendary producer Alfredo Ripstein Jr., father of Arturo, acquired the film rights to two novels by Egyptian novelist Naguib Mahfouz, winner of the 1988 Nobel Prize in Literature. The acquisition was a personal impulse: he simply was very impressed with Mahfouz's novels and, as a man who had produced cinema for nearly five decades, from the late years to the Golden Age and through the entire "cinema of solitude," he clearly saw the potential for those works to become films. In fact, this intuition was spot-on. As Hassan Al-Nemi extensively shows in a dissertation on the topic, Mahfouz's work is highly translatable to cinema and many of its topics and structures had parallels in the Egyptian film industry.[26] It is also telling that Mahfouz served in the Egyptian ministry of film. Ripstein chose two of Mahfouz's novels, the family drama *Beginning and End* and a community story named *Midaq Alley*. These novels share a series of topics: the confrontation between Islamic morality and everyday life, the trials and tribulations of the Egyptian working class, and the conflicts around social mobility and power faced by residents of Egypt. Adnan Haydar and Michael Beard have emphasized Mahfouz's contributions to social realism, as well as his "unornamented, colorless, plain style" where "experiences inaccessible to language" lurk (4). Other critics, most notably Pamela Allegretto-Diiulio, have pointed out a strong concentration on gender, both in the construction of masculinity and in the representations of "female entrapment." In any case, as Sarah Lawall points out, the Nobel Prize allowed Mahfouz to transcend the regional Egyptian context to become a bona fide global literary figure, which in turn became the basis of his transatlantic interpretation in Mexico.

The first film yielded by this purchase was Arturo Ripstein's *Principio y fin* (1993). This movie tells the story of a family in the wake of the patriarch's death. As Vicente J. Benet aptly describes, the family is structured around the "slow, irrevocable decline of each family member ending finally with another death—this time a double suicide" (203). This plot served Ripstein's aesthetic quite well. Like his 1970s masterpiece *El lugar sin límites,* also a literary adaptation (from Chilean writer José Donoso's novel), *Principio y fin* carefully constructs an asphyxiating, self-contained world that connects his characters' lives and inexorably leads them to decay and destruction. Ripstein's taste for sordid spaces like nightclubs is evident, along with the dark-colored palette that characterizes the cinematography of many of his works. The translation of Mahfouz's fiction to Ripstein's visual language is perhaps the most notable element for my analysis. As Benet has noted, Mahfouz's novel is fundamentally based on a Muslim society's codes of honor and dishonor, placing the characters' decline against a religious backdrop, while the "instinctual" behaviors of his characters drive the plot forward, notably erasing the religious undertones of the source text (204).

Ripstein decidedly shapes the movie according to his own idiosyncratic style but some aspects of this specific adaptation are noteworthy for my argument. First, critics have noted that this particular film demonstrates Ripstein and screenwriter Paz Alicia Garciadiego's preoccupation with the limits of melodrama (Benet 206–7; Paranaguá, *Arturo Ripstein* 234–36). While this exploration is usually discussed in light of its formal and stylistic consequences, it must still be examined within the larger frame of neo-Mexicanist aesthetics. Unlike his remake of *La mujer del puerto,* which is perhaps more an exercise in style than a true intervention in the Mexican cinema of his time, Ripstein's *Principio y fin* points toward major reconfigurations of film aesthetics, and it is an early example of the ways in which film adaptations of literature have allowed Mexican filmmakers to transcend the limits of inherited visual codes.

Principio y fin's work with the limits of melodrama is particularly paradigmatic here. As Darlene J. Sadlier has argued, melodrama is historically the most predominant mode of cinematic discourse in Latin America, and even some attempts from the New Cinema generation of the 1970s to rebel against it fell right into its structures. According to Sadlier, some of Brazil's Cinema Novo works, like those of Glauber Rocha or Nelson Pereira dos Santos, "can provoke emotional responses on the order of those elicited by the very melodramas that they reacted against and often critiqued," resulting in both Cinema Novo and melodramas that "now reside alongside one another in Latin America's cinematic archive" (12). Furthermore, Sadlier shows that "audiences preferred melodramas and musical comedies to neorealist films and political critiques" (12). In the Mexican case, an important attempt to break with melodrama came from Luis Alcoriza who, according to Marvin D'Lugo, was original in his "approach to the undoing of melodrama's aura" by relying "on a complex interrogation of representation rather than on a deflating of melodrama's presumed psychological authenticity" ("Luis Alcoriza" 126). However, as I discussed above, the price to pay in Alcoriza's wager was a highly problematic and somewhat derivative representation of popular classes, who are strongly subject to a barbarizing gaze and to a ruthless critique of their social and political immobility.

What makes *Principio y fin* such a notable movie is that, rather than engaging in a radical critique of melodrama or creating an alternative neorealist world, it opts for a subject matter that brings the emotional codes of melodrama to a point of insufficiency, in which the inevitable decay of the characters ultimately exhausts any possibility of affective identification with them. The movie uses certain devices and plot twists that are particular to melodrama in order to grab the audience's emotional attention. This is particularly true of Gabriel Botero (Ernesto Laguardia), played by an actor who had a prominent career in soap operas and TV entertainment. Laguardia came to fame in the early 1980s with the TV variety show *Cachún Cachún Ra Ra,* and became a star thanks to his role as the hero and main love interest in the 1987 *telenovela Quinceañera,* a landmark show in the history of Mexican television. By the release date of *Principio y fin,* Laguardia was the star of *Los parientes pobres,* 1993's most successful *telenovela,* a fact that undoubtedly contributed to attracting some audiences to the theater. By casting a highly identifiable actor, with a career of playing likable characters, who at the time was considered one of the most attractive figures in Mexican television, Ripstein not only contributed to the success of the film, making it one of his few movies to achieve real commercial distribution, but also inserted a hook in the visual world of the movie to attract affective engagements from melodrama consumers. The movie portrays Gabriel as a dedicated and joyful high school student, and begins with someone entering his classroom to notify him of his father's death. Gabriel is considered the most promising member of the family, which directly connects to Mexican ideas of social mobility, another theme closely associated with melodrama. The film's gaze is, in principle, consistently sympathetic to Gabriel's plight, as we follow his inability to get into college because of an act of corruption. At this moment, Ripstein introduces a key dissonance that sets the tone for the rest of the movie. Gabriel, furious at his inability to fulfill his college aspirations, takes out his anger on his girlfriend, Natalia, in a disturbing scene where he violently rips her clothes off and takes her virginity by forcing his hand into her vagina. The scene is brutal and we see Gabriel's hand covered with her blood. The scene concludes with Natalia kneeling next to him and begging him: "Do everything to me."

By creating a likable character and casting an actor famous for his roles as a *telenovela* hero, Ripstein effectively short-circuits the whole narrative imaginary of melodrama in this very scene. Ripstein breaks the affective contract with the audience and shocks spectators with a plot twist that is both brutal and skillfully constructed through melodramatic language, where the woman begging for the violent man's love goes back to familiar storylines from Golden Age film. Ripstein here is in fact invoking the film stereotype that Sergio de la Mora calls the "Midnight Virgin," following a famous *bolero* (21–67). According to de la Mora, Golden Age melodramas developed the figure of the prostitute as "an allegory of the nation" that "reveals the social relations that have historically shaped the private and public regulation of women's sexual agency" (67). With the female figures in *Principio y fin,* Ripstein strategically follows this melodramatic structure, by contrasting Natalia's status as a virgin with Mireya's role as a prostitute. Not surprisingly, Mireya, Gabriel's sister, plays a central role here. At the end of the movie, Gabriel falls into the trap of corruption, gets a college scholarship through a recommendation, and ultimately rejects Natalia's love. At this point, Natalia is pregnant and refuses to have an abortion. In a crucial scene, Gabriel's brother, Nicolás, agrees to marry Natalia, which prompts Gabriel to discard his last shred of honorability and to tell his brother, in a piece of dialogue reminiscent of 1930s melodramas, "I left her broken in and trained [*estrenada y entrenada*] for you." The movie finishes when Gabriel tries to "rescue" his sister from prostitution. Gabriel ultimately persuades Mireya to kill herself, given the supposed fact that she is unredeemable and unable to carry out her predestined role as a "good wife." Once he sees his sister's corpse, Gabriel suffers an emotional shock that leads him to kill himself. Gabriel's pathos is designed to disrupt the audience's identification with his character, as embodied by Laguardia, and to emotionally exhaust the viewer's tolerance for melodramatic narrative. Ripstein never goes outside the narrative codes of melodrama, but rather uses them to undermine the genre by constructing Gabriel as a dissonant figure. Furthermore, it is important to note that the movie is quite long, nearly three hours, which contributes to the movie's attempt to wear out the spectator.

The act of literary adaptation is the foundation on which this film is built. It allows Ripstein to be far more successful in *Principio y fin* than in his previous movies, and *Principio y fin* is far more successful than the movies of Ripstein's contemporaries in the "cinema of solitude" in its critical engagement with melodrama. Ripstein uses Mahfouz's expansive, naturalist family saga by extracting two main topics, social mobility and moral constraints, to use as disruptive elements in the melodramatic form. In this, Ripstein shows a new potential for literary adaptation in the revision of Mexicanist cinematic codes. While *Cabeza de Vaca* circumvents the traditional engagements of history with the imagined community, in using adaption as a way to avoid melodramatic and operatic renditions of the historical narrative, Ripstein shows that adaptation may actually introduce into structural elements received cultural forms that allow filmmakers to undermine narrative practices from within. By extracting a story that is familiar enough to Mexican culture, but ultimately produced in a different sociohistoric context, Ripstein is able to strategically adapt elements into his highly idiosyncratic cinema in order to go further than ever before in the critique of national forms of cinema. While remakes such as *La mujer del puerto* fail to achieve a truly self-reflexive use of melodrama, Gabriel's pathos incorporates familiar visual and narrative codes into a storyline that lacks the sociocultural engagements and limitations of Mexican national literature or of inherited nationalist films. In other words, by reaching beyond Mexico to adapt a novel written in Egypt, Ripstein manages to break out of the networks of cultural nationalism that bound both writers and filmmakers throughout most of the twentieth century. The story line in *Principio y fin* denaturalizes melodrama's codes of meaning, allowing Ripstein not only a true, self-reflexive exercise of the genre, but also, and more importantly, one of the most compelling explorations of its limits as the privileged narrative structure of Mexican cinema. I contend that this exploration, which will repeat itself constantly in other literary adaptations, is an essential part of the process that allows some contemporary Mexican filmmakers to escape from the prison-house of melodrama.[27]

The understanding of such a unique geography of adaptation, in which an Egyptian mid-century novelist becomes an element of transformation in end-of-the-century Mexico, allows important reconsiderations both of the role of literary adaptation in Mexican cinema and of the conceptualization of adaptation within film studies. In her book *De la literatura al cine,* Adriana Sandoval documents an important trend of numerous Mexican novels adapted into cinema between 1918 and 1968. While Sandoval's interests are admittedly narrow, mostly focused on the films as instruments of literary criticism of the books (9), her objects of study offer a meaningful example of the main trends in adaptation: most films that actually attempted to do it were by and large based on canonical romantic and naturalist novels (such as Federico Gamboa's *Santa,* the first and most frequently adapted Mexican novel), with a subset of films based on Mexican Revolution fiction (such as novels like Rafael F. Muñoz's *Vámonos con Pancho Villa*).[28] In other words, literary adaptation was not much more than a validation of the existing nationalist and Mexicanist codes that were already present in cinema production. If anything, dialogue with literature of that kind did nothing but emphasize the narrative structures already present, and variations between versions of the same book, such the many remakes of *Santa,* were usually minor, and had more to do with casting decisions than with major aesthetic reinventions. Ripstein produced what is perhaps the most interesting pre-1990s foray into film adaptation, *El lugar sin límites,* which was crucial to the construction of his personal aesthetic but still not quite beyond the restrictions of the "cinema of solitude," or of the narrative codes put forward by the narrative generation of the Boom, to which José Donoso's source novel belongs.

The fact that adapting Boom fiction under these parameters does not produce any particularly interesting results in Mexican cinema is further demonstrated by another Ripstein film, *El coronel no tiene quien le escriba* (1999), adapted from Gabriel García Márquez's highly acclaimed novella. In spite of the fact that the film had a remarkable budget, a very strong cast that included Salma Hayek in her first Mexican post-Hollywood role, and a strong publicity campaign, not to mention the name recognition of a highly successful García Márquez book, the film is reminiscent of some of the least interesting movies of the 1970s and 1980s. *El coronel no tiene quien le escriba* is a dull film that, lacking the exact prose of the book, turns it into a slow paced, exceedingly safe story further diluted by an out-of-place Ripsteinian aesthetic more apt for the sordid worlds of the Donosian underworld than the nostalgic vistas of García Márquez's fiction. I would even contend that the problem was that García

Márquez's aesthetic was too safe a territory not only for Ripstein, but also in comparison to the cinema that had already been produced. In comparison to *Cabeza de Vaca* or *Principio y fin,* not to mention *El callejón de los milagros* or *El crimen del padre Amaro,* it represents an involution in the potential of neo-Mexicanist film.

In view of this, Alfredo Ripstein Jr.'s selection of Mahfouz as a subject of adaptation is even more crucial because it clearly shows that the choice of books that were at the same time foreign and translatable gave his son Arturo and Jorge Fons (the director of *El callejón de los milagros* [1995]), a tableau in which they could explore issues of class, morality, and gender in terms that went beyond the languages of the "cinema of solitude" while allowing them to keep the key elements of their visual and structural aesthetic. One of the theoretical challenges that the Mahfouz connection elicits lies in the fact that most literary adaptation studies, which have been developed in considerable bibliographies in English, French, and Spanish, ignore Mexican and Latin American cinema altogether, and, perhaps with the exception of passing references to the cinema of Akira Kurosawa, do not offer any sustained reflection on transcultural adaptation.[29] The question that matters for my argument does not lie in issues of fidelity or intermediality, which point to more secondary formal considerations than to the true core of these films. Rather, I propose understanding transcultural adaptation in the context of 1990s Mexican cinema as a practice that allows for the reconfiguration of cultural codes that can be imbricated in film discourse, by presenting similar (or translatable) topics in semiotic logics different from the ideological commitments present in national film traditions. In his foundational article on adaptation issues, Brian McFarlane argues that film draws on a "battery of semiotically charged tools" that allow it to pursue similar interests as the novel, like the representation of place of the "interest in revealing 'lives' in a fullness perhaps denied to others," in ways that "necessarily involve a complex response from the alert viewer" (23–24). In a way, *Principio y fin* is a prime example of this, given that it takes the lives narrated by Mahfouz, transforms them into culturally different but morally similar lives as embodied by the Boteros, and ultimately uses those lives to elicit an affective response via instruments such as film length, editing, and a visual palette that reengages those lives into a newly meaningful semiotic space. To use an old Russian formalist notion, the transcultural adaptation provides an element of "estrangement" to existing visual and cinematic languages in order to then reconfigure its aesthetic and ideological consequences.[30]

Principio y fin remains perhaps too inscribed in Ripsteinian aesthetics to fully illustrate this point, but Jorge Fons's *El callejón de los Milagros,* adapted for the screen by dramatist and novelist Vicente Leñero, offers clear insights into the role played by adaptations of Mahfouz's fiction in a major reinvention of neo-Mexicanist aesthetics. *El callejón de los milagros* tells the story of an apartment building in downtown Mexico City. Structured around the patrons of a local bar, the story focuses on three characters. Don Rutilio (Ernesto Gómez Cruz) is a married man in the closet, who starts publicly seducing a young man. Word of this situation gets to his family, and he reacts in anger by violently beating up his wife. In the end, his son, Chava (Juan Manuel Bernal), runs into his father and his lover in a public shower, and, consumed by rage, kills his father's lover. The second story revolves around Susana (Margarita Sanz), the landlady of the building, a forty-something woman seduced by an attractive young man, Güicho, who marries her to defraud her. In the process, Güicho really does fall in love with Susanita, but realizes this fact too late, as she rejects him when she discovers he has been robbing her. Finally, in the longest story, Alma, the role that made Salma Hayek a household name, is a young and attractive girl who, in spite of the promise of her boyfriend, Abel, to marry her after his return to the United States, decides to marry a well-to-do, older businessman. When her fiancé dies before the wedding, Alma accepts the advances of José Luis, who gradually turns her into a prostitute. When Abel returns, he finds out the truth and confronts José Luis, who kills him. In the final scene, Alma holds a dying Abel in her arms as his life fades away.

As this plot description shows, *El callejón de los milagros* keeps strong identifications with melodrama, enough to keep it within certain familiar frameworks. However, a closer look shows many innovative ideological and stylistic points that further illustrate how adapting Mahfouz resulted in new paradigms of neo-Mexicanist discourse. Perhaps the first significant change lies in a deep transformation of the representations of working classes. The Buñuelian aesthetic that determined representation of poor people as *lumpen,* echoed by Alcoriza and even by Ripstein, is simply not present. In addition, Fons's gaze does not exercise any form of moral or judgment values of its characters: unlike Gabriel Botero's clearly defined spiral of decadence in *Principio y fin,* the characters in *El callejón* are presented in a more multilayered ethical and moral framework, clearly breaking with the good-versus-bad narrative logic of traditional melodrama. Rutilio illustrates this well. As a viewer, it is easy to identify with his plight as a gay man trapped in a traditional patriarchal culture where he is expected to play the role of father and husband. Rutilio, however, is not merely a victim of patriarchy, since he has no qualms about exercising his patriarchal role throughout the movie. When his wife finds out about his gay escapades and confronts him, he violently assaults her, thus asserting his masculine authority. When his son returns at the end of the film, married and with a child, it is up to Rutilio whether or not to allow him back into the family. Rutilio clearly shows how *El callejón* departs from *Principio y fin.* Ripstein exercises a critique of form by stretching the limits of melodrama and using his characters in order to engage the spectators' affects and expectations. In contrast, Fons's film is less complex stylistically, but places a strong focus on the lives of his characters. As a result, rather than offering a preordained trajectory for Rutilio, the story reveals a highly ambiguous ethical persona whose actions cannot be fully accepted or condoned. Rutilio's story offers no clear moral: rather, it presents the complexities of a man constantly faced by a power structure of gender that he embraces as much as he tries to escape from it.

Another important element here lies in the slight but significant transformation in the use of the urban space. As Hugo Lara Chávez points out, *El callejón de los milagros* recovers a variety of spaces that have been canonized in national film history: the *vecindad* (a type of high-density, low-class living arrangement), the cantina, and so on (215). Historically, these spaces have been used to represent either the stereotypes that defined certain popular characters within the paradigms of the Mexican self (like the cantinas in the movies of Jorge Negrete and Pedro Infante), to emphasize the marginality of urban popular subjects in the social fabric of the city (like Buñuel's *Los olvidados*), or to present a community that is able to overcome adversity through solidarity (as in Ismael Rodríguez's *Pepe el Toro* trilogy). Fons appropriates this urban popular geography in order to emphasize the emerging confrontation between the old social order and a modernizing Mexico. Rather than emphasizing the class distinctions typical of old-school social melodramas (two of the *Pepe el Toro* movies are called *We the Poor* and *You the Rich*), *El callejón* shows us the stories of denizens whose conflicts and decisions have more to do with the social issues of the 1990s: gender equality and gay rights in the case of Rutilio, or immigration to the United States in the case of Chava and Abel. In a way, it could be said that the Mexico City popular class presented by *El callejón* is closer to the one put forward by *Danzón,* a working class strongly tied to traditional value systems faced with the challenges of a modernization that makes their forms of life outdated.

David William Foster has suggested that Fons uses the alley (the place where the stories take place) as a synecdoche of Mexico City, representing both the neighborhood culture that defines the city and the commonalities between working-class lives across its geography (46–47). In these terms, *El callejón de los milagros* appropriates Mahfouz's story of an Egyptian community facing the modernizing pressures of World War II and turns it into a reflection on a community unraveled by the pressures of an increasingly modernized and liberalized Mexico in which the hierarchical structures that sustain life are becoming increasingly anachronistic. The fundamental choice, in my view, lies in the fact that Fons does not appeal to nostalgia, not even the reflective kind. There is no lost paradise in *El callejón de los milagros.* While we are witnesses to a community in a gradual process of decay, this decay does put forth a series of power and economic structures that are problematic in themselves. The fact that Alma ends up as a prostitute has a lot to do with a social network that makes single motherhood unacceptable (leading her mother to try to "place" her with a "good" husband) and with a clearly hierarchical dynamic of gender that pushes a young woman into an inescapable position of sexual servitude to men. Abel's ultimate defeat in his idealistic attempt to marry Alma is more a condemnation of this antiquated social environment than of her. Abel, like many other young Mexican men of the 1990s, pursues a better life in the United States through illegal immigration. The movie reproduces a social narrative in which Abel ultimately achieves this pursuit, and he returns having triumphed economically. However, the fact that Alma is irrevocably entangled in prostitution and that Abel's alternative life is not an option for her shows that keeping traditional communities intact creates a social trap that keeps the working class subject to patriarchal power dynamics.[31] In short, the remarkable achievement of *El callejón de los milagros* lies in its capacity to recover the spaces of traditional Mexican cinema for a narrative that neither paints the *barrio* as an idyllic or solidarious space nor falls for the judging intellectual gaze of 1970s cinema. Fons's neo-Mexicanist language, empowered by a story that once again originates in a text in which the economy of inequality and power is not organically related to Mexican history or Mexicanist ideology, produces an unprecedentedly multilayered reflection on the urban popular classes.

In an intelligent analysis of the movie, Andrea Noble suggests that *El callejón de los milagros* emerges in the connection between body and urban space. In these terms, Noble reads Alma as a figure who self-reflectively rehearses the cinematic tradition of the prostitute while registering "stasis in this national cinematographic narrative" (119). Noble's reading of the movie shows the fine line that neo-Mexicanist cinema walks, as represented by the two Mahfouz adaptations. On the one hand, filmmakers are strongly aware of the weight of the cinematic tradition behind them, opting for a cinema that uses its inherited visual and structural codes to undermine its own ideological and social implications. While Alma and Mireya are characters similar to the prostitutes from the movies of Arcady Boytler or "El Indio" Fernández, the cinematic representation of these figures emphasizes the underlying structures of gender power in their lives. As a result, the film does not elicit the same affective or moral response, since it does not operate within the pedagogic modes that defined cinema in the Golden Age period. On the other hand, just like *Danzón* or *Como agua para chocolate*, the cinematic legacies invoked by Ripstein and Fons sustain a certain impasse, as filmmakers in the early nineties were still struggling to find aesthetic and narrative languages that truly broke away from tradition. Yet, both *Principio y fin* and *El callejón de los milagros* open a path in which transcultural film adaptation is a crucial instrument in the process of the development of such languages, a process that will gradually unfold throughout the 1990s. To fully illustrate the extent of this transformation, another transcultural adaptation produced by Alfredo Ripstein Jr. comes to mind: Carlos Carrera's *El crimen del padre Amaro* (2002).

Adapted from a nineteenth-century Portuguese novel by José María Eça de Queirós, *El crimen del padre Amaro* had all the elements to become a box office powerhouse. It features a story with attractive melodramatic undertones, revolving around a young priest who falls in love with a girl in the town where he is assigned. It boasts the presence of the two major stars of recent Mexican cinema (Gael García Bernal as Amaro and Ana Claudia Talancón as his love interest, Amelia), as well as some popular actors from Mexican film and TV (like Angélica Aragón and Pedro Armendáriz). It was directed by Carlos Carrera, who had already delivered some of the most important Mexican films of the 1990s.[32] The movie's visibility came from an entirely different source: a cultural and political scandal where major figures of the Mexican right wing, including the country's pro-life organization and the hierarchy of the Catholic Church, tried to block the film's release and to boycott its distribution.[33] Misha MacLaird, who narrates the incident in detail (*Aesthetics* 92–97), points out that both the film and the right wing benefited greatly from the media exposure.[34] In this film, we have an even clearer example of the way in which transcultural adaptation of literature into cinema creates languages that cut deep into received sociocultural and cinematic notions.

Unlike *Principio y fin* and *El callejón de los milagros,* whose visual representations are full of nods to classical cinema and of elements that question their modern-day character (including apparel, music, and even the color palette), *El crimen del padre Amaro* is decidedly a present-day story and, even if located in a small town, the film is clearly inscribed in contemporary time. Thus, Carrera achieves a quite interesting visual world that presents the colors and practices of provincial communities without engaging in codes of nostalgia. The point is not only that the small town is not idyllic, but that it is also fully inscribed in the sociopolitical dynamics of Mexico at large. Amaro's love affair is at the center of the scandal, which is fueled in part by the ending, when Amalia dies from an illegal abortion to terminate the pregnancy that resulted from her relations with the priest. However, the most meaningful elements of the movie lie in its politically charged subplot. As the movie progresses, we learn that Father Benito (Sancho Gracia), the head priest of the parish, is having a love affair of his own with Amalia's mother (Angélica Aragón). On top of this, he is also financing the construction of a modern facility for the sick with money provided by Chato Aguilar (Juan Ignacio Aranda), a local drug lord. Benito is not only unapologetic about the connection, but he has an open friendship with the kingpin. We also learn that another priest, Natalio (Damián Alcázar), who serves a community in the middle of a tropical landscape, may be implicated with guerrilla groups made up of peasants who arm themselves to protect their interests from the drug cartel. This subplot unfolds when Rubén (Andrés Montiel), Amalia's original suitor, publishes both stories in the local newspaper. As a result, the local bishop (Ernesto Gómez Cruz) organizes a cover-up operation in which Amaro is complicit, convincing the mayor of the town (Pedro Armendáriz), a cynical politician from the conservative party, to say that he is the actual source of the financing. The bishop also expels and excommunicates Natalio from the church for refusing to abandon his community.

As we can see, *El crimen del padre Amaro* uses various mechanisms of melodrama, from its nineteenth-century source text to the intense love story and the soap-opera-like structure of its plots and subplots, to question the very moral economy that melodrama sustained for decades. MacLaird correctly points out that the film "is undeniably open to ambiguous readings" and does not offer "a clear instruction on personal ethics beyond laying out the minimal amount of gray area in issues that are presented as Manichean in politics and religious instruction" (*Aesthetics* 96–97). As MacLaird also indicates, the movie cannot conclusively be read as pro-choice or pro-life (as Amalia's death can be read in either sense), nor does it directly condemn Benito for his use of drug money, since the existence of a children's hospital may actually elicit sympathy from the viewers (97). It is precisely this type of ambiguity that makes the movie innovative in its use of neo-Mexicanist aesthetics. The political tones of the narrative are, in actuality, a deliberate result of the adaptation. Helena Bonito Couto Pereira shows in her comparison of book and film that the latter "intensifies the ideological appeal of the novel" (99; my translation). The connections between church and State were undoubtedly a subject of naturalist narrative in the nineteenth century, but their resurgence in twenty-first-century Mexican film is somewhat unexpected, since such a choice of narrative had largely been used to sustain conservative positions. The tradition of naturalist adaptations was, as I mentioned before, most commonly engaged in texts that exercise a clear moral judgment on their characters (like *Santa*), resulting in films that used the figure of the prostitute, or the "Midnight Virgin," to make clear points about public morality. In *El crimen del padre Amaro,* however, we have a naturalist narrative in which the prostitute and the virgin figures are absent, presenting instead a young girl who is not defined by either stereotype. In doing so, the focus shifts to the double morality of religious institutions, where the ultimate cover-up of the events is far more significant than the moral lesson provided by the female figure: at the end of the movie, Amaro is officiating at Amalia's funeral mass and it is clear that most of people in the town claim that the child was Rubén's. On the other hand, according to Couto Pereira, Natalio is a character who bears less resemblance to the corresponding book figure (102). Thus, his presumed participation in guerrilla activities deliberately recalls liberation theology, which plays a role in contemporary Mexico via the Zapatista uprising. Yet, just like Benito, the movie does not directly question Natalio's motives. Rather, the story confronts his commitment to the welfare of his town with the political interests of the church structure. It is an ideological rather than a moral clash.

What is at stake here is a critique of the structures of power that underlie moral Catholic practices, from the corrupt politician who gets elected by exploiting his relationship to the church, to the priest who sells his soul to better serve his community. This is significant in the context of post-2000 Mexico. The electoral victory of Vicente Fox brought forward an empowered cultural right wing, represented by Fox's party, the Partido Acción Nacional. In these terms, the film became one of the first major interventions against the narrative of "democratic transition" that the Fox administration used to legitimize its power.[35] In this context, *El crimen del padre Amaro* activates a set of familiar figures (like the town priest, the devoted but somewhat crazy old woman, and the rural politician) and a web of conventional melodramatic and narrative structures by investing them with a quite unprecedented political charge. A significant point is that the movie was the result of a collaboration between figures involved both in the "cinema of solitude" (like producer Alfredo Ripstein Jr.) and in the early forays of neo-Mexicanist aesthetic (like screenwriter Vicente Leñero and even director Carlos Carrera). *El crimen del padre Amaro* is perhaps the most successful example of a film that employs traditional cinema aesthetics without endorsing a particular discourse of power or hegemony. Instead of caving to the political narratives of the Mexican transition, like many of the movies discussed in Chapter 3 do, *El crimen* became one of the earliest and most public critiques of the right wing as an institution of power in Mexico. By resisting the temptations of pedagogy and moralism, *El crimen del padre Amaro* became a rare but fundamental instance in which a commercial movie constructed by cinematic languages inherited from national tradition and literary languages from abroad was, at the end of the day, more critical and innovative than many political films of the period.[36]

Provincia and the Afterlives of Neo-Mexicanism

A final but important undercurrent in neo-Mexicanist aesthetics is the role of the interior, *la provincia,* as a cinematic space that competes with Mexico City for the representation of Mexico. In many of the movies I have mentioned so far, the *provincia* is a central but unproblematized concept, a place that allows Mexicanist aesthetics and ideologies to reenter the stage. In *Danzón,* for instance, Julia Solórzano's journey takes her back to Veracruz, a city that, in contrast with the modernizing space of the capital, remains a repository of tradition and solidarity. In *Desiertos mares,* the protagonist takes a memory-driven journey to the interior as a necessary part of his quest to find himself.

El crimen del padre Amaro, as critical as it is of the power structure, still relies on a provincial space to fully emphasize the problematic relation between faith and politics. In an article on the representation of the *provincia,* Emily Hind has shown that some films present the interior "as a permissive space that facilitates social freedom" ("*Provincia*" 26). In this assertion, Hind describes the end-point of a process that, in my view, starts with *Danzón* and that requires further exploration. María Novaro's Veracruz does present the *provincia* as a liberating space, but this liberation is highly dependent on the emancipatory role of traditional popular culture and of underground gendered spaces that are a product of her aesthetic rather than a frame of the social fabric of the interior. In fact, as welcoming as Novaro's Veracruz may be to her gay characters, in reality gays and lesbians in Mexico actually have better chances of acceptance in Mexico City than in the conservative capitals of the *provincia.*[37] Historically *provincia* plays a role as prominent as the *barrio* in the foundations of cultural nationalism. As Carlos Monsiváis demonstrates, Fernando de Fuentes's *Allá en el rancho grande* (1936), the first major movie of the Golden Age, can be read as a glorification of the values and traditions of the interior against the process of modernization brought about by the revolution (*Aires de familia* 58–61). Mexican cinema of the 1990s engaged with this discourse by undertaking a parodic reading of the interior, which, in turn, produced some of the most significant films of the post-1990 period. To be sure, Mexican cinema consistently produces movies in which the return to the interior is a factor of rediscovery for characters lost in modernity.[38] Nonetheless, the capacity to use *provincia* as a critical space is essential to understanding the final aspects of the neo-Mexicanist cinematic transitions.

The most important movie in this trend is Roberto Sneider's *Dos crímenes* (1995), an adaptation of a novel by Jorge Ibargüengoitia.[39] The movie tells the story of Marcos González (Damián Alcázar), a Mexico City graphic designer who, through a misunderstanding, becomes implicated in a murder case. Marcos flees to the fictional province of Cuévano, where most of Ibargüengoitia's novels take place, to take refuge in his wealthy uncle's house. Marcos's presence in Cuévano proves quite disruptive, since all his other family members are waiting for the uncle's impending death in order to distribute his estate among themselves. Most of the film develops as Marcos becomes gradually more involved in this situation, until, at the end, he resigns his part of the inheritance after being turned over to the police and after one of his cousins tries to kill him. The first element to note here is that Marcos is a graphic designer, which aligns the movie with the social types developed in the romantic comedies that I will discuss in Chapter 2. In the meantime, the other important issue is the fact that the movie is essentially a parody of the return-to-the-province narrative so prevalent in films like *Danzón.* Cuévano, which is inspired by Ibargüengoitia's home state of Guanajuato in central Mexico, is never presented as a repository of narratives of origin or as a place where one can go to find oneself. Rather, this location symbolizes the profound corruption and everyday absurdities of modern Mexico.[40] By adopting a fictional space that had already earned prestige as a critical stance against provincial conservatism, Sneider activates a representational device in cinema that questions the idea of the interior, and by extension the nation, as a redemptive space of origin to which one must return. In *Dos crímenes,* Cuévano acts as a synecdoche for the entire *provincia,* designed to expose the dynamics of power behind traditional social orders. Marcos's uncle is, at the end of the day, a local oligarch who controls the economics and politics of the region, while the rest of his family vies for that power.

By living in Mexico City and working in graphic design, an industry that represents a source of wealth different from the "old money" culture of his Cuévano family, Marcos had managed to escape that oligarchical order and to live a life outside the constraints of the local morality: he could have a sexual relationship with a woman without the imperative of marriage, throw parties in his apartment and, in general, live in a city presented as a space of social (though at times shallow) freedom. It is very telling that Marcos's return to Cuévano is not triggered by an identity crisis, like that of the protagonist of *Desiertos mares,* or by a nostalgic search for culture or tradition, like Novaro's Julia. The driving force behind his return is, in his own words, a "violation of the Constitution," a police persecution. That is, the return to *provincia* results from a loss of Marcos's space of freedom in the city; its purpose is to restore that freedom by obtaining money from his uncle. Marcos's misfortunes continue to grow in Cuévano, however, precisely because he willingly participates in the corrupt logic of his family by cheating his uncle out of a sizable amount of money through a made-up investment. In these terms, *Dos crímenes* establishes what will become a significant trend in comedic cinema, in which a constant critique of the interior as a repository of outdated cultural values and, in this particular film, political and social corruption undoes the emancipatory and idealized ideas of the *provincia. El crimen del padre Amaro* operates within the same ideological framework, depicting a Mexican interior still subject to the traditional powers of the church and to corrupt local politicians, and a newcomer, Amaro, who entangles himself in this logic at the expense of his soul. Both *Dos crímenes* and *El crimen del padre Amaro* invert the provincial synecdoche by using the spaces of the interior to denounce the persistence of political and cultural logic inherited from the times of the PRI. In the end, *Dos crímenes* manages to strike a tone that modernizes mainstream comedy and trades the vulgar, raunchy traditions of 1980s *sexycomedias* for more tasteful forms of humor and a more cutting political critique. The film became a major contribution to the reinvention of national comedy. Critic Jorge Ayala Blanco said as much following the release of the movie: "Ultimately, *Dos crímenes* represents an average benchmark that would be desirable in the practice of comedy by current Mexican cinema" (*La fugacidad* 174).

A more radical presentation of *provincia* comes from Alejandro Springall's *Santitos* (1999), adapted by María Amparo Escandón from her homonymous novel. *Santitos* tells the story of Esperanza Díaz (Dolores Heredia). After her daughter dies from a botched tonsillectomy, Esperanza starts seeing an apparition of Saint Jude the Apostle, patron saint of desperate causes, in her oven. This apparition tells her that her daughter is alive, which, along with a (false) rumor that a doctor had kidnapped the daughter to take her to a brothel in Tijuana, triggers a search that takes Esperanza from her small town to the border and all the way to Los Angeles. After a journey in which she gets involved with a cartoonish pimp and prostitutes herself to raise money, she meets "The Angel of Justice," a *lucha libre* wrestler who falls in love with her. Upon her return home, she finds that the woman who shares her living quarters has cleaned her oven, which results in an inability to see any more saints in it. However, her daughter appears to her in a mirror, helping her cope with her loss. In the end, "The Angel of Justice" tracks her down, and the movie ends with Esperanza and the wrestler driving away to a new life.

The movie operates on the basis of very complex imagery that interweaves magical realism, religious iconology, and cultural geography. For instance, Marilyn Ríos-Soto points out the symbolism behind the names: the protagonist is called Esperanza (hope); her daughter, Blanca (white, pure); the town priest, Salvador (savior); the wrestler, Angel; and the pimp, Cacomixtle, a Náhuatl term etymologically connected to the word "thief" (109n3). Visually, we also see Angel wearing a white outfit with wings, Cacomixtle characterized as the devil, and the saints appearing as reproductions of their clay effigies and of their pictorial representations. Furthermore, Esperanza's town is an idyllic, traditional space that stands in sharp contrast to the more sordid life in Tijuana and L.A. In short, it seems to have all the ingredients for a nationalist movie constructed upon cheap, obvious metaphors. What gives *Santitos* an edge is its thoroughly parodic and satiric tone. Dolores Heredia's over-the-top performance characterizes Esperanza both as a charmingly innocent woman and as someone whose religious devotion clearly borders on the absurd. The prostitution scenes in Tijuana are not dramatic, but farcical; the pimp (Demían Bichir) is a quite humorous character as well. Consequently, the movie does not hold any romantic or nostalgic view of the *provincia* it represents. As Ayala Blanco puts it, the movie may be read as "a deliciously extreme testimonial of the Era of the Perfect National Defenselessness, an illumination of the happiest artificial simplicity of Mexican folklore" (*La fugacidad* 451). This "extreme testimonial" is a reductio ad absurdum of the cultural codes of national identity. By embracing them and their carnivalesque extremes, it shows their meaninglessness while constructing a comedic edifice with their icons.

Some critics, such as Darryl Caterine, argue that the film's sympathetic representation of Esperanza can be read as a positive portrayal of Catholicism and as the redemption of a devotionalism rooted in Mexican history (290). In my view, this reading completely misses the point. Caterine is right in contending that Esperanza's religious practices have deep connections to Mexican popular history, but the movie actually focuses its critical gaze on this very history. The key point to sustain my reading lies in the ending of the movie. Ríos-Soto points out that the movie concludes when Esperanza "substitutes her Catholic mythology for her personal mythology," when Blanca appears to her instead of St. Jude, and when she redirects her devotion to "The Angel of Justice" (108). Ríos-Soto reaches this conclusion after discussing the way in which Esperanza's feminine gaze structures the story, claiming that Esperanza is "an active agent of the gaze" (108). According to this line of inquiry, the movie is parallel to *Danzón,* in that Esperanza's journey results in her liberation as a woman. In my view, this reading misses the crucial implications of the ending, since Esperanza is neither liberated from patriarchy (given that she was not subject to a man in the first place) nor from neoliberal economics (since the movie really does not engage with her character's socioeconomic situation). Also, tradition is not the instrument of her liberation and anagnorisis. Quite the contrary: she is existentially bound to her devotion. The ending thus points to the fact that Esperanza's ultimate liberation was from religion and not from the grief of losing her daughter. While she is in a state of grief, the voices of the saints colonize her imagination. When her roommate cleans her oven, this opens the space for Blanca to appear and for Esperanza to cope with her death and move on.

In these terms, one could argue that *Santitos*'s gendered narrative follows, in comparison with *Danzón,* the opposite route. Julia's liberation is, in a way, framed by the tradition she adores, and dancing with Carmelo at the very end of the movie restores the traditional imagery and the idyllic world that allows her to escape her life as a phone operator. In contrast, Esperanza's emancipation is possible only when she breaks away from the imaginary world that leads her, among other things, to subject herself to a pimp and to engage in prostitution. Under the humorous tone and sympathetic presentation of the character, the film exercises a quite critical gaze on her faith. At the end of the day, the film is as critical a reading of the social practice of Catholicism as *El crimen del padre Amaro.*

Besides faith and tradition, new perspectives of the historical narrative cinematically undid previous constructions of *provincia.* This is clear in Alejandro Gamboa's *El tigre de Santa Julia* (2002), a comedic retelling of the story of a legendary revolution-era bandit. The film is based on his quarrels with other bandits and with the federal government, as well as on his sexual escapades and all the women who were attracted to him and who followed him into banditry. *El tigre de Santa Julia* goes back to the same period as *Como agua para chocolate* and casts an entirely different light on it. In lieu of presenting the kitchen as the privileged space of female emancipation, the movie adopts the female revolutionary figure and presents a group of women who are openly sexual and fully engaged in banditry. The film shamelessly exploits its sexual content: both the poster and the DVD cover feature all the major female characters naked and in bed with El Tigre, facing the camera with defiant gazes. In fact, the presentation of female empowerment in the film goes so far that, as Hind convincingly argues, males "depend on the guidance of criminally inclined women" who manipulate them into committing crimes ("*Provincia*" 33). It is relevant to know that there is a 1974 version of *El tigre,* directed by Arturo Martínez and very much focused on a nationalist retelling of this story. The fact that the 2002 version is such an inventive and humorous reinvention of the myth speaks to the ways in which filmmakers of the early 2000s were working with a more complex Mexicanist palette than their predecessors. Moreover, as in *Santitos,* the critique of *provincia* is accompanied by a reconsideration of the role of women in traditional societies: Esperanza escapes her religious chains, while the many women who populate Gamboa's film assume traditionally male roles and carry a great deal of the weight (and the agency) of the plot. While the 1974 movie is strongly focused on the male characters, a wide array of female bandits play major roles in the plot of the 2002 version. Most certainly, as Hind points out in relation to *El tigre de Santa Julia* (33), movies like this or like *Santitos* are contradictory from a feminist perspective, since their empowerment of female characters is accompanied by an occasionally subservient relationship to men. Nonetheless, in their own particular way, both films attack the network of traditional values that has been usually identified with the interior.

Alongside issues of gender, national history is also a major point of contention in *El tigre de Santa Julia*. The film is set during a foundational moment for the nation, at the outset of the revolution, and engages its period with a tone and a visual language that not only operates outside any conceivable code of "official history," but also resists the romantic presentation of the bandit. Still, in a crucial moment of the film, we learn that the origin of El Tigre's rebellion lies in a particular event. While he was serving in the federal army, his superior ordered his troop to shoot at unarmed protestors. El Tigre refused to participate in the massacre, and he was punished with a whipping. This scene, the sole serious moment in the film, shows its libertarian streak: the motor of the action, as in *Dos crímenes,* is the entry into the corrupted space of the interior in search of freedom, something that Esperanza also experiences in

Tijuana. By virtue of this plot device, the interior is presented in a way that simultaneously criticizes the corruption and hypocrisy of its traditional values, and becomes a space the film's characters must escape in order to truly find or emancipate themselves. By utilizing a spectrum of cultural codes ranging from religion to political history, many movies on the *provincia* undertake a gradual but decisive break with the representational politics of twentieth-century cinema. When *El crimen del padre Amaro* came along, a few years after these other films, viewers and filmmakers were already attuned to this critique, and Carrera's film's success was due, in part, to the creation of a cinematic language that exceeded the nostalgic drive that constructed films like *Danzón*. Ayala Blanco aptly characterizes the film's style as "anti-nostalgic" (*antiañoranza*) (*La grandeza* 229). There is no desired restoration or reflection of loss, simply a humorous recasting of an age that should remain in the past.

In conclusion, it is important to realize that, regardless of the many transformations undergone by the different discourses of Mexicanism, neo-Mexicanism remains an ambiguous, aporetic form of cultural aesthetics. In spite of the critical work achieved by some major films of the past two decades, neo-Mexicanism is still represented as a repository of authenticity or of national and local identities. An otherwise unremarkable film may help to illustrate this point. In his movie *Chiles Xalapeños* (2008), Fabrizio Prada presents a cast of characters from the city of Xalapa, capital of the state of Veracruz. The movie holds an ambiguous relationship with the past discourses on the *provincia*. Visually, the film's Xalapa has all the makings of a modern city: we see characters dressed in contemporary clothes and engaged in contemporary professions, and the film makes no gesture whatsoever to history or nostalgia. Still, the characters are meant to be social types, and these types cover the traditional gamut: everything from the beggar to the corrupt politician to the sexy nurse. By appealing to resources uncannily similar to those used by Mexploitation movies of the 1970s (such as speech bubbles shaped like jalapeño peppers or bikini-clad young women giving lap dances to older men), *Chiles Xalapeños* exercises an uncomfortably regressive ideology that typecasts the inhabitants of Xalapa in a space between the nationalist stereotypes of Golden Age picaresque films and the cheap characters of *fichera* cinema. The fact that this typecasting happens in an otherwise modern *provincia* is what makes the movie most disconcerting. It ultimately shows that the very languages that helped undo some of the most resilient problems of nationalist cinema may also give those problems and *aporias* a new life.

Perhaps a good, recent example of the many impasses that still plague neo-Mexicanist aesthetics, in spite of nearly two decades of challenges and renovations, is *Arráncame la vida* (2008), Roberto Sneider's high-profile adaptation of Ángeles Mastretta's well-known novel. The movie enjoyed a similar publicity apparatus as *El crimen del padre Amaro,* minus the censorship. It had similarly high-profile actors, including Ana Claudia Talancón and Daniel Giménez Cacho, and was based on one of Mexico's bona fide literary bestsellers. Unsurprisingly, the movie is, to date, one of the highest-grossing Mexican movies in the country's box office history. The most striking thing about *Arráncame la vida* is how uninteresting it is, particularly when compared to *El crimen del padre Amaro.* The film is set in Puebla and shot in a somewhat nostalgic sepia palette. The predictable plot revolves around a woman, also played by Talancón, who marries a very powerful politician with questionable ethics but then falls in love with a younger, more passionate man, an orchestra conductor. Mastretta's novel is largely based on the figure of Maximino Ávila Camacho, a *caudillo*-turned-politician from the 1940s who, besides being the president's brother and a ruthlessly corrupt man, is reputed to be the most powerful man in Puebla's history. To any spectator of movies like *Dos crímenes* or *El crimen del padre Amaro,* the uncritical presentation of corruption stands out in comparison. Rather than use this corruption as a device to articulate any sort of political or social critique, the movie presents it as a matter of fact, and decides to focus solely on the protagonist's quest.[41] In doing so, it not only erases Mastretta's subtle critique of the politics of the PRI regime, which in Puebla remained very much in place at the time of shooting, but it also shows how a nostalgic, nationalistic cinematic language, full of references to a lost cultural splendor, still holds sway over the imagination of filmmakers and spectators.[42] The point is driven home by the fact that Roberto Sneider, who over a decade earlier had questioned the politics and aesthetics of cinema nationalism, was the director of the film. It shows that, when working within the framework of neo-Mexicanism, directors still face major creative and ideological impasses, and that nationalism still appeals strongly to audiences. The transformation of Mexican cinematic nationalism, as one of the processes resulting from neoliberalism, can be read as a spiral that in many ways returns to its place of origin. It started with a popular book, *Como agua para chocolate,* written by a woman and constructed on the basis of traditionalist codes. The result was a film that translated Mexican identity to the conservative middle classes. In 2008, we have a similar product: a film based on another popular book by another female author, one whose critique of traditional codes of masculinity and identity becomes, in the film version, an affirmation. It gives us a nostalgic view of a time that, regardless of its corruption and dangers, remains a beautiful alternative to the modern present. In the context of a country with a conservative presidency, and shot in a state where the government functions in parameters that have not evolved much since the 1940s, this cinematic outcome shows the critical and cultural limitations of cultural nationalism in contemporary Mexico. While it still holds many creative possibilities, it can easily be defanged by its incessant return to familiar semiotics.

The remaining transitions discussed in this book may be seen as different attempts to engage with this problem. In the next chapter, I will discuss films that radically depart from Mexicanism and promote a contemporary Mexico that decidedly breaks away from the traditionalism of the past and the interior. Ruled by the romantic comedy, this new cinema comes to terms with Mexico's increasing Americanization and modernization in the context of NAFTA, and in doing so achieves many important, sometimes controversial, transformations of film practice.

2

PUBLICISTS IN LOVE

Romantic Comedy, Cinema Privatization, and the Aesthetics of the Middle Class

In *Modern Love,* David Shumway illustrates the cultural prevalence of the emotion by studying the different ways in which "love stories permeate our lives" (2). Shumway extensively demonstrates how the evolution of these stories in literature and cinema has an important impact on the values and practices of love in a society. Moreover, the representation of love in cinema is a symptom of different kinds of social dynamics, from relations of gender and class to the social economies of affect. Shumway restricts his analysis to what he calls "the marriage crisis"—namely, the loss of the meaning of marriage as its social functions gradually eroded away in the wake of feminism. For my purposes, the book points to romance and intimacy discourses as reflective of a large array of ideological, cultural, and affective engagements, pursued by the consumers of romance in film and literature. A similar intuition has been at the core of an important tradition of film studies on Mexico, spearheaded by Carlos Monsiváis. In *A través del espejo,* Monsiváis and Carlos Bonfil argue that, in the Golden Age, cinema was the "great interlocutor of society" (91; my translation). Monsiváis and Bonfil contend that an important set of social behaviors, including sexual morality, national identity, and love, has an organic relation to film spectatorship. The prevalence of melodrama in Mexican cinema established a cinematic code that occupied a hegemonic place in the sentimental education of national audiences. As Monsiváis and Bonfil famously argue in this book, melodrama is a privileged vehicle of cultural secularization and modernization, as it creates popular imaginaries detached from religion and tied to the processes of urbanization. It also establishes strong links between viewers and the Mexican imagined community. By the late 1980s, in spite of the decline of cinema distribution, melodrama remained the primary cultural discourse of sentimental education, thanks to its reproduction in a wide set of cultural genres, from *telenovelas* to music genres such as *bolero* and *balada*.

While the deep penetration of melodrama in the Mexican cultural consciousness from all the way back to the nineteenth century partly explains this phenomenon, the other important factor is the existence of a de facto monopoly in the media. In the late 1980s, Televisa was the only major media company with national presence, and it controlled nearly 90 percent of television ratings, the most important private film company (Televicine), major radio stations, and the main outlets for the distribution of pop music. They produced and distributed all major entertainment, from *telenovelas* to the commercial cinema designed around their talent roster, as well as the most popular songs on the charts. This chapter discusses the consequences of the dissolution of this system, and the ways in which film reflected a diversification in the uses of media in Mexicans' sentimental education. Of course, I am not contending that *telenovelas* are no longer relevant or that melodrama no longer exists: my study of neo-Mexicanist cinema in the previous chapter should make it clear that they still have a role to play. Instead, I will show how, during the process that broke up, at least to some extent, Televisa's nearly total media monopoly, cinema was able to engage middle-class audiences with new aesthetics that provided different languages for discourses such as intimacy and romance. These discourses affected cultural consumption and identity in certain sectors of Mexican urban populations. Thus, this chapter will explore two simultaneous processes that are closely related to each other. On the one hand, I will trace the emergence of American-style romantic comedies as the major genre in commercial cinema and as a contender for the representation and socialization of affect. On the other, I will discuss the increasing displacement of Mexican cinema from a genre directed at the popular classes to a cultural niche for the consumption of urban middle and high classes. While melodrama was essential for cinema to become an influential genre across the social spectrum in the Golden Age, romantic comedy and other genres constructed upon its aesthetics resulted in an opposite phenomenon: an increasing separation between the cultural languages of different social classes and social geographies. This, as I will demonstrate, closely reflects two key elements of the neoliberal process in Mexico: the emergence of a self-referential, wealthy, and Americanized culture in the realm of the middle class, and the economic and cultural exclusion of different sectors of society from that middle class. In this context, I contend that the transformation of affect and the reconfiguration of what Shumway calls "romance discourses" and "intimacy discourses" shows the ways in which Mexican cinema exceeds its traditional function as a vehicle for national identity, thus allowing for the emergence of a new set of visual aesthetics and cultural ideologies.

La tarea and the Reconfiguration of Cinematic Emotion

At the outset of the 1990s, some filmmakers were already producing movies that sidetracked melodrama and tried to explore the social dynamics of romantic interaction in different ways. One of the most important films in this trend is Jaime Humberto Hermosillo's *La tarea* (1991), one of the first major box office hits of national cinema and a quite daring departure from the logics of the "cinema of solitude." By 1991, Hermosillo was already a leading figure in Mexican film and had produced an important body of work, largely centered on issues of gender and sexuality. As Aaraón Díaz Mendiburo discusses in *Los hijos homoeróticos de Jaime Humberto Hermosillo,* his films are notable because of their early discussion of sexual diversity, even at a time, the 1970s, when the topic was by and large taboo in cultural circles.[1] Even so, *La tarea* was in some ways a departure for Hermosillo, showing the first signs of important trends that would take over film production in the latter part of the 1990s. *La tarea* is constructed on the basis of a very simple situation: Virginia (María Rojo), a communications student, invites a former lover, Marcelo (José Alonso), to her house. She installs cameras in the house to tape their interactions. The movie essentially works in two parts. First, Marcelo is unaware of the taping and we see him trying to re-seduce Virginia. About halfway through the film, Marcelo notices the camera and, after an initially negative reaction, decides to stay and play along. Most of the action takes place in Virginia's apartment, in front of the camera. The movie became somewhat notorious for its explicitness, since it features, among other things, a graphic scene in a hammock, which takes place after Marcelo becomes aware of the camera.

While this explicitness is typical in Hermosillo's cinema, and certainly did not hurt the movie's box office earnings, its critical interest in the context of contemporary Mexican cinema lies elsewhere. The first thing to note is that the movie is set entirely in a middle-class, urban apartment. Hermosillo's engagement with sexual issues usually displaces national identity concerns to a distant second place, sidestepping his generation's imperative to engage urban popular subjects. In consequence, Hermosillo not only gives voice to practices of intimacy rarely engaged by Mexican cinema at that time, but also to an urban professional class that plays an unusually protagonistic role in his work. To be sure, pre-1990 Mexican cinema is full of raunchy, highly sexualized films, but Hermosillo's work operates in a more sophisticated space, reflecting on the notion of the private, and on the erotic practices unsanctioned by public discourse. While Hermosillo explored these issues for almost two decades before his unexpected success with *La tarea,* the fact that this particular movie became a hit is telling in terms of the ways in which it represents emergent forms of imagining affective socialization. If one places this film side-by-side with *Danzón* and *Como agua para chocolate,* which were also released in the early 1990s, the issue that stands out is that those movies' melodramatic discourses are constructed in nostalgic, idealized spaces, while *La tarea*'s protagonists engage with each other within the framework of a deliberately unadorned realism. Rather than operating in historical or social contexts that use nostalgia to provide a certain level of cultural fantasy and solace, Hermosillo makes no claim regarding the cultural languages that structure his characters' identities. Instead, he fully focuses on their interpersonal affectivity and desire. It is important to keep this point in mind because, as I will show, romantic comedies operate in a similar way, by altogether evading national identity issues and constructing their characters largely through the discourses of romance and intimacy.

The fact that Hermosillo's characters are not meant to represent any particular form of national identity gives him the space to focus on middle-class characters, who traditionally are not represented by the discourses of Mexicanness. While Hermosillo's groundbreaking work on gender leads critics to emphasize his focus on women and LGBT characters, he is also a major storyteller of the urban middle class. The success of *La tarea* cannot be explained solely by the audiences' morbid attraction to sexual scandal. It is also due to its representation of the private lives and obsessions of social agents that are rarely the subject of Mexican cinema. The second question is closely related to this idea. If one tries to trace *La tarea* back to Mexican cinema of the 1970s and 1980s, including Hermosillo's own previous work, it will be obvious how much of an anomaly it is. In terms of sexual representation, it lacks the narrative elaboration of even Hermosillo's prior films, and it is clearly far and apart from the work of contemporaries like Ripstein, Cazals, Alcoriza, or Arau. In fact, if one reads Ramírez Berg's analysis of some of Hermosillo's 1970s films in *Cinema of Solitude* (81–88), the first thing that stands out is how melodramatic the plots are, full of dysfunctional families, dominating men, virginity issues, and even illness. All of this is very obviously absent from *La tarea*'s bare-boned, matter-of-fact presentation of sexuality and desire. If one focuses on the main structural conceit of the film, the metacinematic use of the camera within the camera, an interesting reference emerges: Steven Soderbergh's *Sex, Lies, and Videotape* (1989), in which the main character Graham (James Spader) conducts and tapes interviews with women, and asks them about their sexual fantasies and experiences. In a comparison of the two films, *La tarea* takes the power of the gaze claimed by Graham in Soderbergh's movie and places it in the hands of Virginia. Then, in a twist typical of Hermosillo's critical engagement with gender issues, the film uses this device to problematize Virginia's relationship with sexuality. While she controls the gaze of the camera for most of the movie by being aware of its presence and by performing for it, at the very end she becomes as emotionally uncovered as Graham's subjects: after Marcelo leaves, she unexpectedly starts crying.

In short, Hermosillo appropriates Soderbergh's device. Rather than constructing a multicharacter plot around it, however, he decides to explore the act of filming the private. In the end, the resolution of both films results in the same dilemma. According to Alice Templeton, in *Sex, Lies, and Videotape*, "rather than solving their ethical and sexual problems, the promise of liberation moves both characters [the protagonists] into a more complicated kind of freedom charged with moral and erotic meaning" (18). The same can be said about Virginia and Marcelo: their acceptance of a sexual freedom exercised in the realm of the private is still charged with the strong semantics of the moral, the erotic, and even the social. While one indeed may argue that claiming this influence is problematic, *Sex, Lies, and Videotape* came out only two years before *La tarea;* it played a prominent role both at Sundance as well as at the Academy Awards and it enjoyed ample commercial distribution in Mexico. Consequently, it is hard to imagine that the film, which so closely relates to Hermosillo's concerns, was not on his radar. In addition, Hermosillo's movie uses a metacinematic device that, while very prominent in *La tarea*, was very rarely employed in his previous body of work. Hermosillo's implicit reference to *Sex, Lies, and Videotape* provides a consistent explanation for this departure.[2] Still, the connection to Soderbergh is very significant beyond the specific elements adopted by Hermosillo, or even to any claim of influence. As James Mottram extensively documents in *The Sundance Kids*, "*Sex, Lies, and Videotape* did not just make a commercial impact on the industry. Its artistry made an immediate impression too, spearheading a series of films that came to define what people understand by the term 'American indie'" (17). In view of this, I would go as far as to claim that *La tarea*'s anomalous but highly successful aesthetic comes from its early adherence to the codes that would come to define contemporary American independent cinema. In the context of my arguments, this connection has two important implications. On the one hand, Hermosillo's use of a language of intimacy coming from a new form of independent American cinema allows him to represent the erotic conundrums of his characters outside the codes of melodrama. Hermosillo manages to depart even from his own allegiances to melodramatic modes of discourse by enacting an imported cinematic language that allows him to focus on the psychological dimension of his characters rather than on their social identities, which is more typical of U.S. cinematic traditions. More importantly, this enactment also permits him an increased focus on their relation to the patriarchal structures of power at the center of both his previous work and Mexican melodrama at large.

In itself, *La tarea* occupies an uneasy place in Mexican film history, since its work on gender remains influential, but its departure from neo-Mexicanist codes of identity would not have followers until late in the decade, when romantic comedy reintroduced Mexican cinema to Sundance-style aesthetics.[3] Hermosillo himself returns to his plot-driven explorations of patriarchy in films such as *Esmeralda de noche vienes* (1997)—a farcical story of a polygamist woman who charms her way out of her trial and ultimately seduces her judge—leaving behind the elegant, two-character drama of *La tarea*.[4] Still, Hermosillo's rare but groundbreaking reliance on the languages and aesthetics of American independent cinema makes *La tarea* an important predecessor to the work of many filmmakers; I will discuss the precedent it set as I lay out my arguments. For now, the second important implication is that Hermosillo opens the door for a new cinematic practice that closely focuses on discourses of romance and identity and that steps away from the allegorical and symbolic modes of discourse characteristic of neo-Mexicanist cinema. Hermosillo's work is too cutting-edge to be trendsetting, so the renewal of middle-class representation and cinema's affective engagement will continue to develop elsewhere. As I will show in the rest of this chapter, however, Hermosillo did create an opening for romantic comedy to ultimately become the site of reconfiguration of film discourses on affect and love in Mexico.

The Neoliberal Networks of Affective Engagement: *Sólo con tu pareja* and the Birth of Contemporary Romantic Comedy

Romantic comedy is a genre located at the very core of Hollywood cinema, with major representatives in classic works by directors like Ernst Lubitsch, but it is a somewhat new practice in Mexican film. I say "somewhat" because a subgenre of romantic comedy, musical comedy, does have a vast history in Mexico, from Pedro Infante's many lighthearted films to the 1960s rock films starring singers like Angélica María, all the way to 1980s vehicles for Televisa-sponsored singers like Lucero and Manuel Mijares.[5] However, plot-based, nonmusical romantic comedies never really emerged in Mexico, largely because of the prevalence of melodrama as the language of affect and to the use of romantic comedy as a vehicle to promote musical celebrities. The origins of the genre in Mexico in the early 1990s follow the important success it enjoyed in the United States in the 1980s.[6] Two noteworthy sources appear in Frank Krutnik's ample accounts of American romantic comedy. On the one hand,

Woody Allen's work, particularly in movies like *Annie Hall* (1977) and *Hannah and Her Sisters* (1987), gave the genre an aura of cultural prestige by undermining its basic assumptions and formulas (Krutnik, "Love Lies" 23), and by thoroughly inscribing it into the codes of what would later become American independent cinema.[7] On the other hand, Rob Reiner's *When Harry Met Sally* (1989), which was an overwhelming commercial and critical success, showed the enormous potential of situational romantic comedy as a mainstream cultural product. It was quickly followed by juggernauts such as Gary Marshall's *Pretty Woman* (1990) and Nora Ephron's *Sleepless in Seattle* (1993), turning this kind of romantic comedy into a frequently visited and highly successful genre in the 1990s.[8] Mexican romantic comedy emerged in the middle ground between both categories: as an attempt to renew the paradigms of urban cinema through a sophisticated, dialogue-oriented comedic discourse that drastically contrasted with the *sexycomedia* exploitation aesthetics, and as a way to appeal to the emerging commercial possibilities of the Mexican middle class made evident by the success of *La tarea* and *Como agua para chocolate*. As the first contemporary romantic comedy of the period, Alfonso Cuarón's groundbreaking *Sólo con tu pareja* (1991) stands at the point where these two trends meet.

In *Sólo con tu pareja*, we meet Tomás Tomás (Daniel Giménez Cacho), a womanizer whose life is turned around by a prank: one of the women he slept with and left behind, a nurse in a clinic, tampers with the results of a test so that he thinks he is HIV positive. Tomás subsequently falls in love with a beautiful flight attendant, Clarisa (Claudia Ramírez), while watching her rehearse the airline security demonstration. After a series of confusions and misunderstandings, until, at the very end, Tomás and Clarisa, whose boyfriend cheats on her with another flight attendant, decide to jump from the top of Mexico City's Latin American Tower. In the end, Silvia, the nurse, admits to her prank, preventing the suicide and providing the movie with a happy ending. When the movie opened in 1991, criticism was quite divided about it. On the one hand, Nelson Carro, an influential film reviewer, praised the movie, arguing that it "raised expectations of a public that rarely goes to see Mexican films but lately has been attracted by certain movies [Carro refers to *La Tarea* and *Como agua para chocolate*] that present a novel and different image than is usually shown by Mexican cinema" (cited in Mora 200). Conversely, Jorge Ayala Blanco attacked the movie by arguing that, behind its "neo-obnoxious gags," there was a tasteless movie about AIDS (the title comes from a government AIDS awareness campaign) directed toward "prettified middle-class youths with aspirations of preppiness [*alindados jóvenes clasemedieros con aspiraciones de pirruris*]" (*La eficacia* 254). These two opinions, nonetheless, point toward the same reading: *Sólo con tu pareja* is a movie that represents a whole new sector of the audience, and its appeal is directed toward those who "rarely go to see Mexican films"—namely, the middle class whose film tastes were Hollywood-centric. What distances Carro and Ayala Blanco is essentially a value judgment: Carro sees *Sólo con tu pareja*'s class appeal as a necessary element in the modernization of cinema, while Ayala Blanco, a noted leftist intellectual, rejects it as a reflection of the values of the local bourgeoisie. This early dilemma, as reflected in the view of these two critics, shows the nature of the transformation announced by Cuarón's movie. After decades of cinema aimed at the popular classes, we have a film that directly and shamelessly appeals to the middle class. As Armida de la Garza shows, this movie will begin a trend of showing a Mexico beyond the world of its urban popular classes, with moral codes different from traditional conservative representations, and a country that, in her view, is as Western as it is Mexican (146–49). These changes ultimately contributed to making the movie illegible even to film critics. Néstor García Canclini shows that, in the nineteen reviews published in print media at the time of the film's release, "it is not only impossible to obtain . . . a minimally shared assessment of the movie. There is not even an agreement among critics about what the movie's central theme is" (*Los nuevos espectadores* 129; my translation). Even at the most basic structural level, the movie was operating in an entirely different ideological, cultural, and visual language. García Canclini, without the benefit of hindsight, lamented the lack of value assessment in the criticism of the movie, but considering the later success of romantic comedy as a genre in Mexican film, it is clear that the more symptomatic point in the critics' lack of consensus results from the film's novelty. The centrality of *Sólo con tu pareja* in understanding the profound impact of neoliberalism as a cultural mechanism in contemporary Mexico rests on the fact that it records major transformations at the level of social and cultural subjectivity and consumption as they were happening, even before the film industry transformed itself accordingly. It was a movie predicated on the aesthetic languages of the 2000s, playing on what remained of the distribution and production systems of the 1980s. In understanding the way in which the film prefigures the full-fledged incorporation of neoliberal culture into cinema, it will be easier to assess not only its precursory role, but also the necessary transformation of film consumers in order for romantic comedy to become the hegemonic film language in contemporary Mexican cinema.

A surprisingly significant element in Cuarón's movie is Tomás Tomás's profession: he writes jingles and slogans for an advertising agency. This choice of trade has many important ramifications. First and foremost, it speaks clearly of the transformations underlying the economic life of the middle class, which contribute to its emergence as a subject of cinematic representation. Rather than opting for a more traditional middle-class profession in Mexico, such as law or medicine, Cuarón invests his protagonist with a trade clearly related to the new economic configurations of neoliberalism. As Deborah Riener and

John Sweeney have shown, NAFTA and the changing nature of the consumer market in Mexico created a major transformation in the advertising industry: "Advertisers must now think in terms of the 'message,' be it through promotions, sponsorship or television and radio ads. Successful marketing is no longer just a matter of buying commercials, because of the growing sophistication of the consumer" (181). In his decision to write Tomás Tomás as an author of slogans and as a creator of the messages that appeal to the new generation of "sophisticated" consumers, Cuarón locates his movie squarely within this logic. Thus, the middle class represented by Cuarón and by subsequent romantic comedies is neither the newly modernized traditional family present, for example, in Golden Age melodramas like *Una familia de tantas,* nor the middle class that claims its roots in its family inscriptions in national history, like the narrator of *Como agua para chocolate* does. Rather, it is a middle class whose wealth and social status stem from the economic and social dynamics brought about by neoliberalism. The publicist will be a quite ubiquitous character in romantic comedy and other genres, figuring prominently in highly successful movies like González Iñárritu's *Amores perros,* where the main character of the second part is a publicist who has an affair with a model, and in romantic comedies like *Ladies' Night* and *Cansada de besar sapos,* where the action unfolds in advertising agencies. I will address these movies later.

This new kind of cultural subjectivity has been at the heart of many debates in Latin American cultural theory. Perhaps the most important example of this is Néstor García Canclini's *Consumers and Citizens,* in which he contends that "changes in the modes of consumption have altered the possibilities and forms of citizenship" in Latin America (15). García Canclini's argument unfolds along two axes. First, García Canclini proposes understanding consumption as a critical act in the public space of the market, a form of agency overlooked by old understandings of the consumer as a passive object of publicity. Second, he proposes a revision of the notion of citizenship from older practices of political participation (such as elections and public demonstrations) to a "private realm of commodity consumption and the mass media" more prevalent in political subjectivities than "the abstract rules of democracy or collective participation in public spaces" (15). Tellingly, García Canclini's first example, which sets the tone of his book, comes from marketing, and from the use of advertising as an essential part of electoral campaigns. The increasing role of advertising in the construction of citizenship and agency created a new class of celebrity marketing executives. Two prime examples are Santiago Pando, who was responsible for some of the most creative advertising campaigns of the 1990s and, as a result, ended up running Vicente Fox's electoral campaign, and Alejandro González Iñárritu, whose successful marketing career in the 1990s helped finance and launch his work as a film director.[9] The consistent presence of the publicist in Mexican cinema as a privileged subject of the middle class clearly reflects these new understandings of citizenship. By establishing the publicist as the representative of the new subjectivities and affects of Mexican cinema, Alfonso Cuarón begins a trend in which film becomes increasingly focused on the "consumer-citizen" described by García Canclini. Surprisingly, García Canclini overlooks this very point in his short engagement with contemporary cinema, when he argues that films like Cuarón's are popular because they "deal with topics of interest to youth" (120). I would argue, rather, that *Sólo con tu pareja* succeeds because it is able to reflect the experiences of a middle class whose social and cultural identities are framed by discourses of consumption, such as advertising. The film's title further exemplifies this point: it comes precisely from a landmark advertising campaign that was omnipresent at the time in print and electronic media. The experience of AIDS as represented by the movie is not medical or physical: it is mediatic. The movie does not attempt a critical look at the AIDS epidemic. It frames its love story in the context of the media frenzy brought about by the campaign. The subjects of the movie, then, are first and foremost characters constructed by their mediatic relationship to the world at large. This is one of the reasons why Cuarón can opt for romantic comedy: the controversial subject of AIDS is a comedic device insofar as it comes from advertising and not from any political or medical standpoint.

In *The Secret Life of Romantic Comedy*, critic Celestino Deleyto offers a useful definition of the genre, stating that it can "be described as the intersection of three, closely interrelated elements: a narrative that articulates historically and culturally specific views of love, desire, sexuality and gender relationships; a space of transformation and fantasy which influences the narrative articulation of those discourses; and humour as the specific perspective from which the fictional characters, their relationships and the spectator's response to them are constructed as embodiments of those discourses" (45–46). Some key words from this description help in gauging the workings behind *Sólo con tu pareja*'s recalibration of Mexican cinema. Deleyto's emphasis on "culturally specific views of love, desire and sexuality" illustrates well the nature of the displacements present in a movie like this. Armida de la Garza writes that the sexual behavior of characters in contemporary Mexican romantic comedy is a departure from the conservative Catholic values one identifies with the country (148). While this is relevant, de la Garza's reading still points toward a notion of national identity that is supposed to be evolving. However, the cultural specificity of the discourses of romance and intimacy at play in *Sólo con tu pareja* has to do with the way in which the characters experience everyday life rather than national identity. In fact, the claim that *Sólo con tu pareja* departs from codes of morality is not quite accurate. It is indeed true that Tomás Tomás is a womanizer cast in a sympathetic light, but, in fact, he is "punished" by an AIDS scare, and redeemed when he makes a commitment to love and monogamy.

The film's message lies elsewhere, and is better exemplified by Clarisa. In one of the film's turning points, Clarisa leaves her husband after he cheats on her with a blonde flight attendant working for Continental Airlines. The fleeting reference to the other woman's employer is meaningful in itself, given that the husband's preference for a flight attendant working for a U.S. airline is a subtle parody of Mexicans' preference for U.S. culture. When describing her feelings to Tomás after the breakup, Clarisa describes it as "worse than an emergency landing" and a clipping of her "wings." When the idea of committing suicide together takes shape, Clarisa emphasizes that she wants to die in the air. This scene demonstrates Deleyto's point about cultural specificity in a very telling way. Unlike Julia Solórzano in *Danzón,* Clarisa's entire affective world is configured not by popular culture but rather by her life in the corporate world of air travel. However, Clarisa does hold an interesting similarity to Julia: the airline industry, like the phone company, was a target of privatization. The film, in fact, emphasizes Clarisa's status as a worker: it shows her wearing her uniform in different scenes, including the one when Tomás falls in love with her. Thus, what defines the language of her experiences is her life within capitalism, in a trade that, regardless of its connection to the State, is also not identified with traditional middle-class professions, but rather with Mexico's increasingly international status. The same thing may be said of Tomás, whose relationship to culture is entirely defined by his writing of slogans and the commercials he works on. At the beginning of the movie, Tomás is working on a commercial for a brand of *chiles jalapeños,* featuring an indigenous man giving the *chiles* to a conquistador. These two characters reappear later in the movie during a dream Tomás has after a night of drinking. The fact that his subconscious is fully determined by his commercial work illustrates how his affective imaginary is equally mediated by his labor relationship to capitalism and consumerism.

Humor becomes a factor in this very point. Ryan Long has pointed out that the movie does use icons of national identity, but only through a "sophisticated satire of the shopworn clichés of Mexican national culture" (7). Long refers to a particular scene: Mateo, Tomás's friend and physician, asks him to entertain two Japanese doctors while Mateo and his wife go see an Akira Kurosawa movie. Tomás takes the doctors to Garibaldi, a plaza in Mexico City famous for its cantinas and mariachis. As Long points out, this particular site of national culture only appears when Tomás validates "the kitschy stereotypes of his own nation" (7). Tomás's drunken dream also forms a key component of Long's argument, as it features not only the conquistador from the commercial, but also a mariachi singing opera like a castrato, and a masked wrestler. Long reads this sequence as the appearance of a cast of characters from Mexico's past whose authenticity is as canned and pre-produced as the jalapeños from the commercial (8). This analysis correctly points out Cuarón's devastating critique of national identity, which, of course, may be contrasted with the many nostalgic discourses of neo-Mexicanism discussed in Chapter 1. However, these two scenes carry another very important dimension that goes unnoticed by Long. When Tomás is in Garibaldi with the Japanese doctors, he starts talking about his love misfortunes while in a cantina and surrounded by liquor. This scene updates a stereotypical site of Mexican Golden Age cinema: the cantina as a homoerotic masculine space in which alcohol and male bonding are ways of dealing with heartbreak. The comedic device rests on the fact that the Japanese doctors speak no Spanish and the only word uttered by Tomás they understand is "hara-kiri," when Tomás speaks of killing himself. At this point, one of the doctors starts speaking to Tomás in Japanese, in a very serious tone, apparently trying to dissuade him from committing suicide. The fact that male bonding overcomes cultural difference is, in a way, a reductio ad absurdum of the typical cantina scene of nationalist masculinities.

The parody of traditional film genres is also a factor in Tomás's dream. The appearance of the wrestler appeals to a large tradition of national cinema directly connected to urban popular experiences. As Doyle Greene shows, wrestling cinema comes from the popularity of the sport among members of the working class, based on a good-versus-evil narrative embodied in the two styles of wresting, "rudo" (rough or rule-breaking) and "técnico" (technical or rule-following) (54–55).[10] By showing a wrestler with a cartoonish resemblance to El Santo, the protagonist of the most celebrated wrestling movies, Cuarón is not only questioning national identity, but also parodying another important national film genre. Both the cantina and the dream sequences can be read as an exorcism: Cuarón uses humor to cast out the ghosts of nationalist imagery. While neo-Mexicanist filmmakers like Carrera or Springall work on the inherited imagery of the nation as a way to critique preexisting power, gender, and religious structures, Cuarón's parodic inversion of nationalism as something that only matters to tourists or in the middle of a drunken dream assumes that such cultural codes are useless in contemporary Mexican cinema. Thus, since the characters' affective construction cannot have any relation to national identity, they inhabit a private sphere that only the languages of capitalism can construct.

The third element in Deleyto's definition comes into play here: the "space of transformation and fantasy" in which the characters' romantic relationships take place. Deleyto argues that the "comic space" is the "fictional space in which [the characters] exist, a fictional space which represents the social space of cultural discourses on love, sexuality and intimacy" (36). Furthermore, romantic comedy operates in a space that "allows the spectator a glimpse of a 'better world,' a world which is not governed by inhibitions and repressions but is instead characterised by a freer, more optimistic expression of love and desire" (36). Space in *Sólo con tu pareja* has primarily been identified with its location in the city, and most academic readings of the film center on its urban setting. Miriam Haddu, for instance, argues that Cuarón deliberately presents the urban as "aesthetically pleasing," in contrast to the Golden Age's grimmer version of the city ("Love on the Run" 196). Furthermore, Haddu puts forward the notion of Mexico City as "postmodern," a space where national identity, as embodied by the Tómas's dream, coexists with the modern (201). This reading is problematic, since it overlooks the obvious parody of national icons and understands Cuarón's reference to wrestler cinema as homage rather than critique. In other words, one could say that the interaction of the modern with the national in Cuarón's visual language does not result in a "hybrid" city where both coexist, but in a clear argument where the modern exists as a matter of fact, while the national is solely an object of mockery. Still, what is telling in Haddu's reading is her idea of presenting the city as the core of the movie, and her analysis of *Sólo con tu pareja* is by and large related to this subject. Manuel F. Medina develops an intuitive reading of urban space in the film. He claims that Mexico City is a "public space that traps one of its inhabitants," a situation that also extends to Tomás's apartment and other private spaces (252). Medina's main line of analysis is the contrast between the public and the private, which, in my view, is suggestive but secondary. Still, by showing the predominance of the private in the film, Medina unwittingly sets forward an element that questions the centrality of Mexico City as an issue in the movie, undermining both his own reading and Haddu's.

Without a doubt, *Sólo con tu pareja* is a deliberately urban movie. However, Mexico City is more a setting than a character. Cuarón does use landmark spaces of the city, such as the Latin American Tower and the restaurant at the top of the World Trade Center, but the actions do not establish any substantial cultural connection to those spaces. The Latin American Tower is the setting of the final scene largely because it was, at the time, the highest building accessible to the public, but any high-rise construction could have served the same purpose. Besides, as Medina shows in his analysis, most of the action actually happens in closed spaces: Tomás's apartment and the surrounding building, Mateo's clinic, the cantina (which might have been a public space, but functions as private since the scene is shot mostly through close-ups of Tomás and the Japanese doctors), and so on. Following Deleyto, one could argue that the central space is not Mexico City in itself, but rather the "transformational" and "magic" space where the protagonists' love develops and that the spectator may read as "better" than reality. By focusing on interior spaces, the film in fact creates a love story where space is emotional but not cultural: what matters is Tomás's intimate world and not Mexico City at large. Emmanuel Lubezki's highly aestheticized cinematography, full of darkly luscious colors, conveys this very sense. Rather than the gritty urban landscapes of 1970s social cinema, *Sólo con tu pareja* presents an unprecedentedly attractive representation of urban spaces, which clearly breaks with any notion of social or cinematic realism. *Sólo con tu pareja*'s status as a romantic comedy consequently requires a break with the issue of representation of the city, since the film's space is, after all, more attuned to the characters' love experiences and woes than to any visual or textual claim vis-à-vis Mexico City. The Latin American Tower, then, is only relevant in that it plays a role in the construction of the characters' pathos and the articulation of their love relationship. It is in this space that Clarisa and Tomás kiss and make love for the first time and the one in which the resolution of the main obstacle to their relationship, his alleged HIV infection, takes place. In these terms, any tall building (even one in another city) would have been equally useful to the plot.

Up to this point, thanks to the elements of romantic comedy, we can see that *Sólo con tu pareja* operates in a radically different niche than any other movie produced in the first half of the 1990s. Its unapologetic superficiality and its refusal to negotiate with the affective code of melodrama cuts deep into the paradigms of Mexicanism and neo-Mexicanism described in Chapter 1. The movie entails an important displacement of the characters subject to cinematic representation by giving the consumer-citizen described by García Canclini a visual language to unfold as a privileged figure of the neoliberal imagination. Cuarón also provides an important opening in the possibilities of film subjectivity in Mexico. While *La tarea* shows the possibilities of characters solely constructed on psychological premises, detached from any meaningful tie to the social and the national, Clarisa and Tomás are thoroughly constructed through a sphere of experience that displaces the social from the nation to the market. As the rest of this book will show, of all the major movies released in Mexico between 1990 and 1992, *Sólo con tu pareja* is ultimately the most visionary, since it heralds the directions that would be privileged by commercial cinema for the following twenty years.[11] Still, until the release of Rafael Montero's *Cilantro y perejil* in 1995, *Sólo con tu pareja* was an aesthetic anomaly, completely out of place in a cinematic landscape still dominated by neo-Mexicanism. For romantic comedy to become a predominant genre in Mexico, a series of transformations in the affective economy of Mexican audiences and the cultural cartography of Mexican cinema would be required.

The Reinvention of the Audience: The Privatization of Exhibition and the Emergence of Middle-Class Spectatorship

In the five to seven years that followed the release of *Sólo con tu pareja*, romantic comedy operated within an identity crisis of sorts. While Cuarón had set a bold new pathway in the construction of characters and the visual aesthetics of romance discourses, many films of the mid-1990s approached the new genre hesitantly. This is clear in Carlos Carrera's *La vida conyugal* (1993), which retroactively tells the story of an old married couple after the wife has killed her husband. Unlike Cuarón, Carrera opts for a more traditional construction of the affective world for his characters, setting his story principally in the 1950s and the 1960s. *La vida conyugal* thus avoids confronting the genre's contemporary articulations by adopting a retroactive view in which the characters' affective sphere can be constructed, like in *Danzón,* through reflective nostalgia. Another notable example is Ernesto Rimoch's *El anzuelo* (1996). This movie focuses on a couple's wedding day and the conflicts that ensue following the disappearance of the money meant to pay for the music. Like *La vida conyugal, El anzuelo* is a film clearly articulated in the discourse that Shumway calls the "marriage crisis," which is at the core of contemporary American romantic comedy. Still, Rimoch follows a thematic line closer to the one developed by Hermosillo, with a character consistently taping the events at a wedding and with the action centering, by and large, on the family's middle-class apartment. Of course, *El anzuelo* does not include an exploration of intimacy as daring as the one put forward by Hermosillo, and its use of its video element is contrived, providing little contribution to the structure or development of the film. Another case, perhaps the most clearly symptomatic of the incapacity of romantic comedy to fully emerge as a contemporary genre in the mid-1990s, is Rodolfo de Anda's *Alta tensión* (1997), a poorly constructed romantic comedy following a beautiful reporter's attempt to win back her ex-boyfriend. The major problem of *Alta tensión,* though, lies elsewhere: it is almost an infomercial of Mexico's State-owned electric industry, framing the romantic plot in an obviously propagandistic presentation of a new electric plant and its role in the future of Mexico. The movie, which concludes with a dedication to the electric workers of Mexico, is the low point of a creative impasse that plagued directors of romantic comedy, who proved unable or unwilling to fully assume the creative and cinematic challenges set forward by *Sólo con tu pareja* or even *La tarea.*[12]

The lack of immediate successors to the new aesthetic created by Cuarón is related to a set of structural problems faced by Mexican cinema in the mid-1990s. While the early part of the decade was characterized by a surprising wave of successful movies against the backdrop of a distribution crisis, a parallel crisis of production materialized as a result of the December 1994 financial crisis. The Mexican cinema industry remained fueled by a steady though aesthetically questionable flow of movies from Televicine, which kept producing low-budget films with Televisa's talent. These were distributed on their TV networks and, in a few selected cases, in some privately held theaters. In addition, even though private production outside of Televicine was hardly viable, the newly created National Council of the Culture and the Arts maintained a significant budget for the production of national cinema. When, in December 1994, Mexico faced its biggest economic crisis in decades, following a financial meltdown that required a substantial bailout from the U.S. treasury, the State became paralyzed in its capacity as a film producer. As Misha MacLaird documents, the State produced only five films in 1995, and seven per year in 1996 and 1997 (*Aesthetics* 28), lowering the industry's total output to less than a dozen movies per year by 1998.[13] The conditions that would have permitted the production of expensive, highly stylized romantic comedies in the wake of *Sólo con tu pareja* were just not there. As MacLaird fittingly points out, this period corresponded with the disappearance of the institutional structures that had made cinema accessible to the popular classes, given the disappearance of State-owned theaters that charged affordable admission. This impasse would be in place at least until 1998, when the creation of FOPROCINE (Fondo de Producción Cinematográfica de Calidad, or Fund for Quality Film Production), a State-sponsored entity, allowed the State to resume its role as a source of media financing.

This crisis in production opened a space in which major transformations of the audience would take place. While it is true that cinema was not producing attractive romantic comedies (or anything else) to engage audiences commercially, Cuarón's style remained alien to the media languages that most Mexicans consumed. The primacy of Televisa as the nearly sole provider of audiovisual content on the airwaves meant that audiences did not have a cultural language to relate to cinema outside the familiar structures of melodrama and Mexicanism. However, the mid-1990s were the site of major transformations in the ideologies and expectations of audiovisual audiences in Mexico. In 1994, a group of sociologists led by García Canclini produced a landmark study of cinema and television audiences in Mexico, entitled *Los nuevos espectadores,* which recorded an unprecedentedly clear image of their habits and views. The scholars represented in the book emphasize the role of videoclubs as a factor that draws audiences away from film theaters. In a study of film audiences in Mérida, Fanny Quintal and Guadalupe Reyes show that theater and videoclub audiences are essentially the same (García Canclini, *Los nuevos espectadores* 275), suggesting that those two distribution channels compete with each other for the same audiences, which explains why, lacking modern theaters, many opted to rent movies and watch them at home. However, the book's most telling findings lie not in the spaces of cinema consumption, but in audience preferences. In a survey of attendees at a Mexican cinema retrospective, the sociologists found that a group made up of housewives, small business owners, and factory workers preferred national over foreign cinema, while a group composed of self-employed professionals and people in managerial positions stated the opposite preference. The sociologists highlight that a group composed of students, teachers, and artists showed no preference, given that people in these trades tend to focus their tastes on critical rather than national parameters (58–59). This emphasis overlooks the most significant finding in the poll: the radical class division between those who prefer national cinema and those who prefer foreign movies. The absence of an audience for commercial romantic comedies produced in Mexico is obvious in this survey. A staggering 79.8 percent of respondents consider the Golden Age their favorite period of Mexican cinema, while contemporary cinema is only mentioned by 1 percent (64). Even with the commercial success of *Cómo agua para chocolate* and *Sólo con tu pareja*, the audience of contemporary Mexican film came by and large from a very small sector of the population.

A salient point here is that, regardless of the presumed quality of films released in the early 1990s, film audiences lacked the cultural literacy necessary to connect with the languages developed by Cuarón. The working classes kept defining their affective experience in connection with the romance discourses already constituted by melodrama, which were then recycled in the near omnipresence of *telenovelas* on the airwaves and in the constant broadcasting of Golden Age cinema in the primetime spaces not covered by soap operas. In fact, as Nora Mazziotti shows in her study of the *telenovela* industry, Mexican soaps of the early 1990s were notorious for their "essentially melodramatic model," with a tradition of conservative plotlines constructed around traditional family values (47–51).[14] At the same time, the middle and upper classes, the implicit audience of *Sólo con tu pareja*, had no affective relationship to national cinema. In García Canclini's survey, members from these social strata mentioned Hollywood-style melodramas such as Peter Weir's *Dead Poets Society* when asked which film they remembered the most (García Canclini, *Los nuevos espectadores* 59). Movies like *La vida conyugal* and *El anzuelo* were configured through aesthetics and narratives meaningless to this audience: the films partly relied on the familiar codes of melodrama present in traditional Mexican audiovisual culture, while picking up some of the middle-class elements developed by Hermosillo and Cuarón. As a result, they were unable to attract either demographic, forcing them to rely on State-sponsored circulation in international film festivals to enjoy some exhibition.[15] Still, what the studies in *Los nuevos espectadores* show is the radical distance between film production and the audiences that had to be overcome for Mexican cinema to attain commercial viability.

The lack of sociological or econometric studies on Mexican audiences after *Los nuevos espectadores* remains a major obstacle in the understanding of the social nature of film consumption in the country. Since the present book is concerned mostly with the aesthetic and ideological changes brought about by neoliberalism, a thorough sociological study falls outside of both my aims and my scholarly training. However, a development evident in the practices of moviegoing must be highlighted: the emergence of privately owned cineplexes. In 1994, the U.S.-based exhibition company Cinemark opened four multiplexes in cities like Monterrey and Aguascalientes, followed in 1995 by a twelve-screen theater in Mexico City on the grounds of the newly built National Center for the Arts, a complex that encompasses theater forums, a school for the performing arts, a film school, and film studios.

Compared to the moviegoing experiences described at the beginning of this book, this first Cinemark complex in Mexico City provided a major transformation of the film-watching experience. The theaters were clean, the concession stand had edible food, the seats were quite comfortable, and the investment in technology was obvious. The complex featured DTS surround sound, the first of its kind in Mexico. The screens were somewhat small, in comparison to those of the old, massive single-screen buildings, but so were the theaters, so a shorter distance from the seat to the screen compensated for the decrease in screen surface. Some trade-offs were also quite clear. The chain refused to hire workers from the Sindicato de Trabajadores de la Industria Cinematográfica (STIC), an old union that ran COTSA theaters, and in spite of the short-lived protests staged outside the Cinemark, the theaters' workforce was composed of young, underpaid workers who compensated for their lack of experience with a well-trained, positive attitude that contrasted with the almost proverbial crankiness of unionized workers. Of course, this meant that while audiences were very pleased with the perceivable improvements in the quality of customer service, the working conditions in the exhibition industry were downgraded from the salaried, benefits-oriented unionized jobs to precarious, short-term, hourly positions. It became an example of Mexico's quick transition from the welfare State to the service economy.

Moreover, Cinemark introduced a new class distinction in movie attendance, as it was clearly aiming at the middle classes for its market niche. Cinemark profited from a provision in a 1992 law that liberalized ticket prices. This reform overrode a price control law from 1952 that had been designed to make cinema affordable to the lower classes (Berrueco García 52). As a result, the admissions prices at the Mexico City Cinemark were set at around thirty-five or forty Mexican pesos (about four to six U.S. dollars at the time), two to three times higher than the price of tickets at State-owned theaters, and roughly the same amount as two and a half days of minimum wage (which equaled 13.97 pesos a day in 1994 and 16.42 in 1995). Tellingly, this particular Cinemark was clearly designed for drivers: while it featured an enormous parking garage, it was nearly inaccessible by public transportation. Located on Río Churubusco, an inner highway, it was a long, unsafe walk away from the closest subway station and outside major public transportation routes. While one could certainly arrive by taxi, it was nearly impossible to flag one on the way out. The message was loud and clear: moviegoing had started its transformation into an activity for the privileged.

The success of Cinemark made movie exhibition a very attractive business from very early on: the theaters boasted sold-out shows and huge lines in the parking garage. Later in 1994, Organización Ramírez, a Morelia-based operator of one-to-three-screen theaters around the country, introduced Cinépolis, its own cineplex concept. These cineplexes were aggressively constructed throughout the country, making Ramírez the largest exhibitor in Mexico to date. In addition, as MacLaird documents, a group of Harvard Business School graduates organized around a failed bid for COTSA and decided to open their own chain. Acting in spite of the financial crisis, they secured investment money to open their first complex, Cinemex Manacar, in 1995 (*Aesthetics* 48). Cinemex would go on to become the third-largest operator in the country and the second largest in major urban markets like Mexico City and Guadalajara. Finally, MM Cinemas, a Monterrey-based corporation born from a conglomerate for small theaters in the interior, decisively entered the cineplex business in the late 1990s. While it lacked a complex in Mexico City, it became the second-largest chain in the country, thanks to its strong presence in the interior. Cinemex and MM Cinemas merged in 2009, under new ownership, in a bid to take on Cinépolis. In 2013, Cinemex acquired the Lumière cinema chain, and Cinemark announced it was selling itself to Cinemex, establishing an exhibition duopoly. According to 2011 data from Canacine, a professional guild that includes exhibitors, distributors, producers, and video companies, Cinemark, Cinemex MMC, Lumière and Cinépolis operated 4,595 screens, 89 percent of the total in Mexico.[16] In other words, in a little over a decade, film exhibition became almost exclusively controlled by a business model that successfully lured middle classes into what has become a quite profitable industry, controlled by a small number of companies. According to the website Box Office Mojo, which tracks international box office receipts, a typical week in Mexico yields between six and eleven million dollars in receipts, and some Hollywood movies have grossed over thirty million dollars in the national market. This massive theater attendance, of course, translates into very profitable concession stands and the attraction of customers to any surrounding eateries and shopping malls.

In addition, the commercial success of the cineplex ventures produced exactly what a viable production industry required: a reliable audience with the economic means to go to the movies (and to pay elevated ticket prices). In 2002, for instance, *El crimen del padre Amaro* grossed over sixteen million dollars in the domestic market, a previously unthinkable figure. According to numbers compiled by Lucía Hinojosa Córdova, in 1995, at the bottom of the market, total film attendance was around sixty-two million. By 2001, this had already increased to 138 million (481). While all theaters profited, a significant number became particularly successful. According to Canacine figures, the Cinépolis Plaza Universidad complex alone attracted over two million attendees in 2008. The other key factor here is the astounding multiplication in the number of screens, which went from around 1,400 at the bottom of the market in 1993 to slightly over five thousand today. Combined with a 1999 law that requires theaters to use 10 percent of their screens for Mexican cinema, this means that available screen space nearly quadrupled, diversifying cinema offerings beyond Hollywood blockbusters and creating a new demand for Mexican movies to fill the screen time requirements.[17] This provided, from early on, unprecedented spaces for Mexican films. As soon as Cinemark opened, Mexican films were able to obtain screen space: during its first year of operation, the Mexico City multiplex exhibited Roberto Sneider's *Dos crímenes* and Ignacio Ortiz's *La orilla de la tierra*.

The increase in the number of screens and in the size of the potential audiences, though, has to be understood side by side with the irreversible redefinition of moviegoing as an activity reserved for the country's wealthier classes. By controlling 89 percent of total screens, cineplexes meant the evolution of moviegoing into what Ana Rosas Mantecón calls "new processes of urban segregation." Rosas Mantecón, one of the very few scholars to address the question of film audiences from sociological perspectives, decries the loss of film exhibition as a space of mass sociability and argues that the most important effect of the expansion of cineplexes in Mexico City, the focus of her research, is the transformation of moviegoing into an "elitist" activity ("New Processes" and "Auge"). In a similar study conducted in film theaters in Monterrey, Hinojosa Córdova finds that moviegoing is tied to "a high level of education and being employed, which leads to the conclusion that many people are excluded from it" (91; my translation). This assessment, though, overly simplifies the role of the cineplex in the new cultural geographies of Mexican cities. The fact that the new movie theaters are not accessible by the working classes does not mean that they do not constitute spaces of sociability. In fact, as Charles Acland has shown in a study of the megaplex in Canada, "cinema complexes are hubs of community and public life. They do not situate conditions of spectatorship alone; they also construct relations between public and cinematic practices" (119). What this means for the Mexican context is that cinemagoing has reemerged as a social practice for the middle classes, related to activities such as dating and after-school entertainment. The economic segregation that resulted from this reemergence was unfortunate and undesirable, but in places like Mexico City, where the middle class is made up by millions of people, it also meant a restoration of cinema as entertainment for a significant part of the audience. This is more so the case today, since ticket prices have risen at a rate lower than inflation: today, they are around fifty-five to seventy pesos, more or less the same as a day of minimum wage. In other words, the cost of the ticket relative to income is about half today what it was in 1995. Moreover, if one follows Acland's analysis, this transformation is what allowed a revival of moviegoing despite the competition from television, video, and the Internet: "In light of a historical economic convergence of industries, it is fundamental that we consider the intermedia linkages of texts, production and reception and reveal the process establishing specificity and distinction in those three realms, whether publicly situated or not" (122). When applied to the Mexican case, this argument shows that the emergence of the cineplex was as important as the emergence of romantic comedy or the transformation of Mexicanist discourse: it was the condition of possibility for the emergence of the viable industry and the reliable audience needed for the aesthetic and ideological reformulation of Mexican cinema.

Precisely because the new audiences are identified with the educated middle classes, in the mid-1990s, the traditional cultural codes of melodrama and Mexicanism, geared toward the popular classes, were gradually displaced out of Mexican cinema. Some movies that moved away from melodramatic codes found early spaces in the new commercial market, even though a much-needed transformation in taste and in production values had yet to take place. *Los nuevos espectadores* hints at an element that may contribute to understanding the evolution of taste in the new middle-class audiences: cable television. In the study of Mérida mentioned earlier, the authors show that Cablediversión had almost twenty-two thousand paying customers in its first two years of operation, located mostly in higher-income neighborhoods (García Canclini, *Los nuevos espectadores* 273). A similar process was observed in Tijuana, where the seven thousand subscribers to cable in 1993 were in upper-income areas (313). Finally, in Mexico City, combined subscriptions for cable, satellite, and DTH outlets were at around 1.25 million households (Sinclair, *Latin American Television* 57), a number that concretely illustrates the size of the audiences sought by romantic comedies and the cineplexes. Early studies of NAFTA's impact on Mexican media, such as the ones compiled by Emile McAnany and Kenton Wilkinson in *Mass Media and Free Trade,* explore this question in terms of national identity, wondering whether the entry of new media outlets providing American content would have an impact in redefining it. Of course, this framing remained within the theoretical ideologies of Mexicanness, and, in hindsight, the main value of those studies remains in their demonstrations of the consistent preference of the audience for national content. Later works on media and communication studies, though, show that the real consequence of the expansion of pay television in Mexican media consumption rests on the class stratification of audiences in the country. According to Joseph Straubhaar and Luiz Duarte, marketing data in Latin America show that 90 percent of subscribers to cable and satellite TV are in the top 50 percent of the income scale (228). In other words, the penetration of pay TV, represented by local cable and satellite companies and by transnational dish networks, echoed the patterns observed in the formation of cineplex audiences. They are mostly urban professional customers who use these new cultural venues as a form to evade the traditional content provided by broadcast TV.

As John Sinclair shows, the growth of the Spanish-language Latin American market allowed transnational media companies to operate TV channels addressed toward Latin America but with a strong level of U.S.-produced content. While MTV produced a specific channel for Mexico, and while some regional chains did possess channels of their own, in 1996 90 percent of the content came from the United States ("International Television" 200). What matters for my argument is the nature of the content presented by the new cable networks in fictional genres. Besides film and sports networks, one of the most interesting developments was the emergence of highly successful channels whose content was largely made up of American primetime fiction shows. These channels, which included Sony Entertainment Television, the Warner Channel, and Fox Latin America, started the distribution of landmark television shows of the 1990s, like *Seinfeld, Friends, Mad About You,* and *Ally McBeal,* with great acceptance from local audiences.[18] An observation of this emerging media landscape allows an understanding of the ways in which cable contributed to the consolidation of romantic comedy in the tastes of the newly acquired middle-class audiences. The people who attend the cineplex are essentially the same ones who subscribe to costly cable systems, with subscription fees that run at about 50–100 percent of the monthly minimum wage. While one of the issues in cable expansion, as studied in *Los nuevos espectadores,* was the creation of a new alternative venue for the distribution of Hollywood films, this content was already available in theaters and video rentals. TV series, on the other hand, were a different matter. Broadcast TV did dedicate some of its stations, like Televisa's XHGC, to some shows like *Dallas* or *Dynasty,* but they were sometimes broadcast years after their American premiere, dubbed in Spanish and circulated in spaces that did not compete with the primetime broadcasting of *telenovelas.*[19] Sony Entertainment Television and the Warner Channel brought subscribers an important array of TV series not offered by Mexican broadcast channels. This meant not only that there was an increasing availability of content accessible only to the middle class, but also that the main product introduced to those audiences in the period was the situational comedy, or sitcom, which had never been part of the Mexican media landscape. If one considers that between *Sólo con tu pareja* and the Mexican romantic comedy boom of the late 1990s, sitcoms were one of the two new media products introduced into the Mexican market (the other being music videos via MTV Latin America and local stations like Telehit), it is plausible to argue that the audiences that would make the genre successful in the 2000s were, at least in part, formed by this new type of programming.

In his study of the sitcom, Brett Mills, drawing from an article by Larry Mintz, emphasizes three aspects that help define the genre: a setting "focused on recurring places and characters"; an aesthetic based on the "artificiality" of the text; and narrative constructed upon repetition (28). While Mills does not fully subscribe to this definition, because its elements may also apply to other TV genres, I find it useful in understanding the narrative and visual formulas introduced by cable channels in Mexico. If one returns to *Sólo con tu pareja*, the merits of this definition are evident. We have a very clearly defined setting centered around Tomás's apartment and the small cast of characters who circulate through it; an artificiality sustained by Lubezki's aestheticized photography and by carnivalesque instances such as Tomás's dream and the over-the-top behavior of the Japanese doctors; and a narrative constructed within the conventions of the romantic comedy genre. To be sure, Mills's focus is on an array of sitcoms, not just those based on romantic interactions. However, the concrete programs successfully broadcasted by Sony and Warner do show a strong preference for sitcoms connected to romance and intimacy discourses: *Friends*, with the many romantic interactions of its characters; *Mad About You*, an archetypal series focused on a married couple; or *The Nanny*, whose main storyline traces the development of a romantic relationship between Fran Drescher's character and her boss. Even in series that do not quite share the comedic structure of the sitcom, the romantic framework is still quite obvious: *Dawson's Creek* is a good example of this. My point here is that U.S. primetime shows introduced by Mexican cable familiarized audiences with a new form of aesthetics surrounding romantic discourse, allowing both audiences and producers to create a media space in which the relationship between melodrama and affect is no longer predominant. The sectors of society with access to these new forms of media production and consumption would develop their tastes in favor of these new forms of cultural engagement.

An early example of this trend is one of the few box office hits of the mid-1990s, Rafael Montero's *Cilantro y perejil* (1995). This movie focuses on the separation and ultimate reunion of a married couple, Susana (Arcelia Ramírez) and Carlos (Demián Bichir). The existence of the film in itself illustrates significant points in relation to the transitions taking place in the 1990s. Coproduced by IMCINE and Televicine, it was the first such collaboration between the two Mexican production behemoths. *Cilantro y perejil* was a significant departure from the films pushed by both companies. On the side of IMCINE, it was a change from the prevalence of neo-Mexicanist works produced by the State and indicated an impulse on the part of the institute to support private production. This mixed system of financing would become the staple of many productions in subsequent years. For Televicine, *Cilantro y perejil* meant the emergence of a new philosophy of production under the leadership of Roberto Gómez Bolaños, a legendary TV comedian appointed as director in 1995. Before this movie, Televicine's productions consisted of raunchy comedies directed at the fading but still profitable urban popular market, and vehicles to exploit the success of Televisa's *telenovela* and comedic talent. *Cilantro y perejil* was neither: it focused on a middle-class world overlooked by Televicine's previous productions, and the protagonists were played by actors whose careers in cinema overshadowed any work they had done on TV. Many important films from the mid-1990s would be made under this type of private/public coproduction scheme, directed at a similar target market, including García Agraz's *Salón México,* Sabina Berman's *Entre Pancho Villa y una mujer desnuda* (1996), and Juan Antonio de la Riva's *Elisa antes del fin del mundo* (1997). While Televicine would gradually cease to be a major force in film production, this transition shows how the film aesthetic it had sustained up to this point was becoming largely outdated. The new audiences of cinema were no longer looking for movies populated by the television talent who had been gradually displaced by the new cable options. The fact that Televisa decided to invest in this new form of middle-class, commercial cinema is telling: even such a major force in media production had to recognize and respond to the new trends in audiences' tastes and preferences.

For all its commercial success and its role in the history of 1990s cinema, critics and scholars have seldom addressed *Cilantro y perejil.* In his otherwise exhaustive history of Mexican cinema, Carl Mora makes no mention of it, and major studies by Miriam Haddu and David William Foster also overlook the film. While Misha MacLaird considers it, correctly in my view, to be a transitional movie, she fails to notice the role of the film in the reinvention of production schemes, even though her book is strongly focused on institutional developments (*Aesthetics* 51–53). In Mexico, Jorge Ayala Blanco dismisses the film as a representation of a "reheated femininity" and of the irrelevant nervous breakdowns of a "couple of yuppies" (*La fugacidad* 378). In my opinion, the film is far more significant. It is inscribed, as MacLaird herself notices (52), in the larger trend of representing the marriage crisis, and both she and Ayala Blanco (*La fugacidad* 380) compare the movie's topic to that of *El anzuelo.* Despite some superficial similarities, like the use of video and the topic of the decay of marriage, these movies have more substantial differences that show exactly why *Cilantro y perejil* would play a stronger role in defining the romantic comedy genre. The movie's exploration of the misunderstandings between the couple works within an altogether different language from *El anzuelo,* in which the structure of the wedding party has strong nods to Mexican identity and working-class sociability (for example, the musicians play traditional music).[20] I would argue that an identifiable narrative and aesthetic source of *Cilantro y perejil*'s main elements is *Mad About You,* the sitcom starring Paul Reiser and Helen Hunt, whose first run both in the United States and in Mexico took place during the 1992–1993 season.

Both the movie and the sitcom feature a married couple that is part of the "creative class": Paul Buchman, Reiser's character, is a documentary filmmaker, and Jamie Buchman, Hunt's character, is a public relations specialist.[21] In both cases, the couple's closest social relationship is with the wife's younger sister, played by Anne Ramsay in *Mad About You* and by Alpha Acosta in *Cilantro y perejil*. The dynamic of the couple is also similar. Paul and Carlos are aloof and distracted, and have a hard time pursuing domestic work without their respective wives' help: *Cilantro y perejil*'s title refers to Carlos's inability to distinguish between the two herbs (cilantro and parsley), while *Mad About You*'s recurring gags are related to the contrast between Jamie's order and Paul's chaos, as well as his dependence on her. And, finally, the action of the movie takes place in the same defined settings of the sitcom, such as apartments, supermarkets, and restaurants.

While some readers may deem it problematic to claim a direct influence on the basis of these similarities, the fact is that the structural language of *Cilantro y perejil* is constructed within the same narrative paradigms as *Mad About You*. Its successful run on Mexican cable television indicates, at the very least, that Televicine was aiming at the audience that consumed the very kind of sitcoms that its own broadcast networks did not have. The reason that *Cilantro y perejil* may be considered a transitional movie is not simply because it is a romantic comedy. It has to do with the changes in the Mexican renderings of the genre brought about by the film. *Sólo con tu pareja* was constructed upon an aesthetic code that owed more to Woody Allen's romantic comedies than to any form of television discourse, but *Cilantro y perejil*'s production values were clearly extracted from television: it features clean, unpretentious photography (in contrast to Lubezki's lush work in *Sólo con tu pareja*), a set of plots and subplots that resemble many television narratives (*Sólo con tu pareja* has no real subplots), and a narrative structure that, not unlike marriage sitcoms in the style of *Mad About You*, is focused on the ramifications of a misunderstanding that is ultimately (and unsurprisingly) resolved in the end.[22]

To be sure, many filmmakers resented this new transition, and considered the new commercial pressures unacceptable. The most iconic example of this resistance is Gabriel Retes's bold *Bienvenido/Welcome* (1995), an indictment of the commercialization and the lack of political freedom felt by filmmakers from the older generations. The movie, which uses the device of a film within a film, tells the story of a group of Mexican filmmakers trying to shoot a movie on the question of AIDS, a clear allusion to *Sólo con tu pareja*.[23] This second story focuses on a married man who sleeps with a blonde woman on a business trip, resulting in an HIV infection that wrecks his life. The movie's title comes from this subplot, since the blonde leaves the man behind after writing in the mirror, "Welcome to the world of AIDS." Language is the distinguishing element between both plots: the main storyline is shot in Spanish, while the movie within the movie is in an English spoken with a heavy Mexican accent. The movie has a bitter tone throughout. The sections in English are long and contrived, and clearly mock the urban professional middle class: we see a man who is essentially punished for preferring an American-looking woman over his Mexican wife, and is ultimately fired from his job at a transnational corporation because of his infection. This character has clear parallels to Clarisa's unfaithful fiancé in *Sólo con tu pareja* and his preference for American and European flight attendants. Conversely, the Spanish section is plagued by a strong didacticism that emphasizes ad nauseam the limitations faced by the film troupe. While critics like Ayala Blanco show strong preference for *Bienvenido/Welcome* over any romantic comedy, Retes is ultimately protesting against an impending and inevitable creative crisis: he is a film author within a long trajectory of political cinema whose work is gradually becoming outdated and unviable. In the long run, the movie remains a rare and valuable document of the transition suffered by Mexican cinema in the mid-1990s. It also clearly illustrates, at least from the perspective of directors like Retes, that the victory of middle-class culture and romantic comedy took place at the expense of the creative freedoms and political possibilities that had been afforded by the "cinema of solitude" paradigms.[24]

Perhaps the most important consequence of *Cilantro y perejil*'s sitcom aesthetic is its recognition of the effect that the new media landscape could have on film consumption. The movie was released at the bottom of the market, when the exhibition infrastructure that would allow Mexican cinema further economic growth was still a work in progress. I contend that *Cilantro y perejil* shows that romantic comedy in the mid-1990s was also a work in progress, as the movie still had an awkward and unnecessary element of self-reflection. Nora (Alpha Acosta), Susana's sister, is shooting a documentary on love, and Carlos and Susana's separation occurs partly because of his late arrival at the session where they were to discuss their love in front of the camera. As I have shown earlier, this plot element comes from *La tarea* and it reappears in other romantic comedies. In *Cilantro y perejil*, though, this metacinematic element feels contrived and out of place, and contributes little to the main plot. While Nora's story focuses on her attempts to become a video professional, the movie lacks the strong psychological work that Hermosillo invests in the camera's gaze. The awkward presence of this element shows how *Cilantro y perejil* still suffered from a certain identity crisis. On the one hand, it seeks to explode the commercial potential of romantic comedy.[25] On the other, just like *Sólo con tu pareja*, it relies on some elements from independent cinema that, in this case, do not correspond to its otherwise commercial nature. The consecration of romantic comedy required further action to filter out these out-of-place artistic pretensions while reshaping romantic comedy to respond to the new commercial realities of media consumption. Antonio Serrano's *Sexo, pudor y lágrimas* (1998) takes this next step.

The Rise of Emotional Capitalism: *Sexo, pudor y lágrimas* and the Film Commodity

In *Cold Intimacies,* Israeli sociologist Eva Illouz proposes a reading of capitalism and modernity in terms of the study of emotions: "My claim is that the making of capitalism went hand in hand with the making of an intensely specialized emotional culture and that when we focus on this dimension of capitalism— on its emotions so to speak—we may be in a position to uncover another order in the social organization of capitalism" (4). She goes on to sustain her claim in more precise terms, with the argument that "market-based cultural repertoires shape and inform interpersonal and emotional identities, while interpersonal relationships are at the epicenter of economic relationships" (5). Illouz's work provides an apt language for studying Mexican romantic comedy in relation to the emergence of cinema as a practice reserved for the wealthier social classes. First, at the level of film analysis, it provides an approach to conceptualize the affective engagements in movies beyond the vocabularies of psychology, thus allowing for the identification of the socioeconomic and cultural elements at play in the cinematic representations of interpersonal relations. Second, insofar as romantic comedies belong to an order of discourse that shapes the romantic and intimate practices of its audiences, it helps explain the ways in which the affective engagements of cinema audiences in Mexico morphed from a tightly controlled system connected to national and social identities to the creation of cultural commodities that engage affect through the market. Before 1998, Mexican romantic comedy had already experienced the processes involved in the new cinematic representations of love, as I have shown in the cases of *Sólo con tu pareja* and *Cilantro y perejil.* Still, the capacity of those films to fully participate in the cultural product market, especially with the necessary depth to challenge melodrama as a language for the public configurations of affect, still had major limitations. The changes in exhibition and audience constitution in the mid-1990s had created new cultural spaces for cinema to conquer, but as it was facing its lowest output in history, it proved unable to seize the opportunity in terms of production. This would change in 1998, when the release of Serrano's *Sexo, pudor y lágrimas* created a blueprint for Mexican cinema to interact with new audiences.

Sexo, pudor y lágrimas is a comedy of manners about two couples and two single characters. The story centers on the relationship between Ana (Susana Zabaleta) and Carlos (Víctor Hugo Martín), which is crumbling because of

Carlos's lack of sexual interest. Significantly, Carlos belongs to the creative class (he is an aspiring writer), and his frigidity parallels his inability to finish his book. The action begins when Ana's former boyfriend, Tomás, a free-spirited adventurer, temporarily moves in with them after having lived in Singapore. Simultaneously, the movie focuses on the conflicted marriage of Miguel (Jorge Salinas) and Andrea (Cecilia Suárez), which is clearly dysfunctional and even turns violent at some points. Miguel is another member of the creative class: he works as an international account executive for an advertising agency. In contrast to Carlos's sexual disinterest and professional impotence, he is an unfaithful womanizer and a well-to-do professional, establishing a significant parallel between masculine sexual prowess and economic success. This second story develops after Miguel's former girlfriend María (Mónica Dionne), a zoologist, returns from Kenya after breaking up with her British husband. The movie's central comedic device occurs when, after a series of fights, all of the men move into Carlos's apartment, while the women move across the street with Andrea. The film is largely grounded in the conventions of romantic comedy, but it also carries a strong dramatic weight, mostly through Miguel's increasingly abusive stance toward Andrea and in Tomás's psychological breakdown, which leads to his suicide close to the end of the movie. This last turn, I would contend, has to do with the movie's origin as a theater play, where drama is regarded as more artistic, and is quite dissonant in the context of the movie, which lessens the dramatic impact present in many scenes of Serrano's original play.

As we can see, the movie constructs both couples according to a precise and symmetrical formula. Both couples sustain long-term relationships, and the triangles are defined by Ana and Miguel's conflicts between their socially acceptable relationships and the remnants of their love for people who do not belong to the economic and social landscape of Mexico City's middle class. In other words, we have characters who belong to a clearly delineated socioeconomic space and whose construction of affect is grounded on the choice of either adjusting to the social expectations of their situation or breaking away from it by returning to a relationship with a person who never became fully integrated into neoliberal values. This is clear in the reunion scene between Miguel and María. After a chance encounter at a party, María asks Miguel why he ultimately did not direct the movie he had been working on when they broke up. Miguel responds that he had to "change" and accept reality, which took the form of accepting an offer to work in advertising. María asks Miguel, "What about social commitment?"—a question Miguel cannot answer. This conversation emphasizes a social choice faced by many members of the Mexican middle class after the 1980s. María and Tomás represent those who decided to pursue their ideals, which, significantly, is only possible by leaving the country. Carlos and Miguel represent those who stay in the country and conform to the social standards of neoliberal Mexico. Interestingly, when Tomás and Ana have a similar conversation, she emphasizes that the apartment she lives in is fully owned by Carlos's mother, and that she does not belong there. In response, Tomás replies, "Is this not my home?" Ana longs for an alternative, while Tomás seeks to take over Carlos's middle-class life. *Sexo, pudor y lágrimas* ultimately is about the ways in which the middle class defines its affective sphere, in the space between the cultural ideals of a left-of-center creative class and the social realities of neoliberalism.

At the end, the movie definitively establishes the neoliberal social order, pushing the rebellious characters out of the picture. Tomás ultimately proves unable to adapt to the "real world," and decides to kill himself. In the final scene, Carlos and Ana return to each other and he expresses sexual desire for her, fully restoring their relationship. No reference to Tomás is made and they display no visible signs of grief. María leaves Mexico to take a job at the San Diego Zoo, and tries to reconcile with her British husband, indicating that she ultimately does not wish to belong in the Mexican social sphere. Miguel tries to return to Andrea, admitting his mistakes and accepting his life in spite of having given up on his ideals. However, in this story line, Andrea leaves him, since his abuses ultimately had to be punished. Still, Andrea does get a job, clearly showing that her personal redemption must also be framed by her own incorporation into the economic system (one could even claim that she was vulnerable to Miguel's abuses and to alcoholism because she was not employed). The development of the characters, in every case, points to the same idea: the acceptance of the middle-class order, either through the final surrender of the people already within it or through the expulsion or death of those who dared to challenge society's standards in order to pursue their ideals.

This unapologetic representation of middle-class social values has led some critics to decry Serrano's cinematic world. David William Foster, for instance, laments that "the difficulties of surviving in postmodern Mexico City are not an issue in Serrano's film" (38), while Jorge Ayala Blanco chastises the film as an "insubstantial" and "cartoonish" movie constructed upon an "irresponsible film language," and based on the lives of the elite (*La fugacidad* 439–44). Critic Francisco Sánchez also laments the movie's aesthetic by presenting it as paradigmatic of what he calls "the light genre" (*Luz* 226–27). It is important to note here that these three critics write from an intellectual stance positioned in some form of political ideology that runs contrary to the values put forth by the film's cheerful acceptance of neoliberal culture: both Sánchez and Ayala Blanco are left-wing intellectuals who tend to celebrate overtly political films, while Foster, a U.S.-based leading authority on gender studies, clearly prefers Hermosillo's groundbreaking work on women and LGBT social issues over Serrano's more superficial and elitist use of urban space. Whether one shares their perspectives or not, the fact that *Sexo, pudor y lágrimas* became by far the most successful Mexican movie in history in its time, with a domestic box office of over twelve million dollars, requires reading the film beyond aesthetic or ideological preference.

As we have seen in the analysis of the film's content, the characters' interpersonal relationships fit neatly into the emotional capitalism defined by Illouz, given that the "market-based cultural repertoires" of contemporary Mexico are as evident here as they are in *Sólo con tu pareja:* the professions of the creative class (designer, publicist, writer), the self-referential adoption of a wealthy part of Mexico City as a location, the presentation of the characters' wealth by using their well-to-do apartments as the main settings for the film, and even the construction of love practices in which marriage is optional (Carlos and Ana are not married, and neither are Clarisa and her boyfriend, while Andrea finds redemption through divorce). In fact, both Ayala Blanco and Foster highlight *Sexo pudor y lágrimas*' location in the upscale neighborhood of Polanco as evidence of the movie's hesitancy to represent the class and social conflicts that plague contemporary Mexico City. Nonetheless, reading this choice as a mere symptom of elitism misses the point in many ways. At the formal level, the movie does respond to the idealized and self-referential space of the romantic comedy genre as described by Deleyto, thus following a trend in presenting the city from the characters' affective perspectives and not through any sociopolitical stance on the city itself. Foster shows that in *Sexo, pudor y lágrimas* the balcony "functions as a promenade, giving access to a panoramic view of the city, with the effect of 'owning' or 'controlling' the city as an important correlative to the financial status of the apartment's residents" (40), a similar argument to the one made by Haddu and Medina about Tomás Tomás's apartment in *Sólo con tu pareja*. This reading rightly focuses on the economic status of the characters, but Foster attributes the space's self-referentiality to a similarity with *telenovelas*.[26] I would rather contend that, unlike *telenovelas,* whose fictional worlds are usually constructed upon wider and more diverse representations of the social spectrum, romantic comedies are particularly apt for presenting life among members of the new wealthy classes, as they self-isolate from other sections of Mexico City. While Foster is right in pointing out that Polanco is more diverse than the movie shows, it is also true that, at the time of the movie's release, one of the most obvious urbanization trends was the construction of private streets and residential complexes, showing the middle and upper classes' will to isolate themselves from the rest of the social spectrum. If anything, romantic comedy's self-referential space emerges as an adequate device to cinematically reflect this aspiration, which in turn shows that critiquing their lack of realism misses the mark.

The objections to the film's elitism also sidestep the trendsetting production and marketing strategies set forward by *Sexo, pudor y lágrimas,* which help explain its financial success and the ways in which romantic comedy started to engage the affective imagination of the new film audiences. The film follows *Cilantro y perejil*'s example in the construction of a private-public coproduction scheme, but the participants in *Sexo, pudor y lágrimas*' financial design represent more complex manifestations of such a scheme. Misha MacLaird describes the participants: "IMCINE's FOPROCINE funds; film upstart Titán Producciones . . . Argos Cine, part of larger Argos Comunicación, whose television side co-produced the two *telenovelas;* and Tabasco Films, one of Mexico's more successful production houses since the early 1990s, having produced the work of María Novaro and Carlos Carrera and backed by billionaire Carlos Slim" (*Aesthetics* 54). This description aptly shows the new financing mix behind the movie, but it is important to further underscore some significant implications and ramifications behind such a scheme. FOPROCINE, created as a result of the 1996 reform to film legislation, operated within new financing formulas that redefined cinema production by moving from the more centralized model pursued by IMCINE in the earlier part of the decade to an outsourcing model that supported private production initiatives. This would become the main form of financing in the following years. As MacLaird also documents, Titán Producciones was partly owned by Christian Valdelièvre, a former broker at JP Morgan, who played a role in the foundation of the Cinemex chain and who, according to MacLaird, was fully aware of the economic potential of the new audiences (48). Tabasco, a studio with a successful track record, provided further cinematic expertise, as well as the financial backing of Carlos Slim, one of the wealthiest men in the world.

Still, Argos Cine is, in my view, the most significant player. Founded by powerful media producer Epigmenio Ibarra, Argos Comunicaciones was responsible for the two most groundbreaking Mexican *telenovelas* of the 1990s: *Nada personal,* an unusually political soap loosely based on the scandals of President Salinas de Gortari and his family, and *Mirada de mujer,* which broke with the traditional schemes of melodrama by addressing a love story between a woman and a much younger man. It is significant that Serrano is credited as the main director of *Nada personal,* which shows that Argos was, in part, expanding upon its existing talent in television production and acting when branching into film. Moreover, Argos's *telenovela* work is based on Ibarra's attempt to change the cultural languages behind the Mexican audiovisual market. Both *Nada personal* and *Mirada de mujer* struck at the prevalence of family-values melodrama in the Mexican media landscape; the fact that, at their peak, both *telenovelas* were able to surpass Televisa's productions in the ratings charts speaks of an audience that wanted to transcend the production formulas push forward by traditional broadcast TV. *Sexo, pudor y lágrimas* extended this process to cinema, by breaking with the neo-Mexicanist aesthetics privileged by prior IMCINE productions and by improving the production values prevalent in the works backed by Televicine or Tabasco Films. While one may, as MacLaird does, read and critique this process as the displacement of audiences from civil society to target market (*Aesthetics* 45-49), the significant issue here is the film's unprecedented capacity to actually engage those audiences, given that the construction of a target market had been as much a concern of Televicine and every other private film production house since the 1940s. What is missing in MacLaird's account and in the readings of critics like Ayala Blanco or Foster is the way in which *Sexo, pudor y lágrimas* operates at the level of neoliberal cultural economics as well as in the construction of a new form of emotional capitalism. Argos is the paradigmatic case here, since it is the one company that, unlike Tabasco (which had produced the Novaro and Carrera films), had dared to strike at the heart of received melodramatic traditions of romantic discourse and affective engagement, which remain part of its television business.

A key to understanding the success of *Sexo, pudor y lágrimas* in a systematic way lies in the marketing device that played an important role in the movie's success: its soundtrack. According to MacLaird, the film's producers intentionally used the soundtrack as a promotional device, factoring its production into the budget following "a U.S. business model"; they ultimately sold 120,000 copies of the CD (*Aesthetics* 54), a remarkable number in a country where music piracy is endemic. The use of the soundtrack as a promotional mechanism had indeed reached maturity in the U.S. market, not only with the advent of the CD as the prime instrument for delivering music, but also as the use of music in marketing campaigns became standard. Examples range from the indie world (like Quentin Tarantino's iconic *Pulp Fiction* soundtrack) to Hollywood blockbusters (such as Whitney Houston's "I Will Always Love You" from *The Bodyguard* and Celine Dion's "My Heart Will Go On" from *Titanic*). The soundtrack of *Sexo, pudor y lágrimas* was led by a song with the same title as the film, written and performed by Aleks Syntek, a singer with crossover success in pop music and alternative rock. The song's lyrics were clearly designed to correspond to the movie's romantic comedy appeal, with a message that focuses on the desire to surrender to a lover after a previous failure to do so. Of course, this closely mirrors both the affective arc followed by Carlos in the movie, from his incapacity to love Ana to his ultimate surrender to her love and Ana's insistence on staying with him in spite of his coldness. The soundtrack constructs a landscape made up of Syntek's mainstream appeal, dance songs such as Litzy's "No te extraño," and acts that parody popular music genres and incorporate them into paradigms closer to middle-class tastes. The album also includes "Supermambo," from Argentine band La Portuaria, and even the classic song "You Sexy Thing," by Hot Chocolate. This point sets forward a dimension of the film soundtrack overlooked by MacLaird and completely ignored by all other critics of the film: the use of music in the construction of film as an affective commodity.

While music became a full-fledged promotional device in the 1990s, it has been a staple of romantic comedy since very early on. Of course, the examples of classic Hollywood musicals and their parallel Golden Age mariachi movies come to mind. In the 1980s and 1990s, many romantic comedies used music as a language to articulate romance and intimacy and as a vehicle to express their characters' affective world. The paradigmatic case is Cameron Crowe's iconic 1989 film *Say Anything*, in which Lloyd Dobler (John Cusack) famously expresses his love for Diane Court (Ione Skye) by standing outside her window with a boom box, playing Peter Gabriel's "In Your Eyes." Also, the creators of many landmark romantic comedies aimed at youthful audiences hired famous musical acts to write songs with the same title as the movie, as the Psychedelic Furs did for the movie *Pretty in Pink* (Howard Deutch, 1986). Finally, romantic comedies strategically chose music that corresponded to the musical tastes of both its represented characters and its target audiences. A case whose strategies may resemble those used by *Sexo, pudor y lágrimas* is Ben Stiller's 1994 film *Reality Bites*, in which the leading single from the soundtrack, Lisa Loeb's "Stay," corresponded to an emerging form of female-oriented adult alternative music popular with women in their twenties. As Chuck Klosterman has argued, *Reality Bites* became iconic thanks to its capacity to transmit the culture behind the "hyper-conventional ideal of such a short-lived era" (155). The movie's soundtrack formed an essential part of that ideal by engaging the emotional codes of its young professional target audience. In these terms, the soundtrack had to be an integral part of the affective codes expressed by the movie. While the use of music as a promotional device works across a large spectrum of genres, the affective identification of the audience with the songs promoted alongside the film is particularly critical for romantic comedy, because the genre requires a sustained affective identification to work as a commodity.

The comparison to *Reality Bites* provides further clues to understanding *Sexo, pudor y lágrimas*. Stiller's film presents its main character, Lelaina (Winona Ryder), with a choice similar to the one faced by Serrano's characters. The plot follows Lelaina's relationships with Troy (Ethan Hawke), an unemployed musician, and a successful video executive named Michael (Ben Stiller). It may be evident at this point in my argument that we are again faced with characters who articulate the relationship of the creative class with capitalism. Lelaina, an aspiring video director, must choose between an "authentic" musician who, like Carlos, lives dysfunctionally outside the capitalist system, and a media executive who, like Miguel, has successfully reconciled his creative talents with the demands of the neoliberal social sphere. The resolution here is, tellingly, the opposite, since Lelaina ultimately chooses Troy, reflecting her generation's disappointment with the neoliberal system as experienced in the transition between the first Bush presidency and the Clinton administration. As Klosterman explains, this decision reflected a generational aspiration to transcend the economic pressures faced by Generation X (155), thus responding to the aspirations of the disillusioned young middle-class moviegoers at whom the movie was aimed. The long life of this film in the U.S. cinematic imaginary attests to this. Conversely, *Sexo, pudor y lágrimas* belongs to a sociocultural moment, when the middle class was living through a new cultural and economic boom after the financial crisis of 1994. The movie was clearly representative of the values of young urban professionals whose cultural world was decidedly separated from the working classes and from the historical mandates of national identity. Lisa Loeb's "Stay" offered an ideal vehicle to express the romantic idea of being in love against the grain of difficult times, but Syntek's "Sexo, pudor y lágrimas" identifies the ultimate success of love with the capacity to become a functional part of society. These examples show that romantic comedy is, at heart, a codification and a cultural articulation of the social pathos of a given sector of society. Its success thus rests in the films' capacity to create affective identification in audiences who belong to the social sector codified by their romantic discourse. This is why understanding the movie soundtrack as a mere publicity device only tells part of the story: the analysis of its components evidences the cultural languages articulated in the realm of romantic comedy.

In *Consuming the Romantic Utopia,* Illouz shows that the consolidation of love as a topic of cinema went hand in hand with the emergence of the advertising industry and its use of romance to encourage consumption (31–39). Her argument rests on the idea that ideologies of love and practices of capitalism are not only closely related, but also influence each other's workings and structure. While Illouz's analysis focuses on the construction of a sociology of interpersonal relations in general, her insights are still useful in understanding the problem of neoliberalism's true impact on culture, and the way in which romantic comedy played a central role in integrating cinema into neoliberalism. The symbiotic relationship between the films and their soundtracks operated against the backdrop of emerging practices of affective identification, which were closely knit to the transformation of the media landscape that I previously described.

Besides romantic comedy, another important mediatic factor at play was the advent of the music video genre as a language to articulate affective identity. García Canclini locates the emergence of MTV in Latin America as part of a "redefinition of the sense of belonging and identity," through the participation in "deterritorialized communities of consumers" (*Consumers* 24). This was an important factor in the constitution of Mexican emotional capitalism, particularly at the level of the urban middle classes, precisely because these new communities of consumers constructed themselves in relation to media outlets that offered alternative forms of identity to the ones that had been promoted by media monopolies and the State a decade earlier. The effectiveness of *Sexo, pudor y lágrimas*' use of pop music depended upon the existence of such media outlets. While Syntek had enjoyed a certain degree of success prior to his participation in the film's soundtrack, his music had not belonged to any of the paradigms promoted by Fonovisa, Televisa's music arm, and was a far cry from the *balada* genre that dominated Mexican pop music well into the 1990s. It was significant, then, that his song "Sexo, pudor y lágrimas" found fans at both MTV and Telehit, the most important music stations in Mexican cable at the time, allowing for the distribution of a video that closely tied the music to clips from the movie. When the song became popular prior to the movie's release, the music video helped attract middle-class audiences into the theater, by identifying the film with the music channels' urban aesthetic, which was clearly distinct from the paradigms of neo-Mexicanist cinema rejected by audiences such as the ones represented by the polls in the mid-1990s.[27]

In sum, *Sexo, pudor y lágrimas* paved the way for the new trends of Mexican cinema, enabling them to tie the new cultural world represented by its aesthetics to a successful engagement with audiences both at the commercial and the emotional level. The film conveys the pathos of a middle class conforming to the life and values brought about by neoliberalism. Unlike the disappointment with neoliberal economics at the core of *Reality Bites*, *Sexo, pudor y lágrimas* ultimately validates the choice of conforming to the new social standards, as shown by the unusually cruel fate of Tomás, introducing a dramatic dissonance within the film's lighter tone. As Emily Hind proposes in a very suggestive reading of this scene, Tomás can be read as a character with "potential queerness" and, while his "presence in Polanco enlivens the comedy . . . the neighborhood lives up to its conservative elitist origins when Tomás intentionally plunges down an elevator shaft that the passively onlooking characters know to be out of order" ("Pita Amor" 157). Furthermore, Hind argues, "the characters' quick return to normality illustrates their easily recuperated self-absorption" (157). The startling elimination of the character that least belongs to the new Mexico is therefore a necessary precondition for the validation of the new social order, even at the expense of introducing an excessively somber plot element that does not correspond with the film's generally lighthearted mood. This validation, tellingly, connected with large audiences, by presenting itself in a language of affect and romance that resonated deeply within the cultural languages consumed via sitcoms and U.S. romantic comedies. Additionally, it responded to a new set of social ideals embodied by the romanticization of the creative class as synecdoche of the aspirations of young urban professionals. *Sexo, pudor y lágrimas* represents the culmination of Mexican cinema's commodification, on two levels: by becoming a film product based on intermediatic strategies, such as the film soundtrack and its promotion on MTV, and by turning the affective imaginaries of the emerging middle class into a reliable cultural product that would be packaged in diverse ways by many other romantic comedies. In the final section, I will explore the normalization of this phenomenon, through the emergence in the mid-2000s of films that wholeheartedly embrace the commercial aspects of emotional capitalism.

Lost in the City, Found in Marketing: The Triumph of Romantic Comedy

The prevalence of romantic comedy as a major genre in the 2000s is exemplified by one of the most telling and most drastic aesthetic shifts in the work of a film director. In 2002, Nicolás Echevarría, director of *Cabeza de Vaca*, released his first and only romantic comedy, *Vivir mata*. As I discussed in Chapter 1, Echevarría became a household name in the early 1990s through a movie that broke with many of the restrictions behind neo-Mexicanist discourse and became a quite bold statement on colonization and history in the middle of the Columbian quincentennial celebrations. After *Cabeza de Vaca*, Echevarría mostly worked on documentaries and soap operas, until *Vivir mata*, his second and only other fiction film. Echevarría's choice to venture into a genre so alien to his previous work is symptomatic of the increasing clout of romantic comedy as the reference point for film stylistics in Mexico. The genre did offer many interesting advantages to filmmakers: it allowed the construction of fictional worlds liberated from the imperatives of Mexicanism, as well as the opportunity to create an economically viable cinema, with potential commercial distribution. *Vivir mata* constitutes another important achievement that can help us understand romantic comedy's articulation in the national cinema industry, because it represents an almost unique example of a film directed by someone who had never before shot such an openly commercial movie, resulting in a product that juggles the superficiality and visual appeal of the genre along with the artistic pretensions of its creators.

Vivir mata rests entirely on a misunderstanding between its characters. The protagonists, Hugo (Daniel Giménez Cacho) and Silvia (Susana Zabaleta), meet by chance in a hotel lobby, where a reporter is running late for an interview with a writer. Upon hearing the reporter ask for the writer, Silvia decides to supplant her, and starts looking for the writer herself. She asks Hugo if he is the writer; since he is attracted to her, he pretends that he is. After spending the night together, they both admit that they are not who they say they were, prompting Silvia to leave. However, Silvia discloses her true identity as a radio host, which allows Hugo to look for her in the city's chaotic streets, following a mobile vehicle used by her radio station to distribute gifts among listeners. Besides the flashbacks to their encounter, most of the movie happens in two spaces: in the radio station, where we see the conversations between Silvia and a coworker; and in a car, where Hugo is stuck with two fellow painters. The plot's formula lies well within the parameters of urban romantic comedy.[28] Its execution, however, presents some important departures compared to other romantic comedies of the time.[29] The first significant element is the script, written by famed novelist Juan Villoro. The film is heavy on dialogue, clearly inspired by Woody Allen's New York-based romantic comedies and Villoro's own urban aesthetic. Since the plot requires little movement in space, the film rests strongly on the characters' reflective and self-reflective speech, particularly on their constant musings about the nature of love. It is also a film in which character development focuses mostly on self-fashioning and retrospective reflection. As Manuel F. Medina argues, a central concept in the movie is a "coherent message regarding human relations. Lying and assuming identities are preferable to exposing ourselves" (255; my translation). Therefore, all the characters constantly discuss the tension between their real selves and the masks they have to put on in order to function in society. Hugo, a frustrated artist, is accompanied in the car by two other artists, Chepe (Luis Felipe Tovar) and Heliut (Emilio Echevarría), whose conversation revolves around the choice between producing profitable art or being true to personal aesthetic values. In this, *Vivir mata* shows a literary bent rarely developed by Mexican romantic comedy. Indeed, *Sexo, pudor y lágrimas* is based on a play, and has a clear focus on dialogue. However, *Vivir mata* depends on a more contrived text, in which dialogue overtakes verisimilitude at some points, and, unlike the plain conversations in *Sexo, pudor y lágrimas*, clearly privileges the text over character interaction.

Vivir mata's heavily literary script allows it to present an unusually critical perspective on the creative class characters who populate romantic comedy. The plot privileges a frustrated artist, Hugo, over Chepe, the one who has given in to publicity. This is a somewhat unusual occurrence, given that Tomás from *Sólo con tu pareja* was a successful advertiser, and Miguel from *Sexo, pudor y lágrimas* had no problems with working as an advertising executive. The subplot that unfolds between the three painters in the car stuck in traffic involves a confrontation between Heliut and Chepe. Heliut, an artist from an older generation, reproaches Chepe for his willingness to participate in advertising. Heliut, though, is not presented as an immaculate figure either: we learn that Heliut designed a graffiti mural (which was illegal to paint), enlisted Chepe and Hugo's help, and then did not show up to help them paint his own design. Hugo and Chepe were arrested while painting the mural, and thus resent Heliut's absence that day. Still, the film casts an even more unforgiving gaze on Chepe. He is involved in a campaign for a shoe company, based on graphic ads centered around the slogan "¡Viva Zapato!," tying the Spanish word for "shoe" to both Emiliano Zapata, a central figure of the Mexican Revolution, and the Zapatista movement. In depicting the ad campaign, the movie not only criticizes the trivialization of Mexican politics in the world of marketing (Medina 255–56), but more importantly, it exposes the absurdity and shallowness of the cultural products of the new mediatic world. This point symmetrically reflects the world of Silvia, who, despite her talents as a broadcaster, has to spend one day every month in a carnivalesque van that gives away turkeys and microwave ovens to people who repeat the station's slogans to the radio host. Villoro's script creates an obvious parallel between the identity crises of his protagonists and the cultural crisis of neoliberal Mexico. Unlike *Sólo con tu pareja*, which openly constructs its characters in terms of neoliberal ideology and culture, *Vivir mata* presents the redemptive potential of love as a form of resistance against both the enormity of the city and the shallowness of media culture. To use Illouz's terms, *Vivir mata* represents a unique example of the "romantic utopia," an ideology of affect that "asserts the privilege of sentiments over social and economic interests" (9). In this, *Vivir mata* is closer to the ideology of *Reality Bites* than to the acceptance of the neoliberal cultural grammar implicit in *Sexo, pudor y lágrimas* and the vast majority of Mexican romantic comedies.

Vivir mata also offers an atypical critique of the urban imagery created by Mexican romantic comedy. The three paradigmatic romantic comedies of the 1990s (*Sólo con tu pareja*, *Cilantro y perejil*, and *Sexo, pudor y lágrimas*) presented an urban landscape that placed Mexico City's demographic chaos under erasure, privileging the closed living spaces of the middle class over the busy streets of the city. Echevarría opts for the opposite, placing Hugo's story line in a hyperbolically rendered traffic jam across Mexico City's center. In addition, he does not restrict his movie to beautified wealthy neighborhoods like Polanco. The final scene of the movie, in which Hugo and Silvia finally reunite, occurs in front of the *Cabeza de Juárez* monument, a huge, awful statue of Benito Juárez's head located in an overpopulated lower-class neighborhood. Some scholars have been critical of the movie's urban landscape, considering it overwhelming and overdone (Ayala Blanco, *La grandeza* 45), while others present it as a beautiful and liberating space (Medina 258). The issue, though, lies in the fact that the city is not just the pleasant setting through which the characters articulate their affects. The city's complex and plural social tissue plays a crucial role in defining its denizens, offering an experience of modernity that does not necessarily comply with the codes imposed by neoliberalism. Even if Hugo and Susana resist the commercial pressures of their endeavors, the city's chaos maintains the continuous threat of the uncertainty produced by late capitalism. While the movie was not as commercially or as critically successful as other landmark romantic comedies, *Vivir mata* remains an original use both of romantic comedy and of urban space, a rare alternative in a cinematic world caught between the outdated codes of neo-Mexicanism and the postmodern anxieties of the creative class.

Vivir mata would ultimately be a mirage of the possibility of using romantic comedy to critique the neoliberal status quo, and the genre would reach the peak of its prominence in the mid-2000s, with a series of movies that repeated the formulas created by Cuarón, Montero, Serrano, and Echevarría in derivative ways. This generated an astounding number of films about the creative classes' love issues, cementing the centrality of film subjects who had emerged during the privatization and class displacement of Mexican cinema. The films achieved different degrees of commercial visibility, but a few examples are worth listing here to give a quick overview of the films that appeared in the next few years. Carlos Sama's *Sin ton ni Sonia* (2003) deals with the love tribulations of a man working at a film dubbing company; René Bueno Camacho's *7 mujeres, 1 homosexual y Carlos* (2004) is a clumsy film about a young advertising executive who becomes inexplicably popular with women only after getting married; Issa López's *Efectos secundarios* (2006), a rehash of the two-couple, two-apartment formula employed by *Sexo, pudor y lágrimas*, focuses on the high school reunion of a group of people in their twenties, and its DVD package includes a CD with the soundtrack; Eduardo Lucatero's *Corazón marchito* (2007) revisits the topic of friends who are actually in love with each other; Luis Eduardo Reyes's *Amor letra por letra* (2008) is a comedy of errors about a young writer who mistakenly receives a cash deposit from a woman he ultimately falls for; and Fez Noriega's *Te presento a Laura* (2010) tells the story of a young woman who has thirty days of life left, because she arranges her own assassination, and meets a young actor whose life is coming apart.

This sample shows the formulaic development of the genre post-*Vivir Mata,* in which production models follow the basic blueprint developed in the 1990s (middle-class art- or advertising-oriented characters; the challenge of finding love in the modern city; the portrayal of either the marriage crisis or the difficulties of single life) and rarely stray from it.[30] Some manifestations of the genre have demonstrated how romantic comedy has gradually been exhausted as an aesthetic choice. Recent movies have started to fully repeat the plots of previous movies: Gustavo Adrián Garzón's *Volverte a ver,* one of the most popular movies in 2009, focuses on a creative director from a fashion company who has a chance meeting with a radio host who uses a pseudonym, a clear repetition of *Vivir mata*'s basic conceit. In other cases, some romantic comedies have introduced dissonant elements in the attempt to create original movies. This is the case with Salvador Garcini's *Divina confusión* (2008), where the characters' lives are determined by the will of Mexicanized versions of the Greek gods, an idea taken from Woody Allen's *Mighty Aphrodite* (1997).

Similar efforts along these lines include Salim Nayar's *Tú te lo pierdes* (2005), in which the male protagonist spends the movie in the afterlife, and Joaquín Bissner's *Mosquita muerta* (2007), a botched attempt to revive the musical romantic comedy. While romantic comedy was reborn through the work of directors who had a clear aesthetic engagement with cinema, like Cuarón and Echevarría, the genre became predominant precisely because it established itself as middlebrow. Romantic comedy has been, at least for the past ten to twelve years, a reliable genre that regularly produces commercially successful movies (Alejandro Springall's *No eres tú, soy yo,* a romantic comedy, was the highest-grossing Mexican movie in 2010) and that has influenced the ethos and aesthetics of Mexican cinema at large.

Despite the disappointing cases listed in the last two paragraphs, romantic comedy remains an interesting focal point for the understanding of the cinematic cultures of neoliberalism. Some mid-2000s directors managed to fruitfully use the genre to create successful films with commercial appeal and interesting cinematic elements. A very popular film in this vein is Gabriela Tagliavini's box office hit *Ladies' Night* (2003). This film starts with Alicia (Ana Claudia Talancón), a young comic-book writer, on the eve of her marriage to Fabián (Fabián Corres), who is sexually attracted to Ana (Ana de la Reguera), a magazine editor whose open sexuality and confrontational personality contrast with Alicia's portrayal as virginal and innocent. Alicia's life is transformed when Ana hires Roco (Luis Roberto Guzmán), a stripper, for her bachelorette party, prompting Alicia to fall in love with him. Predictably, the movie concludes when Ana confesses her affair with Fabián, prompting Alicia to seek out Roco. The movie follows many of the narrative and commercial formulas developed by *Sólo con tu pareja* and *Sexo, pudor y lágrimas*. We have, once again, a love triangle between members of the creative class who face a conflict between their real feelings and what is socially acceptable. At the production level, *Ladies' Night* is notable for being the first Mexican venture of Miravista, a production company financed by Spanish telecommunications giant Telefónica and by Disney (Gabriela Martínez 92); competing with Carlos Slim's Tabasco Films, Miravista established a coproduction agreement with both Argos and Videocine, Televisa's new film arm. At the marketing level, the film's success can be attributed in part to the title song, "Desde que llegaste," by Reyli Barba, a contained but intense ballad that reached the top of the Mexican charts and gave Barba the opportunity to leave behind his alternative rock band to establish a solo career. *Ladies' Night* grossed nearly seven million dollars, a remarkable feat when one considers that its commercial run occurred during the holiday season; it outperformed Hollywood releases such as *The Cat in the Hat, Mystic River,* and *Stuck on You* in its opening weekend. From this perspective, *Ladies' Night* is undoubtedly one of the most successful examples of both the production schemes and the narrative formulas of romantic comedy in Mexico.

Furthermore, *Ladies' Night* is a significant movie because it challenges the gender economy of Mexican romantic comedy. It was not only the first major romantic comedy directed by a woman, but also the first one to center on female characters. The main characters are represented somewhat schematically (the innocent girl vs. the sexually experienced woman) but their opposition synthesizes into an alliance in which they both help each other in overcoming their conflicts, in spite of Ana's relationship with Fabián, Alicia's fiancé. The cast further emphasizes the focus on women: Ana Claudia Talancón plays Alicia, in her first major role after the huge success of *El crimen del padre Amaro,* while Ana de la Reguera takes the other leading role, having established her name through her participation in Juan Carlos de Llaca's road movie *Por la libre* (2000).[31] Conversely, the actors playing the masculine roles do not have such strong public profiles. The film thus constructs its allure through its women, which is both a recognition of the need to appeal to a female audience that has historically constituted the bulk of romantic comedy, and an opening of a cinematic space for women's representation, which in the 1990s was mostly defined within and against neo-Mexicanist discourses.

Alicia's character is particularly telling. At the outset, her persona is based on a highly fantasized version of *Alice in Wonderland,* and sustained within a deliberately stereotypical notion of the "good girl." Under that surface exists a reality that the movie presents without any particular judgment: her fiancé is cheating on her with a woman who represents the exact opposite values that she does, and Alicia gives the sense of being trapped in the fantasy world of the upper class. If we read the movie as the process of Alicia's liberation from her social constraints, the fact that a male stripper is the vehicle for her emancipation carries some meaning: Roco represents a notion of masculinity diametrically opposed to that of the ideal husband and that evidently belongs to a different social class than Alicia. While the film appears to sustain the class logic behind the romantic comedy, these elements subtly undermine it from within. It is through its very superficiality that the movie succeeds in renewing the gender conventions of the romantic comedy. Even Ayala Blanco recognizes as much when he argues that the "bipolarity" of the main characters is original, because it "imbricates two different but complementary movies" (*La fugacidad* 250; my translation). Another interesting element in the gender equation of the movie is the fact that Ana, the "bad girl," is actually the narrator of the movie, giving the main voice to a woman who does not correspond to the standards of femininity idealized in characters like Cuarón's Clarisa or Echevarría's Silvia. Ana lacks the ethereality that the male gaze confers on women in many Mexican romantic comedies, and Tagliavini presents her as a refreshingly vulgar and very intelligent character. It is Ana's ethical choices that set the movie in motion, since she hires Roco to annoy Alicia. Still, when the moment comes to reestablish her relationship with Alicia, Ana's actions become, until the end of the movie, the condition of possibility for Alicia's search for herself and for Roco. Tagliavini's impeccable directorial work and the movie's capacity to work on gender issues within genre conventions as adverse as the ones presented by the Mexican romantic comedy are notable, and show the potential that this aesthetic can develop when unfolded outside intimate and romantic discourses.

Before I discuss that that point further, however, another movie should be mentioned: Jorge Colón's *Cansada de besar sapos* (2006). This movie tells the story of Martha (Ana Serradilla), a young publicist who, sick of her fiancé's infidelities, goes online to establish noncommitted relationships with a set of men whose comedic traits border on the absurd. This plan is thwarted when she starts falling for Javier (José María de Tavira), an aspiring actor who works as a barista in her uncle's coffee shop. It is important to point out that she does not meet Javier online, which can be viewed as a defense of in-person courtship against the emergence of online dating and its neoliberal implication of "shopping" for a date. This movie is not as original in its treatment of the genre as *Ladies' Night*, but still has some elements of note, particularly in the task of tracing the role of romantic comedies in contemporary Mexican cinema. *Cansada de besar sapos* is, like all the other films, a decidedly urban movie. Nonetheless, it presents a unique—and problematic—visual rendition of the city. Rather than placing the movie in Polanco or any other middle-to-upper-class neighborhood, Colón opts for the colonial buildings of Mexico City's recently revamped historic center. The interesting part is that we never get to see the "real" Centro, the chaotic, busy streets that surround the center of the city. Instead, Colón morphs the colonial architecture into a fictional neighborhood constructed upon a contrast of spaces. Martha's apartment, located in a colonial building on a street facing an old church, is in its interior a modern loft with a heavily designed aesthetic. Javier's coffee shop offers another example of the contrast in spaces: it is a spacious, bohemian site full of artwork on a street where such a venue does not really exist. Colón's Mexico City transforms the spatial self-referentiality of romantic comedy into a proactive instrument of the constitution of cinematic space. We see not only the habitat of the privileged classes presented by *Sexo, pudor y lágrimas*' Polanco, but also an altogether redefined city in which the film's gaze appropriates and reinvents highly identifiable geographies like the historic downtown area or Coyoacán.

Cansada de besar sapos also introduces a twist in the gender economy of romantic comedy. Not only is the protagonist a woman, she is also an advertising executive, a position that other movies almost exclusively assign to men (the other exception, of course, is Ana in *Ladies' Night*). If we revisit the movies I have discussed so far in this chapter, even when women had jobs in media, they were largely the muses of creative men: Clarisa inspires Tomás Tomás in *Sólo con tu pareja,* Ana is the model for Carlos's book in *Sexo, pudor y lágrimas,* and so on. In *Cansada de besar sapos,* however, the creative figure is Martha, and Javier is her muse: the gender roles constructed through the portrayals of the creative class are reversed. Certainly, the movie cannot be characterized as feminist, considering that, in the end, Martha chases Javier all the way to Barcelona to seek his forgiveness for her fooling around with men online. Even so, within the parameters of romance discourse, Martha still appears as an independent, creative, hardworking woman who has a coveted job thanks to her own talents. In the problematic realm of gender representation in the Mexican romantic comedy, this is regrettably quite an exception. Martha is complemented by another interesting female character, Andi (Ana Layevska), her neighbor. Andi is a psychologist whose lines of dialogue mostly focus on her detailed analysis of Martha's love life and her own. Besides being another independent, professional woman, Andi is even more in control of her own romantic life than Martha. After deliberately avoiding a serious relationship, Andi falls for one of her patients, a narcoleptic—a funny reversal of the Sleeping Beauty archetype.[32] In doing so, Andi resists the fairy-tale romance pursued by most women in romantic comedies, openly asserting her power to select her partner when Martha questions her about it.

While Mexican romantic comedy still has a long way to go in the portrayal of women, these two recent movies show the genre's potential to gradually evolve by questioning its own assumptions. In fact, romantic comedies with strong female characters like *Te presento a Laura* keep emerging in Mexico. This is a crucial point, given the prevalence of romantic comedy's aesthetic in many areas of Mexican cinema. The process I have described so far refers to a form of cinema that has ably developed within the genre: a visual language that speaks to new audiences and constructs affective arrangements and social identities without directly engaging with the legacies of Mexicanism and neo-Mexicanism. The large impact that the genre has on the constitution of many other areas of cinema—including political film, action movies, feminist cinema, and even auteur cinema—cannot be underestimated.[33] In this sense, romantic comedy may become a language that allows for the emergence of more critical perspectives on neoliberal culture. This speaks of yet another process that merits discussion: political cinema and the way in which the advent of neoliberalism has reformulated the very meaning of the relationship between politics and film. This is the subject of Chapter 3.

3

THE NEOLIBERAL GAZE

Reframing Politics in the "Democratic Transition"

One of the most discussed and perhaps most important functions of cinema within a nation and its civil society resides in its role in shaping and reshaping the discursive and visual boundaries of political discourse. In the late 1980s, as Mexico entered the early stages of its "democratic transition," Jorge Fons's *Rojo amanecer* (1989) played just such a role. The movie was the first feature film to fully focus on the October 1968 student massacre in Tlatelolco Square, and it did so by constructing an unprecedented approach to an event that had been effectively silenced by the official controls of public memory. To be sure, the "cinema of solitude" had ventured into some forms of antigovernment political discourse, including veiled allegories of the massacre—one might remember, for instance, Felipe Cazals's proverbial *Canoa* (1976), a recreation of the murder of four University of Puebla students in a conservative sierra town. However, up to that point no commercially released movie had produced such a frank portrayal of the dark events of October 2.[1] As Francisco Sánchez describes (*Océano* 88), *Rojo amanecer* operates both as a testimonial of the event and as a re-creation of middle-class Mexico City life on the eve of the event. This double articulation recast a diverse set of issues revolving around Mexican film in the last moments of the "cinema of solitude" wave. Scholars have already shed light on some of the issues related to *Rojo amanecer* and to the imagination of the Tlatelolco massacre in public culture: a critique of the mass government urbanization promoted in the 1960s and 1970s (Gallo; Foster 2–13); the limitations of cinematic discourse in the engagement of past traumas (Haddu, "Historiography"; Maciel 217–18; Rojo; Steinberg); the film's connections to other movies (Rangel); and the film as a representation of the early moments of the Mexican "democratic transition" (Velazco, "*Rojo amanecer*"; Porras Ferreyra). As the 1968 massacre became a subject of public discussion and debate in subsequent years, it is now possible to say that *Rojo amanecer*'s true importance in the history of recent Mexican cinema lies in its pivotal spot between 1970s cinema legacies and the emerging paradigms of the late 1980s and early 1990s. Fons's work opts to recount the massacre through a mediated vantage point constructed around a middle-class family. In other words, rather than producing a testimonial narrative of the event, or a narrative of any character directly involved in the massacre itself, Fons presents a quasi-costumbrist view of the massacre as a disruption of everyday life in the realm of the middle class. By making this choice, Fons juxtaposed the leftist ideological commitments of "cinema of solitude" with the new cinematic gaze that re-centers Mexican film upon the experience of the middle class. Thus, *Rojo amanecer*'s role in reframing political discourse in Mexican cinema is not only connected to its representation of the massacre per se, but also, and perhaps more importantly, in its construction of the middle-class urban subject as the privileged witness of the contemporary. The fading of traditional Mexicanist aesthetics and of melodramatic structures of feeling, as described in the previous two chapters, is complemented by the waning left-wing paradigms inherited from the 1960s and the corresponding rise of a transitional politics defined by its concerns around democracy, economics, and corruption. Political film, in the wake of *Rojo amanecer,* is about the politics of a middle class that feels itself in a state of constant siege amid a crisis that never seems to recede.

If one is to read Mexican political cinema from such a perspective, an important obstacle emerges from the shortcomings of existing analytical and theoretical languages on the subject. Latin American political cinema has, by and large, been discussed under the aegis of "Third Cinema," a concept that responds to 1960s geopolitical and geocultural understandings that posed non-Western cinematic traditions of social commitment as necessarily resistant to "First Cinema" (i.e., commercial cinema) and "Second Cinema" (i.e., art house and author cinema). While the notion of the "Third World" has basically vanished from most serious discussions of Latin American global engagements, the idea of "Third Cinema" remains a very active concept. In his 2001 book *Political Film,* critic Mike Wayne argues for a recovery of this conceptual vocabulary in terms of its dialectic relationships—namely, the way in which these three concepts problematize each other and interact in the global sphere. Still, these notions feel outdated in the context of a global film industry that has effectively commoditized both "Second Cinema" and "Third Cinema" into a single continuum of cultural capital. Ultimately, Wayne's book illustrates well the conceptual impasse that emerges from narrowly defining political cinema in terms of social or ideological "commitment." It produces a worthy and impassioned argument for the recovery of forms of political cinema, but a very limited critical model for the reading of actual political films in historical contexts where the 1960s notion of *cinéma engagé* is simply not applicable.

This issue may be extended to other forms and practices of film criticism: it is present in the previously cited work of Jorge Ayala Blanco, the single most influential film critic in Mexico, whose assessment of political movies tends to be connected to their ability to conform to a narrow set of ideological expectations constructed more or less around the same parameters that define "Third Cinema." In any case, I would argue that both Wayne's book and Ayala Blanco's work are symptomatic examples of a professional and ideological bias that plagues many practitioners of film criticism and film studies. "Political cinema" in Latin America is thus traditionally identified with the representation of subaltern and marginalized social groups and their struggle for justice, or with the production of movies openly identified with paradigms of the 1960s cultural Left, as present in iconic movies such as Argentine Fernando Solanas's *La hora de los hornos* (1968) and Bolivian Jorge Sanjinés's *El coraje del pueblo* (1971). Indeed, this understanding of political cinema has a lot to say when engaging left-leaning auteurs such as Solanas, Sanjinés, Fernando Birri, or Glauber Rocha, but in Mexico, where filmmakers did not even produce a national cinema as politicized as the one from their South American counterparts (Mora 105–49), this theoretical approach seems to miss the mark. In a way, *Rojo amanecer* is perhaps the last major Mexican movie that can be productively read from a "Third Cinema" perspective, as it was an independently financed production that had to overcome censorship and other obstacles in order to be able to present a politically urgent subject to film audiences.

The construction of an entirely new set of institutions of cinema in Mexico, with complex networks interconnecting the State, private investment, and individual filmmakers, requires an understanding of political film in a new way. "Third Cinema" represents an idealistic paradigm for approaching film as an instrument of direct social change or, at least, as a testimonial of the voices that had been silenced by years of repression and marginalization. This is not the story of post-1988 Mexico, where political films were usually able to reach their audiences, even when censorship was an issue. Furthermore, the politics framed by post-1990 Mexican cinema have little to do with subalternized voices or radicalized social commitment. The films' subject matter is the daily struggle of middle-class Mexicans with a system in perpetual decline and crisis. It is worth remembering that the State remains a major source of financing, even as private financing becomes prominent, so films that present Mexico in an exceedingly negative light are rather rare. In this context, Mexican films rarely focus on marginalized silenced perspectives, to use a term close to "Third Cinema" paradigms. Being political in contemporary Mexican cinema means to engage with the systemic failure of the Mexican State in preserving the spaces of modernity enjoyed by the new moviegoing audience. While the idea that the State finances some of these films, critical as they are to it, may sound puzzling, this financing of a moderately critical perspective has historically been a part of the Mexican government's claim that it fosters democracy and freedom of speech. As I will show in individual cases, censorship and controversy emerge in diverse ways, but in the new marketplace of private distribution, they tend to contribute to a movie's success rather than silence it.

Taking all these factors into account, I believe that contemporary Mexican political cinema is readable only through an approach that understands its organic and problematic relationship with the politics and economics of neoliberalism, while acknowledging the ideological consequences of the class shift in spectatorship delineated in Chapter 2. When addressing the corpus of political movies produced in Mexico after *Rojo amanecer*, it is important to resist the temptation to read any transformational power in these movies or the urge to romanticize any engagement with the poor and the marginalized as inherently political. In fact, as I mentioned in Chapter 1 in reference to the cinema of Luis Alcoriza, representations of the Mexican working and marginalized classes are hardly progressive, and reading them as such usually results in projecting a political ideal onto films that may in fact represent the opposite view. Rather, "political film" must be understood in this context as a practice that utilizes cinema for the formulation of the politics and interests of a moviegoing audience that looks to the genre to make sense of the transition out of the post-revolutionary regime as experienced in the wake of the 1988 election, and the consequences of this historical movement in the configurations of the urban middle class.[2]

The notion of reading political cinema in relation to its legibility vis-à-vis average moviegoing audiences as opposed to the focus on the agency of the filmmaker in pushing a political point has an important history in non-academic film criticism. This is well documented, for instance, in Jonathan Rosenbaum's *Movies as Politics,* a compilation of three decades of reviews and articles about ostensibly political films. In the preface, Rosenbaum connects enjoyment and politics in a suggestive way, arguing that "what is designed to make people feel good at the movies has a profound relation to how and what they think and feel about the world around them" (3). This insight points to an issue central to understanding films in which the commercial and the political intersect: there is a close relationship between affective and ideological engagement. From a more theoretical perspective, Mas'ud Zavarzadeh contends that "seeing films politically" is a matter of concentrating on "the ideological conditions of possibility of the formal" and the way in which films produce "the kind of reality supportive of the existing socioeconomic arrangement" (8). It is important to make clear the means by which films articulate their "ideological conditions of possibility"—namely, the political and cultural ideals brought about by neoliberalism and shared by the specific demographic groups attending movie theaters. One must also read the interactions between the "existing socioeconomic arrangement" behind the economic and social structures of neoliberalism (and its corresponding political counterpart in the idea of the "transition to democracy") and the affective languages constructed by each movie in order to identify the ways in which the films appeal to their actual or purported audiences. I will thus unfold these two perspectives into a reading of films engaged in critical moments in the arc of Mexican neoliberalism.

1988 was a crucial year in the Mexican political imaginary, and it is usually described as a transitional year in the Mexican social landscape as well. Matthew Gutmann describes the mood in his study of the public performance of "democracy" in post-1968 Mexico: "Pundits and proletarians uniformly look back on 1988 as a watershed year that literally opened the floodgates to subsequent opposition victories" (162).[3] Political cinema in Mexico must be understood in part as a result of the reconfiguration of political forces and ideologies in the wake of this episode. Cuauhtémoc Cárdenas's candidacy in particular was an important event in Mexican left-wing politics for two paradoxical reasons. On the one hand, it allowed the incorporation of a large array of political currents—Marxism, socialism, communism, urban popular movements, and the actions of former guerrillas, among others—into the formal electoral process after years of marginalization and cooptation. On the other, insofar as Cárdenas and many members of his political group were former PRI members, it meant a deactivation of the most radical components of the Mexican Left.[4] It is not trivial to remember that Cárdenas is the son of Lázaro Cárdenas, the socialist president from the 1930s who is widely credited with the formation of the modern Mexican State. This fact fostered a nostalgic view not only of the role of the left wing in constructing the postrevolutionary political hegemony, but also in understanding Cuauhtémoc Cárdenas's candidacy as a restoration of revolutionary ideas at the outset of a neoliberal project that was threatening important revolutionary achievements. Cárdenas's candidacy also meant a major transformation in left-wing politics, where practices associated with more radicalized stances (such as the guerilla movements of the 1970s) migrated to the backburner of society and culture. As such, left-wing politics was able to stake its claim in nostalgic nationalist politics that mirror, for instance, the cultural ideas put forward by *Danzón* and other neo-Mexicanist films discussed in Chapter 1. In the realm of cultural discourses like cinema, this created an ideological void that allowed films to become a perfect means for representing both the sense of loss experienced by members of more politicized generations and the new agendas of citizens who were raised and consequently fully embedded in the neoliberal moment. Thus, as the process of displacement of audiences unfolded as described in Chapter 2, and as the use of Mexicanism as a privileged cultural discourse entered the gradual decline described in Chapter 1, cinema became a vessel for the expression of the topics and subjectivities that would dominate cultural discourses in the age of neoliberalism.

I believe that my contention of cinema as a genre organic to the neoliberal process is proven in the most literal sense by the political films of the period. No other cultural discourse articulated such a deep adoption of the topics of neoliberalism so early in its implementation in politics and economics. In fact, political cinema in Mexico registered the idea of a transition out of traditional structures of the State in the earliest stages of the neoliberal process. An interesting example is Alfredo Joskowicz's 1992 movie *Playa azul,* the story of a politician who shuts himself away in his family-owned hotel in the wake of a corruption scandal. The politician, played by iconic "cinema of solitude" actor Sergio Bustamante, is never able to recover from the accusations, a situation unthinkable in reality during the years of PRI dominance. More significantly still, the character is never granted redemption by the film. While the movie is still deeply inscribed in the gritty aesthetics of "cinema of solitude," the use of corruption as a symptom of the decline of the existing political order, and the story of this politician as an allegory of a system unable to overcome its shortcomings, would foreshadow films from the latter part of the decade. In any case, understanding the ways in which the main preoccupations of neoliberalism infiltrate and colonize cinema is vital to understanding the transformations within the industry in the 1990s and beyond. Before entering the realm of neoliberal politics, it is fundamentally necessary to analyze the way in which film registered the erosion of older paradigms of political cinema. Two crucial movies, Gabriel Retes's *El bulto* (1992) and Juan Carlos de Llaca's *En el aire* (1995), will offer an opening into this problem.

Paradise Lost: *El bulto, En el aire,* and the Erosion of the Political

El bulto is a very peculiar product of the 1990–1992 cadre of Mexican movies. Unlike neophytes like Alfonso Cuarón and Carlos Carrera, or filmmakers with bona fide commercial or critical successes like Arturo Ripstein and Alfonso Arau, Gabriel Retes was a well-established independent director and producer whose work had faced many hardships related to censorship and economic failure in the 1970s and 1980s.[5] Still, Retes was an unlikely beneficiary of the early process of privatization in exhibition. After being rejected by IMCINE and FOPROCINE, *El bulto* was ultimately produced through independent financing mustered by Retes and his production company, Cooperativa Río Mixcoac; he raised the movie's $700,000 production budget by mortgaging his family home. Retes and his wife, screenwriter Lourdes Elizarrás, respectively play the protagonist and his love interest, a decision undoubtedly aimed at saving the equivalent of two actors' salaries. Nonetheless, *El bulto* was able to recover its initial investment thanks to the fact that, as COTSA was winding down, private chain Organización Ramírez picked it up for distribution, making it one of the first non-Televicine Mexican films fully distributed by the private exhibition system. *El bulto* was also a precursor of another strategy of financial viability, home video sales, which, as Retes himself admits, helped the movie to be profitable (Medrano Platas 282). The fact that an openly political, self-financed movie became one of the first to benefit from the decline of State structures of exhibition speaks to the unexpected freedom of speech brought about by privatization. While COTSA had had the power to relegate uncomfortable movies (like Retes's own *La ciudad al desnudo* in the mid-1980s) to marginal theaters, programmers in a private outfit like Ramírez would in fact see economic benefits in bringing controversial movies to audiences. And while *El bulto* was clearly the object of the structural censorship inherited from *echeverrista* financing frameworks, it ultimately reached a wider audience through the incipient private distribution system.

El bulto is built upon a clever, yet familiar, premise. The protagonist, Lauro (Gabriel Retes), is a left-leaning journalist who goes into a coma in 1971, while covering a clash between leftist activists and right-wing shock groups. The movie is focused on his awakening in 1991, having to adjust to the realities of a Mexico at the high point of *salinismo*. Along with his physical recovery, he must come to grips with a reality in which his formerly leftist friends are completely institutionalized in the neoliberal State or the business community, and where his political ideals are hopelessly outdated. Carl Mora (207) and Patricia Hart (29) remind us that this narrative device dates back to Washington Irving's "Rip Van Winkle," something highlighted by Lauro himself. Of course, *El bulto* is not the only movie that uses this conceit to represent the shock of a social transformation associated with market and democratic reforms: in recent years, Wolfgang Becker's *Good Bye Lenin!* (2003) used it to chronicle the collapse of socialism in East Germany. One could also draw a connection to Penny Marshall's melodrama *Awakenings* (1990), where Robert De Niro plays a patient who wakes up after thirty years in a coma. Considering the time it took Retes to raise money to shoot his film, it is hard to claim that *Awakenings* was an influence, but not completely implausible. In fact, Retes's melodramatic tone and the focus of part of his movie on family issues echo some of the topics developed by *Awakenings*. *El bulto*'s similarities to forms of melodramatic discourse more closely related to Hollywood would speak to an exhaustion of national models of melodrama in Mexican cinema, since the focus on Lauro's family fallout definitely moves away from romantically oriented melodramas of the Mexican cinematic tradition. In any case, by constructing his narrative upon this premise, Retes is able to avoid the imperative of a realist presentation of the *Halconazo,* by instead posing the June 10, 1971, massacre as the beginning of a parenthesis in political discourse that closes in 1991.[6] The movie is, in a way, a reflection on how the very demonstrators repressed back in the 1970s became complicit with the neoliberal reforms that, in Lauro's (and Retes's) eyes, betray the left-wing ideals of the past. The movie could even be read as an implicit rebuttal to *Rojo amanecer,* as it suggests that the truly shocking event was not the 1968 massacre or its irruption into the everyday life of the bourgeoisie. Rather, what Retes finds even more shocking is that the political process started by Tlatelolco and the *Halconazo* ultimately results in a complete surrender of the country to neoliberal capitalism.

In a telling conversation with his friend Alberto (Héctor Bonilla), Lauro catches up with the events following June 10. He finds out that a mutual friend was disappeared by the government. Soon after, Alberto presents him with José Agustín's countercultural history book *Tragicomedia Mexicana* and a video copy of *Rojo amanecer,* as aids to sum up the years that had passed. Alberto also highlights the 1985 earthquake, presented here as evidence of surviving forms of social organization, while chanting, "The people united will never be defeated." Lauro is shocked by the realization that the Soviet Union has fallen and that Mexico, in the wake of the Cárdenas candidacy, no longer has a communist party. The fact that the radical transformation that completely banished the Mexico that Lauro knew could be related in the course of a short conversation is clearly geared at showing the role of neoliberalism and transition ideologies in destroying the values held by Lauro's (and Retes's) generation. As Alberto narrates the passing of Spanish dictator Francisco Franco, the persistence of Fidel Castro in power, and the existence of a television commercial where people dance with Canada-brand shoes in Moscow's Red Square, it becomes clear the present renders Lauro's past political ideals meaningless. If anything, this is the scene in which *El bulto* strongly counters *Rojo amanecer,* deactivating it through its presentation as nothing more than videotape, thus scenifying the futility of memory in contemporary politics and culture. If neo-Mexicanist films like *Danzón* staked a claim on nostalgia to resist the winds of neoliberal change, the general tone of *El bulto* is that of resignation and defeat in the face of a struggle that, in hindsight, is void of any significance.

This depiction of the issue of historical memory is unique in the context of the early 1990s. It illustrates how Mexican cinema develops early on a quite distinct politics of memory, in contrast to postdictatorial traditions like that of Argentine cinema. Furthermore, it shows the ways in which cinema, even in its most politicized manifestations, represents a society subsumed by the neoliberal process, while other cultural productions undertake the task Claudio Lomnitz has termed "narrating the neoliberal moment" with an excessive reverence for history: "Given the prominent role that intellectuals played in this transition, it is not surprising that a kind of 'excess of history' marked the period as a whole or that a number of professional historians were drafted by the press or by television. . . . [History] provided politicians and public intellectuals with a succinct and abbreviated moral vocabulary and with a set of images that could handily stand in for long-standing arguments or even for entire doctrines" (54).

Here, cinema stands in stark contrast with literary fiction, which produced a wave of historical novels throughout the 1980s and early 1990s. Unsurprisingly, the most important and most successful novel in the early 1990s, Héctor Aguilar Camín's *La guerra de Galio* offers a long historical recreation of the very period reduced to anecdotes by Retes. One of the novel's main characters is also a 1970s journalist and historian, and his fate is to face those years of political decadence that Lauro missed while he was in a coma. The story presented by Aguilar Camín is that of a betrayal of the ideals of the 1960s or, as Alberto Moreiras puts it, of a moment of "suture" between ethics and politics (80). Comparing Retes's movie to Aguilar Camín's book shows that *El bulto* ultimately works against the grain of the historiographic trend of Mexican public and cultural discourse at the time. Cinema becomes, in cases like *El bulto*, a unique site for resisting the neoliberal politics of history. Retes opts for a story that emphasizes the present at the expense of the past. The movie never uses flashbacks as a narrative device. In fact, Lauro's past is completely absent as a subject of narrative representation and the only scene from the past is a black-and-white documentary-style presentation of the *Halconazo* in the opening credits. By representing only this past event in a style deliberately distinct from the rest of the movie, and with no other referential connections to the plot itself, Retes resists the urge to narrate the past or to make any point about it. Thus, the movie's whole point and its ideological thrust rest solely on Lauro's present story, while his past is as absent from the movie as it is from the public consciousness of neoliberal Mexico. This makes *El bulto* surprisingly more political than Aguilar Camín's novel or the work of historians like Enrique Krauze, the target of Lomnitz's critique.[7] Unlike works produced in the heyday of *salinismo*, when the 1968–1988 period was narrated as a transition to democracy and the beginning of a "desirable" modernity—an idea articulated in the movie by Toño, Lauro's brother—*El bulto* narrates the present against the teleological grain of the period's historiography and ultimately contends that neoliberalism is not the result of the 1968 movement, but rather proof of its defeat. Some commentators have taken this political intervention even further: Miriam Haddu, for instance, suggests that the unmasking of the underlying social inequalities of neoliberalism and of the mirage of *salinista* prosperity foreshadows the Zapatista rebellion (*Contemporary Mexican Cinema* 22–27). This interpretation is an example of certain voluntarism I criticized before: it connects Retes's movie to parts of the Mexican political process completely unrelated to it (the Zapatistas). Nevertheless, Haddu is right in emphasizing that *El bulto* stands almost by itself in the public discourse of 1992 as a denunciation of the falseness behind the neoliberal narrative of modernity.

One of the most salient features of *El bulto* is its technical sloppiness. The movie is clumsily edited, with implausible transitions and awkward camera angles. In the sole scholarly article on the film, Patricia Hart interprets some of these traits as a formalization of Lauro's marginalization in the present and a larger dichotomy between reality and ideal in the movie's narrative structure (29–35). This reading grants, I would argue, too much credit to Retes's technical skills, given that all of his movies have major stylistic shortcomings, including preachy dialogue, shoddy editing, hesitant camera work, and implausible narratives. The fact is that, beyond the budgetary constraints obvious in some parts of the production, the film has important elements of formal dissonance that speak to the outdated nature of Retes's filmmaking. The clearest example of this is the musical score. The deft use of soundtracks by commercial cinema in the late 1990s is missing here. Instead, the movie consistently returns to an anachronistic and unnecessary cue: every time a dramatic revelation takes place, the film presents the audience with a strident tune straight out of *telenovelas*. While Retes's plotline resists nostalgia, his formal devices do not. In contrast with the sophisticated filmmaking of other early-1990s directors like María Novaro and Alfonso Cuarón, his work shows clear signs of formal and narrative exhaustion. Furthermore, Retes's work can be read in contrast to the slick filmmaking of *Sólo con tu pareja*, which features extraordinary cinematography by Emmanuel Lubezki, much stronger narrative pacing, and skillful editing. The difference between Retes's aesthetic and Cuarón's is not casual, of course: it highlights the contrast between a filmmaker, Retes, whose priority is the transmission of a political message regardless of technical limitations, and another, Cuarón, who is evidently more aware of the connection between a film's style and its commercial viability in the emerging cinematic ecosystems.

The ending of the movie offers some clues to reading the formal and conceptual challenges faced by a director like Retes, formed in the margins of "cinema of solitude," when addressing a new contemporary reality. After developing a relationship with one of his daughter's friends and recovering his job as a journalist, Lauro—clean-shaven for the first time in the film—returns to his home, where he finds all his friends and family throwing a party for him. Once he greets some people and after a heartfelt reconciliation with his estranged son, all the other characters start rapping a song about his story. After overcoming his surprise, Lauro integrates himself into the song as the scene fades away into the credits. Patricia Hart reads this ending as a narrative of redemption, where Lauro ultimately encounters "flexibility and forgiveness." Hart concludes: "And where reconciliation is possible for an individual, perhaps it may be as well for a country, if the country manages to face the past" (35). While this interpretation is plausible at first sight, thanks in part to the strong melodramatic subtext expressed by the soundtrack up to this point, a redemptive conclusion stands in direct contradiction to the narrative of ideological disenchantment at the core of the film. The final scene is striking because of its surreal, almost nonsensical nature. A rap song that emerges out of nothing at the end of a film that follows realist narrative conventions cannot possibly be representative of an act of reconciliation within the aesthetic framing of the movie. A closer look shows that the lyrics of the song are not redemptive, but in fact quite aggressive. After reconciling with Lauro, his son, Daniel, prefaces the musical scene by saying, out of the blue, "It's because of you that Grandma cannot live in peace," later followed by another character repeating, "We have to go to the hospital every morning to give therapy to this animal." Rather than representing any redemption, the "rap del bulto" ("bulto" being a word that, incidentally, refers to a bag or a bulky object) mocks his predicament ("one morning he did not do so well," "for being so nosy, they put him to sleep"). Ultimately, when Lauro intervenes in the song, he criticizes himself ("he was so old"). In the very last frame of the film, we see Lauro violently laughing. His expression, which communicates both joy and rage, is frozen for a moment before the credits and the melodramatic soundtrack take over. This finale can be interpreted in two alternative ways. If one stretches the last scene's possibilities a little, the very surreal nature of the song and its focus on his coma, not to mention that all the other singers of the rap basically ignore him, points to the possibility that he did not actually wake up and that he was dreaming the present. This reading may certainly be implausible, and the violence of the "rap del bulto" and Lauro's angry laughter can be interpreted in a second way: as Retes's way of refusing the ideological closure that his story of redemption may suggest. The fact is that the final scene is dumbfounding, and a clumsy way to finish the movie as well, considering that the previous scene had already provided a redemptive conclusion in Lauro's reconciliation with Daniel and the rest of his family and friends. It is thus not far-fetched to argue that Retes, a director whose films tend to have major narrative shortcomings, does not know how to conclude his movie. In the end, Retes's sympathy for Lauro results in his redemption, but this redemption, as Hart shows, may ultimately be an acceptance of the neoliberal present, embodied in his return to the newspaper and a final conversation where his brother tries to recruit him to the neoliberal project. This seems to contradict the ideological perspective presented by the early part of the film. I would contend that in awkwardly prolonging the film beyond the reconciliatory moments and ending it in such a strange way, Retes maintains Lauro's heroic struggle with his personal reality without fully embracing a closure that would deem the neoliberal present acceptable.

In any case, *El bulto* is a narrative of defeat, a movie highly aware of the impossibility of the politics of the past. Regardless of its technical defects, which make the movie almost unwatchable to anyone used to the aesthetics of romantic comedy that was developing at about the same time, the commercial success of the film in a moment so inauspicious for national cinema speaks to the resonance of its political message with audiences. The triumphalist narrative of *salinismo* was still a year and a half away from its demise in 1994, but the social contradictions of the period were obvious to many people in Mexico. Not unlike the telephone workers in *Danzón*, the working and middle classes of Mexico were suffering the radical dismantling of the social networks of protection, while political discontent with the PRI regime was growing both in a left wing persecuted by Salinas de Gortari and in a right wing headed by newcomers like Vicente Fox, which spearheaded a new form of confrontational politics. *El bulto*'s articulation of disenchantment clearly resounded with its audiences, as evidenced by its success at the box office and in home video rentals. It was also the first step in a new tradition of political film that would later focus on the crumbling of postrevolutionary political ideology.

A surprising phenomenon in the wake of *El bulto* is that, in the 1990s, the remaining filmmakers of the "cinema of solitude" paradigm eschewed political film altogether. Fons went on to direct *El callejón de los milagros,* where veiled criticisms of neoliberalism are present, but they are a far cry from the discourse in his controversial *Rojo amanecer;* Retes himself opted to do a metacinematic movie, *Bienvenido/Welcome* (which I discussed in Chapter 2), followed by an adaptation of a nonpolitical novel by Eusebio Ruvalcaba, *Un dulce olor a muerte* (1999); Cazals, after shooting a historical film based on Father Kino, a colonial figure, dropped out of sight for the rest of the decade, which is notable considering how prolific he has been otherwise; and Hermosillo's explorations of gender and sexuality were never really concerned with political or economic transformations to begin with. *El bulto* signaled the exhaustion of any political ideals of the 1970s generation that had survived the structural censorship of *echeverrismo* and *lopezportillismo.*

This is not to say that political cinema was entirely absent; on the contrary, even during the production and exhibition crisis of the mid-1990s, some political movies were able to emerge. A good example is Mitl Valdez's *Los vuelcos del corazón* (1996), a free adaptation of a story by Marxist writer José Revueltas on the vicissitudes of the Mexican Communist Party in the 1940s. The movie is a very successful and detailed period piece that resists the idealization of the past in order to present both the affective and ideological conflicts that haunt its characters. Still, the movie is more a study on the contradictions of a long-gone left wing, a political movement defined by its debates on dogmatism. It is also the re-creation of an affective culture tied to political radicalism. The way in which *danzón* music overtakes the plot at some points departs even from Novaro's nostalgic investment in the present. While shooting a remembrance of the most radical moment of the Mexican Left in the middle of the neoliberal storm may be read as a political act in itself, the fact is that *Los vuelcos del corazón* ultimately evades the present.

In the mid-1990s, Mexican political cinema was clearly haunted by the void left behind both by the institutionalization of the left wing in the Party of the Democratic Revolution (PRD) as well as the fall of the Berlin Wall and the subsequent demise of radical politics as a vehicle of social articulation. This is the case of less successful films such as Hugo Rodríguez's *En medio de la nada* (1993), an unskillful thriller centered on the kidnapping of a retired union leader's family. The story line makes reference to the demise of labor organization in Mexico. The film's union leaders, just like the communists of *Los vuelcos del corazón,* speak to a former political order, but in a more contemporary way. One of the most salient results of *salinismo* was the dismantling of many powerful unions, through the incarceration of long-standing labor leaders like Joaquín Hernández Galicia, the president of the oil workers' union. Thus, thrillers like *En medio de la nada* attempted to work the siege against labor organization into their plot allegories. A similar strategy is pursued by a later and much better movie, Francisco Athié's *Fibra óptica* (1997). This movie centers on a journalist, played by Roberto Sosa, hired to investigate the murder of a union leader after a Brazilian woman was falsely accused of the crime. *Fibra óptica* is a sleekly produced movie that centers on the corrupt underworld of Mexican politics. The movie title makes reference to a Mexico increasingly overtaken by electronic communications (cell phones were becoming a prominent side business for Carlos Slim and other industrialists). This is an important factor, because the movie shows an interesting departure from other political films in its willingness to assume the new forms of modernity developed under neoliberalism. Thus, *Fibra óptica* presents an almost unique premise: an adoption of the urban aesthetic and urban subjectivity of the new middle class to denounce the underlying structures of intrigue and corruption at the base of the new modern project.

Still, the fact is that in the mid-1990s most movies were still caught in the void left by the demise of radical politics. In this sense, the most symptomatic movie of the period is Juan Carlos de Llaca's *En el aire* (1995). The movie focuses on Alberto (Daniel Gimémez Cacho in the present; Plutarco Haza as a young man; Sebastián Hiriart as a child), a DJ for a psychedelic radio show who reminisces about his past as a hippie in the 1970s while broadcasting his last show before the station closes down. The main plotline makes a direct reference to the erasure of the past conducted by neoliberalism. The station, called "Radio Púrpura" (which can be read as a reference to Jimi Hendrix's "Purple Haze"), is part of a larger communications conglomerate, and Juan (Alberto Estrella), the general manager, tells Alberto early on that the station may remain open only if he and his team agree to include more commercial programming, such as English lessons and a quiz show.[8] Alberto promptly refuses, deciding to close the station at midnight and leave the media corporation behind. This general framework may be read as an allegory of the erasure of radical political history on the eve of the implementation of NAFTA.

Radio Púrpura was a nine-month-old project at the time of its closure and had been founded as an attempt to revisit the lost ideals of Mexican hippie culture. By attempting to "modernize" the station through demands that respond to the increasing commercialism behind media, the corporation as represented by Juan ultimately exercises a market pressure that renders the past unprofitable. It is important here to point out that Juan was also a hippie, and became acquainted with Alberto when they both lived in the same commune in the 1970s. Juan, like Lauro's brother Toño in *El bulto*, stands for a generation of radicalized middle-class students who were ultimately co-opted by neoliberal capitalism. Juan, now a media manager, originally accepts the establishment of Radio Púrpura as someone who understands Alberto's nostalgia for hippie culture, but in the end surrenders to the market pressures of the corporate media environment. Juan's success in the media landscape is ultimately a slap in Alberto's face, a punishment for his inability to integrate himself to the new economic reality.

In his study of the relationship between memory and redemption in contemporary cinema, Russell J. A. Kilbourn argues that the "characteristically ironic value of redemption in the narratives of many contemporary memory films reveals it to be a hollow promise, a myth, a fiction," resulting in two possible scenarios: "(a) the protagonist gains this knowledge and yet remains dissatisfied at the end, acquiring no 'closure'; or (b) s/he fails utterly in this quest and yet (therefore?) acquires a kind of negative knowledge that grants the narrative an ironically negative closure" (97). *El bulto*, as I read it in this chapter, falls squarely into the first outcome, as suggested by Lauro's frozen expression of apparent despair in the final shot of the movie, despite the turbulent process of reconciliation with his country and his family. *En el aire* presents us with a form of the second outcome. The plot moves along two story lines: the closure of Radio Púrpura and a set of flashbacks related to Alberto's on-and-off relationship with Laura (Dolores Heredia), the love of his life. The flashbacks also reach back to the 1970s, a time when Alberto was a hippie who escaped his middle-class life to join a commune in Guerrero, a hotbed of guerilla activity during that decade. Alberto was not a particularly committed individual. His self-exile from his bourgeois family was completely related to Laura. Alberto and Laura are forced into marriage to make their relationship socially acceptable. The situation becomes unsustainable very soon, which leads Laura to flee the marriage. As a result of his family's role in his breakup with Laura, Alberto decides to move out and leave his bourgeois life behind.

Later on, Laura appears again in the popular theater commune where Alberto lives, rekindling their relationship. Laura leaves again at the end of this period, after a few months; she does not reappear until Alberto summons her to the radio station during Radio Púrpura's final broadcast. At the end of the movie, after a brief meeting, Laura leaves again, this time apparently for good.

En el aire's ending is as strange as *El bulto*'s. While chasing Laura's taxi down the street, Alberto encounters a little girl from his past (a kindergarten classmate who protected him from bullies) who has repeatedly appeared in the movie during different dream sequences. Thus, de Llaca does not conclude the film with either a redeeming moment or a reckoning with reality. Rather, ending the movie with a final dream sequence and with a character who gives Alberto solace only in the realm of fantasy results in what Kilbourn calls "an ironically negative closure." Both of Alberto's objects of desire in the film—the radio station that preserved the last shreds of his hippie values, and the woman with whom he wanted to rekindle a relationship—are lost in the end, leaving him with no discernible hope or future. Still, by allowing him to return to the foundational moment of his life as embodied by the little girl, the negative closure points to an undefined but perhaps redemptive future, mostly because de Llaca opts to conclude the movie with a dream sequence of sorts. Alberto's "negative knowledge" rests on the realization of the banality of his past values. In this, *En el aire* signals a more resigned perspective on facing neoliberalism than *El bulto*.

It is relevant to point out that, while de Llaca activates the same radical moment of the 1970s as *El bulto,* he does so in a more deliberately tangential way. Alberto's stay in the theater commune is disrupted by political turmoil. Juan's brother, Paco, is involved with a guerrilla cell in Guerrero's highlands, where the movement headed by Lucio Cabañas was based. Paco's cell kidnaps the son of an ambassador, thus attracting attention from the Mexican police. In light of this, Paco asks Juan and the commune to hide the cell's weapons so they do not have to carry them through military checkpoints. While the theater troupe is clearly divided on whether to assist Paco, they eventually accept the premise that they are helping a friend's brother and that they are contributing to the material realization of the liberation ideas embodied by the troupe's lifestyle. Still, the outcome of this event is the breakup of the troupe in the wake of Paco's arrest. The past utopia where Alberto's ideals reside is paradoxically destroyed when he is forced to move from political theory (the commune) to real politics (aiding the guerrilla). In this way, the commune can be read as a mise-en-scène for portraying the ephemeral nature of Mexican hippie ideals, as well as the brutal interruption that radical politics meant in a utopian lifestyle that was also a bourgeois way of life. The ultimate outcome of this event is a recognition of the emptiness of left-wing ideals. As Alberto contemplates his bedroom on the eve of leaving the commune for good, a voice-over of his present-time self clearly identifies the endpoint of the values that had sustained him: "With the commune, the illusions of hippie-ism, cooperativism and romanticism ended. Skepticism, postmodernism and individualism survived. We destroyed a way of life but we did not have time to build another one." In this reflection, Alberto conveys the way in which his generation, like Lauro's in *El bulto*, regards neoliberalism as a palpable demonstration of the end of their ideals and dreams. De Llaca's subsequent career, in fact, shows that his work fully overcame any nostalgia for 1970s values. His 2000 film, *Por la libre*, is a lightly plotted road movie in which two teenagers go to Acapulco to scatter their grandfather's ashes—a perfect allegory for the need to overcome the past—while his most recent film, *Así es la suerte* (2011), is a blatantly commercial comedy about a man who suddenly becomes unlucky. In short, de Llaca's full departure from political cinema is indicative of the impact that the industry changes laid out in Chapter 2 had even on filmmakers who had tried to articulate political issues in their earlier work.

Precisely for this reason, it is very important not to read *El bulto* or *En el aire* from an idealistic perspective that understands Alberto and Lauro as fallen heroes in the struggle against history. One should always remember when watching films like *El bulto* and *En el aire* that both characters are rebellious sons of the traditional middle class and, by virtue of this, the movies contribute as much as the romantic comedies of the 1990s to establishing the urban professional middle class as the privileged subject of post-1988 Mexican cinema and to privileging its gaze as the prime vantage point of the framing and visualization of history and the contemporary. *En el aire*'s memory devices are mostly focused on the countercultural experience of the bourgeoisie. Radio Púrpura, for instance, is conceived as a vehicle to preserve the left-wing ethos of the generation of 1968, mostly college-educated youngsters caught up in political activism or the sexual revolution. Still, the radio station is, from its inception, part of a corporate media organization that ultimately absorbs it. The fact that de Llaca locates Alberto's last stance of freedom in radio—that is, in electronic media—is not accidental, because it exhibits yet another dimension of the creative class represented by publicists in the romantic comedies discussed in Chapter 2.[9] In a very telling coincidence, Daniel Giménez Cacho, the actor who portrays Alberto, also plays the part of Tomás Tomás, the protagonist in *Sólo con tu pareja*. In a way, Cuarón's publicist and de Llaca's hippie are two sides of the same social coin, members of the creative media class idealized by neoliberalism. In fact, radio hosts, like publicists, appear both in movies that are aligned with the ideals of the wealthy moviegoing audiences (like the female protagonist of *Vivir mata*, discussed in Chapter 2, a radio host who spends her time conducting commercial promotions across Mexico City) and opposed to them (like in María Novaro's 2010 movie, *Las buenas hierbas*, where the protagonist works part time as a radio host at a left-leaning independent radio station). These incidences of the privileging the media personality as the subject of representation, regardless of the ideological stance of the films and their directors, add up to one of the best and most precise examples of the way in which neoliberalism reconfigured the ideologies and practices of the contemporary cultural space in Mexico. The movies do not all share the same politics, but they all share a cultural language created by and large by social and political transformations that find their ideological articulation in the aspirations of the middle class. It is no wonder that one of the most popular college majors in Mexican private universities during the 1990s was communication sciences: therein resided the aspirations of young members of the middle class who considered media to be the ultimate space of social success. In this, it is very clear that political cinema in Mexico, despite its many attempts to question neoliberalism, was by 1997 already bound to a cultural language where political agency, much like the affective agency explored in Chapter 2, was the almost exclusive prerogative of a very precise social subject: urban professional middle classes.

Redefining Political Film: *Entre Pancho Villa y una mujer desnuda*

The class displacements at the heart of Mexican film and culture in the wake of the 1988 election were a symptom of the demise of postrevolutionary nationalism's wide-ranging ideological scope, which had managed to keep large sectors of Mexican society within a common culture despite differences in class, gender, and race. The decline of the "imaginary networks of political power" (to use Roger Bartra's term, discussed in Chapter 1) that had ruled Mexico for many decades was behind the creation of the class-specific cultural spaces exemplified both by romantic comedy and by the emerging forms of political cinema. Still, as the cohesive sense of national identity historically fostered by Mexican culture began to lose its hegemonic place, new forms of social identity created spaces of articulation for previously marginalized groups. In Mexican society at large, this was represented by the Zapatista uprising, which gave voice to indigenous groups in the Chiapas highlands. However, as access to cinema production and consumption became a prerogative of the urban intellectual class and of middle-class citizens, the articulation of social identities in film was reclaimed by an intellectual ideology and practice that had become prominent in 1980s Mexico: feminism. In his book *Mexican Masculinities*, Robert McKee Irwin shows the pervasive and long-standing relationship between masculinity and national identity, the pinnacle of which came in the wake of the revolution, when conservative intellectuals like Julio Jiménez Rueda argued that a truly national culture had to be "virile." The symbolic complicity between masculinity and national culture meant that women's cultural agency was limited to a series of "plotting women," to use Jean Franco's term, able to operate within masculine master narratives of modern culture. Still, as Franco herself recognizes, the masculine hegemony in cultural enunciation starts to come apart at the same time that the edifice of revolutionary nationalism suffers its first major cracks in the wake of the 1968 student movement. According to Franco, the entrance of mass media into Mexican culture led to an "internationalization" that allowed for the weakening of Mexican nationalism and, subsequently, for the development of gendered forms of alternative culture, which resulted in the creation of a "feminist public sphere" in the mid-1970s (*Plotting Women* 184). By the late 1980s and early 1990s, feminist intellectuals and artists already occupied an important role in Mexico's urban intelligentsia: there were performance artists like Jesusa Rodríguez and Astrid Hadad who constructed ironic representations of Mexicanness, introducing gendered actualizations of the nationalist cultural repertoire, as well as intellectuals like Marta Lamas, founder of the journal *Debate feminista* and to this day the public face of feminism in Mexico.[10]

It is not coincidental that, in this landscape, cinema had the potential to become a major vehicle for the expression of women, given not only the role that media had in the breakup of traditional notions of gender in Mexico, but also the existence of gendered performance artists and cultural critics who provided a new generation of female actors and directors with both the ideological discourses and cultural languages to create a cinematic practice. Besides María Novaro's *Lola* and *Danzón,* which spearheaded a new wave of cinema by women filmmakers, one could recall Busi Cortés's *El secreto de Romelia* (1988), in which a divorced middle-class woman explores the secrets of her family's matriarch, and Guita Schyfter's *Novia que te vea* (1994), a film about the coming of age of two young Jewish women in 1960s Mexico. In *Palabra de mujer,* critic Isabel Arredondo documents the chronological period that frames these two movies, which was distinctly characterized by an uptick in the production of films by women directors. It is telling that this period neatly coincides with Salinas de Gortari's presidency, which may be read as an indication that the undermining of cultural institutions brought about by neoliberal reform was one of the conditions of possibility for the decisive emergence of women and feminism in parts of the cultural landscape. Still, women directors of this period were bound by the limits of inherited cultural discourses, and cinema by women in the early 1990s was not nearly as politically radical as the work of Jesusa Rodríguez or Astrid Hadad, perhaps because of the limitations posed by the cost of producing a movie.[11] If one considers *Danzón,* as I did in Chapter 1, as a prime example of cultural nostalgia, and then compares it with *El secreto de Romelia*'s fixation on making sense of the past and *Novia que te vea*'s idealization of a Jewish immigrant legacy eclipsed by Mexico's ideas of national identity, one could conclude that major movies by women directors were unable to articulate a strong critique on the cultural signifiers of postrevolutionary Mexico, such as the one undertaken by feminists in activities like performance art, journalism, or literature. One could argue that, since women directors first held a stake in cinema when cinematic discourse was in a phase of deep stagnation, they were ultimately unable to decisively provide alternative film languages that would allow cinema to break the impasses of an industry in the middle of an aesthetic crisis. This is obvious not only in the aforementioned directors and their focus on nostalgia, but also in directors like Maryse (Marisa) Sistach, whose *Anoche soñé contigo* (1992), discussed in Chapter 2, is a timid representation of affective relations, deeply rooted in traditional melodrama, in a time when Jaime Humberto Hermosillo and Alfonso Cuarón were reinventing the discourse of love and sexuality in cinema.

Perhaps the most iconic example is Dana Rotberg's *Ángel de fuego* (1991), a Buñuelian film about a fourteen-year-old trapeze artist (Evangelina Sosa) who, after realizing she is pregnant with the child of her recently deceased father, begins an odyssey that leads her to survive a twisted attempt to "redeem" her by a troupe of fundamentalist Christian puppeteers. In the end, she kills herself while burning down the entire circus where she worked, something that the movie presents as redemptive from the protagonist's perspective, but as a defeat from the perspective of the spectator. Rotberg's movie undoubtedly has artistic and ideological merits, such as extraordinary performances by the actors and the courage of presenting a narrative of the most abject urban poverty in the middle of *salinista* neoliberal triumphalism. However, at this point in my analysis, it is obvious that she was working within an aesthetic dead end, closer to the languages of the "cinema of solitude" than to the mainstream cinematic discourse that became predominant just a few years later. In presenting an unredeemable *lumpenproletariat* defined by its sordid existence (the plot outlined here gives plenty of examples of this), Rotberg is closer to Luis Alcoriza's dismissive characterizations of the lower classes than to any form of political cinema from the 1990s.

Novaro herself would go on to direct three films—*El jardín del Edén* (1994), *Sin dejar huella* (2000), and *Las buenas hierbas* (2010)—in which her style and ideologies were notably and uncompromisingly represented while continuing to obtain acceptable commercial releases.[12] Nonetheless, the first movie by a woman filmmaker to truly enter the realm of neoliberal cinema did not come from the *salinista* generation, but from a playwright whose problematizations of gender and neoliberalism made her one of the landmark figures of contemporary feminism in Mexico: Sabina Berman, who adapted her successful play *Entre Villa y una mujer desnuda* into the movie *Entre Pancho Villa y una mujer desnuda* (1996), with the assistance of codirector Isabel Tardán.[13]

In the wake of *salinismo*'s boom of women filmmakers, Berman and Tardán's movie is a highly refreshing cultural artifact, a fast-paced humorous narrative that stands in stark contrast with the slow tempo favored by Novaro and Rotberg. This is perhaps because both Tardán and Berman were outsiders to the Mexican film scene. Berman had made her name as a playwright and novelist, and *Entre Villa y una mujer desnuda,* which opened in 1993, became an unprecedented box office success and enjoyed a two-year run in Mexico City's theater scene, a feat rarely achieved by Mexican plays. Meanwhile, Isabel Tardán was an accomplished television producer whose work in landmark *telenovelas* in the late 1980s and early 1990s as well as in major advertising campaigns gave her an instinct for the kind of commercial media that was absent from the projects of directors like Novaro or Cortés. The combination of Berman and Tardán's experiences produced a groundbreaking film in the landscape of the mid-1990s: *Entre Pancho Villa y una mujer desnuda* is a meeting point between Berman's deft understanding of the contradictions within neoliberal feminism and Tardán's ability to appeal to audiences formed in the emerging mediascapes. By virtue of this, *Entre Pancho Villa y una mujer desnuda* is a landmark film that ultimately broke through the nostalgia that plagued both the political cinema produced in the arc between *Rojo amanecer* and *Fibra óptica,* and the work of *salinismo*'s women filmmakers.

Entre Pancho Villa y una mujer desnuda focuses on the relationship between Gina (Diana Bracho), a successful businesswoman, and Adrián (Arturo Ríos), a left-leaning historian and journalist intellectually obsessed with Pancho Villa. Their relationship is casual at the beginning, depicted mostly as cycles of Adrián showing up at Gina's house, having passionate sex with her, and disappearing for a long time. The film's plot unfolds when Gina expresses her need for a more committed relationship, which leads her to break up with Adrián and to find a younger suitor, Ismael. As Adrián loses his dominating role in the relationship, Pancho Villa (Jesús Ochoa) appears next to him and advises him on how to restore his masculine power. Not surprisingly, most criticism of Berman's work pays more attention to the play than to the film and gives a predominant role to issues of gender and feminist subjectivity. The play has been read as a contradictory collage of various representations of femininity (Rogers), as a representation of a shift in the balance of gender-based power (Wehling), and as a rewriting of the "mythic family" of a nation through the reinscription of women erased by a masculinized history (Magnarelli 145–70). The film, meanwhile, has been discussed as constructing a feminist gaze and spectatorship in the context of representing gender violence (Forcinito 211–22). While gender issues are undoubtedly crucial to understanding Berman's work, in the play's translation to film the political implications of its narrative and its formal stake vis-à-vis cinema by women in the earlier part of the decade become just as relevant. In particular, I would contend that the crucial issue in both the film and the play is class. While María Novaro and Dana Rotberg opted to tell stories of working-class and *lumpen* women, Berman and Tardán's protagonist is a member of the upper class privileged by neoliberalism, the owner of a *maquiladora*.

Gina thus represents an important displacement in class subjectivity in female cinematic characters, akin to the one performed by romantic comedies vis-à-vis the creative class. Rather than focusing on the women left behind by neoliberal economic policy, *Entre Pancho Villa y una mujer desnuda* constructs a farcical upper middle-class world where Gina's ambiguous relationship to her sexual liberation—as a divorcée and as a woman trying to transform her occasional lover into a more committed partner—is framed by the fact that her direct participation in the neoliberal economy is the very condition of possibility of her gender agency. In other words, Gina's two lovers, Adrián and Ismael, symbolize the upper middle-class conflict between the allegiance to the nationalist-leftist ideals of the 1960s generation (represented by Adrián and literally embodied by Pancho Villa) and the privileges and social emancipations brought about by the rise of the creative class (to which Ismael, a graphic designer, belongs). In post-1988 Mexico, *Entre Pancho Villa y una mujer desnuda* turns this allegory into a political film on two levels: the gender politics of a middle-aged woman dealing with the pitfalls and desirability of Mexican traditional masculinity and the choice of the upper middle class between the preservation of the postrevolutionary status quo and the promise of neoliberal modernization. I would even go as far as to suggest that Adrián and Ismael could be read allegorically as the choice in the 1988 presidential election, between Cuauhtémoc Cárdenas, the son of the foundational figure of left-wing populism in Mexico, and Carlos Salinas de Gortari, the PRI candidate running on a platform of economic modernization. This is not to say that Berman intended this parallel. Rather, the point is that Gina's objects of desire are a representation of the political and ideological conundrum faced by the upper middle class in Mexico, between the nostalgia for a nationalist past and its seductive ideologies and the promise of a more dynamic future that will require giving up some of one's passion for the present. In staging this tension, Berman and Tardán create a radical turn in Mexican political cinema, leaving behind the leftist stances held by directors like Retes and the fascination with the marginalized that dominated Mexican cinema all the way back to Buñuel's *Los olvidados*.

This turn toward the upper middle class as a vantage point for Mexican social cinema may not be surprising, given the decline of Mexicanist ideologies and the emergence of the private exhibition system discussed in the previous two chapters. Nevertheless, the erasure of the working classes carried out by this new class perspective is a key element that distinguishes Mexican cinema of the 1990s compared to the other two major commercial film industries in Latin America, those of Argentina and Brazil. According to Joanna Page, documentary realism was a major tradition in mid-1990s Argentine cinema, balancing a skeptical view of the role of social art in the contemporary world with a nostalgic perspective on cinematic traditions where such a role was assumed (35). This allowed for the rise of major directors, like Adrián Caetano and Pablo Trapero, who focused on the declining working class and marginalized youth, much like María Novaro and Dana Rotberg had done in Mexico during the earlier part of the decade. In addition, Argentine cinema, as Gabriela Copertari reminds us (23), remained embedded in a cultural process highly concerned with the legacy of the dictatorship and its ties with the neoliberal project. Thus, Argentine filmmakers had a sense of social responsibility different from their Mexican counterparts, since Mexico had a less traumatic recent past compared to the Dirty War (even considering 1968), and its middle-class audiences had no unifying cultural trope for radical politicization.

In the case of Brazil, the commercial cinema of the 1990s remained solidly connected with the populist traditions inherited from the 1960s. The most successful film of the decade, Walter Salles's *Central do Brasil* (1998), not only maintains the contrast between the *sertão* (Brazil's vast hinterlands) and the city as a major theme, but also constructs its narrative through melodrama. This is also the case of films on the *favelas,* like Fernando Meirelles's *Cidade de Deus* (2002), another international success. One could even look to smaller Latin American traditions such as that in Colombia, where directors like Víctor Gaviria constructed a unique style of representing the marginalized. In contrast to these cinemas, the aesthetic turning point constructed between 1993 and 1996 by a triad of crucial movies—*El callejón de los milagros* in the exhaustion of Mexicanism, *Cilantro y perejil* in the rise of middle-class romantic comedies, and *Entre Pancho Villa y una mujer desnuda* in the context of political cinema—was based precisely on the departure from the worn-out social cinema traditions inherited from the 1970s and 1980s. Even *El callejón de los milagros,* with its vague subtext of emigration (discussed in Chapter 1), is ultimately a highly aestheticized representation of the working class, lacking the social edge developed by Gaviria or Caetano.

In the context of this chapter's theme, the 1993–1996 generation of films is not only small in number (fewer than ten movies per year), but also highly uninterested in social cinema. The majority of productions in those years could be classified into three categories: the final films of the "cinema of solitude" tradition (the most notable of which is Alberto Isaac's *Mujeres insumisas* [1994]), films that reflect the final years of Televicine as the major force of commercial cinema geared to the working classes (represented by the *La risa en vacaciones* candid-camera film saga), and the rare but major films by the directors working on new paths for Mexican cinema (*El callejón, Cilantro y perejil,* and *Entre Pancho Villa,* along with movies like Daniel Gruener's stylized horror movie *Sobrenatural* [1996] and Ignacio Ortiz's poetic *La orilla de la tierra* [1994]). Tellingly, the only major IMCINE project dealing with the inequalities of neoliberalism at the time, Juan Carlos Valdivia's *Jonás y la ballena rosada* (1994), is in fact a Bolivian movie to which Mexico only provided coproduction resources.[14]

In this context, *Entre Pancho Villa y una mujer desnuda* became a hinge between the leftist political films of the earlier part of the decade and the middle-class-oriented Mexican cinema of the latter part. Aesthetically, Berman and Tardán's film is much closer to the emerging paradigm of the late 1990s romantic comedy than to any of their early 1990s precursors. Regardless of Adrián's leftist aspirations, the working and marginalized social sectors are completely absent and, in the style of Cuarón's *Sólo con tu pareja,* most of the film takes place in self-enclosed Mexico City spaces: Gina's apartment, her business office, a diner, an empty park at night, and so on. In analyzing this use of urban space and the fact that Gina owns a *maquiladora,* David William Foster suggests that Mexico City denizens in the movie "live in disdainful separation from the rest of Mexico" (148). One could take this contention further and point out that Gina is also removed from her *maquiladora,* which we never actually see in the movie. This is not trivial, and we can recall here Celestino Deleyto's point, discussed in Chapter 2, that romantic comedy constructs a "space outside history (but close to it)" (30). Berman and Tardán deftly use self-enclosed Mexico City spaces in a way that never altogether erases the surrounding historical reality for the spectator while preserving the class isolationism of the main characters. Foster, for instance, underscores the fact that the *maquiladora* owned by Gina is located in Ciudad Juárez, which happens to be in Pancho Villa's native state (148). Furthermore, one may also note that the only scenes where rural Mexico and poverty appear take place in the flashbacks to Pancho Villa's past, a space that remains fundamentally disconnected from the present. In her reading of the play, Priscilla Meléndez has suggested that Villa, along with other historical figures deployed across the plot and dialogue, are "textual and intertextual, historical and metahistorical beings who try to embody themselves and interact in Mexico's present and future" (533; my translation).

In these terms, Berman and Tardán create a self-referential space for their characters' romantic interactions—a "space outside history," in Deleyto's terms—under siege by a history that never completely leaves the present. While critics like Maricruz Castro Ricalde have argued that Villa is more relevant here as an icon of masculinity than as a historical figure (11), I would contend that the political implications of choosing Villa as Adrián's imaginary mentor are quite significant. Despite his constant political grandstanding and his complaints regarding the betrayal of the revolution and the defeat of left-wing social movements, Adrián is fully absorbed into the bourgeois middle-class lifestyle: his intellectual performances take place mostly in electronic and commercial media, much like the members of the creative class working in advertising. In addition, Gina, his lover, represents the type of entrepreneurship that would be anathema to any nationalist left-wing intellectual. Villa's ghostly interventions are indeed focused on trying to get Adrián to dominate Gina, but the truly important point is their utter failure. In a crucial scene, Adrián's final attempt to regain Gina's love fails, and when Gina rebukes Adrián, Pancho Villa is shot and killed. In other words, Villa's attempt to reinscribe himself in the present utterly fails, and the victory belongs not only to Gina's ability to hold her own against Adrián's alpha masculinity, but also to neoliberal enterpreneurship's victory over national-revolutionary ideals. Villa's standing in literary and cultural tradition as the untamable emancipatory force that resists the revolution's institutionalization is essential to the film's ends.[15] As such, his defeat is a meaningful allegory, illustrating a paradox: Gina's ability to transcend gender inequality in love and sexuality is accompanied by her successful position in the *maquila* industry, which was itself constructed upon the very undoing of the social conquests of the Mexican Revolution and on the labor exploitation of the lower-class women who make up a considerable part of its labor force. The point here is that, insofar as the romantic conflicts and self-enclosed spaces of the middle class trump the ideological legacies of revolutionary nationalism, *Entre Pancho Villa y una mujer desnuda* creates a language in which the political can be fully subject to the affective and social mores of Mexico's privileged citizens. Unlike the historical films discussed in Chapter 1, and unlike the films of Gabriel Retes or Juan Carlos de Llaca, *Entre Pancho Villa y una mujer desnuda* uses farce and comedy to highlight the fact that there is no possible or desirable nostalgia for the lost emancipatory ideas of the past. This is most strongly emphasized by the fact that the only nostalgic character in the film is also the most demonized: Adrián.

Even though he was originally written for the stage, Adrián is a character who fits perfectly in the canon of emasculated masculine leads of 1990s Mexican cinema. Like *En el aire*'s Alberto, Adrián is a man of the Left whose intellectual work embodies the gradual erosion of 1960s and 1970s ideals. His emphatic masculinity is not unlike Lauro's in *El bulto* in that it is a way to compensate for his lack of social relevance in a country that is transcending the revolutionary ideologies to which he remains faithful as a journalist and a historian. The fact that both Lauro and Adrián are journalists is relevant to understanding these films' articulations of emerging political ideologies in the 1990s. As Sallie Hughes has documented, journalism underwent major changes during the neoliberal period, going from a monolithic, authoritarian media institution to a "hybrid" system encompassing "civic, market-driven and adaptive authoritarian media organizations" (10). Lauro is presented essentially as a man formed in the civic model; he sees the newspaper as a principled media organization. Adrián's case is more complex, as he seems to be negotiating with the different aspects of the new hybrid model. Throughout the movie, we see Adrián expressing his views through the written word and electronic media, making it clear that his preeminence as an intellectual, not unlike many major Mexican intellectuals of the 1990s, depends on his ability to negotiate these new media landscapes. Adrián's project on Villa is one of Hughes's hybrids: it is a civic-oriented subject of inquiry trying to recover the old political values, but these are only valuable insofar as Villa is an easily commoditized and therefore oversimplified figure. In fact, the film preempts the idealization of Villa's political value in the very first scene, one that is not present in the play. Gina and Ismael sit in a dark room, watching footage of Villa riding a horse toward the camera. As Villa rides, we hear Gina rhythmically moaning until she reaches what seems like an orgasm and says, "So much virility! It is the perfect representation of my relationship with Adrián." Gina's inability to read any politics into Villa by privileging his virility, followed by Jesús Ochoa's brilliant and farcical representation of the revolutionary general, casts Adrián's *villismo* as politically empty, reduced to a masculinity unable to assert itself in Mexican contemporaneity. In the middle of his fallout with Gina, we see Adrián making ideological concessions. Adrián is confronted in a television debate by two intellectuals who attack him for leaving his *villismo* behind. Adrián argues that, contrary to what he expresses in his book, he feels that only a revolution that reaches women and changes private life is truly democratic. The interesting issue here is that democracy emerges only as the figure of Villa retreats from the scene: the radical revolutionary ideas embedded in the figure of Villa during much of the twentieth century are no longer valid. A true democracy is possible only when *villismo* retreats. Adrián's *villismo* receives a paradoxical coup de grâce when we learn, through one of his former wives, that his book is for sale in supermarkets: the revolutionary general lives only as a commodity in the neoliberal cultural marketplace. In these terms, the film succeeds in turning Villa into a commodity as much as Adrián's book does so in both the film and the play: in the context of a Mexican modernity seeking to escape its revolutionary legacy, Villa can only be a comic character or a piece of cultural merchandise available for empty consumption.[16] As unlikable as he is, behind the parody of Mexican *machismo* embodied in him, Adrián represents, like Lauro and Alberto, the futility of the ideals dissolved by neoliberal modernization. In his most telling lines in the film, Adrián tells his daughters that one of them will be elected president of Mexico. All four girls reply enthusiastically that they want to become president, to Adrián's exasperation. He silences them angrily and concludes: "You will surely sell the country to North America." The decline of masculinity is the decline of the revolution, and Adrián's attempt to become more democratic and less of a *macho* is, paradoxically, a sign of the defeat of the emancipatory dreams behind revolutionary nationalism.

Berman's play locates the action in Colonia Condesa (160), a meaningful choice given that the professional upper middle class that came to be as a result of neoliberal economics reinvented the neighborhood's social significance. In addition, as Emily Hind points out, Condesa "denotes a live-and-let-live attitude that is at once marginal and increasingly commercial. Hence, Condesa provides a superb backdrop for camp because the idea of spectacle and alterity is one that the neighborhood embraces, at least for those who can pay for it" ("Pita Amor" 152). The choice of Condesa—which is, tellingly, the neighborhood where Berman and many other Mexican intellectuals live—gives the film three important elements: a comedic framework that allows for the construction of a farcical story, a class-determined setting that clearly expresses the social status of the protagonists, and a neighborhood that, unlike the Polanco of *Sexo, pudro y lágrimas,* carries a necessary level of cultural prestige that allows Berman to deconstruct her intellectually pretentious characters. It is important to remember here Celestino Deleyto's point that romantic comedy is not so much a genre in itself, but a narrative device that may be deployed within other genres (38). *Entre Pancho Villa y una mujer desnuda* is, at heart, a farcical romantic comedy consistent with the innovations introduced by the genre in Mexican cinema. Therefore, the Colonia Condesa is part of the generic architecture of the film insofar as the core of the story focuses on the comedy of errors constructed by the triangle between Ismael, Adrián, and Gina. What's important, though, is that romantic comedy here expands into political cinema, and the romantic comedy of errors, as I have tried to show up to this point, grows into a multilayered allegory of Mexico's political and social present from the perspective of the new urban elite.

Berman and Tardán's adaptation of the play into the film includes many telling changes that show both the adjustment of the text into the emerging romantic comedy canon and the highlighting of the story's political undertones at the expense of some of the gender issues raised by the play. Most of the play revolves around interactions between two characters: Gina and Andrea, Gina and Ismael, Gina and Adrián, Andrea and Adrián, and so on. The film introduces many scenes that give Adrián more depth and that tell us more about his ideological fallout: both the television debate and the interaction with his daughters are exclusive to this version. The plot is also based on the irresoluble tension between Adrián's ideology and Gina's role in the new neoliberal economy, which is never truly resolved. The ending delivers this point clearly: an enraged Adrián, followed by a reincarnated Villa, shows up in Gina's apartment. After Adrián confronts her about an abortion she presumably had, Gina ends up running to the bathroom and closing the door, and Adrián and Villa both seem to shoot her from outside through the door. We briefly see an image of Gina with a bullet in her head, but the scene resets to Adrián opening the bathroom door and finding Gina sitting in the bathtub. In the last line of the film, he asks her, "Why won't you marry me?"

This ending is radically different from the play (where Adrián is about to make love to Andrea, but ultimately retreats and tells her that he will never forget Gina) and highlights the inescapable nature of the contradiction that underlies their relationship. This is particularly meaningful if we consider Stuart Day's observation that Andrea is a practical character who ultimately spells out the fact that in order to achieve a change in gender relations we must also give up the positive aspects of Mexican revolutionary ideology. In her analysis of the play, Sharon Magnarelli argues that by removing Gina from the scene and leaving Andrea to interact with Adrián, Berman makes apparent the "breakdown of the mythic family (national and personal)" (169). In contrast, by removing Andrea from the film, this gendered counterpoint to Gina and Adrián is placed in the background and we are left with their reluctance to leave behind that allegorical mythic family. In other words, I believe that the film sacrifices some of the gendered edges of the play in order to give more prominence to the political subtext, by preserving the ambiguous coexistence of neoliberal modernity and revolutionary ideals embodied in Gina and Adrián's relationship. More so in the film than in the play, this is the conflict faced by the social classes represented by the emerging paradigms of Mexican cinema in the mid-1990s.

Entre Villa y una mujer desnuda's adaptation into film illustrates well the changes faced by cinema during the 1993–1996 period, in between the collapse of COTSA and the opening of Cinemark and the other private exhibition chains. The film, like *Cilantro y perejil,* was produced by Televicine, Televisa's production arm, which in itself demonstrates its commercial aspirations. The movie was produced on the heels of the very successful run of the play in Mexican theaters, which guaranteed its attractiveness to middle- and upper-class audiences. In this, *Entre Pancho Villa y una mujer desnuda* precedes the commercial strategies that made *Sexo, pudor y lágrimas,* another play adapted into film, the breakout movie of Mexican commercial cinema in the latter part of the decade. Also, like *Cilantro y perejil, Entre Pancho Villa* uses a very identifiable actress, Diana Bracho, who has had a highly successful career both in television and film and belongs to one of the major family dynasties in

Mexican cinema.[17] In these terms, it is not surprising that the finished product fell so close to the aesthetic of the romantic comedy, given that *Sólo con tu pareja* had already constructed a viable pathway and that *Cilantro y perejil* was following a similar blueprint of love stories and humor as sources of a film language attractive to middle-class audiences. *Entre Pancho Villa y una mujer desnuda,* however, remains a unique film, precisely because it was able to reconfigure political discourse as part of the language of Mexican commercial cinema, something that no other major commercial film of the early and mid-1990s had been able to do.

This is not to say that the film's reception was entirely positive; indeed, some critics attacked its politics. Jorge Ayala Blanco, for instance, laments: "Certain tangential, yet quite perverse, political discourses articulate themselves in the male character's verborrhea" (*La fugacidad* 374; my translation). Ultimately, Ayala Blanco dismisses the film as a poor representation of "turned-on femininity" (*feminidad prendida*) accompanying *Cilantro y perejil*'s "reheated femininity" (*feminidad recalentada*). Ayala Blanco's reading is telling partly because he places both movies within a paradigm of problematic representations of womanhood in romantic movies. However, it is even more telling that, in his reading, as in many readings of both the play and the film, the political point is usually presented as an afterthought, or at the very least as a secondary consideration to the film's presentation of gender issues. I would say that *Entre Pancho Villa y una mujer desnuda* is perhaps more meaningful as a political movie than as a feminist one. Within the ideological frameworks of Mexican cultural feminism, Gina is much less layered than the women constructed by any María Novaro film. However, the portrayal of Adrián as a failed leftist intellectual and of Pancho Villa as an empty political myth opens a fundamental door in Mexican commercial cinema: the ability to reflect the views of an emerging audience facing the exhaustion of the Mexican revolutionary project and its equivocal relationship with a neoliberal promise about to face its first major pitfall (i.e., the 1994 crisis). *Entre Pancho Villa y una mujer desnuda*'s ultimate importance is in its radical redefinition of what constitutes the presence of politics in Mexican cinema: it shows the exhaustion of openly political movies and succeeds by embedding political messages into forms of cinema (like the romantic comedy) previously unsuited to it within the Mexican tradition. This results partly from Berman and Tardán's outsider status: this was their first and only venture as directors, and they would work again in cinema only as scriptwriters for Carlos Carrera's *Backyard/El traspatio* (2009).[18] By introducing major generic and thematic changes developed by Berman's work in theater, and stylistic adjustments from Tardán's work in television, *Entre Pancho Villa y una mujer desnuda* opens the space for a viable political cinema within the parameters of the new commercial cinema. Two of the most important films of contemporary Mexican cinema emerge from this space: Fernando Sariñana's *Todo el poder* (2000) and Luis Estrada's *La ley de Herodes* (1999). I will devote the remainder of this chapter to them.

The Myth of the Citizen: *Todo el poder* and the Politics of Fear

Discussing *Todo el poder* as a political film, perhaps one of the most important in the last twenty years in Mexico, implies an understanding of the deep transformations experienced by the notion of political culture in the mid-1990s. While political film remained scarce in the second part of the decade, Fernando Sariñana was able to craft a production within both the aesthetic parameters of commercial cinema and the political parameters created by the ideologies of the Mexican urban middle classes in the wake of 1994. Cultural producers, including some of the directors discussed in this chapter, remained skeptical of the inequalities within the neoliberal political and economic model, but the Salinas administration was widely praised in political and social circles. As Alexander Dawson documents, "Salinastroika" achieved major reforms and seismic shifts in political and social structures, mostly through its success in dismantling the labor and rural organizational structures, which constituted the PRI's popular base (23–45). Political scientists read the Salinas reforms as a "technocratic revolution" that, in the words of Miguel Ángel Centeno, achieved "democracy within reason." The basis of this transition was the ability of the educated elite to topple the social leaderships inherited by the postrevolutionary bureaucratic structure. This elite, Centeno writes, shared two crucial elements: "the extent to which it is dominated by persons from extremely selective social strata and the increasing homogenization of the elite as a whole" (144). This explains in part the emergence of the upper middle classes as privileged subjects of representation in cinema, since characters like Berman's Gina and Serrano's Miguel are defined by the social values and educational backgrounds of the technocratic elite. The twist that would allow for politicization in the spheres of the middle class was the failure of this model, as embodied by the economic and political crises of 1994.

Jorge Castañeda has described 1994 as "the Mexican shock," a year when the narratives of success and modernization put forward by the Salinas de Gortari administration collapsed. The sequence of events in that ominous year remains staggering in hindsight: the Zapatista revolt in Chiapas; the assassinations of Luis Donaldo Colosio, the PRI presidential candidate, and José Francisco Ruiz Massieu, the Mexican equivalent of the U.S. Speaker of the House; and the collapse of the Mexican peso in December. They deeply undermined the legitimacy achieved by the technocratic elite. Notably, though, the only change that did not take place in 1994 was electoral. Ernesto Zedillo, a leading figure of the PRI's technocratic wing, was ultimately elected president and ruled Mexico for the remaining part of the decade. The result was a state of political and social uncertainty, where, as Castañeda suggested in 1995, it was unclear whether Mexico was in a process of transition, in crisis, or in a new state of affairs in between the two (241–54). The setbacks to the neoliberal model of development were complemented by a political void in the Mexican left wing. Cárdenas's defeat in the 1988 election, the persecution of left-wing politicians and journalists under Salinas, and the dismantling of labor and rural organizing structures led to meager electoral results for Cárdenas in 1994: he wound up in third place, with only 17 percent of the vote. This situation was exacerbated by the general disarray of the Latin American Left in the wake of the fall of the Berlin Wall, which led many former leftists, Castañeda among them, to speak of a "utopia unarmed" that would be based on democratic transition rather than radical political change.[19]

While a more detailed discussion of the political shift would distract me too much from my subject, I would like to underscore two major consequences of 1994 in the construction of the Mexican polity, since they are essential to understanding *Todo el poder* and its impact on political cinema.[20] First, the disenchantment of the middle classes with the ruling of the technocratic elite and the retreat of officialized apparatuses of social organization, along with the concept of democracy as the ideal to attain in Mexico, led to the emergence of "civil society" as a major myth of social organization among educated, middle-class citizens. In cinema, this development was essential because it created a symbolic distinction between the middle professional class (what I have called the "creative class" since Chapter 2) and the upper social echelons. "Civil society," in other words, was in part the emergence of a tension within the elite, turning the professional and creative classes against the business and political classes. Many political discourses about civil society in Mexico were enunciated by the former as a critique of the latter. In this context, Leonardo Avritzer argues that the process behind the formation of a civil society in Mexico had two defining traits: "(1) the dispute with the authoritarian regime regarding the rules of the political game, in particular, the determination of electoral rules, and (2) the dispute with the regime regarding the forms of social organization and state and society mediation" (43). This description clearly shows how the civil society process favored the social agendas of the educated middle classes, given that electoral participation and social organization in the 1990s were two major areas of development among the intelligentsia. In the context of Mexican cinema, I would contend that *La ley de Herodes* and *Todo el poder* succeeded because they were each able to articulate a narrative about one of these areas (electoral reform and social organization respectively). In both cases, the movies resonated strongly with the urban middle classes' disenchantment with the political and social setbacks faced by the neoliberal political and economic elite. I will discuss *La ley de Herodes* and the issues of electoral politics in the following and final section of the chapter. In the meantime, it is important to keep in mind that the notion of "civil society" was omnipresent in the Mexican cultural sphere throughout the 1990s.

The two leading intellectual magazines, Octavio Paz's *Vuelta* and Héctor Aguilar Camín's *Nexos*, provided forums for the translation and discussion of major figures in transnational theories of civil society, including Norberto Bobbio, Jürgen Habermas, and Edgar Morin.[21] In addition, many leading figures of the civil society movement emerged from these publications and attained major media exposure, through television, radio, and print, as well as positions in the Federal Electoral Institute and in local and federal administrations: Enrique Krauze, José Woldenberg, Castañeda, and Santiago Creel are among the most important. The idea of a self-organizing society in Mexico had begun to take shape and gain momentum following the failures of the State to respond to the 1985 earthquake, and acquired increasing importance as the government gradually retreated from crucial areas of public life, such as telecommunications, as well as from cinema itself.[22] This, of course, is directly connected to the neoliberal process in that civil society is ultimately a space in which the market intervenes in social organization. As John Ehrenberg points out in his discussion of Habermas, "the commodification of the public sphere stands behind the 'legitimation crisis' of a political order that is unable to provide the rational justification for state power that it once could" (221). As the Mexican State lost legitimacy in the wake of the 1994 shock, the situation created an incentive for the middle class to use culture as a language to construct alternative ideals of social organization and mediation, a process in which media plays a central role.[23]

The second issue relevant to understanding the role of cinema in this process is the emergence of cultural consumption as an alternative framework for social articulation and citizenship in neoliberal times. Here we can return once again to Néstor García Canclini's *Consumers and Citizens* for guidance. According to García Canclini, "sociospatial" identities defined by territories (like national identity) must be "complemented by a sociocommunicational definition" that recognizes "the locations of information production and communications that play a role in shaping and renewing identities" (29). Cinema is a fundamental vehicle in this process since, as I discussed in Chapter 2, access to it became restricted to a socioeconomic elite able to afford the new admission prices. This inscribed cinema into one of the "sociocultural circuits" identified by García Canclini's work, the "culture of elites," which is "not known nor appropriated by the entirety of society." García Canclini adds that, in recent decades, the culture of elites "has been integrated into international markets and circuits of valuation" (30). While García Canclini refers in this passage mostly to literature and visual arts, it is important to note that cinema in the 1990s belongs to the culture of elites not because of any particular educational requirement for access, but by a mere fact of economics.

García Canclini's larger claim is that consumption redefines citizenship in the age of NAFTA, but an even more fundamental point is that such citizenship can be exercised only by those with the ability to access consumption. The resulting process, of which *Todo el poder* is the most important example within Mexican cinema, is the creation of limited social identities bound both by class (middle and upper sectors) and by nonnational sociospatial demarcations (e.g., cities, Mexico City privileged among them) defined by the economic dynamics and social practices of moviegoing. Following García Canclini's research, Lucila Hinojosa Córdova identifies six models of consumption relevant to cinema. Three of these models operate within political cinema in Mexico: "consumption as the place where social classes and groups compete for the appropriation of social product"—that is, where the unequal structure of economic production becomes a factor in the distribution of symbolic and material goods; "consumption as a place of social differentiation and symbolic distinction among groups," which allows for the creation of a middle and upper class distinct from all other social sectors within the nation; and "consumption as a system of integration and communication," where social subjects articulate common identities through everyday practice and meaning exchanges (70–71; my translation). In the context of post-1994 political cinema, this translates into the emergence of commercial films subject to a consumer market, as opposed to films requiring State subsidy as an indispensable condition to exist and circulate. In these newer commercial films, the work responds to the social identities of an audience newly segmented by class, and its audience finds forms of social and identity articulation that manage to be different from the larger social groups defined by national identity and yet have enough similarities to constitute a common and identifiable social experience.

Todo el poder is a film where the ideology of civil society and the possibility of consuming a new class identity coincide. The film tells the story of Gabriel (Demián Bichir), a failed documentary filmmaker who has become a serial victim of petty crime. Gabriel is in the process of shooting a documentary on crime when, during an interview in the park, his camera is stolen by a lower-class couple. The action of the film is unleashed when Gabriel borrows his wealthy former wife's Grand Cherokee SUV to take his daughter to an event. The night before the event, he goes to a restaurant to meet his friends. An armed squad robs the place and steals the Grand Cherokee during their escape. Fed up with being a victim and with the police's inability to solve the thefts, Gabriel decides to pursue the criminals himself when he spots them driving the Grand Cherokee on the city streets. As the film continues, Gabriel learns that the criminal gang has close ties both with the police and with the higher echelons of Mexico City's security apparatus.

This description already shows many of the relevant elements that place the movie within Mexican political cinema in particular and 1990s cinema in general. Gabriel is a character clearly inscribed in the tradition of cinematic representations of the creative class. However, unlike Cuarón's Tomás Tomás, his work as a creator does not help him achieve any real social status: he is unemployed, and dependent both on the wealth of his former wife, Tere (Claudia Lobo), and the generosity and friendship of Octavio (José Carlos Rodríguez), an upper-class businessman with a considerable fortune and vast political connections. Unlike *Entre Pancho Villa y una mujer desnuda,* where a member of the creative class (Adrián) inhabits the same social space as a member of the business elite (Gina), Gabriel clearly belongs to a different social reality than Tere and Octavio, and his ability to interact with the elite never results from personal achievement. A key moment to understanding Gabriel's social position comes earlier in the film, when his pre-teen daughter, Valentina (Ximena Sariñana), uses her mother's connections to get her father a job interview at an advertising agency. Gabriel reluctantly goes to the agency, where he learns that he would be required to work on a new publicity campaign for Luna (Juan Carlos Colombo), Mexico City's new head of public safety. When Gabriel realizes that the plan is to advertise a decline in crime rates, he flatly refuses to participate in the campaign and storms out of the meeting. The world of advertising is thus presented not as a space for Gabriel's integration into civil society, but as an entity complicit with the State's inability to address the crime problem. Gabriel's principled rejection of the job offer signals a middle-class subjectivity that rejects the purported economic benefits of neoliberal modernization (of which advertising is a major symbol, as we have seen), thanks to the failure of the business and political elite to address the concerns of "average citizens."

This social position is also illustrated by Gabriel's love interest, Sofía (Cecilia Suárez), an aspiring actress and a part-time insurance saleswoman whom Gabriel meets at the advertising agency. Unlike Tomás and Clarisa in *Sólo con tu pareja,* Gabriel and Sofía register the unemployment and underemployment faced by the urban middle classes in the wake of the 1994 crisis.[24] This, in turn, highlights their different social position from those in the higher social echelons, whose wealth and privileges were left unscathed. Clearly, Gabriel and Sofía's relationship follows the symbolic economy of the 1990s romantic comedy at many levels. They are both quirky members of the creative class, and they are played by two actors identifiable by their work in the genre: as readers may remember from Chapter 2, Bichir played the leading role in *Cilantro y perejil* and the role of outcast Tomás in *Sexo, pudor y lágrimas,* the same film in which Suárez gained national fame through her portrayal of abused wife Andrea. In casting them, Sariñana not only appeals to their newly gained commercial prestige in the wake of *Sexo, pudor y lágrimas*' box office success, but also to the symbolic world of middle-class characters constructed by previous movies. Here, Sariñana uses this romantic comedy core to create both humor and affective identification (the two crucial elements of the genre) in order to bring audience members into an expanded world where the "space outside history" is interrupted by the threat of crime and unemployment.

In fact, Gabriel and Sofía fall in love with each other partly because their nonconformity with Mexico's contemporaneity results from a similar inability to integrate themselves into the pressures of neoliberal modernization. When Sofía auditions at the advertising agency, she flawlessly reproduces a scene from the movie *Thelma and Louise*. When she is done, the person in charge of casting scoffs at her and tells her that the audition was for a makeup commercial. Sofía, like Gabriel, tries to be a member of the creative class through self-expression (acting, directing), but the only viable job is advertising, a sellout. Furthermore, it is also telling that Sofía's real job, as an insurance salesperson, is not usually identified with the middle class: in Mexico, it is a job with no security and no benefits and with a lower income compared to most professional jobs. The fact that Sofía drives an old VW Jetta that keeps breaking down, in contrast to Tere's brand-new Grand Cherokee, favored by the upper classes, states this situation clearly.[25] We do not even see Sofía succeed in selling a policy successfully: she spends the whole movie receiving phone calls from the same potential customer.

The middle class in *Todo el poder* is under siege not only from economic and social uncertainty but also from a dysfunctional and corrupt government represented by two characters, Luna and the police lieutenant "Elvis" Quijano (Luis Felipe Tovar). Tovar's characterization of Quijano makes him one of the most memorable characters in contemporary cinema: he is an officer of working-class origins defined by his constant impersonation of Elvis Presley. When we first meet him, in the aftermath of the restaurant robbery, he embodies the stereotypes of incompetence and sleaziness associated with Mexico City's police. He strolls into the scene singing Presley's "Don't Be Cruel," and mocking the restaurant patrons (who had been forced to strip to their underwear by the thieves). Later on, when Gabriel follows the Grand Cherokee and forces Quijano to act, the police commander blames the crime on people that clearly were not involved, and the SUV appears to be found. As the plot progresses, we learn that Quijano is in fact the leader of the criminal gang and that they all work under Luna's command. In the symbolic world of *Todo el poder*, the State is mostly a failed police institution that has abdicated its duty to provide security for the middle and upper classes. An important point here is that the State's other duties—social justice, welfare, and so on—are also completely absent in this portrayal. This is not trivial if one considers that, in 1997, Cuauhtémoc Cárdenas was elected mayor of Mexico City, after running on a platform of social justice and development. In the world of *Todo el poder,* though, crime is not a result of social inequality, but of individual and institutional corruption. Furthermore, the State is represented here as a perverse alliance between a working class that populates the bureaucracy and the upper class of equally corrupt technocrats. On the one hand, the police station appears here as a sub-world of uneducated individuals. When Gabriel arrives at the police station, he is reluctantly greeted by a secretary visibly annoyed by his interruption. Quijano himself is lower class: his place of leisure is a nightclub called *La mazmorra* (The dungeon), a *fichera* bar where women dance with patrons in exchange for drinks and tokens. The fact that *fichera* bars have a longstanding reputation in Mexican cinema as hangouts for criminals and poor people should be noted here. All the police officers and bureaucrats are marked in many ways as lower in class than Gabriel: these include their patronage of the nightclub, their identifiably uneducated idiolects, their darker skin, and, in the case of Elvis, his unpolished and kitschy attempt at adopting a clearly outdated American culture.

In the end, the film gives Elvis a peculiar coup de grâce, when we learn that Quijano's actual first name is Eleuterio, an identifiably lower-class name.[26] On the other hand, Luna is a member of the plutocracy, a highly educated politician with connections at the highest levels of government and business (he is friends with Octavio), who nonetheless is as complicit in crime as Elvis. The State, then, is a corrupt structure where both the upper and lower classes attack the middle class by interrupting its everyday life with crime. The criminal gang in the movie is a clear example: their heists involve robbing patrons in restaurants and movie theaters, both centers of middle-class economic consumption. At the end of the day, the problem from the perspective of characters like Gabriel is the inability to have a normal, middle-class life.

Latin American cultural theory of the 1990s emphatically addressed the question of the relationship between insecurity and social identities. In her well-known introduction to the landmark critical collection *Citizens of Fear,* Susana Rotker argued that "violence rewrites the conditions of citizenship on the exposed body and creates the *potential victim*" (15; emphasis in the original). In other words, beyond the social identities created by traditional liberal citizenship and consumer citizenship—in García Canclini's words, "Twenty-first-century consumers, eighteenth-century citizens" (*Consumers* 15)—there is a citizenship that emerges from the solidarity among individuals who are joined by a shared sense of vulnerability and victimhood. Rotker contends that this solidarity happens across classes, given that poor people and wealthy people are equally vulnerable to violence (16). Still, as Rotker herself recognizes, the result is the withdrawal of the "practitioner of the city" from public space (19)—namely, of the middle class people who primarily use public space as an instance of socialization (the restaurants, parks, and movie theaters where middle-class denizens are attacked in the movie).

While vulnerability certainly affects all social sectors under neoliberalism, the fact is that the culture of fear privileges the perspective of the middle classes, insofar as cultural enunciation is largely the prerogative of a middle-class intelligentsia and cultural consumption the activity of a middle-class audience. *Todo el poder*'s understanding of this factor underlies its commercial success. Its narrative of State failure and its use of the citizenship of fear to construct the protagonists' subjective position allow the movie to lucidly read the social anxieties experienced by the post-1994 Mexican middle class. The political aspect of the movie thus is based not on taking a clearly contoured ideological position, like directors in the "Third Cinema" paradigm did, but instead on registering a general social discontent defined in opposition to the political sphere at large.

This understanding of politics as a wholesale opposition to the political class is central to the narratives of civil society in Mexico. In their landmark theoretical exploration of the notion of civil society, Jean Cohen and Andrew Arato identify civil disobedience as one of its essential components. Cohen and Arato argue for a notion of civil disobedience based on the performance of "illegal acts . . . that are public, principled and symbolic in character, involve primarily nonviolent means of protest, and appeal to the capacity for reason and the sense of justice of the populace" (387). In Mexico, this type of deed is a favored form of political action by the middle classes, and it is duly represented in *Todo el poder*. In an early scene, right after the restaurant heist, we see Gabriel riding in a taxi on the way to his job interview. During the journey, traffic stops to make way for an anticrime protest. This type of protest was common in the late 1990s, taking the form of peaceful demonstrations blocking major avenues (this is the illegal part), with all the demonstrators dressed in white. In the middle of the demonstration, Gabriel and the taxi driver notice that a robber snatches the purse of one of the demonstrators. After noticing this, the taxi driver produces a gun and tells Gabriel that he has been robbed a few times, but the next time he will kill his assailant.

This particular scene has many implications embedded in it. First, it is a particularly keen example of the class-determined nature of civil society. While the middle-class protestors dress in white and march the streets to appeal to the rationality of the citizenry, the lower-class man driving the taxi (once again we know his social status thanks to his accent and his appearance) opts for violence. However, the scene also comments on the futility of purely symbolic assertions of citizenship. If anything, the citizenship of fear and the consumer citizenship deployed by the film advocate more proactive action to counter the State's corruption. The necessary conclusion to this is Gabriel's gradual transformation into a vigilante. Only if the citizen confronts the State directly, rather than doing so through demonstrations and elections, might the problem be solved. One must nonetheless always keep in mind that *Todo el poder* is a comedy and that Gabriel's odyssey against power is more a fantasy enabled by the ideologies underlying the citizenship of fear than a realistic course of action. Still, Gabriel's cathartic experience creates an affective language to which film audiences may relate. It is telling that, in the end, when Gabriel and Sofía prevail in exposing Luna in the media, all of their other problems are immediately solved. During the credits, we learn that Gabriel is finally free to sell out to the advertising agency and make a fortune shooting commercials, while Sofía achieves a successful acting career. Once the middle class is free from the disruptions caused by crime and violence (namely, by the intervention of upper and lower classes in their social sphere), its members are freely able to pursue their idealized livelihood.

It is important to note that Gabriel and Sofía's affiliation with the creative class is ultimately the vehicle of their liberation. The reason why Gabriel is able to expose Luna is his relentless insistence on videorecording everything. When Luna learns that Gabriel will stop at nothing to expose his criminal gang, he opts to kidnap Octavio as an act of intimidation. To rescue him, Gabriel and Sofía decide to kidnap Luna's wife and their dog—which, in a comic twist, is the one Luna truly wants to recover—and to trick Quijano into confessing Luna's participation by having Sofía exploit his womanizing tendencies. Sofia's acting skills become particularly handy here, since she is able to lure Quijano out of *La mazmorra* and into a hotel room by pretending to be a naïve Northern girl freshly arrived to the city. Quijano unexpectedly dies under Gabriel's interrogation, from a heart condition, but Gabriel's filmmaking skills allow him to produce a video where the policeman appears to confess Luna's involvement in the kidnapping. This video forces Luna to arrange a trade with Gabriel, which is also duly taped. In the end, we hear a radio broadcaster—in fact, Fernanda Tapia, an actual radio personality—announcing the surfacing of a video that shows Luna shooting Quijano's corpse and confessing his involvement in Octavio's kidnapping.

If we follow this plot closely, what stands out is that Gabriel's ability to fight back is fully dependent on his filmmaking skills, just like Sofía's involvement in their investigation, which relies on her acting skills. The underlying premise is the existence of the emancipatory abilities of a social identity thoroughly defined by neoliberal social ideals but self-defined in its opposition to the State. This premise registers a major displacement in cinematic political discourse in Mexico. In *El bulto,* for instance, it is clear that neoliberal reform is an action of the State and that the role of the middle-class intellectual, Lauro, is to resist its modernizing pressures. That is why Lauro's brother, Toño, the man who has fully embraced neoliberal modernization, is a member of the government, while Lauro remains hesitant to the very end before finally accepting the defeat of his political ideals. In *Todo el poder*, the opposite logic prevails: citizens like Gabriel and Sofía are the agents of empowering modernization and reform, and they do so through their individual skills as members of the creative class. Here, the State, both in its bureaucratic and technocratic incarnations, is the main obstacle to overcome.

It is quite revealing that the vehicle for citizen agency in *Todo el poder* is media. Following Sallie Hughes's aforementioned thesis on the transformation of journalism in Mexico, one could say that Gabriel is the perfect example of what she calls a "civic-oriented" journalist, a documentary filmmaker who, against all odds, is able to use media and journalism to expose the pitfalls of power. Media is present throughout the movie. Two of the most popular radio hosts in Mexico City, Fernanda Tapia and Olallo Rubio, constantly intervene in voice-overs, while Gabriel becomes aware of the contradictions between the reality of the police organization and its public face through a fictional newscast called *Visión 2000*, hosted by real-life TV reporter Paola Rojas. By using real and identifiable figures of Mexican media, Sariñana appeals to a notion of civil society where communication is crucial for the mediation between the State, civil society, and social reality. As Jesús Martín-Barbero argues, "the true influence of television resides in the formation of collective imaginaries, that is, a mixture of images and representations of what we live and dream" ("City" 29). By giving real life media and its personalities a major presence in the film, *Todo el poder* becomes aware of the role played by radio and television in the construction of the social perceptions inhabited by the film's characters and by its audiences. Fear is both created and alleviated by the mediations of television and radio. In Fernanda Tapia's first monologue, at the opening of the movie, she asks her purported audience whether they "did well" in "their daily crime experience," a statement that satirically reflects the possibility of being a target every single day. In the ending, Tapia herself announces Luna's fall. By intervening in the space of media through his documentary work—and it is important to remember here Hughes's point that all media in neoliberal Mexico is a hybrid made up of civic-oriented, market, and authoritarian journalism—Gabriel is also able to intervene in the social ideologies about crime. Insofar as "film is one of the most potent analyzers of social transformations and one of contemporary society's most efficient mechanisms of reflexivity" (Reguillo 199), Sariñana's meta-representation of media in the film aptly and reflexively registers the importance of media in the definition of the everyday experience of middle-class subjects. No wonder the creative class is such a privileged subject of post-1994 Mexican cinema: by creating media, one also creates reality.

Beyond its political agendas and paradoxes, it is also important to note here that *Todo el poder*'s use of elements of romantic comedy in dealing with

Mexican social issues results in a significant expansion of the cultural vocabularies deployed by Mexican commercial cinema. In the line traced from *Sólo con tu pareja* to *Sexo, pudor y lágrimas,* including of course *Cilantro y perejil* and *Entre Pancho Villa y una mujer desnuda,* a common technique was the construction of self-referential, enclosed spaces where the middle- and upper-class characters could exist in isolation from the contradictory realities of contemporary Mexico. *Todo el poder,* and Sariñana's cinema at large, creates a more expansive view of urban space, where the working-class neighborhoods become visible, even if they do so in an eschewed and limited form.[27] Precisely because the movie's central narrative is about the invasion of middle-class spaces, Sariñana is able to expand the urban landscape represented in the movie. It is not coincidental that the movie's opening credits roll along an aerial shot of the city, beginning on the edges and arriving at the World Trade Center, which locates the starting point of the action in the middle-class Colonia del Valle neighborhood. Gabriel's quest makes him cross urban class lines in both directions. In his pursuit of the Grand Cherokee, he arrives at an industrial neighborhood where he organizes a stakeout of a warehouse presumably used by the gang to hide stolen goods. Also, in their investigation of Quijano, Gabriel and Sofía venture into *La mazmorra,* a sleazy nightclub where they must go in disguise so as to blend in with the lower-class patrons. This setting is clearly inspired by 1970s *fichera* movies, where sordid bars full of policemen and prostitutes were the centers of the action.[28] On the other end of the class spectrum, the movie takes us to a palatial restaurant where the heist takes place, to Octavio's ostentatious mansion, and to the advertising company, located in a building that is an example of postmodern architecture. In other words, the use of public and open spaces in the film—we also see parks and public landmarks, and the movie spends considerable amounts of time traversing the city's streets—stands in stark contrast with romantic comedy's use of apartments and other private places as its privileged settings. *Todo el poder* opens up a new cartography or urban interaction that, as I will discuss in Chapter 4, will be essential for the representation of Mexico City in the transnationalized films of Alfonso Cuarón and Alejandro González Iñárritu.

A final point to be made regarding *Todo el poder* is that it expands the very notion of the middle class in cinema, particularly through certain key uses of cultural languages to frame it. As I mentioned in my discussion of *Sexo, pudor y lágrimas* in Chapter 2, the film soundtrack had become essential not only in the promotion of commercial movies, but also in creating thematic identities. *Todo el poder* uses the soundtrack in a way that emphasizes middle-class culture as countercultural and as a site to contest the neoliberal myth of progress and social peace.[29] The movie opens with El Gran Silencio's "Dormir soñando," a fast-paced ska piece where the lead singer raps about life's uncertainty. A little later in the movie we hear Manu Chao's "Clandestino," a song with hippie undertones, which claims that everyone is ultimately outside of the law.[30] The rest of the soundtrack is made up of songs by experimental and confrontational alternative bands such as Molotov, Plastilina Mosh, Ozomatli, and Azul Violeta, all of them quite successful in middle-class circles and characterized either by a nonconformist social discourse or by their formal questioning of prevailing pop music aesthetics. While Aleks Syntek's contribution to *Sexo, pudor y lágrimas* resulted in a mainstream and attractive form of pop, *Todo el poder*'s soundtrack is a constant reminder of the anger and uncertainty experienced in the everyday life of Gabriel and of the film's intended audience.

In *Performing Rites*, Simon Frith contends that "music constructs our sense of identity through the experiences it offers of the body, time and sociability, experiences which enable us to place ourselves in imaginative cultural narratives" (275). In these terms, a soundtrack like the one constructed by Sariñana is part of a cultural language meant to frame the different aspects that defined the identity of Mexico's late 1990s middle-class: economic and social insecurity, fear, distrust of power, and an ideal based on individual self-expression and creative emancipation through media. Complemented by the use of real-life radio and TV personalities and even by the appearance of Trino Camacho (a famed cartoonist with a strong middle-class following) in the poster art and DVD presentations of the film, Sariñana's film language is constructed upon his ability to create familiar worlds to represent his audience's values and politics.[31] As critic Rafael Aviña points out, the movie achieves a "tone halfway between drama and comedy, not exempt of suspense, which allows the spectator to stand back and have fun while, at the same time, becoming involved in the everyday tragedy of its characters" (122; my translation). Still, Sariñana's political edge is blunted by the limits imposed by the style borrowed from romantic comedy. In the end, the movie's success is due to its creation of an effectively familiar commercial product rather than a fully developed social comment. In the new cinematic world, Luis Estrada is the director who would ultimately succeed in becoming Mexican film's voice of social dissent.

Framing Decomposition: *La ley de Herodes* and the Collapse of Mexican Modernity

In the late 1990s, political Mexican cinema was in full retreat. The withdrawal of overtly political directors either to temporary retirement (like Felipe Cazals and Sabina Berman) or outside commercial circuits (like Retes) severely challenged Mexican cinema's ability to participate in post-1994 Mexico's algid political conversations. Even though *Todo el poder* aptly registered the citizenry's frustration with the ineffectiveness and corruption of the State, its bite was not directed at any of the political parties in contention: the political figures in the film have no clear party affiliation. The film was a diatribe against a vaguely contoured State, rather than an attack on actually existing political forces. This void highlighted the daring political message of Luis Estrada's *La ley de Herodes* when it reached the market. As Misha MacLaird documents (*Aesthetics* 88–90), in an act of unexpected censorship, IMCINE tried to boycott the movie's release, cancelling advance previews and providing a very limited release in which deliberately poor copies were used. This strategy ultimately backfired and propelled *La ley de Herodes* into an otherwise improbable commercial success, achieving box office numbers that added up to over four million dollars. This phenomenon in itself provides meaningful insight into the relationship between culture and the State in a crucial moment of tension between democratic values and the inherited authoritarianism of the Mexican State. However, given that MacLaird provides what in my view is an intelligent and sufficient analysis of this question (88–92), my analysis of Luis Estrada's work will instead focus on his ability to craft a political film, and his contributions to renewing Mexican cinema within a context in which filmmakers were increasingly unwilling or unable to give politics a central role in their work.[32]

La ley de Herodes is a mordacious farce, focused on Juan Vargas (Damián Alcázar), a mediocre bureaucrat recruited to become mayor of a small town called San Pedro de los Saguaros, lost in the middle of the desert. His recruiter is López (Pedro Armendáriz Jr.), the ambitious secretary of the government of an unnamed provincial state. The plot is set not in the contemporary period, but in the late 1940s, during the presidency of Miguel Alemán. We learn at the beginning of the film that the town's majority indigenous population lynched the former mayor after becoming tired of his corrupt management of the town. Vargas originally sees the post as an opportunity to rise through party ranks and to eventually become a congressman. However, when Vargas arrives and contemplates the town's ruinous state, the challenge starts to disappoint and overwhelm him. Facing a lack of economic resources—a result of the previous mayor's exploits and the state government's unwillingness to provide any funds—Vargas starts abusing his legal powers to tax the local population. Ultimately, Vargas falls into the corruption cycle of the town and becomes more corrupt than any other mayor in the past. The controversy surrounding this film rested mostly on Estrada's blunt presentation of all corrupt officials and politicians as members of the very same organizations in charge of Mexico's present. López embodies the PRI's political practices. We see him constantly wearing the party pin on his lapel, and his arguments for drafting Vargas repeatedly tie the country's interests to the party's agenda.

We learn as the movie progresses that López aspires to become the new governor of the state, and when the current governor (Ernesto Gómez Cruz) chooses a different man to run for office, he attempts to organize a murder plot against the new candidate. The movie thus defines the PRI following the public's preexisting perception: as a highly corporatized party where candidates of political office are chosen through the tradition of the *dedazo,* the right of governors and presidents to single-handedly choose their successors.[33] López represents the quintessential PRI politician, a corrupt, power-hungry man whose every action is determined by his political advancement and who acts at the expense of his governing duties. Still, the PRI is not Estrada's sole target. Vargas's nemesis in the town is Dr. Morales, a self-righteous, conservative man and a perennial candidate of the opposition PAN party for the mayoral office. The film initially presents Morales as a man whose Christian values and moral high ground allow him to credibly criticize Vargas. However, when Vargas begins to investigate his opponent for any potentially exploitable weaknesses, he finds credible evidence that Morales is a pedophile and forces him out of town. This critique of the conservative political opposition is furthered through the portrayal of the local priest (Guillermo Gil), who collects bribes from Vargas to purchase a Mercedes Benz and who uses his parishioners' confessions as an instrument of extortion. In other words, the Mexican right wing is portrayed by Estrada as an equally corrupt political apparatus whose vocal and righteous Christianity does nothing to conceal its hypocrisy and ambitions. If one considers that the movie was released the year before the highly anticipated 2000 presidential election, and that the two political parties targeted by the film's satire were bound to be the two most viable options for the ballot, the attempts at censorship and the resonance of the film with audiences are not at all surprising.

While Estrada's story could perfectly well have taken place in the contemporary era, he chose a quite meaningful historical period for his story: the Miguel Alemán presidency (1946–1952). Miguel Alemán spearheaded a major ideological transformation of the postrevolutionary regime. While his predecessor, Manuel Ávila Camacho, veered rightward from the left-leaning path set by *cardenista* populism, which was responsible for the nationalization of the oil industry and the mobilization of labor unions and the peasantry in Mexican party politics, Alemán fully reconfigured the postrevolutionary State and steered it toward a discourse of American-style modernization, with a focus on urban development and a negative stance toward Ávila Camacho's own populism. Furthermore, as Tzvi Medin points out, Alemán is credited with the final institutionalization of the PRI into a strengthened State apparatus cleansed of any traces of its Marxist and labor roots (172). *La ley de Herodes* is constructed upon its ability to present the Alemán presidency as an allegory of contemporary Mexican politics. Daniel Chávez argues that the movie embodies a "new mode of representation" within the traditions of showing the Mexican State on the film screen by presenting forms of political critique "unthinkable" in movies like *El bulto* (134–37). Thus, Estrada's movie shows a frank presentation of the inner workings of the foundational moment of the PRI as a way to suggest that, in the late 1990s, the system still works the same way. This allegory works on different levels. Alemán's claims to modernity are quite similar to the ones made by the Salinas de Gortari and Zedillo administrations in the 1990s. In both cases, the political consolidation and economic legitimacy of the State was based on tilting the scale against the ideas of nationalist populist politicians who, in the wake of the 1988 election, had been forced to leave the PRI and create a new party, the PRD, just like the radical left wing had abandoned the PRI under Alemán to create socialist and communist parties. This shift privileged a capitalistic form of development in favor of the urban middle classes, at the expense of rural areas, which did not benefit from these economic models. Additionally, Estrada's presentation of the PAN follows another achievement of Alemán's presidency, the "institutionalization" of the opposition (Medin 80)—namely, the ability to make opposition parties acquiesce to the rules of the political games. Both the town priest and Dr. Morales are part of the apparatus of corruption in San Pedro de los Saguaros. The priest shows the church's complacent relationship with political power, while Dr. Morales is clearly a critical portrayal of the role of local privileged bourgeoisies in the plight of deeply impoverished towns. *La ley de Herodes'* activation of the *alemanista* past is, ultimately, a clever way to suggest that the PRI and PAN leading the so-called democratic transition are no different from the corporate PRI and the corrupt PAN of the *alemanista* years. The film's spectators, just like its censors, can clearly see that López's PRI and Morales's PAN mirror many traits and practices of their parties' contemporary versions.[34]

A key element in *La ley de Herodes* distinguishes it from most commercial cinema in the late 1990s: its use of *provincia*. One of the underlying trends present in the corpus analyzed so far in this book is the increasing centrality of Mexico City as cinema's privileged setting.[35] This, of course, is directly connected to the rise of the middle class as privileged subject because a disproportionate part of that social sector is concentrated in Mexico City. It also has to do with the type of logic Estrada is getting at—namely, with the fact that neoliberal modernization privileges urban areas. Films like *La ley de Herodes* must simultaneously face three realities: that the economic and institutional structures of cinema tend to grow out of Mexico City, that Mexico City's sizable middle class is the core audience of Mexican cinema, and that the social imaginary of neoliberalism tends to privilege Mexico City as an example of its modernizing feats. *La ley de Herodes* is the first major disruption of Mexico City's primacy in Mexican cinema. In the film, Estrada puts forward a major expansion of Mexican cinema's cultural geography and, as I will discuss when analyzing the cinema of Carlos Reygadas in Chapter 4, allows for the use of wider regions of Mexico to represent the contradictory nature of the neoliberal modernization project. Furthermore, a fictional rural town like San Pedro de los Saguaros makes an important point within Estrada's farcical representation of modernizing discourses: its 1940s reality is not very different from a contemporary rural town in most provincial states.

In other words, Mexico City is an effective signifier for neoliberal modernization because the city has historically experienced vertiginous transformations in its social tissue and economic structure. In contrast, rural areas live noticeably stagnant realities, isolated from most economic development projects. By displacing Mexican cinema's locus from Mexico City to a town as rural as can be—poor, sustained by barely existing agricultural work, and mostly indigenous—Estrada subverts the cultural mirage constructed by romantic comedy. The sites of modernization and its privileged classes are no longer the sole focus of cinematic attention.

In representing San Pedro de los Saguaros, Estrada's film achieves a major departure from the mainstream of 1990s cinema aesthetics and moves away from the social and political languages constructed by romantic comedy and by films like *Todo el poder*. Critics of *La ley de Herodes* have focused significantly on the issue of cinematic style and on the possible genealogies of the movie within the history of Mexican film. Scholars like Salvador Velazco ("*Rojo amanecer*" 74–78) and Jaime Porras Ferreyra (97) have signaled continuities between Estrada and directors like Retes and Fons, somewhere in the last strands of "cinema of solitude." Liz Consuelo Rangel poses a suggestive comparison with Emilio Fernández's classic movie *Río Escondido* (1947), where iconic actress María Félix plays a teacher who, under the commission of the president, tries to incorporate a rural indigenous town into the national educational system. This, Rangel argues, is a parallel to the state government sending Vargas to San Pedro de los Saguaros, at least insofar as both cases involve a centralized government that seeks to bring a rural town into modernity (64). Rangel also suggests that Estrada borrows stylistically from Fernández, particularly to construct San Pedro's iconography (66). One could even make the case that *La ley de Herodes* has deep roots in all periods of Mexican cinema. Daniel Chávez convincingly proposes that the effectiveness of the film lies in part in its ability to combine familiar cinematic styles: we see, according to his analysis, a picaresque style similar to that of the 1940s, the presence of 1970s *sexycomedia* in the graphic presentation of Vargas's sexual escapades, and the demystifying cultural discourse of the 1990s ("Eagle" 137). All of these analyses suggest a reading of Estrada's film as part of a continuum of national Mexican cinema, and also as a politicized reactivation of stylistic legacies of Mexico's major traditions to work against the grain of the aesthetics created by commercial cinema. While these arguments and comparisons have the merit of pointing out Estrada's major departure from the visual languages of neoliberal cinema, I would hesitate to connect *La ley de Herodes* with pre-1998 Mexican cinematic traditions. Certainly, Estrada plays with some iconographic elements, in part to give historical credence to his 1940s setting, but the film also works through forms of genre and comedic tone alien to Mexican cinematic tradition.

The contrast with *Río Escondido* is apt for illustrating the correlation between modernization and rural Mexico during *alemanismo*. However, it is equally important to remember that Fernández's movie preserves the idea of "the State as the *just guardian* of the Revolution," while its main criticism of the State is not corruption but the State's departure from revolutionary ideals (Tierney 158; emphasis in the original). In contrast, *La ley de Herodes* sees no redeeming value in the State, and its thoroughly farcical tone is designed to evade the type of emotional identification invoked by *Río Escondido*'s melodramatic undertones. This same farcical tone creates an important distance from *engagé* directors of the late 1980s. Unlike Retes and Fons, Estrada clearly avoids the presentation of any alternative to or compromise with the social impasse. Furthermore, the credibility of a film like *Rojo amanecer* is based on its testimonial veracity—on the ability to present a silenced truth through as realist a style as possible. Conversely, *La ley de Herodes* presents a deliberately contrived version of the past, since testimonial reality would be an obstacle to the allegorical connection between *alemanismo* and neoliberalism. It must also be said that Estrada's previous work—the Western *Bandidos* (1991), after which he named his production company, and a fantasy movie called *Ámbar* (1994)—never showed any interest in Mexican cinematic tradition. The only salient feature of those films is their polished technical execution, with a carefully crafted artistic direction that corresponded to the norms of their genre. *La ley de Herodes* is also a deceivingly artful film, with no visual features in common with the gritty styles of 1970s or 1980s "cinema of solitude" or with the visibly cheap production values of *sexycomedia*. Even the rundown reality of San Pedro de los Saguaros is carefully crafted through masterly photography and clever character design. This shows that Estrada transcends the purely political implications of his film and that his work is made effective through a careful reflection on cinematic form.

Luis Estrada follows the path of other Mexican filmmakers in looking toward American independent cinema for languages to transform national film. In Chapter 2, I discussed Steven Soderbergh's influence on Jaime Humberto Hermosillo's *La tarea*, as well as the importance of Woody Allen in understanding Cuarón's work in *Sólo con tu pareja*. In Chapter 4, I will discuss the dialogue between Alejandro González Iñarritu's work and the cinema of Quentin Tarantino as well as the impact of the Sundance phenomenon on the creation of transnationalized Mexican cinema. For the purposes of the present chapter, however, it is important to emphasize that Estrada's work has major affinities with an important paradigm of American independent cinema, one that achieved transnational success in the mid-1990s: the cinema of Joel and

Ethan Coen. While they had major critical recognition thanks to films like *Raising Arizona* (1987) and *Barton Fink* (1991), the movie that truly made them internationally recognized figures was *Fargo* (1996), mostly through Joel Coen's winning the Palme d'Or for Best Director at the 1996 Cannes Film Festival. *La ley de Herodes* shares major elements with *Fargo:* the presentation of the rural interior as backward and violent, the use of violence and a dark sense of humor at the core of its aesthetics, the imperfect and picaresque nature of the main characters, and the corruption that touches upon all the members of a given community.

While Estrada is not quite as mannerist as the Coen brothers, his work's detailed iconography is as carefully constructed as *Fargo*'s wintry dystopia. David Sterritt comments on *Fargo:* "The parodic use of regional speech patterns . . . brings us to one of the most important factors in contextualizing their work: their darkly ambivalent attitude toward American culture and, more particularly, their view of Americana as an expression and embodiment of the human capacities for error, immorality and evil" (22). A similar contention may be made regarding *La ley de Herodes:* its parodic use of *provincia* constructs a Mexican reality characterized by the inescapable corruption of all its inhabitants, from Pek (Salvador Sánchez), the bilingual indigenous man who quietly serves all the mayors at the expense of his own people, to the state governor (Ernesto Gómez Cruz), who treats the government as his personal turf. If the traditions of Mexican cinema identified by the aforementioned critics are present in any way, they work in the same way as the Coen brothers' Americana: as a testament to the evil, corruption, and injustice embedded in national culture.

Christopher Sharrett has pointed out that *Fargo* embodies "the bankruptcy of the postmodern American scene" and its solicitations of "nostalgic, if quizzical yearning for a dubious time of innocence, when the small-town community supposedly represented a culture of mutual support and collective values" (56). Estrada similarly undermines the iconicity of Mexican identity in his film by putting forward a foundational moment of revolutionary nationalism as the source of political corruption. Unlike Retes's and de Llaca's nostalgia for 1960s and 1970s political ideals, Estrada does not find any redeeming factor in history, in the past, or in the Mexican interior: there is no hope in the rural world of San Pedro de los Saguaros. Jerold J. Abrams has suggested that *Fargo* is a mise-en-scène of the "end of modernity" (214), manifested by the lack of subjective depth in the protagonist's detective work and the nihilistic lack of culture throughout the film. *La ley de Herodes* constructs a similarly meaningless world, where the characters are either tricksters who value nothing more than their own enrichment (like secretary López, the priest who uses church contributions to save for a car, or the American man who repeatedly tries to cheat Vargas and ultimately runs off with his wife and the money he stole from the town) or people like Vargas himself, a dim-witted idealist who has no choice but to become corrupt. It is not coincidental that the film's publicity slogan uses a popular phrase to make this point: "El que no tranza, no avanza" (he who does not scam, does not advance). Estrada's masterly twist to Abrams's idea is precisely that, in his film, the end of modernity is not in the contemporary world, but in its very outset, where the promises of a developed Mexico were first formulated. In Estrada's world, Mexican modernity has always been located at its failed ending.

The film's ending presents this point in an unequivocal way, showing that Estrada's true originality lies in integrating the languages of Mexican cinema and American independent cinema into a merciless indictment of the Mexican political system, articulating a type of social critique far more mordant that the one constructed by *Fargo*. When López's plot to assassinate his rival for the candidacy of the state government fails, he flees to San Pedro de los Saguaros and tries to extort from Vargas the money that the mayor had raised through shaking down and overtaxing the town's folk. In so doing, López underestimates Vargas, who kills him after finding out that the American had run away with his wife and the money. In a reprise of the opening scene, Vargas is pursued by a lynch mob and saved in the nick of time by the state police. The film ends by juxtaposing two scenes. On the one hand, we see a man who closely resembles Vargas arriving at San Pedro to be the new mayor, with Pek dutifully waiting for him and holding the exact same conversation Pek had had with Vargas when Vargas first arrived. On the other, we see Vargas as a newly minted congressman, giving a speech to the entire congress and receiving thunderous applause from the other politicians. The message is clear: Vargas's corruption was nothing other than his education in the ways of Mexican politics. Having mastered those ways by killing López and turning the murder into a story about how he bravely confronted the killer of the slain candidate, he is ready to enter the national scene. At the same time, San Pedro de los Saguaros remains stagnant, and once again receives a new government official who closely resembles those who have ravaged the town in the past.

La ley de Herodes proved to be a unique film in Mexican cinema, and to this date, no other political film has quite captured the audience success and cultural relevance achieved by Estrada in 1999. This certainly has to do with the absence of major political films in the 2000s. The very few that attempted a political intervention included Maricarmen de Lara's tale of corruption, *En el país de no pasa nada* (2000); Jorge Ramírez Suárez's political thriller, *Conejo en la luna* (2004); and Felipe Cazals's biopic of activist Digna Ochoa, *Digna, hasta el último aliento* (2004). These films received little critical attention or commercial interest and failed at raising any major interest or controversy. In fact, two documentaries—Luis Mandoki's *Fraude 2006* (2007) and, especially, Roberto Hernández and Geoffrey Smith's *Presunto culpable* (2008)—had a much deeper impact on the audience.[36] Still, the other factor was that Vicente Fox's electoral triumph in 2000, which ended the PRI rule, rendered some of the traditional critique against the PRI meaningless. As a result, cultural producers had to explore new options to construct an effective political critique. Estrada himself was caught in this impasse when he tried to follow up *La ley de Herodes* with *Un mundo maravilloso* (2006). In this film, Estrada ridicules the optimistic portrayal of Mexico under neoliberalism. The film is based on the contradiction between the idea of a Mexico on its way to the First World and the deep misery experienced by nearly half of the country's population. In the movie, Lascuráin (Antonio Serrano), Mexico's minister of economics, proclaims internationally that Mexico has won the war against poverty. His optimism is challenged when a beggar named Juan Pérez (Damián Alcázar) is thought to have attempted suicide as a result of his poverty. A left-wing newspaper promotes the story as a way to shame Lascuráin, which leads him to try to help Pérez in an attempt to rebuild his image. The film develops into a carnivalesque story as Pérez resists Lascuráin's efforts to accommodate him into his narrative of development.

Un mundo maravilloso has many elements that could have led to controversy and success. Estrada's casting choices are brilliant. Besides Alcázar's magnificent performance, the film features Serrano, the director of *Sexo, pudor y lágrimas*, as Lascuráin—a joke that can be read as a critique of Mexican cinema's stylistic allegiance to neoliberalism—and Cecilia Suárez as Rosita, a young girl from the slums. Given Suárez's iconic status as an actress in Mexico's most successful movies, primarily romantic comedies, playing Rosita subverts not only her image but, more importantly, the character economy of Mexican commercial cinema. *Un mundo maravilloso* also features a satire of Mexico's historical discourse of modernity (Lascuráin is modeled after Yves Limantour, Porfirio Díaz's minister of the economy) and a no-holds-barred presentation of slums, which, like San Pedro de los Saguaros, are a stark reminder of the broken promises of Mexican modernization. The ending is even more striking than in *La ley de Herodes*. We see Juan Pérez along with his beggar friends having a holiday dinner in a clean, suburban house. The scene initially makes us think that they own the house, perhaps as a result of Lascuráin's attempts at preempting Pérez from embarrassing him in the media. However, as the camera pulls back, and as we listen to Louis Armstrong's "What a Wonderful World," we see the murdered bodies of the house's owners—a family, children included—lying in the backyard, establishing a shocking corollary to the movie's narrative of social inequality and a mordant satire on the discourse of fear discussed earlier. Still, despite the enthusiastic assessments of some critics (Francisco Sánchez, *El cine nuevo* 104–10), the movie failed to make a dent in the box office and went largely unnoticed. This is partly because it lacked the publicity that *La ley de Herodes* enjoyed thanks to censorship, but the primary reason is that by 2006 *Un mundo maravilloso* was stating the obvious, since the inequalities of neoliberalism were far from shocking for the average cinema spectator. In such a context, Mexican political cinema had little to say and no dialogue with the country's civil society.

In any case, there is a possibility that political film may still have a role to play, as Estrada's recent film *El infierno* (2010) surprisingly demonstrated. The film is an acerbic satire of Mexico's drug-related violence, focused on Benny (Damián Alcázar), a middle-aged man who, after being deported from the United States, joins the local cartel of his town. Like Estrada's previous work, the film is constructed upon the premise that everybody is complicit in the country's decay. We see that the leader of the cartel (Ernesto Gómez Cruz) is a man of deep connections, while the main police investigator (Daniel Giménez Cacho) actually works for the criminal organization. The film presents a circle of violence as inescapable as the corruption in San Pedro de los Saguaros and, just like the rural town and the urban slums of *Un mundo maravilloso*, has no qualms with presenting the complete destruction of a Northern Mexican town and its inevitable surrender to the cartel. *El infierno* was a very successful film, partly thanks to its release during the bicentennial celebrations as a reminder of Mexican failures (the film's commercial slogan was "Nothing to celebrate") and ultimately earned box office receipts of 6.7 million dollars. Significantly, the highest grossing film of 2010, the bicentennial year, was not *El infierno* or any of the State-promoted historical films, but a romantic comedy: Alejandro Springall's *No eres tú, soy yo,* which raised 9.9 million dollars.[37]

Even if one considers its box office success remarkable, *El infierno* was a lucky exception. Political film in the 2000s generally faded into the background, just when Mexican cinema was about to achieve—thanks to Guillermo del Toro, Alfonso Cuarón, Alejandro González Iñarritu, and Carlos Reygadas—its peak point as a transnational film industry. One can see this, for instance, in León Serment's 2011 film *El efecto tequila,* a clumsy and unconvincing re-creation of the corruption behind the 1994 economic crisis. The movie's preachy and unrealistic ending, in which a disgraced financier exposes a major politician and businessman's role in profiting from the crisis, is very much the same ending as in *Todo el poder,* but lacking Sariñana's unforgiving gaze and his actors' strong performances. One could add here that Serment's previous feature, *Kada kien su karma* (2008), was a weak romantic comedy that was symptomatic of the fact that the few directors who attempt Mexican cinema have developed their careers through styles and genres that hamstring them and make them less able to shoot effective political cinema. Interestingly, Serment was the director of a TV feature on the Virgin of Guadalupe and a short documentary on Manuel Clouthier, an iconic figure of the PAN, which suggests that his politics are right of center. Thus the plot of *El efecto tequila,* fully based on a flashback that suggests that 1994 was the epicenter of Mexican economic corruption, seems to be an attempt to attack the PRI in order to distract the audience from ten years of PAN rule. In any case, what remains clear in *El efecto tequila* is the rarity of political cinema and the overall inability of political films to construct a convincing cinematic discourse. Paradoxically, the failure of Mexican cinema to construct a durable language for political debate was essential to the legibility of its products both nationally and internationally. The declining portrayal of Mexicanist ideologies, the triumphant romantic comedy aesthetic, and the gradual dissolution of political cinema, which I have discussed in the first three chapters, are the fundamental conditions of possibility of Mexican cinema's newfound success on international circuits. This success, and the elements that allowed the transformations of Mexican cinema under neoliberalism to create truly global film directors, will be the subject of my final chapter.

4

THE THREE AMIGOS AND THE LONE RANGER

Mexican "Global Auteurs" on the National Stage

Of the many iconic moments of Mexican cinema in the past twenty years, the one that best represents the arriving point of all the processes I have been describing took place on the December 20, 2006, broadcast of the *Charlie Rose* show. During this episode, Rose interviewed Guillermo del Toro, Alejandro González Iñarritu, and Alfonso Cuarón, in the wake of the success of their most recent releases at the time, *El laberinto del fauno, Babel,* and *Children of Men,* respectively. The three had already become the most representative and successful film directors in Mexican history, and their work was garnering international critical and audience recognition. Their simultaneous rise in the ranks of global cinema, in addition to the close personal relationships between them, had led to the coinage of the nickname "the three amigos," which shortly became a common reference in the press to the trio.[1] Still, regardless of their common public presence, del Toro, González Iñarritu, and Cuarón are very distinct filmmakers, with radically different aesthetic agendas and few similarities in their formative process. If anything, the only thing that they seem to have in common is the fact that they participated in a similar process of integration into international cinema, and that, as a result of this process, they now collaborate by producing each other's films. According to Salvador Velazco, the three of them produced movies that broke with the formulas and stereotypes of Mexican cinema at the time, which in turn made them all visible at international festivals. As a result, all three shot their second movies in the United States, beginning a process of transnational consecration that resulted in each man's success in Hollywood and on the international art house circuit ("Cineastas mexicanos" 192–97). Still, the most meaningful point about the Charlie Rose broadcast was that, while the episode was billed as an interview with "Mexican filmmakers," none of the three movies discussed can really be called a "Mexican film": *El laberinto del fauno* is a Spanish-Mexican coproduction concerned with the Spanish Civil War, shot in Spain with a completely Spanish cast; *Children of Men* is a US/UK coproduction that circulated widely in international art houses; *Babel* was coproduced by González Iñarritu's company, Zeta, but is ultimately a multilingual film set in diverse global locations and bankrolled by the specialty wing (Paramount Vantage) of a major Hollywood studio.

I highlight this last point because the international visibility of all three directors has led to a flurry of critical interest, both academic and journalistic, which has obscured the origins of these three directors in post-1988 Mexican cinema. Most of the critical literature on the "three amigos" is focused on their non-Mexican films, and in some cases critics are fully oblivious to their Mexican work. Such omissions result in major misreadings and misunderstandings of their work, by inscribing them into cultural dynamics—from Spanish postdictatorial culture in the case of del Toro to Sundance-style independent cinema trends in the case of González Iñarritu—where they, at best, fit awkwardly. In this final chapter, I will focus on the work of these three directors, along with a fourth, Carlos Reygadas, to show how the international success of Mexican filmmakers is impossible to understand without considering the way in which the transformations I described in the first three chapters are the very conditions of the possibility of their work. I include Reygadas, a unique director in the contemporary Mexican landscape, because he shows another route to internationalization, via a ferociously authorial cinema, which renders problematic the narratives of Mexican cinema focused on the "three amigos." My analysis of del Toro, González Iñarritu, and Cuarón will focus on their major Mexican films: *Cronos* (1993), *Amores perros* (2000), and *Y tu mamá también* (2001), respectively. I will show that all three films engage in different ways with the main issues underlying the first three chapters of this book: the decline of Mexicanism, the transition toward middle-class spectatorship, and the erosion of political discourse in cinema. Their internationalization will thus be presented as a process born out of the intersection of post-1988 Mexican cinema with the emergent logics of globalized cinema, particularly in relation to the emergence of a "global art cinema," as well as the turn of U.S. independent cinema into the cultural mainstream. Finally, I will conclude the chapter by analyzing Reygadas's work as an alternative narrative of both Mexican cinema and its transnational projection, to argue that his presence in the contemporary film scene signals an exhaustion of all the aesthetics and ideologies encompassed by the very idea of "Mexican cinema."

The international success of these four directors, along with the emergence of other directors (Patricia Riggen, Gerardo Naranjo), actors (Gael García Bernal, Salma Hayek, Diego Luna), and cinematographers (Emmanuel Lubezki), is also a signal of a fourth crucial process in post-1988 Mexican cinema: its growing connections with international film markets and cultural flows. Cultural internationalization is one of the most prominent consequences of the neoliberal period. It is deeply tied to the growing circulation of economic and symbolic capital across borders, insofar as movies are commodities that belong to an expanding and unequal economic market. Film theorists Jyotsna Kapur and Keith B. Wagner have recently theorized the transition from an idea of "world cinema" as an aggregate of traditions defined by their national origin to an understanding of "global cinema" as "the localized expression of globalized integration" (6). In other words, "global cinema" refers to motion pictures constructed both by the international circulation of cultural practice and by national, regional, and local film heritages. Internationalization, then, is not so much an erasure of the national, but intense negotiation of the national with the global. Elizabeth Ezra makes this point in a slightly different way: "Cinema is not inherently national . . . but it is constantly constricted by the bonds of national identity, just as films are constrained by the artificial generic categories into which they are squeezed for marketing purposes" (38). In these terms, the study of internationalized Mexican directors must ultimately be an engagement with the ways in which their work negotiates the constrains and bonds of national identity, while recognizing their ability to circulate through both the networks of "globalized integration" and the different instances of "localized expression" present in their work. In spite of the important differences between them, del Toro, Cuarón, González Iñarritu, and Reygadas broke away from the pressures of Mexicanism by engaging with distinct forms of globalized filmmaking, both in Mexico and in other global locations (like Spain in the case of del Toro, and Britain in the case of Cuarón). At the same time, they resisted the pressures of Americanization by constructing a diverse array of localized settings. By focusing on their Mexican films, we can explain not only the material conditions of possibility for their internationalization, but also the ways in which their work illustrates Mexican cinema's own role in the globalization process.

One of the consequences of the interaction between the global and the local is the emergence of individually identifiable directors who negotiate this encounter in unique and sometimes idiosyncratic ways. I contend that the four directors I study in this chapter have achieved distinctive styles and careers because of the same underlying process: a negotiation of post-1988 Mexican cinema trends with the shifting realities of cinema at the global scale.

I borrow here Brian Michael Goss's term "global auteur" in order to balance the individual nature of each director's work with the parallels and similarities of their trajectories at the level of institutions and practices. Focusing on Pedro Almodóvar, Michael Winterbottom, and Lars von Trier, Goss uses the term to discuss the intersection of the individual styles and thematic motifs with "the political economy of film, patterns of collaboration, funding streams, sociopolitical climate, and critical response" (53). I would add that the notion of a "global auteur" should recognize that the individual components of the concept, as well as the institutional ones, always result from the negotiation of the filmmaker's national bonds with the pressures of globalized culture. The movies I will analyze here are the filmmakers' answer to the challenge posed by this negotiation, from del Toro's idea of shooting horror and genre cinema in a national tradition where those practices lacked intellectual gravitas to Reygadas's decision to work with an international cast of Mennonite *Plautdietsch* speakers to question the idea that Mexican cinema has to be shot in Spanish. The main argument here is that, while one can indeed emphasize the transnational nature of filmmakers like Cuarón or del Toro, scholarly work on the underlying Mexican processes that defined their cinema remains a central task in understanding their style and their standing in world cinema.

The idea of global authorship also points to an important paradox when considering films that circulate both in national and international markets: films shot as commercial ventures sometimes become "art cinema" when reaching the global market. Rosalind Galt and Karl Schoonover point out that "art cinema articulates an ambivalent relationship to location. It is a resolutely international category, often a code for a foreign film. While certain kinds of popular films can circulate globally . . . for most countries, art cinema provides the only institutional context in which films can find audiences abroad" (7). This peculiar structure of framing and branding cinema for international audiences has deep implications for the study of filmmakers such as the ones discussed in this chapter. Their success is rooted in each filmmaker's impressive ability to appeal both to the urban middle-class audience formed by the romantic comedy in Mexico (we must not forget the foundational role of Alfonso Cuarón's *Sólo con tu pareja*, discussed in Chapter 2, in this process) and to the ideologies of art cinema and independent cinema in transnational contexts. To be sure, the international circulation of Mexican cinema in these instances is not new. As documented in *Premios internacionales del cine mexicano, 1938–2008*, Mexico has consistently submitted entries to all the major international film festivals since 1938, and Mexican movies have won major awards, including the Palme d'Or and the Jury Prize at the Cannes Film Festival, the Silver Bear at the Berlinale, and the Golden Shell of the Festival de San Sebastián (142). What has changed is the fact that contemporary directors are circulating more effectively both in the national market and the transnational one. Here we must consider Arturo Ripstein and Paul Leduc. Although they both won some of these same awards, neither filmmaker had a film that achieved the level of commercial success attained by *Amores perros* or *Y tu mamá también* in Mexico, nor did their films ever quite manage to enter the independent cinema market in the United States.

González Iñarritu, del Toro, Cuarón, and Reygadas also signal an important transition in the very notion of the film auteur in Mexico and Latin America. Auteurs formed in the paradigms of the Golden Age (such as Emilio Fernández and Fernando de Fuentes) or the "cinema of solitude" (like Ripstein, Jaime Humberto Hermosillo, and Felipe Cazals) worked within well-established practices of national cinema, which entered world cinema circuits as representative of local specificities. As Marvin D'Lugo has noted, as early as in the 1980s many Latin American auteurs faced the pressure of declining national audiences, as well as growing pressure to reach international audiences, leading major directors like Argentine Fernando Solanas and Cuban Tomás Gutiérrez Alea to produce films with stronger connections to international audiences and aesthetics ("Transnational Film Authors" 119–29). D'Lugo concludes: "In such a fluid context, the film author becomes a privileged site for the transformation of markets, a mediation between the narrowly-defined local culture and the dominant 'other' culture" (129). As I will show in my analysis, this is the reason why the study of transnational Mexican authors in the national context is a fundamental step to understanding both the implication of their work in global or world cinema, as well as understanding how the changes underwent by post-1988 Mexican cinema allowed its filmmakers and actors to transcend national barriers in unprecedented ways. In following D'Lugo's formulation, I contend that, in the individual study of the four directors I have chosen, one can locate both the ulterior consequences in Mexican cinema of the processes described by the first three chapters of this book and the mutual influence of post-1988 Mexican cinema and global art cinema.

Before delving into the analysis of the specific filmmakers, I want to provide some additional context regarding the transnational market relevant to all four of them. There are two particularly important spaces where Mexican cinema intersects with world cinema and my analysis will limit itself to them. The first one is film festivals and how they insert movies in different ways into the international market. *Los Angeles Times* film critic Kenneth Turan proposes a useful taxonomy of film festivals. According to Turan, festivals have three different kinds of agendas. The "business" festival is a convergence point of different films and film distributors and it seeks to find marketing opportunities for movies outside their national spaces. The two most notable of these film festivals are Cannes and Sundance. The festivals with "geopolitical" agendas gather films in relation to ideological or geocultural concerns. These include FESPACO, aimed at the promotion of African national cinemas in continental contexts, and the Havana film festival, which promotes Latin American films of left-of-center persuasion under the continental-oriented ideology of the Cuban Revolution.[2] Finally, Turan identifies niche film festivals with "aesthetic" agendas, which seek the promotion of specific forms of filmmaking. Examples include the Pordenone festival, devoted to silent film, and the Telluride Film Festival, devoted to high-art independent cinema. While Mexico participates actively in all three kinds of festival, what has defined contemporary Mexican filmmakers on the international stage is their gradual withdrawal from geopolitical festivals and their increasing success at business festivals. Older filmmakers like Ripstein and Cazals have collected many awards from the Havana festival, as well as from festivals clearly devoted to Spanish-language filmmaking, like San Sebastián and Cartagena. Even when they venture out of the Latin American comfort zone, they tend to do so at geopolitical or aesthetic festivals, like the Amiens International Film Festival, which is devoted to alternative European, African, and Latin American film. Conversely, del Toro, González Iñarritu, Cuarón, and Reygadas have all become fixtures at major business festivals, collecting major awards at Cannes and Sundance, and they have even achieved Academy Award nominations and prizes in the United States.[3] In fact, while I was writing this chapter, Reygadas was awarded the Best Director Prize at the 2012 Cannes Film Festival for his film *Post Tenebras Lux*.

For Mexican filmmakers, there is an important correlation between festival exposure and the success achieved in the national and transnational markets. It is not trivial, for instance, that the Mexican movie with the most awards on the film festival circuit (thirty-five total) is *Amores perros*. González Iñarritu's film can boast of success at Cannes (where it won two major awards), at major festivals on the U.S. independent film circuit (such as the American Film Institute and Chicago festivals), at major geopolitical festivals aimed at a Latin American audience (Bogotá, Havana), and at European and Asian aesthetic festivals (Lodz, Tokyo, Porto). The movie also won a BAFTA Award in Britain and an American Latino Media Arts award from the National Council of La Raza. *Amores perros*' international acumen rests on its ability to aggregate these diverse audiences, which in turn gave the film enough cultural capital to draw in an unprecedentedly large Mexican audience.

The second important factor in the understanding of Mexican cinema's recent internationalization is its participation in the rise of independent cinema in the United States during the past twenty years. As critics and journalists like Peter Biskind, James Mottram, Geoff King, John Berra, and Michael Z. Newman have amply documented, American cinema underwent a major institutional transformation that widely opened the doors of filmmaking and distribution to agents outside of the studio system.[4] The emergence of institutions such as the Sundance Film Festival, the Independent Film Channel (IFC), Miramax, and the specialty divisions of major film studios allowed for a widening of the aesthetic range of mainstream American cinema and for the emergence of major figures such as Steven Soderbergh, Quentin Tarantino, and the Coen brothers. In previous chapters, I argued that some of these filmmakers were essential references to post-1988 Mexican filmmakers seeking to break away from the constraints of "cinema of solitude."[5] In turn, the filmmakers discussed in this chapter have acquired international success thanks in part to the U.S. indie scene. Many scholars have repeatedly argued that independent cinema in the United States has created a renewed interest in film authorship, and that Hollywood has actively sought new forms of making cinema by recruiting foreign and independent directors and producers (King, *Indiewood* 148, and *New Hollywood Cinema* 85–115; Dixon and Foster 124–66). The fact that del Toro is a major producer of genre cinema in Hollywood and that Cuarón was hired to direct *Harry Potter and the Prisoner of Azkaban* (2004), an entry in one of the most successful franchises in Hollywood, is a reflection of this. This reconfiguration of what Toby Miller has called "the international division of cultural labor" in cinema (*Global Hollywood 2;* "National Cinema Abroad") not only speaks of the ability of Mexican directors to work elsewhere, but also accounts for what happens when they reinvest their transnational cultural capital in Mexican film ventures.

Finally, it is important to keep in mind that the four film directors I will discuss participate in new forms of distribution that have transformed art, independent, and international cinema into a successful market niche. Shyon Baumann has coined the notion of "Hollywood Highbrow" to present the increasing accumulation of cultural capital performed by cinema in the United States. Baumann argues that, while the number of art houses has declined, the DVD market allows for the construction of specialized audiences (167) and that middle- and upper-class audiences perform their knowledge of cinema trends as "cultural capital" and as "a high-status cultural cue" (171). Mexican filmmakers have benefited from these trends, as they have been able to join the cultural conversations constructed by institutions within this market. IFC Films, for instance, became in the past decade a major distributor of Mexican movies in the United States, particularly after its investment in *Y tu mamá también* paid off.[6] The Criterion Collection, undoubtedly the most prestigious outlet for art cinema in home video, has added *Cronos* and *Sólo con tu pareja* to its catalog, while niche distributors like Desert Mountain Media distribute in DVD, Blu-ray, and instant video streaming Mexican films geared toward the U.S. Latino market. Even Carlos Reygadas participates in these arrangements: his movies are sold by Tartan Video (now Palisades Tartan), a niche house responsible for the distribution, among others, of new Romanian cinema and cult East Asian movies.[7] The growing influence of this marketplace creates a wider variety of aesthetic equations for these directors to balance, as opposed to filmmakers like Fernando Sariñana who seek success mostly within

Mexico itself.[8] When analyzing all four of these directors, I will distinguish the aspects related to specifically Mexican film processes from those that negotiate the frameworks established by global art cinema and American independent cinema, to better assess their location in contemporary Mexican film.

Guillermo del Toro, Genre, and the Reinvention of Film Genealogy

The 1993 release of Guillermo del Toro's melancholic horror film *Cronos* is perhaps the best indication of the newly acquired creative freedoms granted by the crisis of cinema in the *salinista* years. As I have mentioned in previous chapters, the diversity of movies produced in this period (including *Danzón, El bulto, La tarea,* and *Sólo con tu pareja*) signaled a crisis in the models of national cinema inherited by the "cinema of solitude" paradigm. In any case, a film like *Cronos,* which falls outside the aesthetic scope of film production in Mexico to this day, provides a good case study of the limits of the post-1990 paradigms of renovations, and of the advantages gained by Mexican filmmakers through their access to the archives and practices of global art cinema.[9] Del Toro was not an outsider per se. *Cronos* was preceded by his success in the landmark television series *Hora marcada* (1986–1989), a Televisa production that followed in the footsteps of the U.S. series *The Twilight Zone.* Del Toro also served as executive producer of Jaime Humberto Hermosillo's *Doña Herlinda y su hijo* (1985), one of the landmark films of late "cinema of solitude." Rather, his innovations result from the identification of the horror and fantasy genres with some of the campiest moments in Mexican film history, from the low-budget adaptations of *Drácula* by Fernando Méndez and Abel Salazar in the 1950s, to the many monster movies within the masked wrestler genre.[10] This type of cinema reached a low point with movies such as *Alucarda, la hija de las tinieblas* (Juan López Moctezuma, 1978), where the low quality rendition of horror mixes with the raunchy, overly graphic sexuality of *sexycomedia*. For a director like del Toro, whose work was in part an attempt to aesthetically redeem a film tradition that completely lacked symbolic capital among middle-class audiences and art house circuits, it was crucial to move away from this tradition. Therefore, what del Toro's work allows me to show in the context of this book are the ways in which, at the very moment of the class displacement of audiences in the early 1990s, directors like him used their authorial voice to reconfigure inherited cinematic traditions of national cinema, which in turn opened the space through which Mexican cinema decisively intersects with post-Sundance forms of global art cinema.

Cronos tells the story of Jesús Gris (Federico Luppi), an antiquarian who inadvertently discovers in his store a colonial-era contraption—the Cronos device—that seems to grant eternal life through the bite of an insect that apparently lives within it. As he interacts with the device, Gris unwillingly starts to transform into a vampire-like being, a metamorphosis he never quite understands. In addition, he becomes the target of Dieter de la Guardia (Claudio Brook), a moribund capitalist who sends his nephew, Ángel (Ron Perlman), in pursuit of the device. In the company of his granddaughter, Aurora (Tamara Shanath), who has not uttered a single word since the passing of her parents, Gris resists de la Guardia's pressures to the very end. After frustrating Dieter and Ángel's attempt to seize the device, Gris decides to destroy it and immolate himself to vanquish its evil and his increasingly unbearable desire to consume Aurora's blood. Unsurprisingly, the iconic status of *Cronos*, as well as del Toro's success in international cinema, has resulted in a copious critical bibliography.

The point that most interests me in the vast landscape of readings produced by other scholars is the scope of the horror cinema archive that del Toro uses in his movie. First, as Héctor Fernández L'Hoeste has argued, one can read the movie in relation to the long tradition of vampire films I mentioned earlier (43). I am personally not as convinced that this is quite the case, since it seems to me that del Toro's authorial voice seeks to escape this very legacy. In any case, the issue is that there is a vast archive of vampiric references here. Ann Davies, for instance, uses the iconology of the film to develop a theory of the vampire as "embodied heterotopia"—that is, as a "negotiation of the tensions inherent in the dislocations of embodied space that result in the terrifying proximity of the deviant" ("Guillermo del Toro's *Cronos*" 403). John Kraniauskas takes this point further, by suggesting a heavily theoretical reading where the vampire's heterotopia is connected to the return of the specters of Mexico's past (embodied in Gris's antiquarian shop) in the face of the threat of advanced capitalism ("*Cronos*"). Without de-authorizing these readings, I believe that they begin with the assumption that the character is indeed a vampire and then proceed to apply theoretical formulations developed around European and U.S. vampirism to the movie. The truly significant point in the bibliography is that, as Brad O'Brien observes, the film "contains very few conventions of the modern vampire film and parodies most of the ones it does contain" (172), or, as Anne Marie Stock puts it, "rather than merely incorporating often used conventions [from vampire tales], the film distorts and reshapes them" ("Authentically Mexican" 277–78).

As Laurence Davies points out, *Cronos* recurs to a Gothic aesthetic that cannot be fixed clearly into allegory, making it a "mercurial" and "elusive" film where the "shifts are more important than the fixities" (95–97). In doing so, del Toro in fact opens the space to construct a mythology in which vampirism is only one of its components. O'Brien himself has argued that the discourse of science (which ties back to the myth of Frankenstein rather than Dracula) is as crucial here, something echoed by critics like Raúl Rodríguez Hernández and Claudia Schaefer, who point out the technological nature of the Cronos device (90), or Geoffrey Kantaris, whose analysis goes as far as to consider the Cronos device in terms of cyborg theory ("Cyborgs" 54–60). In any case, *Cronos* and its work with a vast genealogy of horror signifiers signal the creative freedom at the foundation of some trends of post-1988 Mexican cinema in its unwillingness to be a formulaic genre film. Rather, del Toro's use of the archive of the horror genre raises the issue of auteurship as an essential component in the processes of renovating Mexican cinema in the age of neoliberalism. This, of course, is not because of a purported "creative freedom" that "resists" the industry's paradigms. Instead, what seems to be underlying *Cronos*' originality is a displacement in the social function of cinema. The formulaic nature of Mexploitation horror cinema, particularly in commercial incarnations like wrestler cinema, connects it to a collective, populist idea of cinema that ruled Mexico for most of the twentieth century. As Andrea Noble has convincingly argued, the rise of cinema and other mass media in Mexico was related to "mass migration to the urban centres," which in turn led to a culture constructed to respond to "the mass mobilisation of the revolution and the accelerated pace of life that came with modernisation" (11).

Cronos is a film made possible by the decline of this populist use of national cinema, not only in terms of the decline in the social validity of Mexicanness in cultural discourse that I discussed in Chapter 1, but also because of the class displacement in consumption detailed in Chapters 2 and 3. In this context, *Cronos* is part of a larger trend of movies that gradually erodes forms of film production chiefly aimed at the lower classes and turns them into objects of intellectual consumption that ultimately appeal to intellectualized middle and upper classes and even to transnational audiences. Stock points out that "in employing the transnational language of cinema, *Cronos* communicates effectively with genre fans across geopolitical boundaries" ("Authentically Mexican" 280). In this, del Toro ultimately registers the same operation performed by *La tarea* in relation to American independent cinema or by *Sólo con tu pareja* in connection to the romantic comedy (see Chapter 2), a reappropriation of transnational codes of film and genre in order to break free from the heritage of national cinema.[11] Or, to put it in the words of Daniel Chávez, del Toro's signature ability is to "reappropriate, reprocess and renew" genres and film traditions to create specific film universes ("De faunos" 379). For the purposes of this chapter, my contention here is that the internationalization of Mexican directors like del Toro fully rests on the process of diversifying the available archives and genealogies of cinema available to filmmakers. The consequence of this diversification is the creation of frames of interpretation that allow Mexican film to connect with those audiences alienated by the traditions of national cinema and "cinema of solitude." These audiences include not only the middle and upper classes that I have focused on so far but also the transnational audience of global art cinema, which becomes crucial to the reinvention of Mexican film. In these terms, *Cronos* is both aesthetically and thematically exceptional, but its exceptionality fully rests in it being one of the first movies to utilize the recasting of its film genealogies in the way I am describing. It is not a movie that constructed a specific film tradition, but it is one that preconized important procedures through which Mexican cinema would operate in the complex intersection between the national and the global.

Because of this, it is not surprising that scholars have registered *Cronos*' exceptional aesthetics as part of the "de-nationalization of the screen" (Segre) in the late 1980s and early 1990s. Most readings of the movie coincide in presenting it as an allegory in which the Cronos device represents a spectral return of Mexico's colonial past, juxtaposed with the fast-paced modernization of the neoliberal era, embodied by de la Guardia's binational self (Segre 36; Kraniauskas, "*Cronos*" 142–43). Rodríguez Hernández and Schaefer offer a more convincing version of this argument when they read the contents of Jesús Gris's antiquarian shop as "wreckage" of the past, collected with "no discernible order" and with "little or no regard as to their origins, chronologies or cultural connections" (88). Rather than having a culturally defined past haunting the neoliberal present, this argument speaks of a wrecked past facing the destructiveness of the present, following Walter Benjamin's well-known image of the Angel of History.[12] In any case, critics place *Cronos* as a film that negotiates the weight of the past with the demands of a present infused with a selfish capitalism. The emptiness of the factories owned by de la Guardia seems to stand for a process that, in the words of Kraniauskas, "involves not only the disciplining of capital but also the subjugation of living labour, the body, to the machine" (146).

While these readings explain in a somewhat sufficient manner the importance of the past and the way in which *Cronos* embodies, at the level of the plot, the tension between past and modernity in Mexico, they still overlook or understate key elements of the movie. In my view, the most important point to be made in the reading of the plot is that de la Guardia is in fact more moribund than Jesús. Thus, his pursuit of the artifact of the past, the Cronos device, seems to contradict in part the idea of a "historical" past versus a vertiginous present, because the present of industrial capitalism is not modern but either on life support (Dieter is alive thanks to an expensive and convoluted setup that conceals his fragile health) or shallow and incompetent (Ángel, Dieter's only viable heir, fails consistently in the task of stealing the device and is mostly concerned with his potential nose job). When scholars overstate the allegorical reading, which attributes to *Cronos* a critique of neoliberalism that is not as obviously present in the plot as it would seem, the role of *Cronos* in Mexican cinema seems lost at times. Still, some other readings have been able to see beyond the dogmatic identification of capitalism with the new. John Waldron, for instance, unconvincingly casts Dieter de la Guardia's technified lair with the "new" ("Introduction" 17), but ultimately focuses on a far more important detail: the fact that del Toro's movie was made possible by the visible decline of what Waldron calls "cultural monopolies" in the early 1990s. As Waldron shows, *Cronos* must be understood in the context of a culture based on a "loss of authority over cultural production and the cultural imaginary," which in turn "replaced the limits imposed by nationalism in the pre-globalizing episteme with the homogenizing weight of the so-called international market" (11). A similar argument is put forward by Stock, who argues that "neither del Toro nor *Cronos* is 'obsessed' with authentic national culture. In fact, they flaunt their migrancy and hybridity" (*Framing* xxvi). If one is to take both Waldron and Stock seriously, what follows is that reading the mythology crafted by del Toro at face value, as a story trying to make a point regarding capitalist modernity and historical specters, misses the point at least in part. Rather, the true, important insight behind del Toro's work is precisely that, in a film tradition that cannot longer claim "authority over cultural production and the cultural imaginary," where the construction of the audience as the subject of a national cinema is no longer possible, the transnational archives of genre become an alternative way of engaging emerging subjects and audiences. If *Cronos* "flaunts its migrancy and hybridity," by casting Argentines and Americans alongside Mexican actors and by effortlessly incorporating English as a complementary language to Spanish, it is because filmmakers like del Toro (or Cuarón, for that matter) work from a position where the collective subject constructed by national cinema is no longer possible or desirable. *Cronos* is not a film that says anything in particular about Mexico. It is a film that, for the first time in Mexican film tradition, assumes that embodying Mexican national culture is no longer possible.

De la Guardia's own decadence is, paradoxically, one of the things that render this point viable. Most readings seem to assume that de la Guardia represents a contemporary capitalism that is at odds with the colonial past embodied by the Cronos device and by Jesús's antiquarian shop. However, if one follows the earlier-cited argument by Rodríguez Hernández and Schaefer regarding the wreckage of the past and the meaninglessness of Jesús's collection of antiques, one can in fact claim that the antagonism between Gris and de la Guardia is not a struggle between the past and the present, but a conflict between two equally outdated and moribund forms of the past. De la Guardia's form of industrial capitalism is not a form of modernity begotten by NAFTA. One could in fact trace the model of Americanized capitalism in Mexico back to the late 1940s, when President Miguel Alemán fostered foreign investment and urbanized industrialization. The very fact that there was a mass migration to the cities, which was the underlying cultural process of Mexican national cinema in the first place, resulted from this. Therefore, to claim that de la Guardia embodies the "new" is quite inaccurate. The fact that he is an old man, someone who could conceivably have started his industries forty-five years before the early 1990s, seems to suggest that his company is not a new company, but a remnant of an older form of capitalism that is unable to find any continuity in the new model of development. The only character that in my view plausibly represents the new is Ángel, whose shallowness and ineptitude make him unable to become a viable heir to the company. Furthermore, a similar logic unfolds on Gris's side, given that his heir, Aurora, is also inadequate: a young orphaned girl who refuses to talk. If horror is an archive that allows for the embodiment of the remnants of the past, *Cronos* is a movie about the exhaustion of two forms of modernity: the baroque/colonial modernity of Fulcanelli, passed on to Gris via the Cronos device, and the capitalist modernity that fails to preserve itself, just like modern medical science fails to preserve Dieter's life. It is not coincidental that the building collapse that kills Fulcanelli and that leads to the first disappearance of the Cronos device takes place in 1937, at the outset of the modernization process of the Mexican Revolution. It is possible to push this point even further: the colonial watchmaker and alchemist dies precisely at the moment when the later stages of the Mexican Revolution and the earlier forms of transnational capitalism begin to provide an alternative to Mexico's longstanding notions of historical heritage. The loss of the Cronos device takes place in the moment of a historical shift, which moves Mexico from its historical past to the promise of postrevolutionary modernization. The reappearance of the device in the early 1990s then signals another historical shift, one that renders obsolete both Gris's nostalgic antiquarianism and de la Guardia's industrial work.

If one ties together both the creative challenge faced by del Toro, as a director, in the context of the early 1990s and this revised reading of the film's story as an allegory of two forms of failed modernity that desperately seek to preserve themselves, del Toro emerges as a visionary figure who is able to creatively deploy a highly flexible set of film languages to compensate for Mexican cinema's fundamental inability to articulate its audience as a subject of history or of modernity. In itself, *Cronos* is the movie that best embodied the exhaustion of twentieth-century models of Mexican cinema, in contrast with films that tried to revitalize them, like *Danzón,* or films that sought to sidestep the question altogether, like *Sólo con tu pareja.* Del Toro essentially de-naturalizes the archive of Mexican history and places it in the larger archive of thematic repertoires of horror cinema, which allows him to recombine identifiable historical signifiers (like Fulcanelli's role in the viceroyalty or his death in the early years of postrevolutionary modernization) with elements from different traditions of horror cinema (such as the vampire and Frankenstein mythologies, and the use of the insect-cyborg). If anything, the genealogy of the *Cronos* device seems to be derived from American cinema rather than from Mexican film: it brings to mind a similar intersection of scientific hubris and insect-human interaction put forward by David Cronenberg in *The Fly* (1986).[13]

Cronos is, then, a film that successfully overcomes the challenge posed by an exhausted film tradition, by forcefully expanding the possibilities of cinema without any regard for the imperatives dictated by "cinema of solitude" and other surviving forms of national cinema. Del Toro is the type of director that is possible only in periods of aesthetic indecision in a national tradition, because his work is founded in the uprooting and reconfiguration of even the most basic elements of film production. This is obvious in one of his earliest projects, his 1990 book on Alfred Hitchcock. In it, del Toro provides a detailed analysis of Hitchcock's films and television shows, carefully examining the style and the devices created by a director whom he characterizes as "the great master of human emotion" (55; my translation). Del Toro reads Hitchcock as a sort of ur-director whose work aims at the basic elements of film itself, including storytelling and feeling. In this, del Toro shows exactly the type of operation that made a film like *Cronos* possible in the moment of aesthetic openness allowed by the crisis of Mexican cinema in the early 1990s. It is a film that truly rethinks what it means to make a movie in Mexico—something accomplished, in del Toro's case, by producing a film that is ultimately denationalized and deliberately disconnected from the legacy of Mexican cinema.

Precisely because the national is heavily regulated in more standard narrative traditions like melodrama, it is not surprising that horror becomes the vehicle where national cinema is preempted in a particularly radical way. In one of the most insightful comments on the film, Waldron argues that the reference to time embedded in the Cronos device (and constantly in the movie via the presence of clocks) brings together two different temporalities of the nation: the linear time of progress and modernity and the mythic time of the archaic ("Introduction" 17). Film theorists have consistently argued that horror and fantasy genres are interventions on the temporality of cinema, insofar as traditional (and national) cinema operates within what Bliss Cua Lim calls "the regime of modern homogeneous time" (11). National cinema proper, the one embodied in Mexico by Golden Age melodramas and "cinema of solitude" political films, belongs to this regime, given that its ultimate goal is to provide homogeneity to a sense of the national that exists both as time and as social identity. This is the case, for instance, of Arau's *Como agua para chocolate*, which, as I discussed in Chapter 1, retells a history of the past to inexorably connect it to the present. In contrast, the fantastic "strains against the logic of clock and calendar, unhinging the unicity of the present by insisting on the survival of the past or the jarring coexistence of other times" (Lim 11). This insight translates in *Cronos* as an operation of unhinging not only the time of the nation, but, more crucially for my argument, the temporality of narrative traditions that underlie national cinema. At the level of content, the film unfolds the contemporary into the mythic time represented by the alchemic knowledge of the Cronos device, and into the linear time of history personified in the aging bodies of Jesús and Dieter. Both, however, belong to the same "regime of modern homogenous time" that underlies a national cinema whose aim is, as it was in Mexican cinema of the twentieth century, to reconcile the different temporalities of its audiences into a single national identity. The crucial operation then takes place at the level of form itself, where del Toro's self-aware use of cinematic tradition allows us/the audience, to use Lim's words, "to glimpse an 'outside' to the regime of modern homogeneous times, one that we might seize as a starting point for more ethical temporal imaginings" (12). By using diverse cinematic and historical semantic archives and constructing a self-enclosed world with it, del Toro achieves a cinema centered in the ability to deploy what Lim calls "multiple times that never quite dissolve into the code of modern time consciousness, discrete temporalities incapable of attaining homogeneity with or full incorporation into a uniform chronological presence" (12). In other words, what del Toro's authorial work with genre achieves is not so much a reinvention of genre cinema itself, given the fact that horror never became a major genre in post-1990 Mexican cinema. Rather, it creates a cinematic world in which the disjointed elements of Mexican history—the colonial and the modern, or the archaic and the progressive—never fully reconcile into anything that could be characterized as a nation or a national identity. This is why both Gris and de la Guardia die in the end: any survival of the ghosts of the past would raise the question of their role in the present. In a way, *Cronos* is as much an exorcism of the codes of national cinema as the dream sequence in *Sólo con tu pareja:* both films want to create a new starting point for the temporal imaginings of Mexican cinema.[14] *Cronos* is one of the first works of post-1988 Mexican cinema in which the imperative to be Mexican is not only ignored, but also thoroughly deconstructed.

Perhaps the best illustration of del Toro's fundamental detachment from Mexican cinema is the fact that he hasn't shot a film in Mexico since *Cronos*. This has to do both with his robust transnational career and with his reluctance to return to Mexico in the wake of his father's kidnapping in 1998. In any case, the point is that del Toro's impact abroad relies on his unique development of genre cinema within the context of post-1998 Mexican cinema, a result both of his emancipation from the imperatives of previous cinematic traditions and of working in a country (Spain) where the Hollywood practices of genre were, as in Mexico, not particularly influential His work in Hollywood and Spain displays the same fundamental technique present in *Cronos,* and its success has to do with his ability to innovate genre cinema through the consistent dialogue with a diversity of film traditions. In *El espinazo del diablo* (2001), for instance, del Toro applies the work on historical time and memory from *Cronos* to the aesthetic of historical memory and childhood developed in Spain by two landmark films: Víctor Erice's *El espíritu de la colmena* (1973) and Carlos Saura's *Cría cuervos* (1976).[15] However, just like *Cronos,* which uses horror to construct a critical distance from the direct representation of the past, *El espinazo del diablo* is not an engagement with direct historical memory but rather a highly idiosyncratic elaboration of the emotions tied to a history that the protagonists and audiences do not fully understand. The most perspicuous readings of the film (Hardcastle; Brinks; Ann Davies, "Beautiful") all concur that the use of the ghost and of Gothic aesthetics allows for the representation of unsymbolized elements that, by materializing in the film language of horror, allow for the emergence of what Hardcastle calls "the on-going emotional dimensions of (especially traumatic) historical events" (129).

By intervening in what Linnie Blake calls "the wounds of nations," films like *Cronos* and *El espinazo del diablo* profit from the inability of most institutionalized forms of cinema to engage with an ideological imperative, by locating themselves precisely in the areas that resist representation. The essential point here is that del Toro locates both *El espinazo del diablo* and his later film *El laberinto del fauno* (2006) at the early stage of *franquismo*, using genre cinema (horror in the first case, fantasy in the second) as a way to short-circuit the imperative of memory, given that del Toro, as a Mexican, lacks an immediate political investment in engaging with the trauma of the Franco regime. This is an important issue when considering how del Toro's films circulate in different markets. As Antonio Lázaro-Reboll points out regarding *El espinazo,* the "film might be defused simply by the mass of non-critical press coverage that is orchestrated around its release" (50), something that is patently true when the audiences and critics of three sites of reception—Mexico, Spain, and the United States—are at play. Thus, just like the story of Fulcanelli and the Cronos device, which provides a space for an alternative reading of the colonial legacy and of the process of capitalist modernization by establishing a monstrous trope that rejects their modernizing promise, the fantasy world found by the protagonist of *El laberinto del fauno* in the interstices of the small town conquered by the fascist commander inscribes a history of hope in a story that historically resulted in utmost defeat. This divergence between history and fantasy, central to most readings of the film (Rose; Thormann; Hairston; Hanley), is made possible by the development of del Toro's cinema in the wake of his Mexican movie.

For the purposes of this book, the central issue raised by del Toro unfolds into two considerations. First, the fact that *Cronos* lacks a visible legacy in Mexico—both in its stylistics and in its work with genre cinema—speaks not only of the challenges faced in the 1990s by any filmmaker attempting work in genre cinema.[16] It shows that the space of creative freedom that originated in the crisis of the early 1990s resulted in a normalization that cast directors like del Toro outside of the new institutional networks of Mexican cinema. Second, and perhaps more importantly, del Toro shows nonetheless the ability to construct a space for directors like him in global cinema, by exporting into the transnational realm cinematic reflections made possible by the neoliberal transition in Mexico. It is in this very point that he can be read as a precursor. Still, del Toro well exemplifies the unique case of a film auteur who moves from the national to the global context by keeping fidelity not to any political stance, but to a certain form of craft. In fact, the politicized and historicized readings of his films are rendered problematic when one considers that his choice of topics is ultimately related to his ability to enter in dialogue with other fantasy texts and traditions. The fact that many of his films (*Mimic* [1997], *Hellboy* [2004], *Blade 2* [2002], *Hellboy 2* [2008], and even *El espinazo*) are directly or indirectly inspired by comic books and genre fiction, and the astonishing level of detail found in the notebooks that he published with all the preliminary work leading to *El laberinto del fauno*, show that his ultimate goal is the mythology and the visual construction of his work.[17] This is, perhaps, one of the reasons why Mexican cinema failed to pursue avenues suggested by *Cronos* or any of del Toro's other works. However, his work with style was the instrument that allowed him to seamlessly move across three distinct cinematic traditions. The de-historicization that Lázaro-Reboll reads in audience reception is embedded in the aesthetic of the films themselves. Del Toro's transnational circulation thus is allowed precisely at the first moment of the de-Mexicanization of cinema, in the early 1990s, proving that the end of Mexicanism discussed in Chapter 1 is an essential component of the transnational success of the "three amigos." In any case, while his aesthetic did not have any major consequences in Mexican filmmaking, del Toro's path created a blueprint for the internationalization of the country's cinema, something that would become patent in the wake of González Iñarritu's *Amores perros*.

Alejandro González Iñarritu and the Neoliberalization of Independent Cinema

The rise of *Amores perros* as the most visible and celebrated film in post-1988 Mexican cinema is first and foremost the result of its position at the intersection of all the processes I have described so far in this book. Its unapologetically urban aesthetic signals a decisive break with the predominance of *provincia* in Mexicanist cinema, a point I discussed in Chapter 1, and concludes the process of imagining Mexico City in 1990s cinema—a process that David William Foster describes in his *Mexico City in Contemporary Mexican Cinema*.[18] It also benefits from the demographic changes in the audience described in Chapter 2, and it deftly builds on the market strategies developed by *Sexo, pudor y lágrimas* and other romantic comedies. Its representation of Mexico, in the context of the 2000 transition to democracy, marks the exhaustion of the nostalgia for 1960s form of political articulation—like the ones represented in *El bulto*,

En el aire, and other films discussed in Chapter 3—and decidedly engages with the complexities of neoliberalism in Mexico. And, of course, it pushes forward and deepens the internationalization of Mexican cinema heralded by Guillermo del Toro. As is well known, *Amores perros* tells three stories intertwined by a tragic car accident. The first one focuses on Octavio (Gael García Bernal), a young lower-class man who enters the world of illegal dog fights in order to raise the money he needs to flee with his sister-in-law, Susana (Vanessa Bauche), and rescue her from the abuse of his brother, Ramiro (Marco Pérez). Octavio crashes his car while being chased by the leaders of the dog-fighting ring. The middle part of the film centers on Valeria (Goya Toledo), a Spanish model who moves in with her married lover, Daniel (Álvaro Guerrero), a publicist. Valeria's life takes a turn for the worse when Octavio crashes into her car, which leads to the slow and torturous erosion of her entire life. In the end, Valeria loses a leg and her modeling career, and Daniel, as far as we can gather, starts cheating on her. Finally, the third part tells the story of El Chivo (Emilio Echevarría), a 1960s social revolutionary who became a homeless hitman. El Chivo witnesses the crash between Octavio and Valeria and rescues Octavio's dog. The core of the story rests on El Chivo's gradual redemption, as he uses his last hit—involving a man who wants to kill his brother—to redeem himself and to attempt a return to his estranged daughter, Maru (Lourdes Echevarría).

Dolores Tierney has called Alejandro González Iñarritu a "director without borders," suggesting that his "Third World authorial specificity can survive the border crossing between Mexico and the United States" ("Alejandro González Iñarritu" 103). While I find the Third World idea problematic—in no small part because González Iñarritu, like most of Mexican cinema, is far removed from the so-called Third Cinema paradigm I discussed in Chapter 3—I share Tierney's belief that recognizing the concerns of Mexican national cinema embodied in *Amores perros* is crucial to understanding González Iñarritu's subsequent work. I would go even further: the success of Alejandro González Iñarritu lies precisely in his ability to translate the paradigm change of post-1988 Mexican cinema into the logics of transnational film, thus inscribing Mexican cinema into the core of the formal and critical conversation surrounding global cinema. This assertion is crucial to understanding two separate yet fundamental issues. First, Mexico's film achievements in the 2000s, including the success of movies like *El crimen del padre Amaro,* are thoroughly defined by *Amores perros'* intervention in the reconfiguration of production, circulation, and spectatorship within Mexico. Second, precisely because González Iñarritu emerged as one of the most influential directors in global cinema after 2000, the nature of his contribution is illegible without understanding his renewal of Mexican cinematic discourse. The importance of this last statement is demonstrated by the constant emergence of readings, both of *Amores perros* and González Iñarritu's work in English, which thoroughly ignore or deny his work. Film critic Terrie Waddell offers an interesting example of this. In her book *Wild/Lives,* Waddell offers, in an otherwise suggestive reading, the idea that the pre-Columbian myth or archetype of Tezcatlipoca (an Aztec deity) and the Nahua idea of the underworld configure the unconscious of the film's plot (123–42). This analysis, based on a superficial reading of Aztec mythology and a lack of knowledge of Mexican cinema and culture of the period, reveals not only a critical voluntarism that necessarily ties Mexico to its ancestral past, but also the denial of the possibility of a modern Mexican culture that is anything other than the return of the pre-Columbian repressed.[19] One of the crucial points that emerges from the analysis I presented in Chapter 1 and from Tierney's contentions regarding González Iñarritu is that his film becomes transnational precisely because he overcomes tokenistic readings and practices of Mexican cinema. This achievement makes films like *Amores perros* relevant to a larger discussion of cinematic modernization.

A full engagement with *Amores perros,* at the level of form and content and as a cultural phenomenon, shows that the film is in fact the point of encounter between progressive cultural forms and conservative political ideologies, reflecting a complex process of cultural modernization that Mexico underwent in the age of neoliberalism. This modernization is tied to the increasing centrality of the urban scene as a place of articulation of the local, the national, and the global. According to Jesús Martín-Barbero, urban cultures embody three complementary dynamics: the desire to improve one's economic situation; the culture of consumption as citizenship (which I discussed via Néstor García Canclini in Chapter 2); and the emergence of communicational technologies (*Oficio* 280). *Amores perros* is, at least in part, an embodiment of these three logics. An important point to raise here is that González Iñarritu is not a film-school director. Rather, his career was a development of his work as one of Mexico's foremost publicists and media personalities in the 1990s. González Iñarritu himself is part of the creative class that Mexican romantic comedies have idealized since *Sólo con tu pareja* (see Chapter 2). By virtue of this, his success is constructed upon pursuing the ulterior consequences of the media privatization process, and by appealing to those filmgoers who identify with the myth of the creative class. As Paul Julian Smith documents in his book on the film, *Amores perros* was made possible by two central decisions: to use an unprecedented amount of private funding (breaking away from Mexican film's reliance on IMCINE funds) and to carefully design a marketing campaign for overseas settings—most notably the Cannes Film Festival (11–13). These actions on behalf of the film appealed to the culture of consumption that overtook Mexican culture in the neoliberal period, while using a new media technology—marketing—as a central component of the production process. Juan Poblete has aptly inscribed *Amores perros* into the "cultural communications complex" that has been central to both the expansion of capitalism and contemporary theories of globalization and culture (214). Furthermore, Poblete points out *Amores perros*' roots in MTV culture, which are obvious considering the film's use of montage and the important debt that its vertiginous pace owes to musical videos of the 1990s (221). This MTV style reflects the impact of cable television on the formation of a distinct middle- and upper-class audience I discussed in Chapter 2—a style that the audience, following the process of cultural urbanization described by Martín-Barbero, increasingly demanded. In their book on González Iñarritu, Celestino Deleyto and María del Mar Azcona argue that his use of the wide-angle shot "becomes a powerful tool in the construction of an urban space that is strongly unified in the intense feeling of violence and pervasive danger that it conveys and in the suggestion of the social conditions that produce such violence" (76–77). If Sariñana's *Todo el poder* is, as I argued in Chapter 2, an embodiment of the neoliberal "citizenship of fear" that unites audiences in a reading of violence as a threat to privilege, *Amores perros* takes this class-determined viewpoint and turns it into the ideological and formal kernel of its story. The interesting part of *Amores perros* is that it pushes both the ideological engagements of middle-class spectatorship in Mexico and the use of these engagements as part of the process of commoditizing cinema to its ulterior—and most successful—consequences.

I argued back in Chapter 2 that a key element in the success of Antonio Serrano's *Sexo, pudor y lágrimas* and other commercial films rested on an intuitive use of the film soundtrack, given that placing a successful single into MTV and radio rotations provided free publicity and a way to bring into the theater audiences who lacked an emotional relationship with Mexican cinema. *Amores perros* has a two-disc soundtrack that includes not only tracks featured in the movie but a set of songs "inspired by" it, mimicking a marketing stratagem common among Hollywood films of the past twenty-five years.[20] Thus, the soundtrack goes far beyond the strategy of placing a single on MTV: it thoroughly adopts the language of alternative music to define the film's tone in relation to the cultural taste and ethos of Mexican middle-class audiences (who, for the most part, were very familiar with this kind of music) and creates an autonomous accompanying product that makes *Amores perros* a mediatic product without precedent in the Mexican cultural market. *Sexo, pudor y lágrimas* found the elements necessary to construct a commercial film industry, and *Amores perros* fully inscribes that industry in the ideological, aesthetic, cultural, and economic terms of neoliberal modernization.

Thanks to its lucid reading of the film market and its audiences both in Mexico and abroad, the politics of *Amores perros* has been the subject of an intense scholarly conversation. Early readings of the film pointedly rested on the relationship between the film and the neoliberal process. Claudia Schaefer, for example, placed the film in a central part of her argument about the relationship between culture, boredom, and modernity in Mexican and Argentine film, and read it as a film of political and social transition (83–107). Building on her argument, some essays point out that the film represents either a conservative viewpoint that subjects Mexico's social problems to the ideological gaze of the neoliberal middle class and to an understanding of society based on ideas of the family (Sánchez Prado, "*Amores Perros*") or as a literal embodiment of a right-wing ethics that allegorizes the penetration of capitalism at all levels of the social in Mexico (Kraniauskas, "*Amores perros*"). Ayala Blanco, the film's most important Mexican detractor, characterized *Amores perros* as an instance of "tacky neotremendism" (*neotremendismo chafa*) that achieves little more than the scandalous presentation of the poor (*La fugacidad* 482). These lines of reading have been problematized by scholars who contend that the "explosion of feeling" and "emotional itineraries" (Cerrato, Perea, and Rentero 29; 49; my translation) lead toward politicized readings that exceed the ideological arguments mentioned before. Earlier critics like Deborah Shaw identified love as a central concern of the film, a feeling that is interrupted by the intervention of power, desire, and other obstacles proper to neoliberalism (*Contemporary Cinema* 67). In a similar vein, Laura Podalsky reads the film as an elaboration of an "affective register" that conveys "an epistemological crisis that has destabilized the subject's understanding of contemporary society and, perhaps, more importantly, his or her ability to make substantive proposals for a better future" (*Politics* 89). This intuition is elaborated further by Hermann Herlinghaus, who ties the film's affective register to a theorization of what Giorgio Agamben refers to "bare life," a community outside the State embodied, for instance, in the social alienation of figures like Octavio or El Chivo (180–81).[21] It is also developed by Dierdra Reber, who reads the story of El Chivo as a process of "moral healing" that, in the end, opens the space for a new political and utopian elaboration, based on the contention that the "politics of love" exceed the realm of ideology (295).

I am not entirely persuaded that the affective register in *Amores perros* exceeds conservative and neoliberal politics. Ultimately, "moral healing" can be a conservative political category that focuses on the individual rather than on the commons, while "bare life" signals the radical exclusion of citizens from the realm of law and human rights. Nonetheless, an objective reading of this debate shows that the true underlying phenomenon is the ideological undecidability of the film, which allows for plausible readings in different parts of the ideological spectrum. This is the precise meaning of Schaefer's contention of the film's transitional nature. Following my analysis from Chapter 3, *Amores perros* can be placed in the exact same historical moment of *Todo el poder* and *La ley de Herodes*, a cinematic culture that read the turmoil of the 2000 election in the context of the decline of politicized discourse in cinema and of the alignment of cultural production to middle-class political ideologemes: civil society, electoral transition, and so on. The fundamental difference is that, in a curious way, *Amores perros* is not as directly engaged in national politics as those two films. While Sariñana (a filmmaker tied to the conservative Partido Acción Nacional [PAN]) and Estrada (a more left-leaning filmmaker) both connect the social reality of their films to a causal relationship with the State's corruption, González Iñarritu opts to erase any political causality within his film. In fact, as some of the most ferocious critics of the film have pointed out (Ayala Blanco, *La fugacidad* 482–86; Sánchez Prado, "*Amores perros*"), the only visible cause of violence relates to family issues, such as Octavio's "bad" mother and absent father, Ramiro and Daniel's adultery, Susana's decision to cheat on her husband, Valeria's decision to establish a relationship with a married man, and El Chivo's abandonment of his daughter for the sake of social revolution.[22] The point here is that one of the conditions of possibility of *Amores perros*' national and transnational success is the gradual erosion of political imperatives in film representation. Unlike *echeverrista* directors like Retes, Cazals, or Alcoriza, González Iñarritu works in a cinematic world emancipated from the social referentiality that Mexican cinema inherited from Golden Age directors and figures like Buñuel, Ismael Rodríguez, or Cantinflas. And instead of appealing to a purely domestic market by embodying the political views of the middle class, like Sariñana or Estrada did, *Amores perros* opts for an aestheticization of social difference through a language that privileges "the space-time concentration caused by the accident [that] brings together not only different individuals but the social classes they respectively belong to" (Sá 45). Rather than politicizing social difference, the film uses its vertiginous aesthetics in order to provide audiences with an affective experience that supersedes the political in terms of the human. This is the main reason why the high emotional charge privileged by Podalsky, Herlinghaus, or Reber does not have a necessary connection to emancipatory politics. They point rather to what Fernando Fabio Sánchez suggestively calls "traumatized contingencies" (172), crises of the subject that beckon the type of moral healing discussed by Reber as opposed to any clear political articulation.

To be sure, the movie does establish a mise-en-scène of class, ethnic, and gender antagonisms at the core of neoliberalism. A whole segment of the critical bibliography points toward this direction. Héctor Amaya, for instance, identifies the use of "racialised masculinities," which construct the characters in a language where "masculinity and race are differentiated between bodies, constituting hierarchies and tragic pathos" and laying "bare race, class and gender tensions in the modern Mexican State, exposing the ways in which ideas of progress and modernity can too easily reconstitute racial and class disenfranchisement" (202). Orla Juliette Borreye contends that the film's representation of masculinity operates "as both a gender performance and as a return to animal instinct" (2); she pursues a line of thought similar to Amaya's, privileging the crisis of the order of genre as a central knot of the film. Likewise, Juli Kroll aligns the film with a "neo-*machista* national consciousness" that "celebrates and critiques modern *machista* cultural frameworks, showing male characters believing that they are behaving honorably even as they digress into aggression, dishonor or tepid reconciliation with the past" (38). All these readings rely on gender, race, and/or class to point out a representation of the social being inscribed into cinematic discourse. It is in these terms that we may also read Marvin D'Lugo's contention that *Amores perros* is "Buñuelian." According to D'Lugo, the film is constructed upon the "tension between the images of violence and order" that underscores "the contradictions of modernity at the foundation of this society" ("*Amores perros*" 228). In constructing a representational aesthetic that does not shy away from identitary and social antagonisms, and in fully assuming the violent nature of the contradictions of modernity, *Amores perros* overcomes the use of Mexico's middle and upper classes as privileged objects of cinematic representation and as privileged subjects of the cinematic gaze. The more debatable premise is that the mise-en-scène of these antagonisms and contradictions is in itself a political act in the context of the 2000 election.

The fundamental problem here is that the social tension represented by the film's content is a manifestation of the contradictions that sustain *Amores perros* at the level of form. Kraniauskas has pointed out that the film "is characterized by a left-wing technical methodology and a right-wing narrative ethic" ("*Amores perros*" 13; my translation). This has to do with the fact that the film operates only partially in relation to the parameters of cultural modernization laid out by Martín-Barbero. The use of marketing and the soundtrack, as well as the MTV aesthetic, respond well to the culture of consumption that frames the circulation of cinema in the neoliberal city scene, where cultural industries and circulation are increasingly determined by private capital. The film is also quite deft at integrating the technological modernization embedded in urban cultures both at the level of form (through immaterial technologies like marketing, and material technologies like video, cinematography, and editing) and content (such as in the reflection of the central role of a machine [the car] in the determination of contemporary urban life [Beckman 179–203; Sá 51]). However, the social demands that emerge from the social inequalities rendered visible by urban development are present in the film's montage, but completely absent from the film's world itself. Even if their destinies were inextricably linked by the car accident, Octavio, Valeria, and El Chivo never leave their respective class locations. While the conservative ideology of the film does construct an interclass narrative based on family trauma, the fact is that the social segregation constructed by Amaya's "racialised masculinities" is never problematized.

Perhaps the truly important consequence of this contradiction is that the success of *Amores perros,* both domestically and internationally, requires this erasure. In Mexico, the film may keep the aura of a vaguely social and postmodern film without contradicting the ideological standpoint of its economically privileged audience. It is crucial to remember that *Amores perros* is a film that decidedly belongs to the exhaustion of national cinema and of Mexicanism discussed in Chapter 1: there is no possible imagined community in a film that only appeals to a specific social sector. Abroad, this erasure of the socially specific allows for a space of open interpretation that facilitates the film's reception in the United States and Europe. It is social enough to elicit the progressive sensibilities of transnational festival audiences who seek political redemption in Third World cinema without obstructing its legibility with an excess of referentiality—one can remember here that other neoliberal social films focused on the postmodern representation of de-historicized marginal subjects, like Fernando Meirelles's *Cidade de Deus* and Majid Majidi's *Children of Heaven,* were circulating at the same time. This explains, for instance, why *Amores perros* functioned so well in international markets, while Estrada's *La ley de Herodes* failed: the Coens' influence in Estrada was overridden by a sense of humor legible only to an audience well informed about Mexican electoral politics.

In any case, the politics of *Amores perros* can be truly understood only when one considers the way in which it relates to the transformation of the uses of politics in cinema described in Chapter 3. Fernando Fabio Sánchez connects the film to Gabriel Retes's *El bulto* (166), which, as we previously saw, represents a watershed moment of the relationship between cinema and politics in Mexico. In Sánchez's rendering, the point is that Lauro's fidelity to revolutionary ideals results from his being asleep for twenty years, while El Chivo spent this time in prison, which led him to "understand that the narrative that gave meaning to his acts of violence had lost coherence in the changing Mexican reality" (166). I would take Sánchez's comparison much further and argue that El Chivo represents the last nail in the coffin of revolutionary politics in Mexican cinema. As I discussed in Chapter 3, Lauro and Alberto, the protagonist of de Llaca's *En el aire,* represent a sort of reluctant integration of the 1960s activist into the neoliberal order. However, both movies conclude with a gesture that refuses to fully inscribe these characters into contemporaneity. While Lauro (like El Chivo) finds redemption in the reconciliation with his family, his facial expression, frozen in the credits, does not show joy but horror. Similarly, Alberto's acceptance of the loss of the woman who represents his idealistic past is sublimated by a dream sequence that points to de Llaca's reluctance to conclude with trauma and heartbreak. In contrast, the ambiguously redemptive ending of El Chivo's saga leads to a completely different conclusion. Herlinghaus has suggestively characterized El Chivo as "a revenant, embodying deep-rooted religious-political myths and masculine moral fantasies" (184). His spectral status within the contemporary Mexico represented in the film—he roams the streets of both lower- and upper-class neighborhoods and intervenes in them through violence—seems to suggest the unsymbolized traumas of social injustice that underlie the country's social antagonism. However, one can most certainly claim that the narrative of El Chivo's section of the film is thoroughly constructed as an exorcism of his phantasmic presence, a push to render his revolutionary subjectivity as anachronistic and exhausted. This takes place in a very significant, visual way. While El Chivo is characterized as a grotesque Karl Marx (semi-long white hair, beard, and so on), his passage to redemption (achieved as he finally dares to establish indirect contact with Maru) is represented by him shaving, and wearing glasses and a suit, representing a damaged bourgeois subjectivity. From this moment on, he can undertake the process of moral healing described by Reber, a process that is possible only through the thorough reduction of his figure as an individual that embraces the path of uncertainty. Unlike Retes and de Llaca, González Iñarritu has no qualms in concluding his film with a definitive renunciation of revolutionary politics (and a return to family values) as the necessary condition of moving toward the future.

The readability of *Amores perros* as part of "global art cinema" rests on its negotiation between its adaptability to a politics of representation fully compatible with neoliberalism and its existence as a work at the level of form that reconciles the aforementioned film aesthetics with the narrative innovations born out of the American independent cinema of the 1990s. In previous chapters, I have argued that Mexican filmmakers engaged with the aesthetics of different figures within post-Sundance American film, including Steven Soderbergh and the Coen brothers. *Amores perros* occupies a central place in another tradition, in the wake of the work performed by Quentin Tarantino in *Reservoir Dogs* (1992) and *Pulp Fiction* (1994). Film theorists have created conceptual elaborations of this type of film: Todd McGowan, for instance, speaks of "atemporal cinema" (*Out of Time*), while Allan Cameron refers to "modular narratives." The problem here is that the film that interests both McGowan and Cameron is *21 Grams* (González Iñarritu, 2003); they ignore the role of *Amores perros* in the international consecration of this type of temporally disjointed narrative. Alejandro Solomianski has noted that González Iñarritu takes the apolitical and aestheticized violence present in Tarantino's works and in another film in this paradigm, Ang Lee's *Crouching Tiger, Hidden Dragon* (2000), and inscribes it into a social-realist narrative (29). While I disagree with Solomianski's contention that *Amores perros* is a film that "de-tarantinizes" this type of cinematic form in order to present a political allegory about Mexico (30), it is true that González Iñarritu's aestheticization of the social antagonism of Mexico is a crucial step in the consecration of this type of narrative in global art cinema. In fact, *Amores perros* had an almost immediate effect on American cinema: movies like Greg Marcks's *11:14* (2003) and, more significantly, Mike Figgis's Academy Award winner *Crash* (2004) fully co-opted González Iñarritu's use of the car accident to structure films that turn the social antagonism of the United States into a liberal fantasy of racial or social reconciliation. This appropriation shows well how the so-called left-wing narrative technique described by Kraniauskas ("*Amores perros*") in fact operates within established forms of independent cinema with less-than-radical ideological engagements. Another take is offered by María del Mar Azcona, who has argued that the "multi-protagonist film" is a central genre of American independent cinema, as attested by the work of directors like Steven Soderbergh, Robert Altman, Paul Thomas Anderson, and Edward Burns, among others (30–32). Without delving too much into the specific parallels between *Amores perros* and these practices, the ease with which one can locate González Iñarritu's work within well-established technical and generic paradigms speaks of the way in which his work decidedly overcame the legacies of "cinema of solitude" and of early neoliberal cinema. As Juan Pellicer shows in his close reading of González Iñarritu's films, his work is characterized by a creative use of montage in the construction of discourse, locating drama away from content (which was the privileged site of narrative tension in the heavily realist paradigms that ruled Mexico for most of the twentieth century) and into formal juxtaposition (12–13). The truly meaningful intervention of *Amores perros* in Mexican cinema lies in this displacement.

Precisely because González Iñarritu's innovations belong to the process of neoliberal modernization of cinema in Mexico, one cannot extricate his later films from *Amores perros*. Tierney is correct in her criticism of both the inability of scholars of Mexican film to fully account for his later work, as well as the ignorance of non-Latin Americanist critics regarding *Amores perros* ("Alejandro González Iñarritu" 102). By claiming that *21 Grams* and *Babel* represent concerns proper to Mexican cinema, Tierney opens an important interpretive space with many potential developments. For my current purposes, a final argument regarding González Iñarritu emerges from this point. González Iñarritu raises the question of considering the material and institutional processes underlying national cinema traditions when reading a global auteur. Beyond the fact that the influence of *Amores perros* on the mainstream of American cinema is placed under erasure when the central film in American criticism is *21 Grams*, González Iñarritu's importance, even in the case of his more global movies, results from the negotiation between the specificities of Mexican neoliberal cinema and the world of independent and art house cinema. For instance, critic Michael Stewart offers a compelling reading of *21 Grams* as melodrama, arguing that the film turns the genre "progressively away from the garishness, irony, and hysteria of Sirkian melodrama, as well as the utopia sentiment of various women's and/or rites-of-passage films, toward nihilism, the abject and what Jeffrey Sconce calls 'cold melodrama'" (49–50).

Stewart's article thoroughly ignores the fact that González Iñarritu comes from a tradition where melodrama (as we saw in the previous chapters) is absolutely crucial in almost every cultural genre and that the turn of melodrama Stewart has identified is already present in *Amores perros*. González Iñarritu is not only turning the genre away from Douglas Sirk's American iteration: he is also moving away from the form as inherited from Golden Age practitioners such as Ismael Rodríguez and Emilio Fernández. In fact, one could argue that the "affecting legacies" identified by Podalsky (81) are first and foremost the result of the problematic engagement between Mexico's contemporaneity and the melodramatic structure of feeling. González Iñarritu's use of melodrama in his non-Mexican films is fully constructed around the same narrative of the family that structures *Amores perros*. This is the case with *21 Grams*, where the accident unravels the family attachments of both the perpetrator, Jack (Benicio del Toro), and the victim, Christina (Naomi Watts), or of *Babel*, where the ordeal underwent by the children of Richard and Susan Jones (Brad Pitt and Cate Blanchett) with their Mexican caretaker (Adriana Barraza) is the direct consequence of their parents' preference for traveling around the world rather than being with them. The family logic is present even in *Biutiful* (2011), where the pathos of Uxbal (Javier Bardem) is defined not only by terminal disease (a melodramatic trope that is also present in *21 Grams* via Sean Penn's character) but also by his dealing with his children and his bipolar wife (his tragic destiny is related to the fact that, unlike El Chivo, he refuses to be an absent father). Some critics have even contended that *Babel* is "reminiscent of classic Mexican cinema" (Sisk, *Mexico* 145) and that its globalized narrative places the U.S.-Mexico border in a constellation of shared human experience (Podalsky 135). Ultimately, the point is that the phenomenon underlying González Iñarritu's cinema is the inscription of neoliberal Mexican cinema and its paradigms into the larger language of global art cinema.[23]

At this point, Mexican cinema enjoyed a domestic market that was as strong as ever and an international market that was already able to receive and process at least some of the work performed in Mexico not only by directors but also by actors and cinematographers. González Iñarritu was instrumental to this process, since he had constructed what Celestino Deleyto and María del Mar Azcona have characterized as "a cinematic style and a very personal yet culturally relevant worldview around the interstices between shots, between places, between nations and between narrative and chronological instants" (119). This worldview emerged, in Deleyto's and Azcona's view, "from a particular moment of Mexican cinema and from a particular place in Mexican culture," and has allowed González Iñarritu to become "the paragon of the contemporary filmmaker by appropriating and expanding the conventions of a new genre and constructing from the edges of empire a new transnational citizenship and, in the process, a new object of cinematic fascination" (119). One can supplement this insight by observing that the reverse process was also at work: a new Mexican cinema was constructed by the appropriation of transnational citizenship and the ethos of worldwide independent and art house cinema. In other words, the point is not only the ability of Mexican film to transcend its national boundaries and emerge as a referent in global cinema, which Tierney, Deleyto, and Azcona aptly analyze. It is also important to fully consider the reconfiguration of Mexican neoliberal cinema through the paradigms of global cinema, because this newly found dialogue allowed Mexican cinema to decisively transcend many of the remaining impasses left behind by the "cinema of solitude" and the crisis of the 1990s. The movie that most adequately represents this juncture is Alfonso Cuarón's *Y tu mamá también*.

Alfonso Cuarón, Commercial Authorship, and the Second Reinvention of Mexican Cinema

If *Amores perros* created unprecedented visibility for Mexican cinema on international circuits, Alfonso Cuarón's *Y tu mamá también* (2001) represents a zenith in the reconfiguration of Mexican cinema suggested by his first film, *Sólo con tu pareja*. While *Sólo con tu pareja* heralded the emergence of a middle-class aesthetic to respond to the cultural pressures embedded in the social transformations of neoliberalism, *Y tu mamá también* is a movie that fully embodies the outcome of the processes of Mexican cinema discussed in the present book. The rough, sentimental education of Tenoch Iturbide (Diego Luna) and Julio Zapata (Gael García Bernal) in their impromptu road trip with Luisa Cortés (Maribel Verdú) is the point where a new Mexican cinematic culture converges with the national and the global, politics and affect, reflecting relationships it had spent the previous decade retooling. *Y tu mamá también* is a film that acknowledges the imperatives of its Mexican origin with an equal dose of sincerity and critical distance, while surrounding the endearing but highly problematic world of two young *machos*-in-the-making with the invisible and contradictory political and social realities that escape their perception. And, even though it is not nearly as ambitious as *Amores perros* in either form or content, *Y tu mamá también* is, in my view, the film that most iconically represents the challenges posed by the neoliberal paradigm both to filmmakers and to film studies.

Not surprisingly, the film garnered ample critical attention in the decade after its initial release. The gender economy deployed by the film, particularly regarding the construction of masculine bodies and subjectivities and the problematic representation of women, has elicited great interest among academics, particularly because of its dialogues with other forms of gender engagement in

Mexican culture. In an oft-cited article, Ernesto Acevedo-Muñoz characterizes *Y tu mama también* as a "counter-epic" that exposes the fiction of the Mexican Revolution's idea of a "class-less society" and that can conclude only with Julio and Tenoch's "discovery of their own hatred and homosexual desires" ("Sex" 47). In a similar line of argument, critics have located the movie as part of traditions related to the representation of "the limits of the homosocial/sexual" (Lewis 177) and "neo-machista consciousness" (Kroll 25), and the film has even been used as an example of the use of fiction in the formation of masculine consciousness (Worrell). These arguments emerge from the strong critique of Mexican machismo embedded in Julio and Tenoch's hormone-laden homosocial relationship, which, at the end of the movie, results in an alcohol-fueled homosexual encounter between them. Other critics have taken the film's work on masculinity to the discussion of its ulterior consequences. Elena Lahr-Vivaz, for instance, reads the film as a "foundational fiction."[24] She argues that there is a potential of rewriting the nation embedded in Julio and Tenoch's homosexual desire, given that they would put together in the same symbolic space their respective social classes (89). Ultimately, this romance fails and, in Lahr-Vivaz's argument, the film "instead calls attention to the imaginary and exclusionary nature of *all* fables of national identity" (93).

Before engaging with this last point, it is important to keep in mind the other gender element developed by critics: the problematic use of Luisa as the female mediator between Tenoch and Julio. Luisa is married to Tenoch's cousin Jano (Juan Carlos Remolina), a somewhat successful writer. The road trip at the core of the movie takes place when Luisa decides to accept Tenoch and Julio's improvised invitation after Jano confesses his infidelity. Luisa has been the subject of ambiguous readings. María Donapetry, for instance, points out that compelling Mexican female characters in the film (such as Julio's sister, a Zapatista activist) are more absent than present, but that Luisa, even though she fails to provide a Mexican role model for female spectators, still elicits solidarity because her questioning of Julio and Tenoch's masculinity is not grounded in a "transnational imperialist or neo-colonialist aspect" (125; my translation). Tabea Linhard identifies in Luisa an example (also present in the films of Agustín Díaz Yanes) of a Spanish female character who appears in Mexican transatlantic films as an instance of "gendered and transatlantic subjects [who] also remain unheard amidst a visual overload of national and nationalist cultural specificity" (46).[25] A more complex reading is offered by Alberto Ribas, who characterizes Luisa as serving "a panoply of functions . . . as translator, conqueror, sexual object and mother." These functions nonetheless are "partially deconstructed" by her illness and death, therefore "destabilizing the position of moral superiority that the spectator has acquired due to the information provided by the voice-over, the vagrant camera perspective and the knowledge of Luisa's marital situation" (470–71).[26] All in all, it is clear that the issue of gender has been sufficiently and successfully engaged by scholarship so far, which in my view opens the space to consider the film beyond this perspective.

A more productive line of inquiry for the purposes of the present book rests on considering the film's complex relationship to paradigms of Mexican cinema. This has to do in part with the location of the film both in the "transatlantic traffic" (Paul Julian Smith) of production schemes and cultural symbols embodied in the movie—including the performance of Maribel Verdú as Luisa and the Spanish business interests of producer Jorge Vergara—and in the "Mexican *nouvelle vague*" (Menne), which allowed the directors considered in this chapter to locate themselves in the cartography of global art cinema.[27] However, the status of *Y tu mamá también* as a product of post-1988 Mexican cinema remains underdiscussed in part because critics have surprisingly failed to consider it in relation to *Sólo con tu pareja* and to Cuarón's original contributions to the process. This is in my view crucial not only because it partly explains Cuarón's unprecedented success abroad, but also because it highlights many important issues in understanding the limits and impasses of representing Mexico in national cinema. Following the arguments I have laid out in previous chapters, the movie can be characterized as an attempt to reconfigure national cinema in the wake of its inextricable relationship with global circuits and from the consciousness of the profound exhaustion of historical paradigms of representing Mexico in film.

It is important to remember here that *Y tu mamá también* is a film produced after Cuarón's return from his first round of work in Hollywood. After *Sólo con tu pareja,* Cuarón participated in two adaptations of British literary classics: *A Little Princess* (1995), an adaptation of Frances Hodgson Burnett's novel of the same title, and *Great Expectations* (1998), a modernized rendering of Charles Dickens's classic. This trajectory makes Cuarón somewhat different from his Mexican counterparts. Del Toro and González Iñarritu's Hollywood ventures kept their directorial identity very close to their genre and narrative interests: Del Toro worked in horror (*Mimic*) and fantasy (*Hellboy*), and González Iñarritu reused the narrative structure of *Amores perros,* completing a trilogy of sorts with *21 Grams* and *Babel.* Conversely, Cuarón has shown far more range and adaptability to the paradigms of English-language cinema. In her reading of *A Little Princess,* Rosemary Marangoly George faults the movie for turning Burnett's book into a "liberal multicultural narrative" (156). Similarly, Ana Moya and Gemma López argue that *Great Expectations* engages identity politics by transposing Victorian reflections on social dynamics into the analysis of "postmodern identity" (186).[28] These two readings illustrate the fact that Cuarón's second and third feature-length movies are closer to the ideologies of American cinema of the Clinton era than to the logic of post-1988

Mexican film. This is not surprising, considering that Cuarón's first venture in the English-speaking world was strictly contemporary to the arc between the cinematic void that took place between the 1994 economic crisis and the release of *Sexo, pudor y lágrimas* in 1998. While *Sólo con tu pareja* foretold the success of romantic comedy as a genre in commercial Mexican cinema more than half a decade in advance, Cuarón's migration to Hollywood was most certainly connected to the fact that his style of filmmaking was out of place in an industry that was still dealing—as I illustrated in previous chapters—with the last threads of "cinema of solitude" in films such as *El callejón de los milagros* and *Entre Pancho Villa y una mujer desnuda*.

Y tu mamá también embodies Cuarón's return from the world of American independent cinema to a Mexican industry that was radically different from the one that engendered *Sólo con tu pareja*. Cuarón brought with him the savoir faire of private independent production, which had achieved an unprecedented level of economic and aesthetic certainty thanks to the success of *Amores perros*. Still, the more fundamental question faced by such a film was how to reengage both the national and the political at a juncture where, as I argued in Chapters 1 and 3, the very possibility of doing so seemed preempted by the nonexistence of current and viable languages for such an enterprise. *Y tu mamá también* solved this conundrum by using this impossibility as a central formal conceit, through its unique use of the voice-over. As viewers of the film may remember, the film features a narrator who talks constantly about politics, the internal workings of the characters' minds, and many other things missed by the self-referential perspectives of Julio and Tenoch. In this narrator, Cuarón invokes a rare device, the disembodied voice-over—that is, an omniscient male narrator whose voice is located completely outside the actions and the bodies of the protagonists. In fact, every time this narrator intervenes in the film, all other sounds fade away and go silent, showing a deliberate attempt to keep the narrator's musings fully outside the film's diegesis. Invoking Kaja Silverman's study of this device, Hester Baer and Ryan Long suggest that the voice-over "disrupts identification with the characters to call the viewer's attention to social, political and historical events that fall outside the purview of the film's immediate story," which, as a result, "functions to construct a hegemonic national memory of Mexico's contemporary political transition" (159).

While Baer and Long are right to emphasize the authoritarian nature of the voice-over as a narrative resource, I think that the use of such an unusual device on the part of Cuarón is not fully explained by the mere will to assert a hegemonic narrative of contemporary Mexico. Rather, the voice-over seems to signal the fundamental impossibility of organically inscribing such political and social stances in the narrative weave of a film fully embedded in the modes of production and discourse predominant in the late 1990s and early 2000s. As I argued in the previous section, another manifestation of this impossibility is present in *Amores perros* and the political undecidability that allows for readings of the film as both progressive and conservative. In the case of *Y tu mamá también*, the voice-over shows how the very narratives of the urban middle class as developed by film at the time were unable to engage with forms of politics beyond the mere class interests of the cinematic subjects. While the two most predominant political films of the period, *Todo el poder* and *La ley de Herodes*, express agendas proper to their middle-class audiences (concerning corruption, electoral democracy, and so on), *Y tu mamá también* cannot comment on massive social inequalities or the contrast between urban and rural life from the perspective of the film's protagonists (or its purported audiences). Thus, rather than inscribing such realities in forms that would either be too contrived (for instance, by narrating Julio and Tenoch's potential acquisition of social consciousness) or too sanctimonious (like tying the characters' failed pathos to a concrete political or social event), the film opts to place the impossibility of political articulation itself as a formal resource.

The fact that Cuarón is the one director inscribing the impossibility of politics into a prominent Mexican film is by no means coincidental. *Sólo con tu pareja* was, as I discussed in Chapter 2, a fundamental landmark in the construction of the detached, depoliticized, and self-referential middle-class stance that would become the norm of Mexican commercial cinema. At the time of the shooting and release of *Y tu mamá también*, this stance had become hegemonic, either by the production of films fully embracing it (like *Sexo, pudor y lágrimas*) or by the validation of the gaze imposed from that class perspective into the social world of Mexico (such as the criminalization of the working class in *Todo el poder* or *Amores perros*). If *Amores perros* embodies the conservative interpretation of Mexico's inequalities through its family-oriented narrative, the voice-over in *Y tu mamá también* represents the left-oriented view of Mexico City elites aligned with the Partido de la Revolución Democrática (PRD), the primary political force in the country's capital. As Vicente Fox achieved the first electoral victory of a non-PRI presidential candidate in 2000, Andrés Manuel López Obrador, the leading figure of the Mexican Left, was elected mayor of Mexico City. In achieving this, the PRD was able to develop strong ties to parts of the Mexican intelligentsia, which in turn resulted in the gradual internalization of the discourse of social inequality in parts of Mexico City's middle class. *Y tu mamá también*'s voice-over might be one of the first manifestations of this alternative ideological stance.

The film's narrator is voiced by Daniel Giménez Cacho, the actor who performed the role of Tomás Tomás, a visible member of Mexico's progressive intelligentsia, in *Sólo con tu pareja*. This inherent citation of Cuarón's previous movie provides a way to see the important elements that differentiate the world represented in both films. The self-referential world of Tomás Tomás took place in the outset of the neoliberal transition, and his unapologetic machismo, reprehensible as it was, was nonetheless framed by the symbolic viability of representing a circumscribed and sheltered "space outside of history" in the romantic comedy.[29] It reflected the aspirations of those who benefited from the early fruits of neoliberal culture and economics. *Y tu mamá también* belongs more to a world where the contradictions and conflicts effaced by the affective shelter of the romantic comedy cannot quite be concealed. Properly speaking, Julio and Tenoch attempt to live in a self-enclosed world similar to that of Tomás, a space where the haunting contradictions of everyday life may be dissolved in the hormonal solidarity of male friendship. Still, the film does not fully place itself within the "space outside history" constructed by Julio and Tenoch's homosocial relationship, a decision that would have inscribed it in the neoliberal tradition discussed in Chapter 2. Rather, Cuarón opts to locate viewers in the border between the neoliberal "fiction of development" (Saldaña Portillo 757) that remains operative in the everyday life of the movie's characters (insofar as they come from a privileged social sphere) and the perspective of a narrator who consistently reminds us of the social costs and contradictions underlying that fiction. And most certainly, the voice-over's ability to represent Mexico's social contradictions has limits of its own. As Deborah Shaw convincingly argues, the film is not "concerned with organized political protest" and "no real poverty is seen, and while State oppression is hinted at in the prominence of the police presence, no explanation is given for the arrests made" ("(Trans)National Images" 124). The limits of the politics embodied by the voice-over are more or less the same as the limits of the progressive middle class represented by it: awareness of inequality, though not of its extremes; a critique of political corruption and privilege (including in the wedding scene, where the boys meet Luisa and the power and privilege exercised by Tenoch's family becomes quite evident), but not an understanding of radical political engagement (even though the road trip ends up on the southern Pacific coast, the fact that those territories have operational armed groups is never considered). Yet, the presence of the elements actually used by the film does move the discourse of Mexican cinema toward an improved ability to consider some of the contradictions within neoliberalism. An example is the story of people like fisherman Chuy (Silverio Palacios), whose livelihood is on the verge of being destroyed by a tourism development, something that very palpably shows the correlation of the privilege exercised by the film's protagonists and the people they encounter during their trip. Such acknowledgment would have been unthinkable in *Sólo con tu pareja*, in *Sexo, pudor y lágrimas*, and even in the class-segregated world of *Amores perros*. Certainly, the solidarity between Luisa and Chuy's family is simultaneously melodramatic (she finds refuge with them, peacefully meeting the end of her life in their company) and problematic (it is the Spanish woman who is able to see the value of non-neoliberal life through her engagement with a subaltern subject, while the Mexican boys are unable to comprehend it). But, in the end, by creating a mise-en-scène that allows the social contradictions of Mexico to coexist in the space of commercial cinema, Cuarón is in fact breaking with the self-referentiality that his previous Mexican movie helped to build.

Even if one accepts the positive assessment of *Y tu mamá también* as more sensitive than other contemporary films to the contradictions and inequalities of neoliberalism, the movie's rendering of Mexico remains problematic. Nuala Finnegan has described the film's perspective as a "tourist vision" that, at times, "indulges in scenes of folkloric picturesqueness" ("So" 32). Finnegan's assessment is based, correctly, on the fact that Cuarón's aspiration to reach a global audience creates an imperative for the film to answer the question "So what's Mexico really like?" (29); that is, to participate in the taste for the local that is part of the commoditization of identities proper to global art cinema.[30] Finnegan's assessment, however, does not quite address the conundrum faced by directors like Cuarón and González Iñarritu: they must equally engage the international audience that requires a measure of cultural "authenticity" in cinema from the global South while addressing a domestic Mexican audience with no desire to return to the tokenism of the country's prior international blockbuster, Arau's *Como agua para chocolate*. My contention here is that the "tourist vision" criticized by Finnegan is not only a device to appeal to international audiences, but also the result of Mexican film's own inability to represent the national in the wake of the collapse of Mexicanism described in Chapter 1. If one recalls the films from the 1988–2002 period, most commercially successful works (including even a neo-Mexicanist film like *El callejón de los milagros*) are set in Mexico City. *Y tu mamá también* is not impervious to this logic. As Salvador Oropesa reminds us, the film does develop a somewhat detailed cartography of the city before the protagonists embark on their road trip (98). Conversely, the few major works that engage with Mexico's interior (such as *Santitos* or *La ley de Herodes*) tend to represent it as a site of superstition, historical regression, and corruption.[31] The films that engage Mexican *provincia* as a site of the contradiction of modernity and neoliberalism (like Carrera's *El crimen del padre Amaro* or Naranjo's *Drama/Mex*) would come later in the decade, made possible in part by the recasting of Mexico in *Y tu mamá también*. The interior in Cuarón's work is, once again, a product of this logic: as Julio, Tenoch, and Luisa travel across it, *provincia* is the site of rural beauty queens, political protest, and the supposedly redeeming authenticity that neoliberalism has pushed to the verge of extinction.[32]

In these terms, Cuarón's film must be regarded as both a product of the impasse defining the relationship between film and Mexicanism in the late 1990s and as a turning point that allows for the reconsideration of Mexico as a subject of cinematic representation. By highlighting the fundamental blindness of the urban middle-class subject when confronted with the rest of the country,

Y tu mamá también also raises the question of the lack of a national memory that involves anything other than the elites. At one point on the trip, the camera shows us two unassuming black metal crosses on the side of the road. Right before seeing them, we hear the voice-over explaining that, if the travelers had driven through the same spot ten years earlier, they would have found broken birdcages in the road, a wrecked truck, two corpses, and a woman crying. This reminiscence is peculiar because it does not draw a social or political conclusion: it does not assert either a repressed political memory or the life story of someone with a clear personal history. It simply states this event. A few minutes later, as Luisa chastises Julio and Tenoch after they fight over her, we briefly see another black cross. The voice-over becomes unnecessary here, since the viewer already knows the meaning of that cross. Two points emerge from this detail. First, when the narrator brings up the story underlying a small detail on the side of the highway—just after Luisa tells her companions about a boyfriend who died in a motorcycle accident—he raises the truck accident to the same narrative level as Luisa's tragedy. In the economy of the scene, it does not matter if the person killed is a truck driver or the protagonist's object of affection. Both stories are revisited, one within the action of the movie and the other outside of it. It is possible to read this scene as a comment on the many untold stories in Mexico's cartographies, and on the inability to tell them from within the narrative parameters of commercial cinema: only the film's unusual narrative voice can account for them, since the self-referential nature of the protagonists makes them unaware of anything other than their personal stories. Still, by investing the crosses on the side of the road with meaning, the narrator effectively inscribes these stories into the cinematic experience of the audience. In consequence, when the camera's gaze fixates for a moment on another cross, the narrator becomes unnecessary, since the potential story underlying it is already part of the rapport with the spectator.

This strategy of recollecting untold stories penetrates even the consciousness of the protagonists themselves. Early in the road trip, the trio drives through a town called Tepelmeme, which, as we learn through the narrative voice, is the birthplace of Tenoch's nanny, Leodegaria, who immigrated to Mexico City at age thirteen and began working for the Iturbide family shortly thereafter. This time around, the narrator does not express an event outside the consciousness of the characters. Rather, we learn of the inner thoughts of Tenoch, who remembers that he used to call her "Mom" until age four. This emphasizes that he had a deeper relationship with her than with his biological mother, Silvia (Diana Bracho), who earlier in the film is presented as a superficial and clueless upper-class woman. The narrator makes a point of telling us that Tenoch did not share this information with his travel companions, which means that its mention is for the benefit of the audience. In this case, the memory of Leodegaria—the rarely told story of one of those domestic servants who silently accompany the life of a Mexican elite—not only brings into the space of cinema yet another subject that had been conspicuously absent in neoliberal Mexican cinema. It also, if briefly, shakes the foundations of Tenoch's class subjectivity.[33] These acts of remembrance not only create a privileged perspective for the spectator. Insofar as the average audience member of Mexican cinema belongs to the class range that spans from Julio's middle class to Tenoch's upper class, *Y tu mamá también* also questions the very social world its spectators inhabit. Andrea Noble argues that "the film radically undercuts the viewer's omniscience and in so doing, the real political charge of Cuarón's film comes into focus, in its exposure of, and thereby challenge to, the will to knowledge in looking and in the ethnographic look in particular" (146). Although Noble restricts this insight to her analysis of the representation of the rural lower classes from the perspective of the protagonists, the point she makes is crucial: even though the viewer "knows better" than the characters, the film is always critical of the social location of the audience. The fundamental difference between *Amores perros* and *Y tu mamá también* emerges from this very point. The social world constructed by Alejandro González Iñarritu ultimately presents social difference in a way that embraces class segregation: the only reason why the film is able to show us a wide social canvas results from the narrative act itself, from the construction, through montage and through the use of an accident, of zones of class contact that would not exist otherwise. Although she is involved in the same accident, Valeria never interacts with Octavio or with El Chivo. Before and after the crash, they belong to altogether separate spheres, which is why *Amores perros* has to consist of three independent episodes. Conversely, *Y tu mamá también* shows that such class segregation is not so much a fact as an ideological perception: from Tenoch's memory of Leodegaria to Luisa's encounter with Chuy's family, the working classes are always already there.

Some readings of the film have made the point that *Y tu mamá también* is unique in its undoing of mise-en-scène Mexico's unequal and segregated class dynamic. Amaya and Blair, for instance, suggest that the film entertains "the notion [that] there is a space, a middle ground, where . . . two classes and races can coexist," although it is "ambivalent, because racial and class differences exist in parallel systems of desire" (59). Ultimately, though, "class and racial inequality, as unnamable differences, remain unbridgeable" (60). This is most obviously illustrated in the film's ending, when we find out that Tenoch will study economics at the ITAM (Instituto Tecnológico Autónomo de México), the elite school identified with Mexican neoliberal technocracy, while Julio is enrolled in a public university's biology program. Their friendship becomes irreparably broken, and both Tenoch and Julio are placed in destinies that will reproduce their existing social positions: Tenoch renounces his aspiration to belong to the "creative class" (as a writer) in order to fully assume his role as a member of Mexico's power elite, while Julio will follow a path where he is expected—not without the uncertainty of having a science major in a country with little science research—to remain in the professional middle class. However, one cannot read this conclusion solely at face value. One should bracket the gender argument set forward by Amaya and Blair—who conclude that the film treats masculinities in a way that poses the melancholia of changing sexual roles in Latin America (61)—because it's too reliant on the plot. What becomes clear when considering my argument so far is that the critical class perspective introduced by the narrative voice (who gets the last words of the film, saying that Tenoch and Julio "will never see each other again") leads to an ending that has two coexisting narrative levels. Within the world inhabited by Tenoch and Julio, it is clear that the class difference was fully asserted and that, in its brutal logic, even the close personal relationship between them was unable to survive the inexorable fate of social inequality. However, precisely because the spectator knows better, thanks to all the elements provided by the narrative voice, this fate is not simply assumed matter-of-factly. When comparing Tenoch and Julio with Tomás Tomás in *Sólo con tu pareja*, it is important to note two meaningful differences. First, neither Tenoch nor Julio dwells in the fantasy of the "creative class." Their career choices are disappointing from the perspective of the audience precisely because the social normalization they represent does not even allow for the fantasy of self-realization. Second, Tomás Tomás ultimately prevails by gaining Clarisa's love, giving *Sólo con tu pareja* the type of happy ending through which romantic comedies allegorize the integration of the protagonist into the social order. In *Y tu mamá también*, there is no happy ending. The awkwardness of the final scene, which, as we learn from the narrator, takes place because it was less uncomfortable for the characters to have a cup of coffee than to ignore each other, serves as a painful reminder that the social order of neoliberalism does not result from personal realization but from renouncing a part of one's aspirations and affects.

A point overlooked by critics in *Y tu mamá también* is Cuarón's use of artificiality to create critical distance. The narrator is undoubtedly an element in this regard. Also, like in *Sólo con tu pareja*, Cuarón uses implausible names for his characters. In *Y tu mamá también*, Cuarón replaces the repetition predominant in his first movie (e.g., Tomás Tomás, Silvia Silva) with the ironic use of last names from Mexican history. Tenoch's last name, Iturbide, recalls Mexico's first post-Independence leader; Julio Zapata is named after the revolutionary; Luisa Cortés after the conquistador; the boys' girlfriends, Ana (Ana López Mercado) and Cecilia (María Aura), are named, respectively, after an independence leader (Morelos) and an infamous counterrevolutionary (Huerta), and so on. Juli Kroll has used these names to claim that "national identity is foundational for the relationships forged in *Y tu mamá también*, a past of identity building that the film references via character names but does not point to overtly in the dialogue" (39–40). In my view, this reading assesses Cuarón's odd naming choices in too literal a manner. Following the precedent of *Sólo con tu pareja,* the names establish a pact of distance with the viewer: there is no way one can find a situation real with people named like that. Through this device, the movie preemptively de-authorizes literal readings of the film as some form of "authentic" representation of Mexico. The interesting part of this de-authorization is that it works only from the perspective of a Mexican audience that possesses the cultural referents to make the names meaningful. By virtue of this, the film in fact invites a non-Mexicanist reading by Mexican spectators while allowing the "tourist vision" from foreign audiences. Furthermore, I think the names belong to Cuarón's effort—represented in *Sólo con tu pareja* by the dream sequence with the cartoonish national icons—to void national signifiers by denaturalizing them. The point is, in my view, precisely the opposite of Kroll's reading: national identity is so irrelevant in the formation of the characters' identities that their being named after historical characters is, at most, an ironic comment on a superficial trait (like the Spanish woman with the last name Cortés), and in most cases meaningless (as is the case with the boys' girlfriends, as well as with Tenoch's nanny, Leodegaria, who is named after a Mexican president of the post-Independence period).

What emerges from Cuarón's appropriation and representation of Mexico is the construction of a national cinema thoroughly uninterested in engaging with the nation as such. This is due, in part, to the collapse of Mexicanism as an apparatus of construction of overarching identitary narratives and, also, to the fact that identity politics—race, class, gender—are a much stronger factor than the nation in the ideological economy of *Y tu mamá también*. Stephen Crofts has discussed the impact of similar displacements in the study of national cinemas:

> Politics, in other words, is a matter of unequal distribution of power across axes of nation, as well as of class, gender, ethnicity, etc. The political engagements that people do (or do not) make will vary with their social and political contexts, and their readings of those contexts. In considering national cinemas, this implies the importance of a political flexibility able, in some contexts, to challenge the fictional homogenizations of much discourse on national cinema, and in others to support them. (44)

While one cannot, in Crofts's words, "underestimate the continuing power of the nation-state" (44–45), *Y tu mamá también* is a film that requires resisting the temptation to assert the "fictional homogenization" of the national in its discourse precisely because it deploys many different dimensions of the "unequal distribution of power" within Mexico. In a way, *Y tu mamá también* is a transformational movie in the Mexican context especially because it resists all typical homogenizations. It does not pose a homogeneous national discourse, as the inherent contradictions of the nation are central to its narrative construction. In addition, the film does not present a homogeneous class fiction, like romantic comedies do, or even a schematic narration of class difference in the style of *Amores perros*. Rather, we are confronted with a complex spectrum of different social strata that constantly interact and problematize each other. One can certainly not claim that either the urban privileged classes or the impoverished rural subjects are homogeneous. There are differences of class among Tenoch, Luisa, and Julio, just like there are among Leodegaria, Chuy, and the people working at the bar near the end of the film, who all belong to distinct social positions. The film works because it resists the construction of social identities both in the overarching national sense (there is no unequivocal Mexicanness, not even a problematic one, to be derived from it) and in the class-specific sense—unlike *Todo el poder*, for example, the film does not attempt to create any fiction of citizenship or middle-class belonging. Hester Baer and Ryan Long have read the film as a portrayal of Mexico "as a nation at an impasse, but it does not provide a satisfactory way out" (164).[34] I would take this conclusion even further: such a "satisfactory way out" is no longer a desirable or possible outcome. The proper role of *Y tu mamá también* in Mexican cultural history is its exhaustion of the symbolic possibilities of the nation in cinematic discourse.

There are two interesting aftermaths to this renunciation of the cultural density of the national performed by *Y tu mamá también*. The first one is exemplified by Carlos Cuarón's *Rudo y cursi* (2008), where Diego Luna and Gael García Bernal reunite to play Beto and Tato, two siblings from a rural town who are recruited by an agent to play in the national soccer league. The film is a farcical comedy centered on the conflicts that arise from Beto and Tato's rise to fame, which result in their mingling with organized crime and a spectacular fall into disgrace. *Rudo y cursi* belongs to the same paradigm as *Y tu mamá también* not only because Carlos Cuarón was a scriptwriter for both films (as well as for *Sólo con tu pareja*), but also because of its unwavering attack on the mythology of soccer as a structure of social ascendance. It is also relevant to note that the film was the first production of Cha Cha Chá Films, a company co-owned by del Toro, González Iñarritu, and Alfonso Cuarón, which also coproduced Rodrigo García's *Mother and Child* (2009) and González Iñarritu's *Biutiful*.[35] One could certainly denounce *Rudo y cursi* as classist, given the exaggerated, cartoonish way in which both Luna and García Bernal play their lower-class characters, not to mention the fact that most of the humor is derived from Beto and Tato's nouveau-riche behavior. This, however, would be too reductive. What underlies the film's comedy is the insurmountable distance between Mexico's rural classes and the pressures of the ruthless capitalist system represented by soccer and the media. It also undermines the success story typical of the sports-film genre in general and the soccer movie in particular. One could remember here the story of social integration embedded in Gurinder Chadha's *Bend It like Beckham* (2002), where soccer is a space for multicultural encounter and for overcoming the limits of tradition, or the *Goal!* trilogy (Danny Cannon, 2005; Jaume Collet-Serra, 2007; Andrew Monahan, 2009), a series bankrolled by FIFA that focused on an illegal Mexican immigrant who begins the movie as a gardener and goes on to achieve international soccer stardom. The fact that both Chadha's film and the first two installments of *Goal!* precede *Rudo y cursi*—and that the latter has Kuno Becker, a well-known Mexican actor, playing the protagonist—suggests the possibility that *Rudo y cursi* may in fact be implicitly critiquing their triumphalism. The point here is that, just like *Y tu mamá también*, *Rudo y cursi* exhibits the ability of commercial Mexican film to operate in forms that no longer seek any identitary claim over its spectatorship. The brand of commercial Mexican cinema spearheaded by the Cuarón brothers shows that the very expression of the cultural exhaustion of Mexican culture and the absurdity of its ideals amid the disappointment with and failure of the neoliberal model is as much a way to draw audiences into the theater as the construction of the creative class fantasy was in the 1990s. Recent films based on the carnivalesque deployment of empty Mexican signifiers seem to demonstrate this point. We can see it in the brutal critique of the mythology of the American dream of Mexican immigration as represented by the wrestler-protagonist of Héctor Hernández and Horacio Rivera's *Los pajarracos* (2006), or, more recently, in the comedic appropriation of traditional Christmas theater for the satirization of Mexico's culture of corruption in Emilio Portes's *Pastorela* (2011).

The second aftermath of *Y tu mamá también*'s success is Cuarón's meteoric rise as a "global auteur." Cuarón successfully articulated himself both to commercial cinema and to art cinema in the English-language world. His sensitivity in developing the distinct personalities of Julio and Tenoch translated well in his recasting of the *Harry Potter* franchise. The fact that he established the tone that would prevail for the remaining six installments—breaking with the childish aesthetic created by Chris Columbus in the first two films—speaks volumes about the way in which his desacralizing approach to characters allows for the creation of psychological depth even when working with the most commercial of materials. Equally notable is the success of *Children of Men* (2006), which established Cuarón both as a formal innovator, thanks to his work with the long take (Udden), and as a filmmaker concerned with crucial political questions regarding race, immigration, and war (Chaudhary; DasGupta). As Samuel Amago has perceptively noted, *Children of Men* grounds its political commentary in the same formal strategy as *Y tu mama también* by presenting the victims of Cuarón's dystopic world on two levels: "Although they are essentially invisible to the characters as they go about their lives, they are nonetheless presented prominently to the viewer, who is invited to see more than the protagonists can" (220). We can see here that the narrative solution devised by Cuarón as a way to overcome the representational impasses of Mexican neoliberal film evolved into an interesting tool for ideologically framing his transnational work, allowing him to break with another representational impasse: the recognition of the subjectivity of the oppressed in the face of their reduction to the status of terrorists or illegal immigrants. Once again, rather than providing a direct allegory of the political issues at hand, *Children of Men* inscribes at the level of form the very representational aporia that characterizes the relationship between film and the political. Cuarón's easy circulation between Mexican commercial cinema, global art cinema, and Hollywood, recently shown by his film *Gravity* (2013), is the result of a transformational operation at the core of post-1990 Mexican cinema: the ability of film to reflect on its own ideological and identitary limits. In doing so, at least in the Mexican context, Cuarón opens the door for a properly post-national cinema—one that, beyond the acknowledgment of the limits of the nation, fully deterritorializes and undermines the codes of the national. This is why Cuarón's intervention is an important precursor to the most radical film auteur in contemporary Mexican cinema: Carlos Reygadas.

Carlos Reygadas and the End of National Cinema

The cinema of Carlos Reygadas—characterized by its bewildering beauty, its carefully crafted technique, and its subtle yet unsettling confrontation of the audience—represents yet another interesting manifestation of the neoliberal process in Mexican cinema. His style and cinematic sensitivity have no obvious precursors and, at times, his work seems to have emerged out of nothing. Nonetheless, his brand of filmmaking, based on an uncompromising attention to form and on the disavowal of the aesthetics and ideologies of the Mexican film industry described in this book, is at the same time made possible by the very process of neoliberalism that his movies so thoroughly deconstruct. An auteur like Reygadas emerges only when there is a solid institutional platform, both national and transnational, that allows not only alternative forms of film production and financing, but also vehicles of distribution within the national industry. Reygadas thus benefits both from the presence of Mexican cinema in international film festivals—bankrolled by IMCINE in the 1990s and consecrated by the success of directors like Ripstein, del Toro, and González Iñarritu across Europe and the Americas—and from the widening of the national market provided by the multiplexes. Discussing Reygadas at this point in my account of Mexican neoliberal cinema highlights three important, interconnected issues. First, it illustrates the fact that a central consequence of neoliberalism in the Mexican film industry has been the creation of a plurality of creative and commercial spaces, which in turn has favored the emergence of cinematic practices that break with established paradigms or inaugurate new ones. Second, in representing the formation of niche spaces within the industry, the discussion of Reygadas allows for a new way to undermine the twentieth-century tradition of national cinema. Rather than contesting Mexicanist ideology through its modern recasting (like in Carrera's *El crimen del padre Amaro*) or its satirization (like in *Y tu mamá también* or *Los pajarracos*), Reygadas's aestheticized approach simultaneously undercuts both the ideological premises of Mexican rural and urban cinema and the marks of modernization developed in paradigms such as the romantic comedy or the political film of the democratic transition. Finally, his movies engage with the process of insertion into paradigms of global art cinema by aligning his work to a genealogy of international film—Yasujiro Ozu, Andrei Tarkovsky, Carl Theodore Dreyer, Robert Bresson, and so on—and becoming readable alongside those of other highly acclaimed contemporary filmmakers: Abbas Kiarostami, Pedro Costa, Gus Van Sant, and Lisandro Alonso, among others. The fact that he was awarded the Cannes Film Festival Best Director Award in 2012, a few days after his film *Post Tenebras Lux* was subject to a violently adverse reaction from the audience, embodies well a paradox central to understanding Reygadas, a director whose illegibility and irritating nature is precisely the condition of possibility of his impact and genius.

The existence of Reygadas in the Mexican cinematic landscape is a sign of the expansion of the post-1988 industry into market niches beyond the commercial circuit described in Chapter 2. If neoliberalism produces, at a certain level, a homogenization of cultural texts (such as the romantic comedy aesthetic), the intersection of capital and globalization also creates a diversification of audiences and cultural products. As economist David Throsby reminds us, "diversity is an important attribute of cultural capital particularly because it has the capacity to yield new capital formation" (57). Thus, the construction of a cinematic market in Mexico not only produced trends in film language, but also opened the space for private exhibition to expand into underserved markets and audiences. As Mexican cinema gradually drew middle-class audiences into the theater, private investors geared the diversification of the industry toward art cinema. Up to the mid-1990s, art cinema was mostly a State-run affair. The venerable Cineteca Nacional was and remains the primary outlet for film festival fare, particularly through its Muestra Internacional de Cine, which has been running since 1971. The Muestra has in fact been an important channel for the domestic release of Mexican art cinema throughout its history. The first showings of many of Ripstein's movies and the work of younger auteurs like Julián Hernández and Amat Escalante have taken place at the Cineteca. In addition, the Muestra, the Foro Internacional, and other activities have provided Mexican audiences with a steady stream of films from a diverse set of countries and directors. The work of filmmakers with strong followings in the country—like Woody Allen, Manoel de Oliveira, Lars von Trier and, more recently, Béla Tarr and Bruno Dumont—typically open there before they are released to wider audiences. This activity is complemented by a variety of small theaters and clubs run by universities and public cultural institutes. Many of these theaters have always enjoyed large audiences—during an average Muestra, the Cineteca may get seventy thousand visitors in one month.[36] In fact, since the mid-1990s, the Cineteca expanded from four to seven screens, as well as partnering with other cultural institutions in Mexico City and in other locations to increase distribution of its fare. Recently, in response to yearly increases in attendance (it reported a 20 percent bump from 2010 to 2011), the Cineteca undertook a major remodeling project so that it could expand its services.

These numbers, and the types of audiences behind them (students, intellectuals, upper-middle-class attendees, and people trying to avoid Hollywood blockbusters), became attractive to private exhibitors, and some of them got into the business. In 1994, a private investor opened Cinemanía, a small three-screen complex in Plaza Loreto, a Carlos Slim-owned mall geared toward adults. Cinemanía has a bar and a bookstore, and shares the mall with a museum (which exhibits the Slim family's private collection), some of Mexico's most exclusive restaurants, and a cabaret. The business became so viable that Cinemanía was able to weather even the 1994 crisis. In September 1996, Cinemex opened its "Casa de Arte" venue in the upscale Polanco neighborhood, where it also benefits from the presence of art galleries and high-end restaurants. Gradually, all three chains got into the art house business: Cinépolis theaters have become sites for various Cineteca-promoted activities, Cinemark has participated in activities promoting Mexican and international cinema, and Cinemex even bankrolled its own festival, FICCO, which ran from 2004 to 2010. Today, it is not unusual for the three chains to devote part of their screen time to a considerable number of Latin American, European, and East Asian films.

It is also important to remember here that the public and private infrastructure of art cinema in Mexico allowed for the release and distribution of domestically produced movies that did not quite correspond with the more commercial paradigms of romantic comedy. Even when the industry hit a financial bottom in the mid-1990s, art cinema directors like Ripstein, Ignacio Ortiz, and Carlos Carrera were producing some of their more important works: one can remember here *Profundo Carmesí* (1995), *La orilla de la tierra* (1994), and *Sin remitente* (1995), respectively. This constant presence of art cinema in the Mexican scene not only affected exhibition, it also allowed producers to take the risk of going beyond the parameters of the new commercial cinema.

In 1998, the same landmark year that *Sexo, pudor y lágrimas* was released, director Jaime Romandía created Mantarraya Producciones, to develop two of his short films. Later on, he partnered with director Pablo Aldrete and turned the company into a major venue for the promotion and distribution of work by young Mexican directors. Mantarraya went on to distribute and produce Reygadas's films, along with works by Amat Escalante and other auteurs. More recently, it has expanded into distribution, securing the rights to films by Argentine director Lisandro Alonso, Thai cult filmmaker Apichatpong Weerasethakul, and French auteur Bruno Dumont, among others.

Thus, when Reygadas broke into the film scene, he benefited from the cultivation of audiences performed by the Cineteca and private distributors, and from the emergence of private venues for funding and distributing auteur cinema. His first movie, *Japón* (2002), signifies in my view the consolidation of many growing trends in Mexican film, both aesthetically and institutionally. *Japón* focuses on a man (Alejandro Ferretis) who withdraws to a remote, small town to die for a reason not disclosed to the spectator. In this town, the man rents a barn from Ascensión (Magdalena Flores), a devoutly religious older woman. Gradually, the man develops feelings for Ascensión, and he eventually has sex with her. However, their relationship is interrupted when Ascensión's nephew, Juan Luis (Martín Serrano), claims the bricks from her barn as his property, the loss of which would sink her further into poverty. The man attempts to prevent Juan Luis from pursuing the claim, but ultimately Ascensión has to cave in. At the end of the film, Ascensión and Juan Luis are killed in an accident while transporting the bricks. *Japón* firmly establishes Reygadas's style and his connections to global cinema. Like his subsequent features, *Japón* is light on plot and contemplative in mood, and relies heavily on a slow tempo constructed through long shots. Reygadas prefers nonprofessional actors because, as he states in various interviews, the performances are more "pure" and the actors are not identified with characters in other movies.[37] In addition, *Japón* shows the way in which Reygadas uses his masterly command of technique in the construction of landscape. The impoverished rural community is a fundamental backdrop to the characters' development, particularly when Reygadas uses different shots (encompassing everything from dried fields to the mountain background) to narrate and deploy the emotions of his mostly silent protagonist. As Jorge Ruffinelli argues, "Reygadas's aesthetic is not based in acting—his actors never act, in the way of [Robert] Bresson—but in a set of elements that unite the spectacular cinematography of the landscape, the human faces (as landscapes in themselves), music, and sound" (251; my translation).[38] In this, Reygadas steers clear of the creative pitfalls embedded in the emerging star system of post-1988 Mexican cinema, where actors like Gael García and Daniel Giménez Cacho frequently override their characters thanks to their presence in a large number of movies. Thus, he establishes his uniqueness in part by moving away from the strong presence of carefully constructed characters—a feature central, for instance, to the work of González Iñarritu and Cuarón—and into more technical areas, such as art direction and montage.

Locating *Japón* in the tradition of Mexican film poses a few challenges. One of the problems of reading Reygadas in the context of Mexican cinema at large emerges from the fact that most scholarly critics of his movies tend to read his works either in isolation or in relation to non-cinematic cases. In fact, part of the critical consensus regarding *Japón* tends to assert that the film is an "exception" in the Mexican and Latin American context, based on its purportedly unique use of cinematic form for the transmission of emotions and narrative (Caballero 156–59). Reygadas's work has been subject to a notable set of interpretations based on the film theories of Gilles Deleuze (Tompkins; Niessen; Game), which promote the idea of considering movies like *Japón* as part of a specific development of global art cinema that is not particularly common in Latin American traditions. Conversely, two critics (Javier Guerrero and William Rowlandson) wrote two separate articles, apparently at the same time, comparing *Japón* to Juan Rulfo's landmark novel *Pedro Páramo*, which narrates the return of a man to the town of Comala in search of his father. While I find the comparison to Rulfo's novel imprecise at best, the point is that the reference to a canonical literary text suggests a certain inability to connect *Japón* to more properly cinematic traditions in Mexico.[39]

Japón is in fact not unique in its representation of the countryside. One can recall here the use of rural communities in films such as Carlos Carrera's *La mujer de Benjamín* (1991), Ignacio Ortiz's *La orilla de la tierra* (1994), and Arturo Ripstein's *La perdición de los hombres* (2000), all of which use Mexico's barren rural areas to tell stories of the conflict between everyday life and the intense, even sinful, passions of their characters. *Japón*'s idea of a protagonist from the city withdrawing to a remote location in the interior has other iterations in post-1998 cinema. For instance, this idea underlies the plot of Carlos Bolado's *Bajo California* (1998), where an artist named Damián Ojeda (Damián Alcázar) tries to face the guilt he carries by seeking the prehistoric paintings in a desolate area of the Baja peninsula. In light of this, I would contend that *Japón* is a radical reconfiguration of existing discourses of the rural in Mexican cinema, rather than an altogether new representation. In contrast to the canonical representations of the interior as a place for backwardness or anti-modernity, *Japón* extricates it from the cinematic traditions of Mexicanism and reconfigures it as a space that confronts the modern individual with secular forms of the spiritual and the sublime.[40]

In order to achieve this reconfiguration, Reygadas aligns his work to forms and traditions of global art cinema with little or no clear presence in Mexican films. *Japón* draws heavily from Andrei Tarkovsky's last film, *The*

Sacrifice (1986), to the point of citing a well-known shot of a tree in the earlier moments of the movie. One could certainly ascribe Reygadas to what Steven Dillon calls, apropos American cinema, "the Solaris effect"; that is, the relationship between artifice and self-reflexivity in post-Tarkovsky cinema. However, when reading Reygadas, the more crucial issue regarding Tarkovsky's influence is the way in which the Russian master's work with form allows him to short-circuit the cultural and ideological expectations embedded in the representation of the rural. According to Sean Martin, "Tarkovsky proposed that if a take is lengthened, boredom naturally sets in for the audience. But if the take is extended even further, something else arises: curiosity. Tarkovsky is essentially proposing giving the audience time to inhabit the world that the take is showing us, not to *watch* it, but to *look* at it, to explore it" (46; emphases in the original). One could expand that by saying that the curiosity elicited by boredom not only allows for the aesthetic contemplation of the landscape but, perhaps more importantly, it also suspends the ideological and cultural meanings present in received cinematic traditions. Landscape is certainly crucial to the national cinema tradition: cinematographer Gabriel Figueroa, the creator of the most influential instances of cinematic language in the Golden Age, extensively portrayed Mexico's landscapes, particularly in his work with Emilio Fernández.[41] The difference is that Figueroa's work is constructed to embed the landscape with cultural meaning, while Reygadas's subjective use of the wide shot gradually strips the meaning out of its images. By allowing his different rural images to remain on the screen, the exploration embedded in Tarkovsky's use of boredom becomes a way for the audience to detach itself from signification and focus on the bare experience of the characters.[42]

A similar thing happens at the level of the characters. Reygadas is not devoid of certain ethnographic clichés, like his representation of the mayor of the town as a picturesque, inarticulate man. However, this may be more an effect of the use of nonprofessional actors (and their lack of histrionic training) than a deliberate construction of rural subjects as folkloric and funny—something that happened often enough in Golden Age cinema and that remains the case in films like *Santitos*. Nevertheless, Ascensión presents a very distinct and unique example of a rural character who breaks out of the stereotype. In her first encounter with the man, Ascensión appears to conform to cliché, mostly because of her exceedingly devout religiosity. As the film progresses, though, Ascensión gradually becomes the object of the protagonist's affection. In a telling scene, the protagonist imagines Ascensión kissing an unnamed young woman (perhaps a former lover of his). Later on, the man actually has sex with her, consummating a relationship that had gradually developed in spite of the protagonist's initial cynicism and detachment. By eroticizing a character who does not belong in stereotypical representations of sexuality, and by doing so from a perspective constructed upon the protagonist's love for her, Reygadas intervenes in the audience's expectations by undoing established forms of reading a diverse range of national characters and landscapes through the very suspension of their inherited Mexicanness. This is why Reygadas resorts to a random, non-Mexican locale (Japan) for the title of his movie: the film operates in the deliberate undermining of the marks of the national.[43] Geoffrey Kantaris uses the notion of "translocality" to describe *Japón*'s ephemeral and "phantasmagoric rural *spaces*" ("Cinema and *Urbanías*" 526), asserting that the cultural identity embedded in it is not a result but an ongoing process. This, of course, does not mean that *Japón* is "beyond the national" or "post-national." As Deborah Saw puts it, "in *Japón* the images of Mexico fit in with art film audiences' expectations that an auteur will bring them this artistic vision of the human condition rooted in a symbolic vision of the local environment" ("(Trans)National Images" 130). Reygadas takes signifiers clearly rooted in Mexican tradition and provides them with a whole new system of meaning, one that disrupts the continuity of nationalist film tradition while allowing his work to belong to global flows of art cinema that had previously excluded Mexican film.

Reygadas's ability to perform such a re-signification of cinematic spaces and characters comes in part from his belonging to forms of cinema heavily concerned with the subjective. Tiago de Luca locates Reygadas in a constellation of global cinema defined by what he calls "realism of the senses"—that is, a new "realist peak in world cinema . . . defined by a sensory mode of address" ("Realism" 187). De Luca places in this paradigm a diverse array of filmmakers, including Gus Van Sant, Béla Tarr, Lisandro Alonso, Apitchapong Weerasethakul, and Abbas Kiarostami.[44] Three elements arising from de Luca's notion are immediately relevant. First, the appeal to the sensory allows all of these filmmakers to transcend highly determined national traditions of cinema (from the hyperrealist melodrama of American independent cinema in Van Sant's case to Kiarostami's critical approach to neorealism in the context of Iranian cinema) to establish themselves squarely into the practice of global authorship I invoked earlier in the chapter. Second, the fact that the "realists of the senses" come from very distinct film traditions from all across the globe suggests that Reygadas's intervention in the national works by the appropriation of forms of cinema that critically engage local tradition: one can remember here the way in which Apitchapong's *Uncle Boonmee Recalls His Past Lives* takes rural folklore (such as the existence of "monkey ghosts" in the forest) and places it in a squarely uneventful, realist setting (Boonmee finds his long-gone son converted into a monkey ghost and has a very routine conversation with him and his dead wife over dinner). While Reygadas's sparse style may seem distant from this type of magical realism, the procedure is fundamentally the same: the erosion of signifiers close to national or local meanings creates a sensory address that denaturalizes their cultural meaning. Finally, one can note here again that Apitchapong and Alonso are both distributed by Mantarraya in Mexico, and that all of the filmmakers listed by de Luca are constantly present on the Cineteca circuits. This fact is not trivial, because it shows the way in which Reygadas's international success allows him to be legible in Mexico, not by means of his national signifiers, but thanks to the construction of a small but important audience familiar with contemporary forms of global art cinema.

This last point is key because Reygadas functions within certain paradigms that had long been present in art cinema circulation in Mexico and abroad. An critical precedent to de Luca's "realism of the senses" is Schrader's notion of "transcendental style in film." Schrader's analysis, originally published in 1972, identifies three directors from vastly different traditions—Yasujiro Ozu, Robert Bresson, and Carl Theodor Dreyer—in a similar mode of exploration of religiosity and the Holy. It is not coincidental that, in many interviews, Reygadas cites all three of these directors as influences, mostly on his continued interest on religious discourse.[45] In fact, as I will discuss near the end of this chapter, his third feature, *Stellet Licht,* directly draws from Dreyer's masterpiece *Ordet.* The influential nature of this "transcendental style" in global art cinema reflected itself on Mexican circuits too: most of the works of all three directors are listed in the Cineteca's database of movies screened. The point, of course, is not that Reygadas necessarily became familiar with these influences in Mexico (he in fact produced his first short films in Belgium, and his preference for the transcendental style can be traced to his time in Europe). Rather, the long tradition of exhibiting this type of cinema in Mexico allowed Reygadas to insert himself into the limits and margins of Mexican cinema, right when the niche market of art cinema was becoming integrated into the neoliberal forms of exhibition and production.

It is certainly hard to establish the impact of Reygadas in Mexico through quantitative means, particularly because his films are released in a somewhat modest number of copies. Álvaro Fernández points out that *Japón*'s release was limited to fifteen copies in Mexico—a very low number even compared to the fifty-seven copies of its release in France (413). Its box office gross was a mere $34,688. Nonetheless, the quantitative data on a film like this does not tell the story of its influence in the industry. As Fernández himself admits, there are directors—like Amat Escalante or Pedro Aguilera—whose work either traces back to Reygadas or achieves a certain degree of visibility thanks to Reygadas's irruption in Mexican cinema. In fact, Reygadas's work contributes in two significant ways to the institutional realignment of art cinema in Mexico. First, the visibility of his work opened the space for the exploration of topics and ideas previously excluded from film circulation. Julián Hernández, for example, is a director whose aesthetic has many important parallels to that of Reygadas.[46] His first feature, *Mil nubes de paz cercan el cielo, amor, jamás acabarás de ser amor* (2003), followed a festival track similar to that of *Japón*, earning the prestigious Teddy Award for Best LGBT Film at the 2003 Berlin Film Festival (an award that directors like Van Sant, Almodóvar, and François Ozon had won in prior years), and a Best Director Award at the Guadalajara Film Festival. Hernández's most significant films (*Mil nubes de paz* and *El cielo dividido* [2006]) become legible beyond their intervention in LGBT culture precisely because their work with slow tempo and with the subjective representation of the body acquires new dimensions in the light of Reygadas's work.[47] This is also the case of Amat Escalante, whose films *Sangre* (2005) and *Los bastardos* (2008) develop Reygadas's approach to nonprofessional acting and observational rhythm into more violent stories. Thus, Escalante achieves in *Los bastardos* a brutal representation of the question of illegal immigration to the United States, through the saga of a character who evolves from day laborer to serial killer. While Escalante's movies have an element of violence absent in Reygadas's oeuvre, his work becomes readable in the wake of Reygadas's redefinition of slow-paced cinema in Mexico.[48]

The true impact of Reygadas's filmmaking emerges in his second, most controversial feature, *Batalla en el cielo* (2005). This film tells the story of Marcos (Marcos Hernández) and his gradual descent into disaster. Early in the film we learn that Marcos and his wife (Bertha Ruiz) were responsible for a botched kidnapping of a baby, who died in the process. Marcos—a middle-aged, dark-skinned, obese man—works as the driver of a military general. The core of the movie's plot unfolds when Marcos gets sexually involved with the general's daughter, Ana (Anapola Mushkadiz), who in turn works as a high-class prostitute. The unexpected solidarity between Marcos and Ana unfolds because they share a secret: Marcos is the only one who knows of Ana's double life, while Ana becomes the only person who learns of Marcos's involvement in the kidnapping of the baby. In the last part of the film, Marcos seeks Ana in her boyfriend's apartment, where he ultimately kills her, prompting him to participate in a pilgrimage to the sanctuary of the Virgin of Guadalupe. As Marcos tries to reach the sanctuary on his knees and with his head covered, the police try to find him in his apartment, having learned both about the kidnapping and the murder of Ana.

In this movie, Reygadas's contemplative style focuses on images meant to openly confront the semiotics of class and race in Mexico. The film is fully centered on the race and class contrast between Ana and Marcos, which is emphasized by the screening of her performing actual oral sex on him in the first and last scenes of the movie, as well as shots of them having sex and lying together naked afterwards. Reygadas appropriates here what Linda Williams has called "an international phenomenon of hard-core art cinema" (295) spearheaded by directors such as Catherine Breillat and Julio Medem. In doing so, Reygadas's use of sexuality achieves, at the same time, cultural credibility in its breaking of moral taboos while using a resource with a clear track record of causing scandal. In 2003, American director Vincent Gallo raised major controversy at Cannes because of a graphic scene of oral sex with Chloe Sevigny in his film *The Brown Bunny*. The transgressive nature of the oral sex scene in *Batalla en el cielo* does not rest solely on morality. It constructs a performance of class and race that directly confronts the notions of male and female beauty and desirability in Mexican media. Many of the actors and actresses who emerged as sex symbols in post-1988 cinema (like Gael García, Ana Claudia Talancón, Alfonso Herrera, and Ana de la Reguera) were clearly aligned to Mexico's class- and race-determined notions of attractiveness, which privilege white-skinned, upper-middle-class actors both in cinema and in television.

As I discussed in Chapter 2, the standard of beauty embodied in romantic comedy female actors like Martha Higareda and Cecilia Suárez was part of a cultural economy of class self-referentiality to which the middle-class audiences of the cineplex could relate. Anapola Mushkadiz, a slim, white-skinned woman, embodies in Ana an edgier version of that standard, which Reygadas challenges through her drug use and her role as a prostitute. It is telling that the female protagonist role was originally written for pop star Paulina Rubio, whose presence in the film would have provided an even more confrontational contrast with Marcos. True to form, Reygadas was inspired to write the role of Marcos by Hernández, who worked as a driver for his father. In doing so, Reygadas deliberately resists even the use of actors who play working-class characters in films geared toward the middle class (Silverio Palacios and Dagoberto Gama, who typically play police officers or criminals, are good examples). Rather, he shows on the screen a man who is clearly outside the aesthetic of Mexican visual media, radically placing in the center of the film the type of working class-subject that the romantic comedy aesthetic excluded from the screen. Through these protagonists, Reygadas clearly disturbs the class economy of middle-class cinema through the construction of a love story that materializes an impossible social encounter. As Tiago de Luca argues: "Averse to all victimization and moral didacticism, *Battle in Heaven* exposes an abyssal social divide by bridging this gap and making this couple possible *in reality*, refusing to acknowledge its incongruity within the social establishment" ("Realism" 201–2; emphasis in the original). I would further insist that the very realization of the couple through the devices of visual exploration that Reygadas obtained from directors like Tarkovsky pushes the audience beyond the naturalized status of racial and class difference in Mexican culture. *Batalla en el cielo* imposes on its viewers the critical engagement with the forms of bodily and social representation on which most films and television shows rely.[49]

Reygadas's attack on audience expectations also focuses on national iconology. The film has a recurring scene in which it shows the daily ceremony of raising and lowering the flag in Mexico City's Zócalo Square. The camera closely follows the ritual and the movements of the soldiers while a martial tune plays in the background. More provocatively, the resolution of the movie takes place in the context of the pilgrimage to the Basilica of the Virgin of Guadalupe, one of Mexico's central religious rituals. To narrate Marcos's final act of penitence, Reygadas appropriates the ritual, in which some of the most committed believers show penance by crawling for miles on their knees to reach the sanctuary. This transformation of Marcos is astonishing because in a scene in the middle of the movie, he shows disdain for a group of pilgrims (he calls them "sheep") and, when his wife asks him to participate in the pilgrimage, he seems uninterested. My impression is that Reygadas does not seek to merely subvert both rituals, the national and the religious, nor does he attempt an ironic take on them. Just like the landscape in *Japón*, which functioned as a way to reflect on the question of spirituality, these rituals are clearly fascinating to Reygadas, and his aesthetic is in part an attempt to encompass them at the level of form. In his reading of the film, Fernando Toledo points to this ritualistic logic, suggesting that Marcos's penance and the constant presence of the flag ritual hint at a structure of spiritual debt connected both to the law and to the nation (105–6). The connection to the national iconicity, however, does not seem to restore any logic, creating what Ilana Dann Luna has perceptively called a "deformation of national allegory" constructed upon the "tension between its signifiers: the national flag, the virgin of Guadalupe, the whore and its signified: the failed project of national unity."[50] Just like he does at the level of the body, Reygadas pushes the viewer to reflect on the symbolic efficacy of the constitutive rituals of the nation by displacing them toward contexts that keep certain elements of meaning while undermining others. In this sense, while Marcos does not participate in the collective logic of the pilgrimage, or in the cultural system that elevates the Catholic image to the status of national identifier, he has a religious experience that seeks to expiate the guilt of his crime. While Luna is right in observing the tensions in Reygadas's iconology, it is nonetheless important to assert that *Batalla en el cielo* preserves some of the human and spiritual effects of the national rituals. As with the tragic yet uneventful death of Ascensión in *Japón*, collective or sacrificial redemption never takes place, so the two male leads (Marcos and the man in *Japón*) experience the power of their spiritual undertaking but never resolve or sublimate the guilt, violence, or contradictions that led them to the realm of the religious.

Another important point about *Batalla en el cielo* is its belonging to the tradition of films focused on Mexico City. Reygadas's cinematic gaze spends a considerable amount of time contemplating the city; the film includes aerial shots of the city's avenues and a very telling 360-degree camera pan that shows a group of buildings while Marcos and Ana engage in sex. *Batalla en el cielo*'s intervention on the urban is crucial, considering the privileged role of Mexico City as a space for the neoliberal middle class in films like *Sólo con tu pareja* and *Sexo, pudor y lágrimas*.⁵¹ This focus on Mexico City is vital precisely because the undermining effect of Reygadas's filmmaking style relates more directly to the type of spectator who actually sees Mexican art cinema. Marcos's presence in the city takes place in two opposing but related ways. On the one hand, he appears to not have really a meaningful relationship to the urban space. In an early scene, Marcos sparsely discusses the kidnapping with his wife in the hallway of a subway station, where she works selling desserts and trinkets. While the scene has an unassuming tone, the semiotic economy of this particular location is relevant, given not only the couple's participation in the marginal spaces of neoliberalism (the informal economy) but also their seemingly harmless appearance, which hides a dark secret that goes unnoticed by the many denizens who populate the subway station. A similar scene takes place in a gas station, where Marcos sees the pilgrims that he calls "sheep." This assertion takes place in the middle of another sparse conversation, with a customer with whom he establishes a superficial connection (Toledo 105). Marcos once again is completely irrelevant to the urban landscape that surrounds him. As his story unravels, his relationship with the urban is modified, turning him into an increasingly uncomfortable and invasive presence. This is clear, for instance, when Ana takes him to the boutique-brothel where she works, where the other prostitutes ask her about the reasons for his presence. It is also clear when Marcos seeks Ana in a wealthy neighborhood, where her neighbors see him as out of place. I should note here that Marcos never appears as criminally threatening in these spaces and that the upper classes are presented from an equally unrelenting perspective. When Marcos is waiting for Ana, for instance, we see a group of rich teenagers, visibly intoxicated, suggesting a sexuality beyond their years. The scene concludes with two of the teenagers urinating into the trunk of a car before the servants get the contents. Therefore, Marcos's out-of-placeness is not, like in *Todo el poder*, a representation of the lower classes as a threat to the security of the rich. Rather, it is part of a mise-en-scène that represents Mexico's inherent social inequalities both through the tensions embedded in the encounter among social classes and in the moral debauchery of the privileged (including Ana's double life and her somewhat exploitative relationship with Marcos).

Read together, *Japón* and *Batalla en el cielo* constitute a major intervention on the very idea of national cinema in Mexico, at least in three possible senses. First, they represent a realignment of cinema made in Mexico, given that Mantarraya and its foreign sources of funding, like the Hubert Bals Fund, set an example for art cinema on how to break, at least in part, its organic relationship to IMCINE.⁵² While Mexican auteurs of the 1990s undoubtedly enjoyed certain freedoms when dealing with transgressive subjects (Arturo Ripstein's confrontational cinema comes to mind), the ability to produce and distribute art cinema privately allowed directors to move beyond different paradigms of

Mexican cinema. Besides Mantarraya, one can remember here Canana Films, a much larger production company backed by Gael García Bernal and Diego Luna, which has supported other art cinema directors like Gerardo Naranjo and Kyzza Terrazas. Second, Reygadas's work intervenes in cinema as a device to represent the nation in Mexico. *Japón* and *Batalla en el cielo* are films that push two distinct traditions of Mexico's cinematic framing to near exhaustion: the aestheticized rural world founded by people like Gabriel Figueroa in *Japón* and the representation of Mexico City's contradiction in *Batalla en el cielo,* a film that goes far beyond *Amores perros* in its indictment of social stratification. Finally, Reygadas intervenes in the signifiers of national cinema that negotiate Mexicanness for foreign audiences. While Shaw is right when pointing out that *Japón* follows foreign audiences' expectations of Mexicanness (130), the film is also clearly self-conscious of its clichés (Tompkins, "Deleuzian Approach" 165). In other words, Reygadas does not simply reproduce or subvert the signs of the national expected by foreign audiences, but forces a moment of reflection on the true content of those signs.

The consecration of Reygadas's undermining of Mexican national cinema can be attested in his third feature, *Stellet Licht/Luz silenciosa* (2007), a true masterpiece focused on the emotional and religious crisis faced by a Mennonite man called Johan (Cornelio Wall) thanks to an extramarital affair with Marianne (Maria Pankratz). The film departs from any notion of Mexican national cinema in its very purpose: it focuses on the life of a community that has never been represented as an organic part of the Mexican nation. Furthermore, Reygadas shot the movie in Plautdietsch, a Low German language spoken by the Mennonites worldwide. The film is based in part on Carl Theodor Dreyer's *Ordet* (1955), a classic film on the question of religiosity, from which Reygadas draws the ending scene, where Esther (Miriam Toews), Johan's wife, comes back to life after being kissed by Marianne.[53] The reference to Dreyer's film clearly establishes a deeper connection to the "transcendental style" mentioned earlier, and shows the way in which Reygadas maintains fidelity to the genealogy that allowed him to create his own brand of art cinema. In addition, there are important aesthetic departures in *Stellet Licht,* such as a deft use of natural sounds instead of the lush music Reygadas had featured in previous soundtracks.[54] Reygadas also employs a new cinematographer, Alexis Zabé, who has helped him further his contemplative style. It is important to note that Zabé is also the cinematographer for another auteur, Fernando Eimbcke, which shows that Reygadas is not altogether disconnected from a larger scene of art cinema production.

Stellet Licht is a movie that departs from Reygadas's commentary on contemporary Mexico, thanks to its focus on a minority community. For this reason, a closer reading of the film is not relevant for my purposes.[55] The more important point here is that the existence of such a unique art film shows the level of institutional and aesthetic development achieved by Mexican film in the 2000s. While art cinema has never been an anomaly in Mexico, the ability to shoot a film in Plautdietsch, with national circulation and strong festival presence, would have been nearly impossible in 1998. Seen together, del Toro, Cuarón, González Iñarritu, and Reygadas represent distinct pinnacles of a cinematic tradition whose institutional development over the past twenty years has been crucial to the current internationalization of Mexican cinema. As I conclude the writing of this chapter in mid-2013, we can see in the work of these four authors plenty of evidence of this internationalization: Reygadas was awarded the Cannes Film Festival's Best Director Award; del Toro is about to release *Pacific Rim,* a blockbuster sci-fi action film; Cuarón recently finished *Gravity,* a drama focused on two astronauts played by Sandra Bullock and George Clooney; and Alejandro González Iñarritu is currently producing the first film by Armando Bo, a screenwriter for *Biutiful.* Thanks to the roads opened by them, younger Mexican auteurs are achieving success on international cinema circuits: Michel Franco won the 2012 Un Certain Regard Award in Cannes, where Antonio Méndez Esparza won the International Critics' Week Award (the same award won by *Amores perros*), while Nicolás Pereda was the subject of an online film festival on the prestigious website *mubi.com* and Gerardo Naranjo completed a tour of many important festivals (Cannes, Nantes, Rotterdam, Rio de Janeiro, New York) for the promotion of *Miss Bala.* Yet one cannot read these directors merely as individual examples. I believe this increasing success on the international circuit rests on an industry that, despite its limitations in the domestic market, has been able to break away from its most outdated ideologies and aesthetics. This type of authorial cinema emerges from the plurality made possible by the end of Mexicanist imperatives, by the diversification of production and exhibition schemes, and through the ability of art cinema to occupy spaces on public and private circuits, among other factors. The erosion of old systems of aesthetics and ideology through the processes described in the previous three chapters allowed the directors studied in this chapter to become instrumental in the consecration of a Mexican film industry at home and abroad. Today, the Mexican cinema industry is, in my view, the most diverse it has ever been. In the conclusion to this book, I will briefly discuss the complex and exciting cinematic landscape of the past five years.

Conclusion

Mexican Cinema after Neoliberalism

Going to the movies in Mexico at the beginning of the second decade of the twenty-first century constitutes an experience far different from the one I narrated in the introduction to this book. When I was in Guadalajara in the summer of 2011, I had the opportunity to see the last installment of the *Harry Potter* franchise—one that contained many elements of the aesthetic that Alfonso Cuarón had instilled in the third episode—at the Cinépolis VIP Andares complex. Located in a high-end mall created to cater to Guadalajara's moneyed elite, this complex provides an astonishingly luxurious cinematic experience, with amenities such as all-leather individual recliners with side tables, numbered seats (which are now a standard feature of all film theaters), a full bar, an extensive food menu (which can be ordered through waiters summoned by a button next to the seat), and a comfortable lobby that resembles a posh café. Such theaters have been gradually developed both by the Cinépolis chain (where they are called "VIP") and the Cinemex company (where they are branded "Platino"), and were recently introduced under the "Premier" rubric by Cinemark. What sets Andares apart is that it is a VIP-only site, while in other locations the VIP theater is only a section within a larger complex. This development illustrates not only the impressive growth of the Mexican film market in the past twenty-five years—which places it as the fifth-largest market in the world in box office numbers and as one of the top ten in terms of number of screens—but also the significant change in the demographics of film attendance during the neoliberal period. Before 1988, cinema was predominantly a form of entertainment geared toward the lower classes. Today, the development of the VIP experience, and the fact that the average ticket still costs the equivalent of a full day of work at minimum wage, show that the market remains firmly rooted in attracting the middle and upper classes.[1] It is certainly true that the lower middle class has an increasing presence in film theaters, given that, proportionally, the tickets are cheaper now than in the late 1990s, when they cost as much as two or three days of pay at minimum wage.

It is also true that Cinemex and Cinépolis have forcefully expanded into both working-class neighborhoods and a larger array of cities. The emergence of the VIP theater is perhaps a result of this expansion, a way to reconstitute the class segregation of audience that brought wealthy moviegoers into the multiplex a decade and a half ago.

Still, these developments have not quite translated into assets for the development of the Mexican film industry. It is certainly true that production is way up from the mid-1990s nadir. According to the 2011 *Anuario estadístico del cine mexicano,* IMCINE's statistical yearbook, an average of sixty-five to seventy-five feature films have been produced every year since at least 2006 (63). But the same report points out that fifty-nine out of seventy-three films produced in 2011 had some kind of government funding, including fiscal stimuli, showing that cinema still requires considerable State support to remain viable (81). Nonetheless, it is also true that Mexican movies have much more sophisticated production resources, thanks to an increase in the average budget per film from 940,000 Mexican pesos (about 94,000 dollars at the time) in 2000 to 22.4 million pesos (about two million dollars) in 2012 (84). While full financial independence remains elusive, Mexican production enjoys a level of technical support and economic strength that results in better-crafted movies. Still, the underlying problem remains the overwhelming ability of Hollywood films and distributors to colonize Mexico's vast market at the expense of the national industry. In 2012, as the president of the Mexican Academy of Film Arts and Sciences, director Carlos Carrera pointed out during his speech at the Ariel Awards (Mexico's Oscars) that Mexican productions struggle in their search for screen time, even though Mexico has a very successful film market. This was echoed by Emilio Portes, whose film *Pastorela* (2011) won the top award. Portes argued that Mexican cinema is not able to truly represent the Mexican people and national culture because of the lack of access to audiences, and demanded that major media companies provide more spaces for Mexican films. These complaints are fully echoed by the numbers in the *Anuario:* 90 percent of the country's box office and screens goes to Hollywood cinema, compared to Mexican cinema's mere 7 percent (17). And, considering that an average of seventy movies are made every year, and only about sixty to sixty-two are released, there are a substantial number of films that never get any kind of commercial circulation.

Still, the very existence of a 7 percent market share and the release of 62 movies a year is, as paradoxical as it may sound, a success story, considering the industry was pretty much in shambles in the wake of the 1995 crisis, thanks to scarce production resources and an audience completely uninterested in domestic films. Despite being dwarfed by Hollywood's promotional machine, which enjoys not only big advertising budgets but also product tie-ins with powerhouses like McDonald's restaurants and Kellogg's cereals,

Mexico manages to produce box office hits every single year, and its films enjoy widespread recognition at international film festivals. If one sees the box office results for Mexican films released in 2011, one can see many interesting phenomena emerging. The highest-grossing film was *Don Gato y su pandilla* (Alberto Mar), a Mexican version of Hanna-Barbera's cartoon *Top Cat*, fully produced in the country. This movie, along with *Una película de huevos* (Gabriel and Rodolfo Riva Palacio), the most popular film in 2006, shows the ability of Mexican cinema to make inroads even in Hollywood's most profitable market: animated cinema. The third-highest grossing movie of 2011, *Presunto culpable,* is a documentary about a man whose conviction in a murder case is questioned through a devastating exposé of the Mexican judicial system.[2] The very existence of the film is remarkable. It was underwritten in part by the William and Flora Hewlett Foundation, which supported its release in the United States as part of the P.O.V. documentary series on PBS. It was also funded by a Gucci-Ambulante fellowship from the Ambulante Film Festival, a Mexican yearly event focused on documentaries. The endorsement of the festival, founded in 2005 by Gael García Bernal and Diego Luna, granted *Presunto culpable* extensive media access and vast circulation in the cineplex network. In addition, the film secured distribution through Cinépolis. Even more notably, the company that produced the film weathered strong political pressure and even a judicial order once the controversy surrounding the misconduct of judges and prosecutors arose. The movie ultimately raised almost six million dollars in Mexico, a figure that would be remarkable even for a documentary with wide release in the United States.[3] The *Presunto culpable* phenomenon illustrates many of the industry's triumphs in the past fifteen years: a system that withstands censorship, receives sufficient support from private financing, experiences acceptable distribution, and enjoys an audience willing to listen when the film has a compelling message to share.[4]

Beyond economics, the Mexican films of the last four or five years have shown that their departure from Mexicanist models of representation is definitive, and their occasional returns to nationalist subjects take place with a considerable amount of critical distance. As I discussed in Chapter 1, Carrera's *El crimen del padre Amaro,* to date the second highest-grossing Mexican film of all time in the domestic box office, went back to subjects typical of Mexicanist production but gave them a devastatingly critical twist that preempted any celebratory perspective of the national. More recent films have pursued this path in ever more confrontational ways. *Pastorela,* the fifth-highest grossing film of 2012 and the winner of the Mexican Academy Award, is a good example of this. The title refers to a comedic Christmas genre of Mexican popular theater, in which pastors have to overcome the obstacles created by a very charismatic and funny representation of Satan in order to reach the birth of Jesus. The film focuses on Jesús Juárez (Joaquín Cosío), a federal police agent whose main source of pride comes from playing the devil in his community's yearly play. When a new priest (Carlos Cobos) and former exorcist is appointed to the parish, he takes the role away from Jesús and gives it to Jesús's best friend, Bulmaro (Eduardo España), who takes the role in hopes of winning a trip to a resort after he hears that the parish's young nun, (Ana Serradilla), wants to go there. Adding insult to injury, the new priest is encouraged to enroll the play in a national competition, which stokes Jesús's anger even further. Jesús attempts to use his powers as a federal agent, which include his ability to employ corrupt police officers as torturers, to stop the play from taking place, and to implicate Bulmaro in the assassination of an assistant to the attorney general. As the film progresses, we are encouraged to suspect that Jesús has some supernatural powers and may in fact be possessed by the devil, which leads to a final confrontation between demons and the police. This plot, I think, shows clearly the degree of distance and irony through which Mexican directors deal with Mexican culture. Portes takes a traditional cultural practice, using the corruption of Mexico's federal police as his film's central comedic device, to thoroughly question the very cultural logic underlying the *pastorela* genre. And, exacerbating the criticism that made *El crimen del padre Amaro* so controversial, *Pastorela* portrays the church as an institution full of politically minded bishops, and priests and nuns who ignore their celibacy vows, as well as using the imagery of demonic possession and exorcism to make fun of the more radical edges of Catholic belief. It is even more notable that a film with such confrontational themes enjoyed wide success (including box office earnings of over three million dollars) without eliciting any controversy from religious or political groups. Furthermore, the film enjoyed corporate sponsorship from two of Mexico's largest companies (the canned foods giant Herdez and the investment bank Ixe), and is distributed by Televisa's branches in Mexico (Videocine) and the United States (Pantelion). The very normalization of this type of confrontational take on Mexicanist culture shows how cinema has found credibility and success in undermining the very cultural imagery that film from the twentieth century helped to build.[5]

In 2010, as the bicentennial celebration of Mexico's independence and the centennial celebration of the Mexican Revolution provided plenty of reasons for patriotic culture, the film industry instead delivered movies with plots and styles surprisingly detached from nationalist agendas. This was the case with Felipe Cazals's *Chicogrande* (2010), a suggestive film focused on the punitive expedition of the U.S. Army against Francisco Villa (Alejandro Calva) in 1916. Rather than presenting Villa, the national hero, at his peak, Cazals opts to tell the story of his demise, when his transformation into a legend was matched by his physical decay. The protagonist is in fact not Villa himself, but Chicogrande (Damián Alcázar), a lieutenant in his army whose failed search for medical help is at the core of the film. Thus, rather than portraying a celebration of the revolutionary general as a founding figure of the nation, Cazals presents a melancholic take on a sad moment in Mexican history, when the social movements behind the revolution succumbed to treason, defeat, and foreign intervention.

Even the three films bankrolled by the vast amounts of money that the government invested in the bicentennial and branded with the "Mexico 2010" rubric failed to deliver a nationalist message. The film meant to celebrate Independence was *Hidalgo: La historia jamás contada* (2010), Antonio Serrano's first movie since his Spanish venture, *Lucía, Lucía* (2003), and an attempt to match the success of his first film, *Sexo, pudor y lágrimas*.[6] The film is a biopic of Father Miguel Hidalgo (Demián Bichir), the first major leader of Mexico's Independence movement, prior to his involvement in the 1810 war. The film narrates the story of Hidalgo's youth as he recalls it while awaiting execution. While the portrayal is certainly positive, Bichir's Hidalgo is focused not on his military prowess or his role as founding father. Rather, the film is most interested in his refusal to submit to the authority of the Spanish Crown, his commitment to treat indigenous peoples and people of mixed race as equals, his relationship to the church, and his feelings about his own human failings, given that he reputedly was a gambler, a drinker, and a womanizer. It is telling that we see Hidalgo's participation in the Independence movement only at the very end, in a scene when he meets General Ignacio Allende (Raúl Méndez), after an austere black screen informs us of his role in the war. Serrano's film thus avoids any representation of Independence as an event to be celebrated and displays more interest in showing the ideals of freedom and equality represented by Hidalgo, ideals that may be easily construed as absent from contemporary Mexico.

The film presumably meant to commemorate the revolution was *El atentado* (2010), Jorge Fons's first feature film since *El callejón de los milagros*.[7] But the revolution was nowhere to be found. Instead, Fons adapted Álvaro Uribe's novel *Expediente del atentado*, which narrates a failed plot against dictator Porfirio Díaz (Arturo Beristáin), which took place during the Independence celebration on September 16, 1897. Like *Hidalgo*, *El atentado* focuses on a period that precedes the historical event and that cannot be commemorated as part of the centennial narrative. Fons's resistance to the celebration itself is strongly declared by the movie. In a scene early in the film, the would-be assassin Arnulfo (José María Yázpik) states in a drunken tirade that he sees no point in celebrating the events of 1810, given that the actual independence of Mexico from Spain took place in 1821, and that the only reason the celebration takes place on September 16 is because it coincides with Díaz's birthday. The film also narrates its story through a discontinuous chronology, focused on flashbacks that gradually connect the assassin with Inspector General Eduardo Velázquez (Julio Bracho), a formerly ardent Porfirista who was in fact behind the assassination plot, and writer Federico Gamboa (Daniel Giménez Cacho), a famed intellectual and diplomat from whose perspective we see the story unfold. In order to further erode any possibility of raising the events of the film onto a historical pedestal, the film introduces a clever device. Every time a major event takes place in the film (the foiled plot, the lynching of Arnulfo, Eduardo's suicide), it gets comically recast by a troupe of popular theater actors who mock the events in front of an audience of lower-class citizens. This device is more complex than it seems, since it not only questions the importance of the elites at the center of historical events, but also emphasizes the fact that Mexico's lower classes will be unable to see the film, and that the solemnity of the history told in *El atentado* can really be nothing but a joke to Mexico's poor. The film is undoubtedly one of the most beautifully produced films in recent Mexican cinema, thanks to its considerable budget of nearly five million dollars, which makes it one of the five most expensive films ever made in Mexico, and to Fons's arrival at a level of craftsmanship far superior to the one displayed in *El callejón de los milagros*. The point here is that Mexican films are able to deal with topics proper to Mexican culture and history, and do so admirably, without returning to the time when cinema was a vehicle for the advancement of the ideological and political agendas of the State.

In these terms, the striking feature shared by *Chicogrande, Hidalgo,* and *El atentado* is their unwillingness to focus on the actual historical events meant to be celebrated in the bicentennial. Instead, these films presented Mexican audiences with the desacralization of national heroes, a nostalgic take on the social ideals lost in the course of Mexican history, and a refusal to participate in the celebratory mood implied by their State funding. In a way, they show that, even if IMCINE remains a major element in film production, it no longer exercises the type of ideological and political controls exercised by the Echeverría and López Portillo regimes during the "cinema of solitude" period. Indeed, the third film released under the rubric of "Mexico 2010"—with the provocative subtitle "Nada que celebrar" (nothing to celebrate)—was *El infierno* (2010), the last installment of Luis Estrada's devastating trilogy of political comedies.[8] The fact that this film went through the IMCINE approval process to be financed and featured in the bicentennial celebrations is astonishing in itself, not only because of Estrada's reputation as a controversial filmmaker, but also because it targets the government's cornerstone policy, President Felipe Calderón's war on drug cartels. The film tells the story of Benny (Damián Alcázar), an undocumented worker forced to return to his hometown after being deported from the United States. With no future in sight, he is enticed by El Cochiloco (Joaquín Cosío), a local hit man, to join the cartel of Don José Reyes (Ernesto Gómez Cruz). As he rises within the ranks of the cartel, Benny learns not only that his whole town is somewhat involved in the drug trade, but also that the network of corruption runs deep in the government and the police. When he meets Don José, Benny notices that he has many photographs of himself with major political figures in his living room, and when Benny tries to leave the cartel to protect his nephew (Kristian Ferrer), he learns that even the federal agent (Daniel Giménez Cacho) supposed to be prosecuting the organization is also in Don José's pocket. The film's climax is perhaps the most antithetical scene possible in regards to the bicentennial. As Don José, recently elected the town's mayor, prepares to kickstart the celebration of Independence in the town's square, Benny appears with a machine gun and massacres everyone on the stage. At the end of the film, we see Benny's nephew, armed and ready to avenge his uncle.

El infierno is, in fact, a comedy, a mordant satire of contemporary Mexico. El Cochiloco is one of the most charismatic characters in contemporary Mexican cinema, and actor Joaquín Cosío is certainly one of the most iconic comedians in contemporary Mexican culture. Yet, its brutal attack on everything related to the war on drugs—the government strategy, the corruption of officials, the participation in and tolerance of organized crime by everyday citizens, and the strengthening of the cartels thanks to the utter lack of economic opportunity in Mexico—made this film the most successful work in relation to the bicentennial celebrations and the most telling example of Mexican cinema's highly critical stance toward the country's contemporary issues. If anything, *El infierno,* like *Presunto culpable,* remains a clear example that Mexican cinema can produce high-quality films, with strong performances and notable production values, that also aim at the core of the political and cultural conversation in the public sphere. *El infierno* was perhaps the first successful and honest portrayal of the drug war in Mexican culture, and definitely superior to most works of literary fiction and television shows trying to deal with the subject. Furthermore, unlike *narcocultura,* which creates a lore of heroism around the figure of the drug dealer, Estrada's humorous take established a language that dealt efficiently both with the cultural and economic seductions that *el narco* provides to impoverished Mexicans and with the relentless destruction of everyday life brought about by the growth in the trade and in government intervention. In doing so, *El infierno* is a prime example of the possible future role that film may have, in discerning the complexities of Mexican contemporary life while creating products that remain appealing to the spectatorship that commercial cinema from the last fifteen years has arduously constructed. In fact, Carlos Bolado's *Colosio: El asesinato* enjoyed considerable success in the middle of the 2012 summer season, competing with franchises like *Spiderman* and *Batman,* thanks to its semi-fictional retelling of one of Mexico's most traumatic events in recent history: the never-solved assassination of PRI presidential candidate Luis Donaldo Colosio (Enoc Leaño) in 1994. The fact that a political film was able to shine while sharing the multiplexes with the most popular blockbusters of the Hollywood machine demonstrates that films that compellingly deal with the concerns of the Mexican audience may actually have a market advantage vis-à-vis American film in the daily struggle for screens and distribution. The future of the industry undoubtedly rests on its ability to discover and exploit this type of advantage. At this writing, Bolado is also on the way toward replicating his success with *Tlatelolco* (2013), a film about the 1968 massacre that is designed around the love story of a working-class boy and an upper-class girl, adapting once again the audience-pleasing narrative of romantic comedy with a political edge.

Beyond the success of *El infierno,* the drug war has provided Mexican directors of different strains and aesthetics with an opportunity to claim social relevance for the film industry and to showcase the versatility of current productions in relation to the culture at large. The second-highest-grossing film of 2011 was *Salvando al soldado Pérez* (Beto Gómez, 2011), with a box office of nearly seven million dollars. A parody both of *narcocultura* and of U.S. war films, *Salvando al soldado Pérez* tells the story of a drug dealer, Julián Pérez (Miguel Rodarte), who embarks on an expedition to Iraq to find his brother, Juan (Juan Carlos Flores), after he goes missing during an operation of his U.S. Army company. This outrageous plot is well executed by the film, precisely because of its ability to use a diverse set of elements from U.S.-Mexico relations and from Hollywood cinema as the basis of its humor. Just like Benny in *El infierno,* Julián and Juan represent the paths chosen by young men facing the inequalities inherent in the neoliberal economic model: either joining organized crime or migrating to the United States. In the character of Juan, the film tackles one of the realities faced by many Mexicans in the United States: the need to join the army in order to perhaps achieve a path to legalization. In addition, the film overcomes its lack of economic resources—required to build a believable war scene—by representing post-war Iraq as a no-man's- land controlled by criminal organizations: when Julián and his fellow cartel members arrive in the Middle East, they rely on Russian mafias and Turkish organized crime to enter the country and obtain supplies. The story of crime and chaos thus criticizes the moralistic tone of films that focus on Iraq, such as Academy Award winner *The Hurt Locker* (Kathryn Bigelow, 2008). Furthermore, the film also caricatures drug dealers, by portraying such characters as incompetent, ignorant, and ruthless. In fact, the success of the mission is due in no small part to Eladio (Jaime Camil), a visibly upper-class, educated man who provides business expertise and technical competency to Julián's cartel. In a way, *Salvando al soldado Pérez* shows another avenue for the representation of Mexico's contemporary issues, one that is not a direct intervention on political conversations, but a creative appropriation of elements from the country's daily life through the fictionalizing abilities of cinema. It is also important to note that *Salvando al soldado Pérez* is an action film, a genre that has recently reemerged in Mexico's neoliberal cinema, thanks to the success of films like

Sultanes del sur (Alejandro Lozano, 2007) and *Ladrón que roba a ladrón* (Joe Menéndez, 2007).⁹ In fact, Lemon Films, a company that has contributed to the action genre's expansion in Mexican commercial cinema, produced both *Sultanes del Sur* and *Salvando al soldado Pérez*. It is important to note that this type of action film performs yet another expansion of neoliberal cinema, one that appropriates subjects like the drug war, which had historically been at the core of films aimed at the lower classes. In doing so, this type of cinema creates a cultural language that better reflects the anxieties of the middle and upper classes regarding these issues—something that requires further study as part of understanding the culture of those benefiting from the neoliberal process— and that improves the production values behind action films in order to compete with foreign movies. The very existence of films like *Salvando al soldado Pérez* points toward the potential ability of Mexican cinema to compete in Hollywood-dominated genres like action by stripping away the U.S.-centered nationalism that typically characterizes these films and reconstructing them through ideologies and satires relevant to Mexico's commercial audience.

As a result of these processes, Mexican cinema has developed in a very short time the ability to use film as a sophisticated language of engagement with the contemporary, which in turn has resulted in films that, in their formal work, reframe the understanding of contemporary issues. In these terms, authorial cinema, particularly the brand that has emerged in the wake of the visibility of Carlos Reygadas and of the increasing presence of Mexican film on the international festival circuit, has begun to more frontally engage social themes.¹⁰ The most notable case of this is *Miss Bala* (Gerardo Naranjo, 2011), an authorial interpretation of the violence lived by everyday Mexicans trapped in the drug war. Loosely based on a true story, the film focuses on Laura Guerrero (Stephanie Sigman), a young woman aspiring to compete in the Miss Baja California pageant. Laura becomes unwittingly involved with a drug cartel when she tries to track down her friend Azucena (Lakshmi Picazo), who went missing during a shootout between the police and a criminal organization in a nightclub. When she tries to get assistance from a police officer, he surrenders her to Lino (Noé Hernández), the local drug lord, who starts using Laura to carry out cartel missions. While Laura is trapped by Lino, he arranges for her to win the Miss Baja pageant, in order to be able to reach a Mexican army general in charge of the drug war. In the end, Laura decides to betray Lino and save the general's life, which leads to her arrest. However, after being shown to the press, Laura is released in the middle of an industrial neighborhood with no explanation, presumably to reward her for helping the general. The film is fully narrated from Laura's perspective, in a dreamy tone with fuzzy cinematography and a constant sense of loss. Laura moves from the city to the cartel and then to the pageant, carried by inertia as actions unfold beyond her control. Naranjo creates his aesthetic through a cinematic reconstruction of the sense of powerlessness experienced by the citizens of towns and cities hijacked by organized crime.

Miss Bala is the point of arrival of many interesting formal and institutional developments that took place in the 2000s. Naranjo emerged out of the authorial paradigm discussed in Chapter 4, and his work stands between the uncompromising personal style of directors like Reygadas and Escalante and the practice of commercial authorship established by Cuarón and González Iñarritu. *Miss Bala* was produced by Canana Films, a studio founded in 2005, like Ambulante, by Gael García Bernal, Diego Luna, and Pablo Cruz. Canana has produced some of its founders' own films, like *Déficit* (García Bernal, 2007) and *Abel* (Luna, 2010), as well as projects that have received transnational recognition, like *Sin nombre* (Cary Fukunaga, 2009), a critically acclaimed film on the plight of Central American immigrants trying to reach the United States. Under the umbrella of a well-funded, prestigious production company, Naranjo has flourished and has caught the attention of international distributors like IFC Films. In addition, *Miss Bala* profits from the intelligent appropriation of youth cinema developed by Naranjo in his prior films *Drama/Mex* (2007) and *Voy a explotar* (2009), which explored the issues faced by alienated middle- and upper-class youths in societies marked by elitism and inequality. Sigman's Laura can be read as an intersection between Naranjo's haunted young female characters (like Tigrillo, the teenager who, in her attempt to become a prostitute, falls in love with an old man because she lacks a sense of family and she is alienated from the classist Acapulco society) and the politics of the drug war. *Miss Bala* thus expands Naranjo's palette of female characters facing their inability to enter a hostile society to women who become victims of the whirlwind of Mexico's contemporary problems.

Still, watching *Miss Bala* raises some of the industry's blind spots. Laura is ultimately a beauty queen and her plight is at times interrupted by camera work that has no qualms about sexualizing her body. The rise of female actresses through the ranks of romantic comedy—women like Ana Serradilla, Ana de la Reguera, and Martha Higareda—has by and large reproduced classist, ethnocentric, and sexist criteria of beauty inherent in Mexico's media ecosystem. Certainly, film representation of women has come a long way since the exploitation films of the 1970s and 1980s. According to a study by Jacqueline Benítez-Galbraith, Elizabeth Irvin, and Craig S. Galbraith, post-NAFTA films have less "sexist roles" than their pre-NAFTA counterparts (180). Nonetheless, like most contemporary film industries, Mexican cinema faces a troubling absence of successful female directors, which in turn has been an obstacle for more progressive representation of women's issues. The boom in female directors from the late 1980s and early 1990s brought figures like María Novaro and Maryse Sistach to the scene.[11] But women filmmakers in the 2000s have not matched the success of male directors like Reygadas or Naranjo. Still, as Joanne Hershfield has compellingly shown in a recent article, even films like Novaro's *Sin dejar huella* (2000) and Sistach's *Perfume de violetas* (2001) "address violence against women *in the abstract* [and] lack the political awareness of particular manifestations of violence that might generate necessary and effective sociopolitical responses" ("Women's Cinema" 182; emphasis in the original). In a market where films like *Presunto culpable* have managed to create awareness of urgent social issues, women's cinema remains unable to reach audiences beyond those who readily identify with feminist agendas, and the lack of spaces for female directors in contemporary cinema has certainly affected the ability of feminism to be a central element in the formation of contemporary cinematic ideologies.

Yet, two recent films show potential blueprints for the ways in which women's issues can shape Mexican cinema's effort to engage with the public sphere. The first one, *Backyard/El traspatio* (2009), is a film focused on one of the most dramatic realities in contemporary Mexico: the two decades of brutal and unsolved femicides in the working-class areas of Ciudad Juárez. Although the film was directed by Carlos Carrera, the script was written by Isabel Tardán and Sabina Berman, in their first film collaboration since the wonderful feminist film *Entre Pancho Villa y una mujer desnuda*, which Berman and Tardán had directed in 1996. Berman and Tardán clearly stamp the film with a feminist aesthetic that allows a discussion of the issue in the realm of cinema, which contrasts with the neglect and lack of interest shown by journalists and politicians in the last two decades. The film focuses on Blanca (Ana de la Reguera), a young detective from the local police assigned to the femicides. Blanca's characterizations already show the way in which Berman and Tardán's vision and Carrera's direction provide a very different representation of women from the one present in *Miss Bala* or in romantic comedies. The film dramatically plays down de la Reguera's sex appeal, and her performance of Blanca results in an androgynous figure defined by her conflicted relationship to the masculine worlds of politics and law enforcement.[12] Furthermore, the narrative of the film focuses on a network of women who participate in the daily struggle against the indifference to the mass rapes and femicides. Blanca thus builds ties with Sara (Carolina Politi), an activist who keeps records of all missing women and runs an organization for shelter victims, while resisting the political pressure exercised by the state governor (Enoc Leaño), a devout Catholic who throws the killings under the rug to protect the sweatshop industry. The film also tells, in parallel, the story of a victim, Juana (Asur Zagada), an indigenous teenager from Oaxaca who gets raped and killed by men gathered around her former boyfriend, Cutberto (Iván Cortés), as a "punishment" for her desire to enjoy her status as a financially independent woman. The film successfully shows the core gender issue of the femicides: the absolute disregard of women's rights (from the right to personal freedom to the right of legal protection from the State), which manifests itself both in the brutality of the crimes and in the ineptitude of the government in prosecuting them. It also exposes the fact that the crimes are not simply the work of a serial killer—a fiction produced both by mediatic attention and by the government's desire for the issue to go away—but an aggregate of acts of violence against women, performed by men in different positions of power, such as boyfriends like Cutberto, uncles who rape their nieces, and men who resent the women's success in the labor force. At the end of the film, Blanca pursues Mickey Santos (Jimmy Smits), a pedophile businessman, when he is trying to kidnap a high school girl to rape her and kill her. When Blanca and her partner Fierro (Marco Pérez) catch Mickey, he gladly surrenders because he knows that his bribes to the police chief and the inefficiency of the judicial system will shield him from prosecution. Furthermore, even though Mickey's businesses are in Ciudad Juárez, he lives in El Paso, which allows him to perform criminal acts on the Mexican side of the border while living the life of a respectable businessman in the United States. To end this cycle, Blanca decides to shoot him. Women like Sara and Blanca thus emerge in the end not as sex symbols or as figures constructed by a masculine gaze, but as righteous social agents who remain the only figures of justice in a society that discriminates against women.

Of course, feminism is not the only instrument to allow women to become central participants in the film industry. Patricia Riggen's *La misma luna* (2007) shows a possible way of breaking with some of the limits of neoliberal Mexican cinema by rehabilitating melodrama as a language of the social. Rather than creating a moralistic tale, like melodramas from the Golden Age did, *La misma luna* is a heartfelt story about Carlitos (Adrián Alonso), a nine-year-old child who, following the death of his grandmother, travels north to escape his uncle and join his mother, Rosario (Kate del Castillo), an undocumented worker living in Los Angeles. Riggen's film became very successful both in the United States and in Mexico, precisely by featuring the type of emotive discourse that Mexican directors of the 2000s tended to avoid. Unlike romantic comedies and other commercial films, which rely mostly on actors with cinema careers, Riggen cast two of Mexico's most popular television actors: *telenovela* star Kate del Castillo and comedian Eugenio Derbez, Rather than focusing on social cinema conventions of representing social inequality, Riggen opted for a story that hooks audiences through an intensely empathic representation of the mother-child bond, a narrative more common in melodramatic canons than in post-1988 Mexican cinema. The combination of the film's smart appeal to *telenovela* sensibilities and Riggen's ability to deploy forms of narrative typically constructed by media aimed at lower-class women resulted in a binational hit, thanks to a box office gross of eight million dollars in Mexico and over thirteen million dollars in the United States.

Riggen shows in this movie that her deep immersion in Mexican popular culture and her use of a subject traditionally associated with women filmmakers (motherhood) have a strong potential to overcome some barriers faced by contemporary Mexican cinema.[13] As Caryn Connelly has discussed, *La misma luna* constitutes, through its emotive discourse, a new way of representing immigrants as "honest, hard-working and family oriented people trying to improve their lives and the lives of their children *and* who make great sacrifices to do so" (18). Interestingly, the codes of melodrama, typically associated with hyperbole and escapism, paradoxically allow Riggen to construct a narrative that humanizes immigrants from the perspective of audiences both in Mexico and the United States, giving Mexican cinema the possibility of intervening in debates crucial to the bilateral relationship. In fact, *A Better Life* (Chris Weltz, 2011), a U.S. film about an undocumented worker (Demián Bichir) and his wish for a better life for his son (José Julián), follows the melodramatic blueprint of *La misma luna* into a further exploration of the human stories behind illegal immigration. The film's impact was such that Demián Bichir—an iconic actor of post-1988 Mexican film who was already a visible figure in United States thanks to his role in the television series *Weeds*—earned an Academy Award nomination for Best Male Performance by an actor, along with Jean Dujardin, George Clooney, Brad Pitt, and Gary Oldman. Bichir's surprise recognition—a nomination for Leonardo DiCaprio had been more widely expected—speaks volumes about Riggen's discovery of melodrama as a language of communication between the film industries of Mexico and the United States. As a result of this nomination, Bichir was cast in 2013 as the star of the FX series *The Bridge,* a police procedural focused on the U.S.-Mexico border. Incidentally, the series's first episode was directed by Gerardo Naranjo.

Furthermore, the casting of *telenovela* actors not only breaks with the class separation between television (aimed at lower classes) and cinema (primarily a middle- and upper-class genre), it also speaks to a new audience in the Mexican community in the United States, one that is already familiar with figures like del Castillo and Derbez thanks to their presence in the programming of the Univision network. Riggen is thus not only an exceptional case of a successful woman director, but also a pioneer in the newly constructed industry bonds between Mexican cinema and the U.S. Latino market. In fact, the success of *La misma luna* led in part to the creation of Pantelion, a joint production and distribution effort co-operated by Televisa and Lionsgate Films. Pantelion is already the distributor of many successful Mexican films in the U.S. market (including *Salvando al soldado Pérez* and *Pastorela*). But, perhaps more importantly, it is working with Mexican studios to produce films in Spanish and English geared to U.S. audiences. Pantelion is very much in the process of constructing an audience for projects that appeal to different levels of the U.S. Latino audience and show some crossover potential. Its first release, *From Prada to Nada* (Angel Gracia, 2011), a Latino retelling of Jane Austen's *Sense and Sensibility*, was modestly received (it grossed only 3.5 million dollars), but it boasted a transnational cast that included Hollywood actress Camila Belle, Mexican actress Adriana Barraza, and U.S. Latino stars Wilmer Valderrama and Alexa Vega. Also, *From Prada to Nada* was a meritorious attempt to bring the romantic comedy aesthetic as developed in Mexico to U.S. audiences, particularly through its unusual focus on upper-class Latinos. This is very significant in the U.S. market given the typecasting of Mexican actors and characters as illegal immigrants and drug dealers. A more recent release, *Casa de mi padre* (Matt Piedmont, 2012), tackles stereotypes through a different route. The film is a mock Western entirely spoken in Spanish, with a cast mostly composed of well-known media actors like García Bernal, Luna, Pedro Armendáriz, and Sandra Echeverría. The central conceit of the film is the fact that the main role, Armando Álvarez, is played with a straight face by comedian Will Ferrell, who has no knowledge of Spanish whatsoever. Ferrell performed all of his lines through phonetics, without ever being sure of what he was saying. The film deftly mocks the U.S. audience's ignorance of the Spanish language and of Mexican culture (given that the Western genre has been a source of stereotypes of how Mexico is supposed to look). In any case, this type of intervention may change the equation of Latino presence in U.S. culture. It is also of note that *Casa de mi padre* was coproduced by Canana Films and Lemon Films, which exemplifies a potentially viable path for Mexican production houses to enter the U.S. market. Two of Pantelion's other films, Carmen Marron's *Go for It* (2011) and Patricia Riggen's second feature, *Girl in Progress* (2012), both aim for the positive representation of U.S.-born Latino girls dealing with the contradictions of their heritage. Ventures like Pantelion may indeed contribute to reshaping the still questionable representation of Latinos in U.S. media.[14]

Back in the Mexican domestic market, the industry keeps providing a reliable stream of commercial films, which at least maintain their market share. Romantic comedy remains a consistent and dependable source of commercial success. In the past few years, romantic comedies with successful runs at the box office included *Te presento a Laura* (Fez Noriega, 2010), a vehicle for Martha Higareda; *No eres tú, soy yo* (Alejandro Springall, 2010), a follow-up for *La misma luna*'s Eugenio Derbez; and *Labios rojos* (Rafael Lara, 2009), the latest film to feature romantic comedy and *telenovela* star Silvia Navarro. Pantelion was the U.S. distributor for *No eres tú* and *Labios rojos*. But the true major development in Mexican cinema since 2005 has been the expansion of commercial cinema toward genres beyond romantic comedy. Production houses like Lemon Films have pushed different boundaries and challenged U.S. cinema in genres traditionally not present in post-1998 moviemaking.

As a result, horror cinema, which was a staple of "cinema of solitude" films and which had not had a major representative since del Toro's *Cronos,* emerged with great force in the second part of the 1990s, led by the box office success of the film *Kilómetro 31* (2006). Paul Julian Smith has aptly described this film, which focuses on telepathic twins involved in a car accident, as a transnational venture that combines a cast composed of Mexican and Spanish actors, familiar strategies from U.S. and global horror films, and a plotline based on a Mexican story ("Transnational Cinemas" 69–70). Director Rigoberto Castañeda's commitment to the genre, though, follows Guillermo del Toro's path to some degree, particularly in its attempt to decouple horror cinema from its unattractive Mexican tradition. Thus, Castañeda's second film, *Blackout* (2008), was shot in English and aimed at the U.S. indie market. Nevertheless, Castañeda's first film provided a blueprint that made horror once again a viable language for Mexican commercial cinema, and many remarkable movies have followed: *Spam* (Carlos Sariñana, 2008), a film about an e-mail that kills people; the *Cronos*-style cannibal story *Somos lo que hay* (Jorge Michel Grau, 2010); and ghost story *Viernes de ánimas* (Raúl Pérez Gámez, 2011), among others. If one tallies up the action and animation films I've listed, along with the steady stream of romantic comedies, the aforementioned horror films, melodramas like *La misma luna,* dramas like *Miss Bala,* and even documentaries like *Presunto culpable,* the resulting landscape of commercial cinema is far more diverse and complex than the one at the outset of the 2000s.

Another peculiar sign of the growing influence of Mexican cinema in the cultural milieu is the recent use of the medium by conservative groups in order to advance a revisionist history of Church-State relations. Mexico is a country that has maintained the separation of Church and State since the 1850s and the conservative right-wing position seeking to undermine that separation has rarely emerged in mainstream culture. In fact, one of the foundational events of modern Mexico is the Cristero War, a civil conflict that resulted from the government's attempt to expel the Catholic Church in the late 1920s. The right wing has long held the Cristeros as defenders of religious freedom, even though organizations espousing these views (like Opus Dei and the Legionaries of Christ) are not representative of mainstream religious thinking or practices in the country. Cinema has recently become a vehicle for the expression of these views, in an attempt to sway audiences to the perspective held by conservative activists. The first notable film in this vein is *2033* (Francisco Laresgoiti, 2009), a science fiction allegory of the Cristero War, set in a futuristic Mexico City. The film takes place in a society where books and religion have been banned, and where all control is held by a corporation through a synthetic food called PECTI. The heroes of the film are a priest (Marco Antonio Treviño) who bravely keeps a library and helps people break their PECTI addictions, and a young man, Pablo (Raúl Méndez), who is being groomed by the elite to take over the corporation but decides to join the resistance. Treviño's character is named Miguel—a clear reference to Father Miguel Agustín Pro, one of the leading figures of the Cristeros. In the world constructed by the film, liberal and neoliberal secularism threaten humanity, and it can achieve redemption only through a full-fledged embrace of religion. The film is tied to the Servitje family (through the director as well as through patriarch Lorenzo, who financed the film), a prominent business clan known for its ownership of the Bimbo Bread empire and its support of radical right-wing causes. More recently, a steady stream of works focused on this narrative has emerged, including *Marcelino, pan y vino* (José Luis Gutiérrez, 2010), which is set in the Mexican Revolution era and is a remake of the infamous 1955 Spanish film of the same name, an iconic work of nationalist Catholicism from the Franco period. But perhaps the most telling film is *For Greater Glory* (Dean Wright, 2012), a binational U.S.-Mexico production starring Andy García. This film is a 150-minute-long re-narration of the Cristero War, presenting it as an epic struggle for freedom of belief. The film was supported both by Latinos in the United States, like García and Eva Longoria, and by the Mexican company Dos Corazones Films, which in the past had produced films on Pope John Paul II and the Virgin of Guadalupe. To date, *For Greater Glory* is the most expensive Mexican film ever made (an eleven-million-dollar budget), which illustrates the producers' faith in the ability of cinema to advance their agenda. Regardless of one's position on the issue of religion in Mexico, the existence of these films shows the growing presence of cinema in the public sphere. Works like *2033* and *For Greater Glory*, religious movies financed by the conservative business elite and circulating in commercial film markets, were unthinkable even in the early 2000s.

The 2010 bicentennial provided another glimpse of Mexican film's future potential. Benefiting from the funding available for the celebration, Canana produced *Revolución* (2010), a compilation of ten short films by their top directing talent, in which the idea of the Mexican Revolution is appropriated in creative and revisionist ways.[15] The arc of the anthology is in fact quite notable. It features works by Naranjo, García Bernal, Mariana Chenillo, Fernando Eimbcke, Rodrigo Plá, and Rodrigo García that are all interesting in their own right, but three other pieces are particularly worthy of attention. Patricia Riggen activates once again her penchant for melodrama and binational Mexican stories in "Lindo y querido," the story of a young woman who returns to her Mexican roots after the death of her father. Carlos Reygadas does not disappoint with his experimental short "Éste es mi reino," which documents the decadent crescendo of a party of the Mexican elite in the town of Tepoztlán. The film is based on a radical *cinema verité* approach: the rich people's utter selfishness and their capacity to devolve into a drunken carnival are contrasted with all the people of the town, who watch in astonishment as the partygoers burn a car. Amat Escalante directed, in my view, the best short, "El cura Nicolás Colgado," where a priest attacked by a lynch mob and left hanging in a tree is rescued by two children. The short, shot to resemble Mexico during the Cristero War of the late 1920s, surprises the audience by having the characters arrive at a modern city and eat dinner at a McDonald's. Escalante uses cinematography and montage to convey a powerful message: Mexico has not changed that much since revolutionary times. In their formal, thematic, and stylistic variety, the films of *Revolución* showcase many avenues for the future development of film and indicate an even more considerable expansion of authorial cinema.

The most notable impact of all is the way in which cinema has reshaped Mexico's most important media industry: television. As Mexican cinema became an important cultural referent for the middle classes, television networks and cable channels in Mexico took note and adopted its languages and starts for new shows addressed at their audiences. HBO Olé, Latin America's version of the U.S. pay channel, produced its first show in Mexico, *Capadocia*, following the blueprint of Mexican cinema. The show stars Ana de la Reguera as a woman who goes to prison after accidentally killing her husband's lover, at a time when the city government has decided to privatize the prison system. The show not only casts film actors like de la Reguera and Juan Manuel Bernal. It also echoes a narrative of State corruption and citizenship of fear similar to Sariñana's *Todo el poder*, which I discussed in Chapter 3. Rather than opting for comedy, *Capadocia* translates this story into HBO's strong work on drama, producing an interesting blend of U.S. premium station serial and Mexican cinema. Another iconic example is *Soy tu fan*, a successful television show produced by Canana Films, Luna and García Bernal's venture. Based on an Argentine television show, *Soy tu fan* is fundamentally a romantic comedy in which the protagonist, played by Ana Claudia Talancón, is involved in a triangle with her former boyfriend, who is a member of a rock band, and a new love interest. The series' episodes are often directed by major players in the film industry, like Mariana Chenillo and Gerardo Naranjo. Also, piggybacking on Talancón's popularity and on the audience's positive reception of Mexican romantic comedies, *Soy tu fan* has managed to establish both a national audience—via the State-owned Canal Once, headed at the time by Fernando Sariñana—and a transnational one, thanks to its rebroadcast in the United States on MTV Tr3s, which has made the series a referent among young U.S. Latino audiences. Even Televisa has moved into series inspired by the film aesthetic, as programs like *El Pantera*, an action series based on a comic book and starring Luis Roberto Guzmán (of *Ladies' Night* fame), garner the attention of audiences no longer interested in *telenovelas*.

Carlos Gutiérrez has recently stated that "the study of film in Mexico remains largely trapped within paradigms of earlier decades" ("*Y tu crítica*" 108). This certainly continues to be a problem across the academic landscape, both in Spanish and English, as critics remain committed to the study of Mexicanness and Mexicanism. As I hope my study has demonstrated, it is imperative to overcome Mexicanism as the predominant form of approaching Mexican cinema, and to read Mexican film production in ways that do not echo the ideological agendas of the critic. Mexican film certainly contradicts many tenets developed by scholars of cultural studies. The absence of women film directors and of representations of women's issues, which I discussed earlier, limits the scope of feminist approaches. In addition, the fact that post-1988 Mexican cinema is first and foremost a culture of the elite, and that films may manifest regressive political positions and problematic representations of race, class, and gender, clashes with the leftist and progressive ideals of most scholars of culture (myself included). Still, in this book I hope that I have shown that one cannot understand the issues raised by Mexican film—the segregation of audiences, the need to negotiate with a domestic market, the pressures of the international market on Mexican filmmakers, the competition against Hollywood, and the need to lure audiences who may hold regressive ideological and cultural positions—by privileging films with progressive agendas or by dismissing the culture of the middle and upper classes. Twenty-first-century Mexican film is no longer a vehicle for the expression of the national, or a form of culture that may be used for the cultural and social democratization of the country. But the industry's brave if problematic success in keeping alive a tradition that would otherwise be vanquished by the Hollywood juggernaut requires critics and scholars attuned to what the movies mean and to the many odds they have to face to even exist. And, as I believe my study suggests, the processes underwent by Mexican cinema during the last twenty-five years have much to tell us: about cinema, about neoliberalism, and about what Mexican society—under the siege of political division, social inequality, and unprecedented violence—has to say about itself.

NOTES

INTRODUCTION

1. For a development of the concept of national culture as invoked here, see Schlesinger 107.
2. See Sánchez Prado, *Naciones intelectuales,* for a discussion of the 1930s and 1940s process in literature; Doremus, for a discussion of the culture at large; and Dever and Noble, for the specific case of cinema.
3. Most of this infrastructure grew out of the Ley de Industria Cinematográfica (Film Industry Act) promulgated by the administration of President Miguel Alemán in 1949. This law was active until it was replaced by a new federal act in 1992. See Berrueco García for a good study of the history of film legislation and jurisprudence in Mexico. In addition, see Flibbert 82–97 for a useful and concise history of the role of the State in Mexican film from the 1930s to 1992.
4. For a description of this global process, see Harvey.
5. As I was revising this book, Frederick Luis Aldama published *Mex-Ciné,* a study that incorporates elements of sociology and cognitive theory into the study of cinema. The book has a peculiar structure, with short summaries of films and chapters with somewhat strange titles. While I do not share the idea of using the term "Mex-Ciné" to talk about Mexican cinema, as Aldama does throughout the book, his work offers some original insights on post-2000 movies.
6. Paz's work is common knowledge among Mexicanist and Latin Americanist scholars and I find it unnecessary to delve into its thesis in the context of my discussion. However, it can be said that Paz understood his book as a diagnosis of a Mexican disease, "solitude," which expressed Mexico's problematic relationship with itself, its history, and modernity in general. By focusing his study precisely on gender and urban popular classes, Ramírez Berg closely follows the scheme of Mexican culture developed by Paz which, to be fair, does have more influence on Chicano and Mexican American scholarship than it does in Mexico. A good discussion of Paz's views of history and modernity, particularly for those not familiar with them, may be found in Quiroga, *Understanding Octavio Paz* 57–87.
7. A study of this tradition is, of course, beyond the scope of this work, but my critical assertions here derive from Sánchez Prado, *Naciones intelectuales* 191–238.
8. Discussions of Cuarón's film will take place in Chapters 2 and 4, while *Cronos* will be discussed in detail in Chapter 4.

9. Discussing Buñuel's full impact on Mexican cinema exceeds my purposes here, but readers interested in the question may consult Acevedo-Muñoz, *Buñuel and Mexico*.
10. And here "specific" must be emphasized. While some movies have been the subject of numerous studies, most of the works I discuss here have not generated any monographic works, so the only available criticism will be that of general discussions of film in the period.

CHAPTER 1

1. In fact, in terms of gender issues, Wu's article represents a consensus regarding the film. Claudine Potvin, for instance, recognizes both the book and the film's attempt to recover popular cultural genres to engage the feminine condition. Still, Potvin argues, "the marginalization of feminine figures remains intact, from the beginning of the movie to the end, without establishing the radical character of the margin or a redefinition of the center, through the characterization of Tita, for instance, or through the subversion/inversion of her tragedy" (64). Another critic, Deborah Shaw, argues that, deep down, the movie offers a very conservative vision of gender and class: "Without this problem [her commitment to her mother], Tita would live an idealized life with the man of her dreams and would be fulfilled, cooking and attending to the needs of her husband and children with the help of her indigenous servants, who are happy to work for her as a kind, considerate mistress of the house" (*Contemporary Cinema* 39). There have been, of course, some dissenting views. Dianna Niebylski, while recognizing the "quasi-reactionary" views of the film, ultimately proposes a reading of both the movie and the book as parodies of traditional Mexican genres. While she shows a strong preference for the book—unlike Potvin, who argues that both texts are essentially the same—Niebylski nonetheless characterizes the film as "sweet and sexy" and "a lovely treat for the eyes" (193).
2. In her landmark book, Doris Sommer uses the term "foundational fiction" to illustrate the ways in which nineteenth-century "national romances," like Jorge Isaac's *María* or Ignacio Manuel Altamirano's *Clemencia*, allegorically represent certain national projects, ideologies, and identities. This notion may be expanded to twentieth-century productions, like the novels of García Márquez or mid-century Mexican melodramas, insofar as they also use affective identification to allegorize national ideas and ideologies.
3. In my view, this reading does not hold, because the movie clearly wants the audience to identify with Tita, a device of melodrama rather than comedy. Also, following the reading by Shaw and Rollet quoted earlier, the audiences who flocked to the movie both nationally and internationally were most definitely not reading the film as a comedy.
4. An excellent study of this figure may be found in Linhard.
5. I owe this point to Olivia Cosentino.
6. Since this book is not a Deleuzian reading of Mexican cinema, explaining the complexities of Deleuze's system is out of my scope. Still, for a development of the question, see Campbell and Martin-Jones. The notions of "time image" and "movement

image" come from Deleuze's *Cinema 1* and *Cinema 2*. For a good study on Deleuzian concepts of cinema, see Bogue.

7. Another well-known phenomenon in this regard is the Frida Kahlo boom in the early 1990s, which included a MoMA exhibit in New York that was backed by a considerable amount of Mexican government money. For a good study on this exhibition, see Franco, *Critical Passions* 39–47.

8. Interestingly, Ripstein's movie is the second remake of Boytler's film. Director Emilio Gómez Muriel used Boytler's script to make a version in 1949, in the middle of the Golden Age.

9. An interesting case in this context is Carlos García Agraz's *Mi querido Tom Mix*, a somewhat successful film based on an older woman's obsession with silent Western films. While García Agraz does not appeal to the Golden Age past, his nostalgia operates in relation to the same affective identification of the audience with cinema, this time represented by a nationalization of a classic foreign genre. The film is hard to classify and thus hard to place in systematic relation to other movies of the period. Still, it can be said that it does possess unusually high production values and is a movie worth consideration. In my argument, it shows yet another example of filmmakers' reflections on the lost public value of cinema. However, other critics have produced interesting readings of the movie. See particularly Stock, whose "Authentically Mexican?" provides a suggestive reading of it in the context of early 1990s cinema.

10. For a good discussion of *Ave María*'s adoption of the colony, see Gordon 109–40. Gordon's discussion is appropriate here, since he understands the film as the "retooling of a national icon" (109).

11. It is also important to note that Pelayo recently wrote an account of the meaning of making cinema during the crisis of the 1980s. The hardships faced by directors like Ripstein, Cazals, and himself are undoubtedly a factor in his nostalgic recasting of Miroslava. See Pelayo.

12. Mora Catlett directed, more recently, a film shot in Purehpecha, another indigenous language. *Eréndira Ikukinari* (2006) is the story of a sixteenth-century indigenous woman who bravely resists the Spanish conquest. While the film is not quite as contrived as *Retorno a Aztlán*, it likewise proves that this style remains a dead end in contemporary Mexican cinema.

13. For a definition and examples of this "Mexploitation cinema," see Greene.

14. For *Cabeza de Vaca*, see the next section; for *Sólo con tu pareja*, see Chapter 2; for *Cronos*, see Chapter 4.

15. A contrast here may be made with a less interesting example of reflective nostalgia: Juan Antonio de la Riva's *Pueblo de Madera* (1990). This movie recreates life in a wood-producing town in the sierra. While it follows many characters throughout the movie, the main plotline is based on two children, who are best friends. One is bound to become a worker in the logging industry, while the other will leave the town at the end of the film. The movie begins with a scene that sets a costumbrist tone for the rest of the movie: a poetry declamation contest, where a child recites a nationalist text. Nostalgia here is represented in the constant tension between the

idyllic atmosphere of the town and the conflicts brought about by crime, poverty, and life. While *Danzón* operates in a sophisticated network of cultural references, *Pueblo de Madera* is very plain and literal: a syrupy reminiscence of an era that is fading away. The fact that Novaro achieved a more multilayered plot using the same structure—the confrontation of affect and modernity—says a great deal about her talent as filmmaker. Still, *Pueblo de Madera* is another important example of the role of nostalgia in the configuration of filmmaking practices in the late 1980s and early 1990s.

16. Schaefer does mention the fact that Julia works for Telmex (62), and argues that in the end the movie is about Julia's integration into the neoliberal order. She also recognizes the meaning of Julia's use of her retirement funds to finance her trip and the training sessions she has to undergo. However, Julia's labor status plays a minor role in Schaefer's argument, which is more interested in issues of culture and leisure.

17. I thank Olivia Cosentino for pointing this out.

18. *Mestizaje* in Mexico refers to the idea that national identity is the result of the encounter and mixture, both cultural and racial, of European and indigenous peoples. This idea became popular in post-revolutionary Mexico, as it was used by public intellectuals like Manuel Gamio and José Vasconcelos as an argument for nation building and continental unity. In the context of 1992, the celebration of Columbus Day (tellingly called *Día de la Raza* in Spanish) was used to re-create this narrative of origin as a foundation of identity. For a good account of Latin American *mestizaje* and its continental development, see Marilyn Grace Miller.

19. That neither *1492* nor *Christopher Columbus* has been commercially released on DVD in the United States is striking, considering both the stature of the directors and cast and the fact that less visible movies are currently getting DVD releases. For my purposes, this further illustrates how these films were instruments of a very specific historical moment and how they have been irrelevant in the long run to contemporary cinema.

20. Of the many possible examples, I would highlight the book *Raíces indígenas, presencia hispánica,* edited by Miguel León-Portilla, a foundational figure of pre-Columbian Mexican studies and one of the leading figures in the quincentennial celebrations. The book gathers the work of dozens of scholars from different areas of expertise, highlighting for the most part the idea of the Conquest as an "encounter between cultures." For a study of the ideologies behind this kind of scholarly work, see Sánchez Prado, "Pre-Columbian Past." A further discussion of this context in Mexican cinema may be found in Haddu (*Contemporary Mexican Cinema* 45–48), where, besides the Columbus films and official narratives, she underscores the parallel emergence of indigenous resistance movements and of films that presented the story in a more "sensitive" way, such as Michael Mann's *The Last of the Mohicans* (1992).

21. To be fair, some recent studies on the historical film genre do present a more complex picture. See in particular Hughes-Warrington, which introduces a more nuanced landscape, including a useful discussion on affect and identity. While some of my concepts are tangentially informed by this work, I focus on Landy's arguments because of their role in shaping debates of historical cinema and their resonance in the study of Latin American historical films.

22. That said, I still believe that the detailed study of Mexican historical cinema remains a pending task of film studies and that no major book on the subject has been produced. I am open to the possibility that even these films mentioned here might be read as interventions against the grain of official discourse, much as I am reading *Cabeza de Vaca*. The point to emphasize here is simply that the automatic connection between historical cinema and national identity is problematic in contexts such as Mexico, and that the theoretical development of these ideas has come mostly from the study of Western European cinema, particularly that of Britain and France, and of Hollywood productions.
23. Another consideration comes from the fact that Landy's work mostly focuses on films from the mid-twentieth century (*British Genres*' framework is 1930–1960), and that more contemporary uses of history in film are not fully accounted for in her models.
24. Still, many interesting arguments have been made regarding *Cabeza de Vaca*'s appropriation of the Conquest as a historical event. See Gordon's excellent study of the film in comparison with the Brazilian Cinema Novo masterpiece *Como era gostoso o meu francés* (47–77).
25. Luis Fernando Restrepo fairly notes that the film omits the parts of the chronicle that more emphatically represent colonial violence and Amerindian resistance (190–91). My view does not attempt to contradict this point. Rather, I am interested in highlighting that, despite its failures, the film does offer a unique and original representation of indigenous peoples, which goes against the grain of a tradition of idealized representations present in film and in other cultural genres.
26. It is important to note here that Al-Nemi does not consider the Mexican movies based on Mahfouz, most likely because they came out right when he was concluding his dissertation.
27. Another example of a film adaptation that points toward the break-up of the melodramatic form is Ernesto Rimoch's *Demasiado amor* (2002), which is based on a successful homonymous novel by Sara Sefchovich. The film tells the story of a woman who, in the process of waiting to join her sister in Spain, meets a man who helps her to rediscover herself personally and sexually. Sergio de la Mora points out that the book breaks with the melodramatic legacy of Golden Age cinema by presenting a woman who is sexual without being stigmatized, but ultimately recognizes the movie as a neonationalist romantic fantasy narrative (*Cinemachismo* 42–46). It is interesting, nonetheless, that de la Mora refers to the book rather than to the movie, even though his study was released four years after Rimoch's film. This capacity to be highly critical of the melodramatic form and still engage with a clear nationalist narrative is part of the appeal behind adapting the book into a movie. However, I do think that the movie is ultimately not nearly as important as the book because it came out in 2002, and so its breaking of melodramatic narratives was not as daring and as cutting-edge as the one Ripstein attempted in 1993. Still, the existence of a movie like this nearly a decade after *Principio y fin* shows the persistence of melodrama as an aesthetic concern for film directors, who are in turn quite able to present a critical perspective on it even in more conventional and less groundbreaking movies.
28. I am not claiming that this was the only literature adapted in Mexico prior to 1968 (this being something that I cannot substantiate either way and that falls outside of

the scope of my study). I am simply emphasizing the fact that the most well-known films were based on canonical Mexican novels.

29. My sample of English studies for this claim included Cartmell and Whelehan, *Adaptations* and *Cambridge Companion;* Kroeber; Carroll; Leitch; and Welsh and Lev. For a French example, see Gaudreault. For Spanish examples, see Sánchez Noriega and Wolf.

30. Russian formalism used this notion to discuss the ways in which original works of literature or criticism allowed for the "transformation of our conventional perceptions of literary history" (Shklovsky xvi). It is in this particular sense that I use the term, since I believe that adapting Mahfouz made it possible for Ripstein and Fons to transform traditional perceptions of the melodrama genre, as well as of the social function of cinema vis-à-vis the scale of values put forward by traditional Mexicanist and even neo-Mexicanist aesthetics.

31. Many critics of Mahfouz have pointed out the central role of patriarchy as a structure of power in his work. See Allegretto-Diiulio. In addition, Hamman Al-Rifal contends that the underlying figures of *machismo* in Mahfouz are translated into the film adaptation, making these gender dynamics one of the central remaining elements from the source text.

32. Carrera's first film, *La mujer de Benjamín* (1991), is a landmark film, and *Sin remitente* (1995) was a somewhat successful film as well.

33. Ayala Blanco correctly asserts that other films, like Ripstein's *El evangelio de las maravillas* (1998), hold an even more anticlerical tone that was overlooked both by critics and censors (*La grandeza* 144). I believe one of the reasons why it was such an issue in Carrera's movie, beyond the advertising that surrounded *El crimen del padre Amaro,* was precisely because this anticlericalism is presented in such a familiar and commercial style, with clear anchors in neo-Mexicanist traditions, while Ripstein's films are rooted in his trademark style, which has only rarely been appreciated by Mexican moviegoers. In other words, this controversy is a very good instance of a situation in which traditional cinematic narrative may actually result in a more effectively critical position than even auteur cinema.

34. MacLaird goes on to offer a suggestive reading of the film and the legal and religious implications of its alleged "blasphemy," as well as the institutional and legal intertwinings of the scandal. Since my analysis is more interested in the use of Mexicanist cinematic codes to undermine hegemonic nationalistic ideologies, I am not as concerned with these controversies, but MacLaird's analysis is undoubtedly fundamental to the full understanding of this movie's significance.

35. The early years of the Fox administration were characterized by a sense that the presidential system of the PRI was over after the election of a president from a different party. However, by 2002, this enthusiasm was curtailed by a gridlock that resulted from a congress made up of three minority parties and the resentment of the right wing of the PAN due to Fox's early decision to appoint nonpartisan figures to significant positions in his cabinet. By this time, there was a backlash against Fox from different angles. See Dawson 142–43. One way of reading this movie is in relation to the growing concern on the liberal left regarding the empowerment of ultra-right-wing groups like *Provida,* which spearheaded the campaign against the movie.

36. For another good reading of the adaptation, see the article by Mónica Figuereido, who discusses the ways in which Eça's critique of religious fanaticism is translated in the Mexican film. I do not quite agree with her reading, however, since I do not find fanaticism to be anything more than a secondary subject in the film.
37. Novaro's Veracruz is not always welcoming. Doña Tí, the owner of the hotel where Julia stays, is actually quite homophobic and she mistreats and mocks Julia's transvestite friends.
38. Two examples come to mind: Óscar Blancarte's saccharine *Entre la tarde y la noche* (2000), in which the protagonist, Minerva, returns to Mazatlán to confront her past and ultimately reclaim her identity; and Ignacio Ortiz's *Cuento de hadas para dormir cocodrilos* (2002), a search for origins that overlaps family history and the history of Mexico in a provincial town. Still, it is significant that this narrative form remains active well into the 2000s, proving the resilience of some of the forms critiqued by more sophisticated films.
39. It is worth noting that another major Ibargüengoitia novel, *Estas ruinas que ves*, was adapted to film in 1979. Unlike Sneider's film, the film directed by Julián Pastor was more focused on the characters' sexual escapades than on constructing any form of critical stance on Mexico. The distance between Pastor's movie and *Dos crímenes* is a good illustration of the process I describe here.
40. For a good study on Ibargüengoitia's fiction, see Campesino.
41. Here, *Arráncame la vida* stands in contrast with Luis Estrada's *La ley de Herodes*, a much more daring movie about the period. See Chapter 3 for an analysis of this film.
42. I refer here to former governor Mario Marín, a politician accused of protecting a businessman and alleged pedophile. Marín was shielded from prosecution both by the State structure of the PRI and by the national party and was known to exercise power quite vertically during his administration.

CHAPTER 2

1. For a larger sample of LGBT representations in cinema, see Schulz-Cruz.
2. Incidentally, Claudia Schaefer suggests in passing a connection, with *Sex, Lies, and Videotape* not as an influence, but as a "cliché" (50). Schaefer does not refer to Soderbergh's movie directly, but rather contends that the trope was so prevalent in the air that it is not surprising Hermosillo decided to use it. I disagree with this perspective because the movies that replicated the "sex, lies, and videotape" concept were not as ubiquitous as Schaefer claims; furthermore, when Hermosillo adopted it for his film, it was a unique choice in the larger landscape of Mexican cinema.
3. *La tarea* is echoed in more than one way by Sabina Berman and Isabel Tardán's *Entre Pancho Villa y una mujer desnuda*, which I will discuss in Chapter 3.
4. Hermosillo did produce a weaker sequel, *La tarea prohibida* (1992), in which a young student invites an older woman (Maria Rojo) to his apartment and starts seducing her while secretly taping the interactions. Even though the woman is also played by Rojo, the character is entirely unrelated to Virginia from the first film. This movie fails because the interaction between the characters is not as strong, and because Hermosillo renounces the Spartan visual presentation of the previous film

for more staged and contrived sexual interactions. For a good reading of *Esmeralda*, see Foster 111–21.

5. See Ismael Rodríguez's *A. T. M.: A toda máquina* (1951) for a Pedro Infante vehicle, Julián Soler's *Me quiero casar* (1967) for a famous Angélica María comedy, and René Cardona Jr.'s *Escápate conmigo* (1987) for a prime example of a Televisa-backed singer vehicle starring Lucero and Mijares. A wonderful discussion of the culture behind the rock movies of the 1960s may be found in Zolov.

6. While *Sólo con tu pareja* is the movie that was ultimately successful in redefining the genre, it was not the first. Other films tried and failed to use the forms of romantic comedy. The most notable example is Marisa Sistach's *Anoche soñé contigo* (1992), in which a young man (Martín Altomaro) experiences his sexual initiation thanks to the visit of his older cousin Azucena (Leticia Perdigón). This movie is not as important or successful in part because it replicates ideas and plot structures from 1980s *sexycomedias,* albeit in a more critical and tasteful way. Even in its framing, the movie belongs to a previous era: the soundtrack is full of tropical music rather than the pop music that would colonize romantic comedy in the 1990s. The movie itself is named after a traditional song.

7. Of course, the discussion of this trajectory would merit a book in itself. However, a short example may illustrate the point: Edward Burns's romantic comedies, which draw many elements from Woody Allen's work, operated in the 1990s and 2000s as bona fide independent movies even though they lacked the literary elaboration of Allen's scripts. For a study on Burns's romantic comedies as indie cinema, see Stilwell.

8. For a very complete account of how romantic comedy unfolded in the United States in the 1990s, see Krutnik, "Conforming Passions." It is also important to note here that Britain would also develop a very important trend in romantic comedy following the success of Mike Newell's *Four Weddings and a Funeral* (1994).

9. More examples may be obtained in the book *Historias personales,* in which José Antonio Fernández F. interviews some of the leading figures of the Mexican advertising industry of the 1990s. For a good history on the development of advertising in Mexico, see *Crónica de la publicidad* 192–219.

10. For an excellent discussion on wrestling as a cultural genre, see Lévi.

11. As the reader may realize, the major movies include *Como agua para chocolate, Cabeza de Vaca, Principio y fin,* and *Danzón.* Other significant movies of this time frame are *El bulto,* discussed in Chapter 3; *Cronos,* discussed in Chapter 4; and *La mujer de Benjamín.*

12. As I revise this chapter in 2013, *Alta tensión* feels even more invalidated by recent events. The government's closure of one of the two public electric companies revealed that the industry fails to meet the country's demands, and is plagued by corruption and inefficiency. The fact that a romantic comedy touted this industry, which was already in a slow process of decline in 1997, shows the aesthetic and ideological regression these movies signified in comparison with *Sólo con tu pareja.*

13. For an exhaustive catalog of movies produced in these years, see Wilt 655–62. Other numbers compiled by Enrique Sánchez-Ruiz show a total output of fifty-six films in the country (both publicly and privately funded) in 1994, fourteen in 1995, sixteen in 1996, thirteen in 1997, ten in 1998, and twenty-four in 1999.

14. To be sure, this cultural frame remains the dominant scheme, and as such is necessary to understand mediatic consumption in the urban popular classes. As Hugo Benavides shows in *Drugs, Thugs and Divas*, a large slice of media culture, music, and popular literature in Latin America remains centered on two melodrama-oriented genres: *telenovelas* and *narco* (drug dealer) dramas. As I will show later on, the evolution of Mexican cinema toward romantic comedy represented a new class division in cultural tastes, leaving melodrama in the realm of the lower classes and opening the space of the middle class to new forms of cultural engagement.

15. *La vida conyugal* had some success at the Amiens International Film Festival: Socorro Bonilla was recognized as Best Actress, while Carrera picked up an award in the Best Director category at the Trieste Latin Cinema Festival. Still, in Carrera's very successful run as a film director, *La vida conyugal*'s reception, as well as its quality, pales in comparison even to his previous film, *La mujer de Benjamín*, proving that well-reputed directors experienced major creative blocks during this period.

16. Other than Cinemex's information, all the rest of this data is publicly available on the websites of the companies (*www.cinemark.com.mx; www.cinemex.com; www.cinepolis.com.mx; www.mmcinemas.com*) and of Canacine (*www.canacine.com.mx*).

17. One should mention here that the requirements are sometimes unenforceable since the law allows for an exception to comply with international treaties. Exhibitors have used NAFTA in order to take advantage of the exception, particularly in the summer season. However, screen time granted to Mexican films is much higher today than before the law. For a discussion of this issue from a legal standpoint, see Berrueco García 78 and 99.

18. While economic studies of the specific impact of cable channels in Mexico are largely nonexistent, some trends echo those developed in the late 1980s in the United States, with the emergence of networks like TNT or HBO. For a study of this period, see Gomery 263–75.

19. While Televisa no longer enjoys the 70–90 percent ratings of pre-cable times, it still holds a strong grip on the national media landscape, by owning Televisa Networks (formerly Visat), which is an umbrella company for an important number of cable channels, and four national broadcast networks. For a study on the ways in which Televisa reframed itself during this period, see Patrick D. Murphy; and Sinclair, *Latin American Television* 33–63. See also Sinclair, "Neither West nor Third World," for a reconstruction of the TV landscape prior to the transformations I describe here.

20. A more appropriate comparison may be Jorge Prior's *Pruebas de amor* (1994), a Romeo and Juliet story featuring Demián Bichir and Claudia Ramírez. The movie has an indecisive aesthetic that lacks the more polished visual language of Cuarón or Montero. It mixes the acting and plot structures of romantic comedy with the *telenovela*'s stories of impossible love. The film went largely unnoticed during its commercial release in Mexico, indicating both the lack of distribution alternatives in 1994 and the film's lack of touch with the new audiences. This is illustrated by the film's ending, in which the main characters assassinate their other lovers before escaping, something that contrasts radically with the lighter tone of the rest of the film, and that disconnects the movie from romantic comedy paradigms.

21. I use the term "creative class" here and in the rest of the book, following Richard Florida's argument that a new social class emerged in recent years, defined by its "economic function to new ideas, new technology and/or new creative content" (8). This class includes people like architects, designers, and artists, as well as those in business fields like marketing, who belong to flexible forms of work that require advanced education and substantial social capital. I do not share Florida's enthusiasm for this social phenomenon, but I find his analysis useful insofar as it idealizes the same lifestyles and professions as Mexican cinema.
22. The subplot of *Cilantro y perejil* focuses on Nora, Susana's sister, who is pursuing a career as a documentarian and a relationship of her own.
23. Ayala Blanco highlights this allusion and celebrates Retes's attack on Cuarón's superficiality (*La fugacidad* 286).
24. I will discuss Retes's *El bulto* in Chapter 3. Retes would keep pressing the point in later movies, including a 2006 sequel of *Bienvenido/Welcome* that focuses on a director whose movie, shot in English, is shown at a series of Latin American film festivals without subtitles, resulting in the scorn of the regional film community. This film lacks the impact of the first, and its defense of filmmaking in Spanish sounds unconvincing given the boom of continental productions in the late 2000s.
25. The marriage crisis will, of course, evolve into a more straightforward commercial cinema conceit, eventually leaving behind the cinematic pretenses still present in *Cilantro y perejil*. A good example of the use of the marriage crisis subject in more recent cinema is León Serment's *Kada kien su karma* (2008), about a woman who is forced to take care of her former husband after he has an accident. The interesting fact about this movie is that, unlike most romantic comedies, the characters are middle aged and the action is focused on the ending of a marriage rather than on the formation of love. After *Cilantro y perejil*, most romantic comedies would not be as focused on married characters.
26. One can certainly sustain this hypothesis through the fact that Serrano was a soap opera director for his production company. However, I feel that the narrative structure of this movie does depart sufficiently from soap opera conventions enough to problematize this reading. Indeed, it is possible to contrast *Sexo, pudor y lágrimas* with films more closely related to soap opera themes and plots, like Enrique Gómez Vadillo's *Desnudos* (2004), which provides a good example of a movie that adopts the middle-class ethos of romantic comedy but opts for a narrative structure closer to melodrama.
27. Emily Hind has argued, somewhat convincingly, that Syntek's song represents the banality of the film itself, considering that the "hyper-sentimental vocals" of the song seem out of keeping with lyrics in which "the soundtrack does not care which of the titular elements prevails" ("Pita Amor" 159). Hind refers to the song's chorus. Still, I believe that one can resist this hyper-literal reading, since the song's emotional music and vocals do highlight the romantic relationship narrated by it, and I think that the spectators who went to see the movie as a result of listening to the song were unlikely to pick up such a subtle point.
28. Another example of a similar conceit can be found in Juan Andrés Bueno's *Como tú me has deseado* (2005), in which a publicist looks for a model he sees on a billboard.

The movie lacks the elegance and nuances of *Vivir mata,* but still shows not only the prevalence of advertising as a topic in film, but also the difficulty of relating to a fellow human being in the middle of the big city.

29. A good contrasting example is Ángel Mario Huerta's *Inspiración* (2001), an insipid romantic comedy about an aspiring musician who falls in love with a beautiful woman in a club and ultimately seduces her through his music. Unlike *Vivir mata*'s visual work or even *Sexo, pudor y lágrimas*' carefully crafted dialogue, *Inspiración* unapologetically works with a very simple, straightforward visual and linguistic palette, resulting in a movie closer to teen-oriented TV shows than to any previous Mexican romantic comedy. Still, *Inspiración* must be recognized as a decisive sign of the fully commercial turn of romantic comedy, given not only its simplicity but also its use of two very popular soap opera actors, Arath de la Torre and Bárbara Mori.

30. An interesting exception to the urban setting is Luis Vélez's *Corazón de melón* (2003), in which a city chef falls in love with two girls from a small provincial town. The movie reactivates the visual codes of *provincia* and builds its characters' identities on the traditional cultures of food, something that resembles *Como agua para chocolate.*

31. It is worth noting that the road movie genre actually gains some prominence in this period. Besides *Por la libre,* whose success made the genre a viable aesthetic possibility, three other major movies fall into this genre: Alfonso Cuarón's *Y tú mamá también* (2001), María Novaro's *Sin dejar huella* (2000), and Ángel Flores Torres's *Piedras verdes* (2001). For a good discussion on the genre, see Oropesa.

32. I owe this point to Sara Potter.

33. A good example of an action movie is Chava Cartas's *Amor Xtremo* (2006), which uses the romantic comedy aesthetic to tell the story of two brothers who travel to Las Vegas to compete in a motocross tournament. Sabina Berman and Isabel Tardán's landmark feminist movie *Entre Pancho Villa y una mujer desnuda* also owes many debts to the genre, including a protagonist who owns factories on the border, which is yet another example of a NAFTA professional. Finally, the works of director Gerardo Naranjo show how even independent auteur cinema became defined in certain ways by the languages developed by romantic comedy.

CHAPTER 3

1. In fact, most prior productions were basically documentaries that featured clandestine recordings of the event or movies like *Canoa,* where the reference to 1968 was indirect and subject to interpretation. For accounts of 1968 in Mexican cinema, see Rodríguez Cruz; Gallo; and Aviña 55–60.

2. The 1988 election, when PRI candidate Carlos Salinas de Gortari defeated Cuauhtémoc Cárdenas, the candidate of a left-wing opposition coalition, is usually recognized as a starting point of the electoral decline of the post-revolutionary regime, not only because Cárdenas mounted the first credible challenge to the party in power, but also because considerable sectors of the Mexican public still believe that he actually won the election and that Salinas de Gortari only won thanks to fraud. It is not coincidental that the first major political films in this regard come in the wake of 1988. They are a symptom of the upcoming change in Mexican politics.

3. A detailed description of the events of 1988 would exceed the purpose of my account. However, a good account of the political landscape of that year and its consequences in Mexico can be found in Preston and Dillon 149–80.
4. For a more detailed account of this process, see Carr 306–28.
5. Retes tells many stories of these hardships in a 2004 interview with Alejandro Medrano Platas. See Medrano Platas 277–98.
6. The *Halcones* was a right-wing group of young students and clandestine military personnel, known also as *porros,* that was allegedly financed by the government. It was usually sent to left-wing rallies to provoke fights with demonstrators. The *Halconazo* refers to a particular event on June 10, 1971, when the *Halcones* quashed a protest and killed at least thirty students. A good account of this event can be found in the documentary *Halcones: Terrorismo de estado,* produced by Canal 6 de Julio.
7. Interestingly, Aguilar Camín was identified as the organic intellectual of the Salinas de Gortari administration, while Krauze is widely regarded as sympathetic to many of the ideals behind the neoliberal process. For an extensive discussion of Krauze's work, see Sánchez Prado, "Claiming Liberalism."
8. I am grateful to Sara Potter for noting the Hendrix reference to me.
9. And, of course, Lauro is a journalist, another way of representing the idealization of middle-class interactions with social causes.
10. For a superb study of this dimension of Mexican feminism, see Laura G. Gutiérrez's *Performing Mexicanidad.* Lamas herself has developed an analysis of this process in her book *Feminismo: Transmisiones y retransmisiones.* For a good, detailed analysis of the intersection between feminism and Mexican thought, see Gómez Campos.
11. I owe this observation to Sara Potter, who also rightfully points out that Rodríguez and Hadad, as performance artists, are able to choose the venues to show their work in ways that a woman filmmaker, tied to the commercial structures of cinema, cannot.
12. Yet, one must not forget here that Novaro's cinema operates within somewhat stereotypical ideas of gender, ethnic, and social identity, as has been pointed out by critic Óscar Robles' idea of "identidades maternacionales" (see Chapter 1), as well as Raciel Martínez's identification of Novaro's *Sin dejar huella* with emerging ideologies of multiculturalism.
13. It is important to note here the distinction between the play's name and the film's name (which adds the first name Pancho). I will use the titles of the play and the film to distinguish between them. The play was published in Berman's *Puro teatro.*
14. The film, based on the homonymous novel by José Wolfgango Montes, tells the story of a teacher's romantic problems in the context of Bolivia's encounter with neoliberalism. While the influence of Mexican romantic comedy is clear in this movie, the visible presence of neoliberalism's conflicts in, for instance, the need of workers to convert their salaries into black market dollars, is an important difference in comparison to Mexican cinema's gradual erasure of the political. It may also be worth noting that Valdivia's most recent movie, *American Visa* (2005), was also a Mexican-Bolivian coproduction. Based on the novel of Juan de Recacochea, the film tells the story of a Bolivian teacher (Daniel Giménez Cacho) who fails to obtain a visa to the United States and, trying to get funds to obtain a counterfeit one, entangles himself

in a web of crime. It is worth noting that both the teacher and his love interest (Kate del Castillo) are played by Mexican actors linked to the romantic comedy paradigm, even though the characters are Bolivian.

15. For a development of this idea and a study of Villa's tradition in literature and culture, see Parra. This legacy is, I would contend, part of the reason why Berman chose Villa. Beyond his masculinity, Villa's significance as a social leader cannot possibly be lost on a Mexican audience that has long been educated to revere revolutionary figures.

16. It may be useful to note that critics of the play, like Stuart Day and Sharon Magnarelli, bring up Ilene O'Malley's study of hero cults in the post-revolutionary period (1920–1940, to be more precise). I would resist identifying Berman's Villa with this analysis, because the mission of the film is in part to resist the iconic legacy studied by O'Malley. Still, her reading (87–112) does raise a valid point in underlining the ambiguous portrayal of Villa both as a revolutionary idealist and as a masculine power-seeker.

17. For a study of Diana Bracho's career and her family legacy, see Ibarra.

18. And in fact *Backyard/El traspatio* shows the encounter between many of the traditions I have discussed in the book up to this point in a single film. We see a very refined gritty neo-Mexicanist aesthetic, developed by Carrera fresh from his success as the director of *El crimen del padre Amaro* and the producer of *Arráncame la vida*. We also see Berman's intuitive and complex work on gender issues, which has proven particularly apt for representing the serial murder of women in Ciudad Juárez. Finally, the protagonist is played by Ana de la Reguera, an actress who became famous thanks to her work in romantic comedies. This brief example shows how the formational processes of Mexican cinema of the mid-1990s remain central to the aesthetics of Mexican cinema even today.

19. See Castañeda, *Utopia Unarmed*.

20. Readers may certainly read some of the vast bibliography written on this period. Besides Dawson, Castañeda, and Centeno, other books include Preston and Dillon; Gutmann; and Domínguez and Poirén. A wider perspective on political change in Mexico during the neoliberal period may be found in Middlebrook. Finally, an excellent sociology of the new political class, focused on the rise of economics as the privileged discipline of State management, may be found in Babb.

21. Discussions of these magazines in the context of Mexican neoliberalism may be found in Van Delden, and in Sánchez Prado, "Claiming Liberalism."

22. See Monsiváis, *Entrada libre*.

23. In fact, major theoretical interventions around the world identified similar processes across different configurations of neoliberalism. The most influential of these interventions, one that informs some of the Latin American cultural theory relevant to this chapter, may be found in Manuel Castells's trilogy *The Information Age*.

24. For a good sociological study of the impact of neoliberalism and the crises it provoked in the livelihood and political opinions of the Mexican middle class, see Gilbert.

25. Many critics of the movie have placed special emphasis on the Grand Cherokee as a signifier of social wealth in the film. See Ayala Blanco (*La fugacidad* 471) and Foster 80.

26. Ayala Blanco is right in one of his scathing critiques of the movie: he argues that the film is constructed upon the use of social stereotypes of both the working class (the policemen, the woman who cleans Gabriel's building) and the upper class (Luna's cartoonish, new age wife) (*La fugacidad* 472).
27. Another example is *Amar te duele* (Fernando Sariñana, 2002), where the rich girl/ poor boy relationship allows Sariñana to represent poor and marginalized neighborhoods usually absent from commercial movies.
28. For a study of *fichera* movies, see de la Mora, "Tus pinches."
29. An analysis of rock as counterculture in late 1990s Mexico City may be found in Castillo Berthier 257–60.
30. See Kun for a good dissection of Manu Chao's cultural significance, along with an explanation of the meaning of the song "Clandestino."
31. A sampling of Camacho's work may be found on his website, *www.trino.com.mx*.
32. MacLaird's argument is mostly that the attempt to limit the film's circulation "maps out a complicated web of power dynamics" based on the interaction between the State and Estrada's own privileged status and ample connections with the Mexican press (*Aesthetics* 92).
33. The PRI's complex system of accepted practices and rituals is in itself a topic of major study. For a good study of this system, with a particular focus on the practices of presidential succession—the ones mirrored by *La ley de Herodes*' fictional state—see Adler-Lomnitz, Salazar-Elena, and Adler. For a strong historical study of the Mexican State's workings throughout the PRI years, see Knight.
34. For a recent analysis of Estrada's invocation of Miguel Alemán, see Price.
35. David William Foster's *Mexico City in Contemporary Mexican Cinema* makes this point quite obvious by identifying a vast number of post-1998 movies where Mexico City is a major component.
36. *Fraude 2006* is an indictment of the presumed fraud that led to the defeat of leftist candidate Andrés Manuel López Obrador by a hair-thin margin in the 2006 election, while *Presunto culpable*, released in Mexico in 2010, is a controversial attack on Mexico's judicial system, as it presented a man who was found guilty of murder even though it was obvious that the evidence was not clear and that the process is structurally stacked against the accused. Both documentaries received major media coverage and achieved far more relevance than any political fiction film in the period. This is also a reminder of the fact that a study of Mexican documentary film remains a pending task. I discuss *Presunto culpable* further in the Conclusion.
37. A group of critical essays on *El infierno* may be found in Hernández Hernández and Cervantes.

CHAPTER 4

1. Deborah Shaw uses the term as the title of her most recent book, *The Three Amigos*, on Cuarón, Gonzláez Iñarritu, and Del Toro. Unfortunately, I was unable to consult it for this study, since it was still forthcoming at the time I completed the copyedits; however, I do make reference to Shaw's published articles on the subject. From what I can tell, looking at the table of contents of *The Three Amigos,* Shaw talks about the

Mexican movies of the three directors, but seems to focus equally on their "transnational filmmaking."

2. It may be interesting to note here that the notion of "geopolitical" seems to be evolving from a clear identification of cinema with specific ideological or regional concerns to the idea of film as a reflection of cultural and political space. González Iñarritu's *Babel* would perhaps be an important example in the context I am discussing. For a theoretical discussion of this issue, see Power and Crampton.

3. In *Historia de un gran amor* (Vega et al.), a chronicle of the cinematic relationship between Cuba and Mexico, we can clearly see that in the past twenty years that relationship has almost completely faded away. This, I believe, is an indicator of the gradual departure of Mexican film from the geopolitical concerns that defined the "cinema of solitude" paradigm in relation to Latin American engagements with the "Third Cinema" movement. See Vega et al. 60–62, where the authors lament the gradual disappearance of Mexican cinema from Cuba and the fact that the films most accessible on the island are typically from the Golden Age. Cuban scholars have recently lamented the decline of inter-Latin American connections and the growing presence of Hollywood and of globalized capital in the local film scene, as well as the "elitism" promoted by international art cinema trends like Dogme 95 (del Río and Cumaná 293–97). As I hope my book makes clear, Mexico is a particularly strong example of these trends, and I think that, of all the major film traditions in Latin America, Mexico's is becoming the most removed from the Latin Americanist practices embodied by the Havana Film Festival.

4. See Biskind; Mottram; Geoff King, *American Independent Cinema* and *Indiewood, USA;* Berra; and Newman, *Indie*.

5. See my comparison of Hermosillo's *La tarea* with Soderbergh's *Sex, Lies, and Videotape* in Chapter 2 and of Luis Estrada's *La ley de Herodes* to Joel and Ethan Coen's *Fargo* in Chapter 3.

6. IFC has been crucial in the distribution of younger Mexican auteurs in the United States. Perhaps the most important one is Gerardo Naranjo, director of *Drama/Mex* and *Voy a explotar,* who has acquired some visibility thanks to IFC.

7. The catalog is available at *www.palisadestartan.com*.

8. It must be said, however, that Mexican commercial films do enjoy some U.S. distribution by mainstream houses targeting the growing Latino audience. In fact, some of Sariñana's most commercial films, such as *Todo el poder,* are distributed by 20th Century Fox.

9. I would contend that the only Mexican movie clearly influenced by *Cronos* is Jorge Michel Grau's *Somos lo que hay* (2010), a grim film about a modern-day cannibal family facing extinction because of the death of their patriarch. The movie connects itself to del Toro's film by recreating verbatim a morgue scene from *Cronos*. In it, a mortician (played by Daniel Giménez Cacho in both movies) is seen carefully preparing the corpse of the movie's monster (i.e., Jesús Gris in *Cronos,* the cannibal father in *Somos*). When he is done, the director of the morgue (Juan Carlos Colombo) praises his artful and dedicated work, but tells him that it was all in vain, given that the corpse will in fact be cremated. Grau's movie not only casts the same actors but reproduces the dialogue word for word. Aside from this overt citation,

there are many stylistic and thematic commonalities between the two movies: the loss of the father figure, a somber palette, and the challenge of a traditional family who has to face an overwhelming modernity. I have written an article comparing these two movies; see Sánchez Prado, "Monstruos neoliberales." This example notwithstanding, the horror movie is an infrequently employed genre in Mexico, and in the few cases where filmmakers work with it, the results tend to fall closer to the middle-class aesthetic discussed in Chapter 2. This is, for instance, the case with Rigoberto Castañeda's very successful *Kilómetro 31* (2006), Mexico's highest-grossing horror film in history.

10. For a good account of the history of horror cinema in Mexico between the 1950s and the 1970s, see Greene.

11. One could see here similar patterns in the Western, which was at the time reclaimed, with less success, by García Agraz's *Mi querido Tom Mix* (1991)—a movie also mentioned by Stock in "Authentically Mexican"—and Luis Estrada's *Bandidos* (1991). A similar pattern has been at work recently in *narco* cinema. It is historically the source of action films aimed at the working class, but has become, in the last two years, a more authorial cinema, thanks to movies like Luis Estrada's *El infierno* (2010) and Gerardo Naranjo's *Miss Bala* (2011). These films have translated the *narco* genre into languages of consumption for the Mexican middle and upper classes (*El infierno* was the second-highest-grossing film in Mexico in 2010) and for the international art house audience (*Miss Bala* enjoyed a widely positive reception at the Cannes Film Festival). I will discuss these films further in the Conclusion.

12. I refer here to thesis 9 of Benjamin's "Theses on the Philosophy of History." See Benjamin 392.

13. *The Fly* tells the story of a scientist (Jeff Goldblum) trying to develop a teleportation machine. When he is conducting a test using himself as a subject, a fly enters the machine. As a result, the scientist gradually morphs into a man-fly.

14. I refer here to Tomás's dream, in which we see cartoonish renditions of characters from traditional Mexican cinema (like a wrestler, as well as a mariachi singing as a castrato). See Chapter 2.

15. For an examination of these two films in the context of memory studies in Spain, see Jo Labanyi's landmark piece, "Memory and Modernity in Democratic Spain." For a good assessment of Erice's film in the context of Spanish cinema, see Zunzunegui. A helpful analysis of the relationship between Erice and del Toro may be found in Derry 315–30.

16. For a further elaboration of this point, see Sánchez Prado, "Monstruos neoliberales."

17. In the case of *El espinazo del diablo*, the film is not an adaptation, but it includes a reference to Carlos Giménez's comic *Paracuellos*.

18. It is also relevant to remember here Geoffrey Kantaris's argument that the film's urban aesthetic has roots in late-1980s and early-1990s Mexico City film, most notably María Novaro's *Lola* (1989) and Francisco Athié's *Lolo* (1993). See Kantaris, "Lola/Lolo."

19. Another implausible mythological reading is offered by Andrea Sabbadini, who interprets the story of Octavio and Susana as an iteration of the Orphic rescue

fantasy: Octavio is an Orpheus who rescues Susana, his Euridice, from the hell of poverty and abuse, but he is defeated because she looks back when she decides to return to Ramiro. Even if one accepts the parallels between myth and plot, it is hard to see what this reading can tell about the movie, because one can easily contend that rescue fantasies are so predominant in Western culture that their appearance in a cultural product does not necessarily entail a direct connection to the source myth. Furthermore, this reading is also based on a denial of the historicity of the film, which results, at best, in a highly partial interpretation.

20. Just to show how predominant this strategy was, it was famously used by two major film franchises of the 1990s: *Batman* and *Mission Impossible*.

21. Herlinghaus's densely philosophical argument relies here on Giorgio Agamben's theory of the "state of exception." According to Agamben, "bare life" refers to social subjects who are not protected by the rule of law and are therefore left unprotected by the guarantees provided by "political life." While Agamben elaborates the argument on the basis of the status of Jewish people in Nazi concentration camps, cultural theorists like Herlinghaus have adopted the notion to refer to people marginalized or excluded by the process of capitalist globalization, such as the millions of people who live in slums or work in sweatshops and conflict zones. In these terms, a member of the very edge of society (like El Chivo) or a young man who has to make a living in the clandestine sectors of the economy (like Octavio) represent "bare life" in the context of neoliberal society. See Agamben.

22. Another way of looking at this issue is with the idea of the figure of the absent father. Deborah Shaw connects *Amores perros* to a tradition of Latin American films where this trope emerges as a symptom of the redefinition of masculinity and as an allegory of the erosion of the State. See Shaw, "Figure."

23. Guillermo Arriaga, who wrote the script of *Amores Perros* and who has an important role in developing the film's narrative structure, has also developed a career of his own in independent cinema by invoking similar structures. The topic of the family is quite central to the interwoven stories in Arriaga's U.S. directorial debut, *The Burning Plain* (2008). His narrative style also finds interesting iterations in the scripts he wrote for *The Three Burials of Melquiades Estrada* (Tommy Lee Jones, 2005) and, especially, *El búfalo de la noche* (Jorge Hernández Aldana, 2007), which opts for an exploration of fragmented narrative not in the context of social realism but in the construction of highly subjective perspectives.

24. Lahr-Vivaz applies here Doris Sommer's well-known concept of a fiction that poses the romantic relationship of its protagonists as an allegory for the consecration of the nation and its values. See Sommer.

25. Linhard refers here to Diaz Yanes's *Nadie hablará de nosotras cuando hayamos muerto* (1996), the story of Gloria (Victoria Abril), a Spanish woman trapped in the network of Mexican organized crime. Abril's character reappears in a sequel of sorts, *Sólo quiero caminar* (2008), where another Spanish woman, Ana (Elena Anaya), marries an abusive Mexican gangster (José María Yázpik). If one adds here the role of Valeria in *Amores perros,* one can see a pattern of using Spanish female characters as a device to either generate or undermine Mexican masculine worlds. This is quite problematic

because Mexican female characters are conspicuously absent and Spanish women are ultimately only an element of worlds that never cease to be masculine.

26. Ribas's reading relies partly on arguments set forward in Noble 145–46.
27. Jorge Vergara, the film producer, is the CEO of Grupo Omnilife, a transnational vendor of beauty products. It also owns a cadre of soccer teams and, more importantly, Producciones Anhelo, one of Mexico's most successful production companies. Vergara's Spanish footprint has to do both with Omnilife's business interests and with his role in the production of Guillermo del Toro's first Spanish film, *El espinazo del diablo*.
28. Readers interested in *Great Expectations* should also consider Michael K. Johnson's superb article "Not Telling the Story the Way It Happened," which reassesses the film in the wake of the success of *Y tu mamá también*, providing a valuable appraisal of Cuarón's aesthetic and ideological contributions to Dickens's story.
29. I use here Celestino Deleyto's previously discussed concept. See Chapter 2.
30. Deborah Shaw also furthers Finnegan's argument by pointing out that Cuarón's world is "almost too obviously Mexican" ("(Trans)national Images" 121).
31. For another discussion of this point, see Hind, "*Provincia*."
32. The film's connection to historical discourses of the nation and the interior is asserted, in a different way, in Andrea Noble's suggestive analysis of *Y tu mamá también* with the representation of Otherness in Sergei Eisenstein's *¡Qué viva México!* (1933). See Noble 123–46.
33. Finnegan reads Leodegaria's story as a "telling reminder of the indigenous in both urban and rural Mexico," which in turn deploys a "destabilizing ability to pierce the national conscience" ("So" 39). I disagree with this reading because nothing indicates that Leodegaria is in fact indigenous (or not). She may well be one of the many *mestizo* rural immigrants to Mexico City. Also, there is nothing in Tenoch's reaction that suggests that his "national conscience" (which for the most part is a nonissue in the film, other than the fact that his name is more nationalistic than he is) is questioned in any way. Rather, I think that the whole issue is about class, revolving around the impact of a lower-class woman on the emotional life of an upper-class boy.
34. While I do not share all of their opinions—such as the idea that the film advocates at times "nostalgia for the national-developmentalist state"—Baer and Long provide what is in my view the most suggestive reading of the film in scholarly criticism so far, not only because of their deft interpretation of the voice-over, to which I refer earlier, but also because they manage to provide an elegant analysis of the ideology of the film without overstating the gender component and without over-interpreting the national and the political in the film.
35. For a study of Cha Cha Chá Films in comparison to IMCINE, see Sisk, "Entre el Cha Cha Chá."
36. I obtained all data related to the Cineteca Nacional's activities and audiences from its official website: *www.cinetecanacional.net*.
37. Critics of Reygadas rely on various interviews. In my case, I find the interviews included in the U.S. DVD releases of *Japón* and *Batalla en el cielo* to be the most extensive and informative available.
38. Indeed, the influence of Bresson (as suggested by Rufinelli) is an important factor. Bresson was a foundational figure of what Joseph Cunneen calls "a spiritual style

in film" that was based on an "unwillingness to offer comforting illusions" and his "avoidance of melodrama, sensationalism and even . . . 'acting'" (14–15). The fact that this assertion can be fully applied to Reygadas shows the long tradition of global art cinema that precedes his style.

39. Certainly, there are common elements between *Japón* and *Pedro Páramo,* such as the narrative of returning to one's origins, the indictment of the unfairness of rural societies, and the interest in spirituality (the reader eventually learns that Rulfo's book is a ghost story). Nonetheless, I find that the comparison does not hold, given that Juan Preciado's search for his father is much different from the nihilism of *Japón*'s protagonist, not to mention the contrast between the fundamentally polyphonic and complex narrative in *Pedro Páramo* (the book has many voices and does not limit itself at all to Juan Preciado's pathos) and *Japón*'s sparse and highly subjective narrative.

40. For an analysis of this tradition, see Hind, "*Provincia,*" and the comments I made on this subject regarding *El crimen del padre Amaro* in Chapter 1.

41. For a study on Fernández and his construction of national cinema, see Tierney, *Emilio Fernández*. For further analysis of Figueroa's cinematography and its role in the creation of nationalist iconicity in Mexican cinema, see Higgins.

42. By the way, this is not the only trope that Reygadas deconstructs. Craig Epplin argues that Reygadas's representation of death (another stereotypically Mexican subject) also breaks with its nationalist tradition, given that it "cannot be recuperated for collective purposes" (294). In other words, Reygadas does not use death as a sacrificial creation of a community or as an event that has to be sublimated for the sake of the living. This is why the film ends with Ascensión's death: her passing is not to be read as a transformational event of any kind, but as something that merely interrupts the protagonist's pathos.

43. Paul Julian Smith points out that the use of random toponyms is common in Latin American cinema: he points to Argentine Lisandro Alonso's *Liverpool* (2008) and Fernando Eimbcke's *Lake Tahoe* (2008). According to Smith, the reasoning behind these obscure titles is to create an aura of complexity that enlists the attention of the critic, whose intervention "is required to ensure that the full social meaning of the film is achieved" ("Transnational Cinemas" 32). I would add that the two directors cited by Smith have, in fact, connections to Reygadas (Mantarraya and Reygadas's No Dream distribute Alonso's *Liverpool*) or, at least, clear debts to his work (*Lake Tahoe* belongs to the same line of reflexive cinema in Mexico).

44. The comparison between Reygadas and Van Sant has also been suggested by Jérôme Game under the Deleuze-inspired concept of "image without organs"; that is, a cinema "without a predetermined frame, without a pre-established montage, without a prescribed rhythm, etc." (151; my translation). Furthermore, Game establishes parallels in both filmmakers' use of the physical and the cinematic body.

45. I rely once again on the interviews included in the U.S. DVDs of his films.

46. For a detailed comparison between Reygadas and Hernández, see Millán, "Le corps-récit." According to Millán, both filmmakers are characterized by the use of the body as discourse.

47. Another interesting example of the use of the body in the wake of Reygadas is Michael Rowe's *Año bisiesto* (2010), an unsettling film on the complex sexual

relationship between two lovers. Rowe's use of sexuality as part of the language of communication between the characters and its representation of the secret past of its female protagonist can be read as iterations of elements developed in Reygadas's films.

48. Fernández has used the term "the slow style of spectacle" (409) to define Reygadas's work. It must be said that Reygadas is not the creator of this slow style. Important movies from the 1990s and the 2000s, such as Carlos Carrera's *Sin remitente* (1995) and Fernando Eimbcke's *Temporada de patos* (2004), are examples of successful slow-paced films. The difference is that Reygadas (like Hernández, Escalante, and Rowe) uses the wide shot, contemplation, and certain specific styles of music and performance to create a cinema with a more organic focus on form than the one present in Carrera (whose work in the 1990s still had a certain melodramatic tone absent in Reygadas) or Eimbcke (whose interest in childhood and innocence distance him from the hard-edged worlds created by Reygadas and Escalante).

49. *Japón*'s critical success gave *Batalla en el cielo* wider distribution and critical attention. *Batalla* had fifty copies for its release, and reached over seventy thousand spectators, which places it below more commercial releases (which average 100–150 copies) but at about the average number of copies for a Mexican film. This level of distribution guaranteed circulation in the venues where art cinema audiences attend, giving Reygadas a forum to confront educated national audiences.

50. Luna made these remarks during her presentation on *Batalla en el cielo* at the conference of the Latin American Studies Association in San Francisco, which took place on May 2012. I thank her for sharing a printed version of her remarks to cite here.

51. As I have mentioned in other parts of this book, the two best resources for study of the representation of Mexico City in cinema are David William Foster's *Mexico City in Contemporary Mexican Cinema* and Hugo Lara Chávez's *Una ciudad inventada por el cine.*

52. The Hubert Bals Fund is a source of funding for art movies in different parts of the production process, backed by the Rotterdam Film Festival. Miriam Ross has studied the way in which this festival has affected Latin American cinema through its privileging of certain specific aesthetic and cultural perspectives and styles. See Ross, "Film Festival."

53. *Ordet* is a film that has been subject to many important critical readings and any interpretation of *Stellet Licht* would undoubtedly need to rely on it. See, for instance, Wahl; Bordwell 144–71; and Drum and Drum 221–44.

54. In his previous films, Reygadas showed a preference for classical music and for contemporary composers such as John Tavener and Arvo Pärt. It may be interesting to note that Tavener and Pärt are very popular in art cinema worldwide: Tavener has been used in the firms of Alfonso Cuarón and Terrence Malick, while Pärt can be heard on the soundtracks of films from directors like Paul Thomas Anderson, Isabel Coixet, and Tom Tykwer.

55. There are, however, very good readings of *Stellet Licht.* See Tompkins, *Deleuzian Approach;* Yehya; Niessen; Foltz; and William Johnson.

CONCLUSION

1. In 2012, the minimum wage was between 59.08 and 62.33 pesos per day (about 4.60 U.S. dollars), while the average Cinemex or Cinépolis ticket was between 45 to 65 pesos (3.33 to 5 dollars), depending on the theater's location and the time of day. A VIP or Platino ticket cost around 115 to 150 pesos (8.50 to 11.10 dollars).
2. *Presunto culpable* was made in 2008, but it was not commercially released in Mexico until February 2011.
3. Just to compare, it is worth remembering that *Inside Job* (2010), the Academy Award–winning documentary on the financial crisis, raised 4.3 million dollars in the United States. I should also mention that the documentary genre is becoming central to Mexican film production, mostly thanks to Ambulante and to the need of producing outlets for political and social stories beyond the duopoly that controls Mexican television and radio. The scholarly study of this trend would undoubtedly be an important contribution and it is certainly emerging as a fundamental future task for academics and critics.
4. In 2013, another film, *Nosotros los nobles* (Gary Alazraki), managed to become the highest-grossing Mexican film in history, raising 26.5 million dollars between March and July, with some copies still in commercial release when I was completing this book. It is notable that a movie can still break that mark, which had stood since 2002, showing that the market remains potentially promising for Mexican cinema. It also shows that appealing to the middle and upper classes remains a key formula for success. The film is about three upper-class siblings who, after their father suffers a heart attack, are made to believe that the family money ran out (which in fact is not true) and have to find real jobs. The movie's sympathetic view of the upper class is well within the parameters of what I have discussed in this book.
5. It may be interesting to note that this questioning does not only take place in the realm of comedy. In drama, one can recall here the wonderful film *Vaho* (Alejandro Gerber Bicecci, 2009), in which one of Mexico's most venerable traditions, the representation of the Passion of the Christ in the Iztapalapa area of Mexico City, is the backdrop for the drama among three friends who, during childhood, were part of a traumatic incident. The film does an excellent job in contrasting the supposed community experience of the religious representation with the true fractures that underlie the personal interactions in contemporary Mexican society.
6. For a discussion of Serrano and *Sexo, pudor y lágrimas,* see Chapter 2.
7. For a discussion of *El callejón de los milagros,* see Chapter 1.
8. As I discussed in Chapter 3, the first installment was the highly successful and controversial *La ley de Herodes* (2000), perhaps the most significant political fiction film in Mexican cinema to date. The second film, *Un mundo maravilloso* (2006), a brutal attack on Mexico's neoliberal fantasy, based on the contrast between the government's development narrative and the point of view of a homeless man, was not as successful. John Waldron, in two conference papers that he graciously shared with me ("Discreet Charm" and "La risa"), argues that the film is in fact the most radical of the three, as it proposes a political return to the commons in its shocking last scene, where the homeless family enjoys Christmas dinner in a suburban house

while the slain bodies of the family who owned it lie on the lawn outside. I agree with Waldron on the assessment that this second film's lack of commercial success had to do in part with its bringing this message to the very lives of the middle-class audience of Mexico City, rather than locating the action, as Estrada's other two films do, in the *provincia*.

9. Historically speaking, action cinema was part of the genres geared to the working classes during the neoliberal period. Films like *Lola la trailera* or the many movies produced by the Almada brothers created a representation of organized crime that informs contemporary *narcocultura*. It is important to say that these films have not completely disappeared: they are produced with very small budgets and circulate via home video in Mexico and the United States, and are regularly programmed by cable channels devoted to Mexican cinema. This type of film is not analyzed here because it belongs to a regime of production different from the one that concerns me, but a scholarly study of the social phenomena underlying this other film market is undoubtedly overdue.

10. See Chapter 4.

11. I addressed this period in my discussion of *Danzón* in Chapter 1. The best study of these directors is Rashkin's *Women Filmmakers in Mexico*.

12. In her analysis of *Backyard/El traspatio,* Emily Hind underscores this point, arguing that the film deliberately hurts its commercial potential by not exploiting de la Reguera's reputation as a sex symbol ("Estado" 29–30). I, however, do not share Hind's harsh assessment of the film. She thinks the movie has an "identity crisis" and concludes her article by addressing the unsatisfying ending with possible alternatives. In contrast, I think that, considering the difficulties in addressing the femicides in contemporary Mexican society, the film resists many temptations, such as exploiting the subject to construct a more satisfying—and more commercially viable—police procedural.

13. For a study on the implications of the representation of motherhood in cinema by both male and female directors, see Fischer.

14. Charles Ramírez Berg has a wonderful book on the subject of Latino stereotypes in film, in which he studies both the mechanisms of stereotyping and the struggle of Latino actors to overcome typecasting. See Ramírez Berg, *Latino Images in Film*.

15. It's also worth reading the accompanying book, *Revolución 10.10,* in which ten young Mexican writers profile the ten directors.

Bibliography

FILMS

7 mujeres, 1 homosexual y Carlos. Dir. René Bueno Camacho. Perfs. Mauricio Ochmann, Adriana Fonseca, Ninel Conde. 2004. DVD. Venevisión/Lionsgate. 2007.

11:14. Dir. Greg Marcks. Perfs. Rachel Leigh Cook, Patrick Swayze, Hilary Swank. 2003. DVD. New Line Home Video. 2004.

21 Grams. Dir. Alejandro González Iñarritu. Perfs. Benicio del Toro, Sean Penn, Naomi Watts. 2003. DVD. Universal Studios. 2004.

1492: The Conquest of Paradise. Dir. Ridley Scott. Perf. Gerard Depardieu. 1992. Spectra Nova. 2011.

2033. Dir. Francisco Laresgoiti. Perfs. Raúl Méndez, Sandra Echeverría. 2009. DVD. Cinema Epoch. 2010.

Abel. Dir. Diego Luna. Perfs. Christopher Ruiz Esparza, Karina Gidi, José María Yázpik. 2010. DVD. Videomax. 2012.

Allá en el rancho grande. Dir. Fernando de Fuentes. Perfs. Tito Guízar, Esther Fernández. 1936. DVD. Facets. 2007.

Alta tensión. Dir. Rodolfo de Anda. Perfs. Juan Manuel Bernal, María Rojo, María Colla. 1997. DVD. Ventura Distribution. 2004.

Alucarda, la hija de la tinieblas. Dir. Juan López Moctezuma. Perfs. Tina Romero, Susana Kamini, Claudio Brook. 1978. DVD. Mondo Macabro. 2003.

Aguirre: The Wrath of God. Dir. Werner Herzog. Perfs. Klaus Kinski, Helena Rojo. 1972. DVD. Anchor Bay. 2000.

Amar te duele. Dir. Fernando Sariñana. Perfs. Martha Higareda, Luis Fernando Peña. 2002. DVD. Distrimax/Lionsgate. 2005.

Ámbar. Dir. Luis Estrada. Perfs. Jorge Russek, Alfredo Sevilla. 1994. Bandido Films. Theatrical release.

American Visa. Dir. Juan Carlos Valdivia. Perfs. Demián Bichir, Kate del Castillo. 2005. DVD. Studio Latino. 2007.

Amores perros. Dir. Alejandro González Iñarritu. Perfs. Gael García Bernal, Goya Toledo, Emilio Echevarría. 2000. DVD. Lionsgate. 2001.

Amor letra por letra. Dir. Luis Eduardo Reyes. Perfs. Silvia Navarro, Alan Estrada, Plutarco Haza. 2008. DVD. Quality Films. 2009.

Amor Xtremo. Dir. Chava Cartas. Perfs. Aarón Díaz, Irán Castillo, Daniel Martínez. 2006. DVD. Distrimax. 2007.

Ángel de fuego. Dir. Dana Rotberg. Perfs. Evangelina Sosa, Roberto Sosa, Lilia Aragón. 1991. DVD. IMCINE/Desert Mountain Media. 2006.

Annie Hall. Dir. Woody Allen. Perfs. Woody Allen, Diane Keaton. 1977. DVD. MGM Home Video. 2007.

Año bisiesto. Dir. Michael Rowe. Perfs. Gustavo Sánchez Parra, Mónica del Carmen. 2010. DVD. Strand. 2011.

Anoche soñé contigo. Dir. Marisa Sistach. Perfs. Leticia Perdigón, José Alonso. 1992. DVD. Venevisión/Condor Media. 2002.

Arráncame la vida. Dir. Roberto Sneider. Perfs. Daniel Giménez Cacho, Ana Claudia Talancón, José María de Tavira. 2008. DVD. 20th Century Fox. 2009.

Así es la suerte. Dir. Juan Carlos de Llaca. Perfs. Mauricio Isaac, Alfonso Herrera, Irene Azuela. 2011. DVD. Videocine. 2012.

A.T.M.: A Toda Máquina. Dir. Ismael Rodríguez. Perfs. Pedro Infante, Luis Aguilar. 1951. DVD. Warner Home Video. 2007.

Ave María. Dir. Eduardo Rossoff. Perfs. Tere López-Tarín, Demián Bichir, Juan Diego Botto. 1999. DVD. Distrimax. 2007.

Awakenings. Dir. Penny Marshall. Perfs. Robert De Niro, Robin Williams. 1990. DVD. Image Entertainment. 2010.

Babel. Dir. Alejando González Iñarritu. Perfs. Rinko Kikuchi, Adriana Barraza, Brad Pitt. 2006. DVD. Paramount Pictures. 2007.

Backyard/El traspatio. Dir. Carlos Carrera. Perfs. Ana de la Reguera, Jimmy Smits, Joaquín Cosío. 2009. DVD. Paramount Pictures. 2010.

Bajo California: El límite del tiempo. Dir. Carlos Bolado. Perfs. Damián Alcázar, Jesús Ochoa. 1998. DVD. Quality Films. 2004.

Bandidos. Dir. Luis Estrada. Perfs. Pedro Armendáriz, Daniel Giménez Cacho. 1991. DVD. Condor Media. 2002.

Barton Fink. Dir. Joel Coen. Perfs. John Turturro, John Goodman. 1991. DVD. 20th Century Fox. 2003.

Batalla en el cielo. Dir. Carlos Reygadas. Perfs. Marcos Hernández, Anapola Mushkadiz, Berta Ruiz. 2005. DVD. Tartan Video. 2006.

Bend It like Beckham. Dir. Gurinder Chadha. Perfs. Parminder Nagra, Keira Knightley. 2002. DVD. 20th Century Fox. 2003.

A Better Life. Dir. Chris Weltz. Perfs. Demián Bichir, José Julián. 2011. DVD. Summit Entertainment. 2011.

Bienvenido/Welcome. Dir. Gabriel Retes. Perfs. Lourdes Elizarrarás, Luis Felipe Tovar. Gabriel Retes. 1995. DVD. Quality Films. 2005.

Bienvenido/Welcome 2. Dir. Gabriel Retes. Perfs. Lourdes Elizarrarás, Gabriel Retes. 2006. DVD. Zafra. 2013.

Biutiful. Dir. Alejandro González Iñarritu. Perfs. Javier Bardem, Maricel Álvarez. 2011. DVD. Roadside Attractions. 2011.

Blackout. Dir. Rigoberto Castañeda. Perfs. Amber Tamblyn, Aidan Gillen. 2008. DVD. Velocity. 2009.

Blade 2. Dir. Guillermo del Toro. Perfs. Wesley Snipes, Kris Kristofferson. 2002. DVD. New Line Home Entertainment. 2002.

The Bodyguard. Dir. Mick Watson. Perfs. Kevin Costner, Whitney Houston. 1992. DVD. Warner Home Video. 2005.

The Brown Bunny. Dir. Vincent Gallo. Perfs. Vincent Gallo, Chloe Sevigny. 2003. DVD. Sony Pictures. 2005.

The Burning Plain. Dir. Guillermo Arriaga. Perfs. Charlize Theron, Kim Basinger. 2008. DVD. Magnolia Home Entertainment. 2010.

Cabeza de Vaca. Dir. Nicolás Echevarría. Perfs. Juan Diego, Daniel Giménez Cacho, Roberto Sosa. 1991. DVD. Quality Films. 2007.

Calzonzin Inspector. Dir. Alfonso Arau. Perfs. Alfonso Arau, Pancho Córdova, Arturo Alegro. 1973. DVD. Desert Mountain Media. 2003.

Canoa. Dir. Felipe Cazals. Perfs. Ernesto Gómez Cruz, Enrique Lucero, Salvador Sánchez. 1976. DVD. Desert Mountain Media. 2005.

Cansada de besar sapos. Dir. Jorge Colón. Perfs. Ana Serradilla, José María de Tavira, Ana Layevska. 2006. DVD. Buenavista Latino. 2007.

Casa de mi padre. Dir. Matt Piedmont. Perfs. Will Ferrell, Gael García Bernal, Diego Luna. 2012. DVD. Pantelion. 2012.

Central do Brasil. Dir. Walter Salles. Perfs. Fernanda Montenegro, Marcos Bernstein. 1998. DVD. Columbia TriStar, 2003.

Chicogrande. Dir. Felipe Cazals. Perfs. Damián Alcázar, Daniel Martínez, Juan Manuel Bernal. 2010. DVD. Venevisión. 2012.

Chido Guan: El tacos de oro. Dir. Alfonso Arau. Perfs. Mario Almada, Fernando Arau, Gabriela Roel. 1985. DVD. Imagen. 2005.

Children of Heaven. Dir. Majid Majidi. Perf. Mohammad Amir Naji. 1997. DVD. Lionsgate. 2007.

Children of Men. Dir. Alfonso Cuarón. Perfs. Clive Owen, Julianne Moore. 2006. DVD. Universal. 2006.

Chiles Xalapeños. Dir. Fabrizio Prada. Perfs. Irán Castillo, María Rebeca, Ricardo Bautista. 2008. DVD. Distrimax. 2008.

Christopher Columbus: The Discovery. Dir. John Glen. Perfs. George Corraface, Marlon Brando. 1992. VHS. Warner Home Video. 1992.

Cidade de Deus. Dir Fernando Meirelles. Perfs. Alexandre Rodrigues, Matheus Nachtergaele. 2002. DVD. Miramax. 2004.

Cilantro y perejil. Dir. Rafael Montero. Perfs. Demián Bichir, Arcelia Ramírez. 1995. DVD. Desert Mountain Media. 2002.

Ciudades oscuras. Dir. Fernando Sariñana. Perfs. Alejandro Tomassi, Jesús Ochoa, Bruno Bichir. 2002. DVD. Quality Films. 2006.

Colosio: El asesinato. Dir. Carlos Bolado. Perfs. Enoc Leaño, Daniel Giménez Cacho. 2012. DVD. Videomax. 2012.

Como agua para chocolate. Dir. Alfonso Arau. Perfs. Lumi Cavazos, Regina Torné, Marco Leonardi. 1992. DVD. Miramax. 2000.

Como era gostoso o meu francês. Dir. Nelson Pereira Dos Santos. Perfs. Arduíno Colassanti, Ana María Magalhâes. 1971. DVD. New Yorker Video. 2007.

Como tú me has deseado. Dir. Juan Andrés Bueno. Perfs. Abraham Ranos, Ernesto Yáñez, Isela Vega. 2005. DVD. Quality Films. 2006.

Conejo en la luna. Dir. Jorge Ramírez Suárez. Perfs. Bruno Bichir, Lorraine Pilkington. 2004. DVD. Lionsgate. 2007.

Corazón de melón. Dir. Luis Vélez. Perfs. Christina Pastor, Daniel Martínez, Ludwika Paleta. 2003. DVD. Quality Films. 2007.

Corazón marchito. Dir. Eduardo Lucatero. Perfs. Ana Serradilla, Mauricio Ochmann. 2007. DVD. Lionsgate. 2007.

Crash. Dir. Mike Figgis. Perfs. Don Cheadle, Sandra Bullock, Thandie Newton. 2004. DVD. Lionsgate. 2005.

Cría cuervos. Dir. Carlos Saura. Perfs. Geraldine Chaplin, Mónica Randall. 1976. DVD. The Criterion Collection. 2007.

Cronos. Dir. Guillermo del Toro. Perfs. Federico Luppi, Claudio Brook, Ron Perlman. 1993. DVD. The Criterion Collection, 2010.

Crouching Tiger, Hidden Dragon. Dir. Ang Lee. Perfs. Yun-Fat Chow, Ziyi Zhang, Michelle Yeoh. 2000. DVD. Sony Pictures. 2001.

Cuento de hadas para dormir cocodrilos. Dir. Ignacio Ortiz. Perfs. Arturo Ríos, Luisa Ruedas. 2002. DVD. Warner Brothers/Venevisión. 2004.

Danzón. Dir. María Novaro. Perfs. María Rojo, Carmen Salinas, Tito Vasconcelos. 1991. DVD. Facets/Macondo. 2007.

Déficit. Dir. Gael García Bernal. Perfs. Andrés Almeida, Fernanda Castillo. 2007. DVD. Revolver Entertainment. 2008.

Demasiado amor. Dir. Ernesto Rimoch. Perfs. Ari Telch, Karina Gidi, Daniel Martínez. 2002. DVD. Quality Films. 2007.

Desiertos Mares. Dir José Luis García Agraz. Perfs. Arturo Ríos, Verónica Merchant, Juan Carlos Colombo, Dolores Heredia. 1992. DVD. Desert Mountain Media. 2005.

Desnudos. Dir. Enrique Gómez Vadillo. Perfs. Karyme Lozano, Rafael Amaya, Carmen Rodríguez. 2004. DVD. Quality Films. 2006.

Digna, hasta el último aliento. Dir. Felipe Cazals. Perf. Vanessa Bauche. 2004. DVD. Distrimax. 2005.

Divina confusion. Dir. Salvador Garcini. Perfs. Jesús Ochoa, Diana Bracho, Pedro Armendáriz. 2008. DVD. Quality Films. 2009.

Don Gato y su pandilla. Dir. Alberto Mar. Perfs. Jorge Arvizu, Raúl Anaya. 2011. DVD. Warner Brothers Mexico. 2011.

Doña Herlinda y su hijo. Dir. Jaime Humberto Hermosillo. Perfs. Marco Antonio Treviño, Arturo Meza, Guadalupe del Toro. 1985. DVD. Strand. 2006.

Dos crímenes. Dir. Roberto Sneider. Perfs. Damián Alcázar, José Carlos Ruis, Pedro Armendáriz. 1995. DVD. Quality Films. 2008.

Drama/Mex. Dir. Gerardo Naranjo. Perfs. Diana García, Fernando Becerril, Mariana Moro. 2007. DVD. IFC Films, 2007.

Efectos secundarios. Dir. Issa López. Perfs. Marina de Tavira, Alejandra Gollás, Arturo Barba, Pedro Izquierdo. 2006. DVD. Warner Home Video. 2007.

El anzuelo. Dir. Ernesto Rimoch. Perfs. Bruno Bichir, Damián Alcázar. 1996. DVD. Quality Films. 2003.

El atentado. Dir. Jorge Fons. Perfs. Daniel Giménez Cacho, José María Yázpik, Julio Bracho. 2010. DVD. Distrimax. 2011.

El búfalo de la noche. Dir. Jorge Hernández Aldana. Perfs. Diego Luna, Liz Gallardo, Gabriel González. 2007. DVD. 20th Century Fox. 2007.

El bulto. Dir. Gabriel Retes. Perfs. Gabriel Retes, Héctor Bonilla, José Alonso. 1992. DVD. Venevisión. 2006.

El callejón de los Milagros. Dir. Jorge Fons. Perfs. Salma Hayek, Ernesto Gómez Cruz, Luis Felipe Tovar. 1995. DVD. Venevisión/Alameda Films. 2006.

El cielo dividido. Dir. Julián Hernández. Perfs. Miguel Ángel Hoppe, Fernando Arroyo. 2006. DVD. IMCINE. 2007.

El coraje del pueblo. Dir. Jorge Sanjinés. 1971. Film. Cinema Guild. 1971.

El coronel no tiene quien le escriba. Dir. Arturo Ripstein. Perfs. Fernando Luján, Salma Hayek. 1999. DVD. Maverick. 2003.

El crimen del padre Amaro. Dir. Carlos Carrera. Perfs. Gael García Bernal, Ana Claudia Talancón. 2002. DVD. Columbia TriStar. 2003.

El efecto tequila. Dir. León Serment. Perfs. Eduardo Victoria, Juan Carlos Colombo. 2011. DVD. 2013.

El espinazo del diablo. Dir. Guillermo del Toro. Perfs. Eduardo Noriega, Marisa Paredes. 2001. DVD. Sony Pictures Classics. 2004.

El espíritu de la colmena. Dir. Víctor Erice. Perfs. Fernando Fernán Gómez, Teresa Gimpera. 1973. DVD. The Criterion Collection. 2013.

El evangelio de las maravillas. Dir. Arturo Ripstein. Perfs. Francisco Rabal, Flor Eduarda Gurrola. 1998. DVD. Quality Films. 2005.

El infierno. Dir. Luis Estrada. Perfs. Damián Alcazar, Joaquín Cosío. 2010. DVD. Distrimax. 2011.

Elisa antes del fin del mundo. Dir. Juan Antonio de la Riva. Perfs. Sherlyn, Imanol, Susana Zabaleta. 1997. DVD. Quality Films. 2005.

El jardín del Edén. Dir. María Novaro. Perfs. Renée Coleman, Bruno Bichir. 1994. DVD. Vanguard Cinema. 2001.

El laberinto del fauno. Dir. Guillermo del Toro. Perfs. Ivana Baquero, Sergi López, Maribel Verdú. 2006. DVD. New Line Home Entertainment. 2007.

El lugar sin límites. Dir. Arturo Ripstein. Perfs. Roberto Cobo, Ana Martin, Gonzalo Vega. 1978. DVD. World Artists Home Video. 2001.

El secreto de Romelia. Dir. Busi Cortés. Perfs. Diana Bracho, Arcelia Ramírez, Pedro Armendáriz Jr., Dolores Beristáin. 1988. DVD. IMCINE/Alterfilms. 2009.

El tigre de Santa Julia. Dir. Alejandro Gamboa. Perfs. Miguel Rodarte, Irán Castillo, Fernando Luján. 2002. DVD. Quality Films. 2006.

El tigre de Santa Julia. Dir. Arturo Martínez. Perfs. Juan Gallardo, Norma Lazareno. 1974. VHS. Quality Films. 1988.

En el aire. Dir. Juan Carlos de Llaca. Perfs. Daniel Giménez Cacho, Dolores Heredia. 1995. DVD. Vanguard/Condor Media. 2002.

En el país de no pasa nada. Dir. Maricarmen de Lara. Perfs. Fernando Luján, Julieta Egurrola. 2000. DVD. Vanguard Cinema. 2001.

En medio de la nada. Dir. Hugo Rodríguez. Perfs. Manuel Ojeda, Blanca Guerra, Gabriela Roel. 1993. DVD. Alterfilms/IMCINE, 2010.

Entre la tarde y la noche. Dir. Óscar Blancarte. Perfs. Angélica Aragón, Lumi Cavazos, Manuel Ojeda. 2000. DVD. Desert Mountain Media. 2006.

Entre Pancho Villa y una mujer desnuda. Dirs. Sabina Berman and Isabel Tardán. Perfs. Diana Bracho, Jesús Ochoa, Arturo Ríos. 1996. DVD. Quality Films. 2005.

Eréndira Ikukinari. Dir: Juan Mora Catlett. Perfs. Xochiquetzal Rodríguez, Alberto Rodríguez. 2006. DVD. David Distribución. 2006.

Escápate conmigo. Dir. René Cardona Jr. Perfs. Lucero, Manuel Mijares. 1987. VHS. Madera Cinevideo, 1988.

Esmeralda de noche vienes. Dir. Jaime Humberto Hermosillo. Perfs. María Rojo, Claudio Obregón, Martha Navarro. 1997. DVD. New Line Home Video. 2006.

Estas ruinas que ves. Dir. Julián Pastor. Perfs. Pedro Armendáriz, Fernando Luján. 1979. DVD. Ventura Distribution, 2003.

Fargo. Dirs. Joel and Ethan Coen. Perfs. William H. Macy, Frances McDormand, Steve Buscemi. 1996. DVD. MGM Home Entertainment. 2003.

Fibra óptica. Dir. Francisco Athié. Perfs. Roberto Sosa, Lumi Cavazos, Angélica Aragón. 1997. DVD. Cinevilla. 2002.

The Fly. Dir. David Cronenberg. Perfs. Jeff Goldblum, Geena Davis. 1986. DVD. 20th Century Fox. 2005.

For Greater Glory: The True Story of Cristiada. Dir. Dean Wright. Perfs. Andy García, Catalina Sandino Moreno, Óscar Isaac. 2012. DVD. Arc Entertainment. 2012.

Four Weddings and a Funeral. Dir. Mike Newell. Perfs. Hugh Grant, Andie MacDowell. 1994. DVD. MGM/UA Home Entertainment. 2000.

Fraude 2006. Dir. Luis Mandoki. 2007. DVD. Zafra Video. 2007.

Frida: Naturaleza viva. Dir. Paul Leduc. Perfs. Ofelia Medina, Juan José Gurrola, Claudio Brook. 1983. DVD. Miramax, 2002.

From Prada to Nada. Dir. Ángel Gracia. Perfs. Camila Belle, Alexa Vega, Adriana Barraza. 2011. DVD. Pantelion. 2011.

Gertrudis Bocanegra. Dir. Ernesto Medina. Perfs. Ofelia Medina, Angélica Aragón, Fernando Balzaretti. 1992. DVD. Altermedia. 2009.

Girl in Progress. Dir. Patricia Riggen. Perfs. Cierra Ramírez, Eva Mendes. 2012. DVD. Pantelion. 2012.

Goal! The Dream Begins. Dir. Danny Cannon. Perfs. Kuno Becker, Alessandro Nivola. 2005. DVD. Touchstone Pictures. 2007.

Goal 2: Living the Dream. Dir. Jaume Collet-Serra. Perfs. Kuno Becker, Alessandro Nivola. 2007. DVD. Genius Entertainment. 2009.

Goal 3: Taking on the World. Dir. Andrew Monahan. Perfs. Kuno Becker, J. J. Feild. 2009. DVD. Metrodome. 2009.

Go for It. Dir. Carmen Marron. Perfs. Aimée García, Al Bandiero. 2011. DVD. Pantelion. 2012.

Good Bye Lenin! Dir. Wolfgang Becker. Perfs. Daniel Brühl, Katrin Saß. 2003. DVD. Sony Pictures Classics. 2004.

Gravity. Dir. Alfonso Cuarón. Perfs. Sandra Bullock, George Clooney. 2013. Theatrical release. Warner Brothers. 2013.

Great Expectations. Dir. Alfonso Cuarón. Perfs. Ethan Hawke, Gwyneth Paltrow. 1998. DVD. 20th Century Fox. 2002.

Halcones, terrorismo de estado. Dir. Carlos Mendoza. 2006. DVD. Canal 6 de Julio/Memoria y Verdad. 2006.

Harry Potter and the Prisoner of Azkaban. Dir. Alfonso Cuarón. Perfs. Daniel Radcliffe, Emma Watson, Rupert Grint. 2004. DVD. Warner Home Video. 2004.

Hasta morir. Dir. Fernando Sariñana. Perfs. Demián Bichir, Vanessa Bauche, Juan Manuel Bernal. 1994. DVD. Condor Media/Venevisión. 2002.

Hannah and Her Sisters. Dir. Woody Allen. Perfs. Woody Allen, Mia Farrow. 1986. DVD. MGM Home Entertainment, 2001.

Hellboy. Dir. Guillermo del Toro. Perfs. Ron Perlman, Selma Blair. 2004. DVD. Columbia TriStar Home Entertainment. 2004.

Hellboy 2: The Golden Army. Dir. Guillermo del Toro. Perfs. Ron Perlman, Selma Blair. 2008. DVD. Universal Studies. 2008.

Hidalgo: La historia jamás contada. Dir. Antonio Serrano. Perfs. Demián Bichir, Ana de la Reguera. 2010. DVD. 20th Century Fox. 2011.

The Hurt Locker. Dir. Kathryn Bigelow. Perfs. Jeremy Renner, Anthony Mackie. 2008. DVD. Summit Entertainment. 2010.

Inside Job. Dir. Charles Ferguson. 2010. DVD. Sony Pictures. 2011.

Inspiración. Dir. Ángel Mario Huerta. Perfs. Bárbara Mori, Arath de la Torre. 2001. DVD. Venevisión/Lionsgate. 2002.

Japón. Dir. Carlos Reygadas. Perfs. Alejandro Ferretis, Magdalena Flores. 2002. DVD. Tartan Video. 2002.

Jonás y la ballena rosada. Dir. Juan Carlos Valdivia. Perfs. Dino García, María Renée Prudencion. 1994. Amazon Instant Video. 2011.

Kada kien su karma. Dir. León Serment. Perfs. Blanca Guerra, José Alonso, Rocío Verdejo. 2008. DVD. Venevisión. 2008.

Kilómetro 31. Dir. Rigoberto Castañeda. Perfs. Iliana Fox, Adrià Collado, Raúl Méndez. 2006. DVD. Videomax. 2007.

Labios rojos. Dir. Rafael Lara. Perfs. Silvia Navarro, Jorge Salinas. 2009. DVD. Pantelion. 2011.

La ciudad al desnudo. Dir. Gabriel Retes. Perfs. Luis Felipe Tovar, Lourdes Elizarrarás. 1986. DVD. Vanguard Cinema. 2006.

Ladies' Night. Dir. Gabriela Tavigliani. Perfs. Ana Claudia Talancón, Luis Roberto Guzmán, Ana de la Reguera. 2003. DVD. Buena Vista Home Entertainment. 2004.

Ladrón que roba a ladrón. Dir. Joe Menéndez. Perfs. Fernando Colunga, Miguel Varoni. 2007. DVD. Warner Home Video Mexico. 2008.

La hora de los hornos. Dir. Fernando Solanas. 1968. DVD. Cine-Sur. 2007.

Lake Tahoe. Dir. Fernando Eimbcke. Perfs. Diego Cataño, Héctor Herrera. 2008. DVD. Film Movement. 2009.

La ley de Herodes. Dir. Luis Estrada. Perfs. Demián Alcázar, Pedro Armendáriz, Salvador Sánchez. 1999. DVD. Venevisión/20th Century Fox, 2003.

La misma luna. Dir. Patricia Riggen. Perfs. Kate del Castillo, Eugenio Derbez, Adrián Alonso. 2007. DVD. 20th Century Fox. 2008.

La mujer de Benjamín. Dir. Carlos Carrera. Perfs. Eduardo Palomo, Arcelia Ramírez, Eduardo López Rojas. 1991. DVD. Desert Mountain Media. 2006.

La mujer del puerto. Dir. Arcady Boytler. Perfs. Angélica Palma, Domingo Soler. 1934. DVD. Facets. 2005.

La mujer del puerto. Dir Arturo Ripstein. Perfs. Patricia Reyes Spíndola, Alejandro Parodi. 1991. VHS. Buena Vista Home Entertainment, 1996.

La orilla de la tierra. Dir. Ignacio Ortiz. Perfs. Luis Felipe Tovar, Jesús Ochoa. 1994. VHS. Madera. 1994.

La perdición de los hombres. Dir. Arturo Ripstein. Perfs. Patricia Reyes Spíndola, Luis Felipe Tovar, Rafael Inclán. 2000. DVD. Venevisión. 2000.

La reina de la noche. Dir. Arturo Ripstein. Perfs. Patricia Reyes Spíndola, Alberto Estrella, Blanca Guerra. 1994. VHS. San Luis. 1995.

La risa en vacaciones 1–8. Dir. René Cardona. Perfs. Pedro Romo, Pablo Ferrel, Paco Sánchez. 1990–1996. DVD. Oxxo. 2004.

The Last of the Mohicans. Dir. Michael Mann. Perfs. Daniel Day-Lewis, Madeleine Stowe. 1992. DVD. 20th Century Fox. 1999.

La tarea. Dir. Jaime Humberto Hermosillo. Perfs. María Rojo, José Alonso. 1990. DVD. Distrimax, 2004.

La tarea prohibida. Dir. Jaime Humberto Hermosillo. Perfs. María Rojo, Julián Pastor. 1992. DVD. Venevisión. 2004.

La vida conyugal. Dir. Carlos Carrera. Perfs. Alonso Echánove, Socorro Bonilla, Demián Bichir. 1993. DVD. Desert Mountain Media. 2005.

Las buenas hierbas. Dir. María Novaro. Perfs. Úrsula Pruneda, Ofelia Medina. 2010. DVD. Axolote. 2013.

A Little Princess. Dir. Alfonso Cuarón. Perfs. Liesel Matthews, Eleanor Brom, Liam Cunningham. 1995. DVD. Warner Home Video. 1997.

Liverpool. Dir. Lisandro Alonso. Perfs. Juan Fernández, Nieves Cabrera. 2008. DVD. Kino International. 2010.

Lola. Dir. María Novaro. Perfs. Leticia Huijara, Martha Navarro. 1989. DVD. Facets. 2007.

Lola la trailera/Lola la trailera 2/Lola la trailera 3. Dir. Raúl Fernández. Perf. Rosa Gloria Chagoyán. 1983–1991. VHS. Film-Mex Entertainment. 1991–2001.

Lolo. Dir. Francisco Athié. Perfs. Roberto Sosa, Lucha Villa. 1993. DVD. Cinevilla. 2002.

Los bastardos. Dir. Amat Escalante. Perfs. Jesús Moisés Rodríguez, Rubén Sosa. 2008. DVD. Kino International. 2010.

Los olvidados. Dir. Luis Buñuel. Perfs. Roberto Cobo, Miguel Inclán. 1950. DVD. Televisa. 2008.

Los pajarracos. Dirs. Héctor Hernández and Horacio Rivera. Perfs. Miguel Rodarte, Luis de Alba. 2006. DVD. Distrimax. 2007.

Los vuelcos del corazón. Dir. Mitl Váldez. Perfs. Martín Barraza, Arturo Beristáin. 1996. DVD. Zafra Video. 2009.

Lucía, Lucía. Dir. Antonio Serrano. Perfs. Cecilia Roth, Kuno Becker. 2003. DVD. Fox Searchlight. 2004.

Marcelino, pan y vino. Dir. José Luis Gutiérrez. Perfs. Mark Hernández, Jorge Lavat. 2010. DVD. Quality Films. 2011.

Mecánica nacional. Dir. Luis Alcoriza. Perfs. Manolo Fábregas, Lucha Villa, Héctor Suárez. 1972. DVD. Laguna Films 2004.

Me quiero casar. Dir. Julián Soler. Perfs. Angélica María, Alberto Vázquez. 1967. DVD. Televisa. 2006.

Mighty Aphrodite. Dir. Woody Allen. Perfs. Woody Allen, Mira Sorvino. 1997. DVD. Buena Vista Home Video. 1999.

Mil nubes de paz cercan el cielo, amor, jamás acabarás de ser amor. Dir. Julián Hernández. Perfs. Juan Carlos Ortuño, Juan Carlos Torres. 2003. DVD. IMCINE. 2003.

Mimic. Dir. Guillermo del Toro. Perfs. Mira Sorvino, Jeremy Northam, Giancarlo Giannini. 1997. DVD. Dimension Films. 1998.

Mi querido Tom Mix. Dir. Carlos García Agraz. Perfs. Federico Luppi, Manuel Ojeda. 1991. DVD. Facets/Zafra, 2007.

Miroslava. Dir. Alejandro Pelayo. Perfs. Arielle Dombasle, Claudio Brook, Milosh Trinka. 1992. DVD. Alterfilms/IMCINE. 2009.

Miss Bala. Dir. Gerardo Naranjo. Perfs. Stephanie Sigman, Noé Hernández. 2011. DVD. 20th Century Fox. 2011.

Mojado Power. Dir. Alfonso Arau. Perfs. Alfonso Arau, Blanca Guerra. 1979. VHS. Madera Cinevideo, 1986.

Mosquita muerta. Dir. Joaquín Bissner. Perfs. Bruno Bichir, Odiseo Bichir, Denisse Gutiérrez, Rocío Verdejo. 2007. DVD. Videomax. 2008.

Mother and Child. Dir. Rodrigo García. Perfs. Annette Bening, Naomi Watts. 2009. DVD. Sony Pictures Classics. 2010.

Mujeres insumisas. Dir. Alberto Isaac. Perfs. Patricia Reyes Spíndola, José Alonso. 1994. VHS. Oxxo. 1995.

No eres tú, soy yo. Dir. Alejandro Springall. Perfs. Alejandra Barrios, Eugenio Derbez, Martina García. 2010. DVD. Pantelion. 2011.

Nocaut. Dir. José Luis García Agraz. Perfs. Gonzalo Vega, Blanca Guerra. 1984. Theatrical release. Cooperativa Kinam. 1984.

Nosotros los nobles. Dir. Gary Alazraki. Perfs. Gonzalo Vega, Karla Souza. 2013. Theatrical release. Alazraki Films. 2013.

Novia que te vea. Dir. Guita Schyfter. Perfs. Claudette Maille, Angélica Aragón, Ernesto Laguardia. 1994. DVD. Desert Mountain Media. 2006.

Ordet. Dir. Carl Theodor Dreyer. Perfs. Henrik Malberg, Emil Hass Christensen, Preben Lerdorff Rye. 1955. DVD. The Criterion Collection. 2001.

Pastorela. Dir. Emilio Portes. Perfs. Joaquín Cosío, Eduardo España. 2011. DVD. Pantelion. 2012.

Pelo suelto. Dir. Pedro Galindo. Perfs. Gloria Trevi, Humberto Zurita. 1991. DVD. Oxxo. 2004.

Perfume de violetas. Dir. Maryse Sistach. Perfs. Jimena Ayala, Nancy Gutiérrez, Arcelia Ramírez. 2001. DVD. Quality Films. 2004.

Picoso pero sabroso. Dir. Óscar Fentanes. Perfs. Luis de Alba, Gabriela Goldsmith. 1990. DVD. Million Dollar Video. 1990.

Piedras verdes. Dir. Ángel Flores Torres. Perfs. Vanessa Bauche, Oswaldo Benavides. 2001. DVD. Venevisión/Lionsgate. 2003.

Playa Azul. Dir. Alfredo Joskowicz. Perfs. Pilar Pellicer, Sergio Bustamante. 1992. DVD. Condor Media/Vanguard Cinema. 2003.

Por la libre. Dir. Juan Carlos de Llaca. Perfs. Oswaldo Benavides, Rodrigo Cachero, Ana de la Reguera. 2000. DVD. Venevisión. 2003.

Presunto culpable. Dirs. Roberto Hernández, Geoffrey Smith. 2008. DVD. Madera Video. 2009.

Pretty in Pink. Dir. Howard Deutch. Perfs. Molly Ringwald, Jon Cryer, Andrew McCarthy. 1986. DVD. Paramount Home Entertainment. 2006.

Pretty Woman. Dir. Garry Marshall. Perfs. Richard Gere, Julia Roberts. 1990. DVD. Touchstone Pictures. 2002.

Principio y fin. Dir. Arturo Ripstein. Perfs. Ernesto Laguardia, Julieta Egurrola, Blanca Guerra. 1993. DVD. Alameda Films. 2006.

Profundo Carmesí. Dir. Arturo Ripstein. Perfs. Regina Orozco, Daniel Giménez Cacho. 1995. DVD. Quality Films. 2004.

Pruebas de amor. Dir. Jorge Prior. Perfs. Demián Bichir, Claudia Ramírez. 1994. DVD. Urban-vision, 1997.

Pueblo de Madera. Dir. Juan Antonio de la Riva. Perfs. Angélica Aragón, Gabriela Roel, Ignacio Guadalupe. 1990. DVD. Desert Mountain Media. 2007.

Pulp Fiction. Dir. Quentin Tarantino. Perfs. John Travolta, Bruce Willis, Uma Thurman. 1994. DVD. Buena Vista. 2002.

¡Qué viva México! Dir. Sergei Eisenstein. 1933/1979. DVD. Kino Video. 2001.

Raising Arizona. Dir. Joel Coen. Perfs. Nicholas Cage, Holly Hunter. 1987. DVD. 20th Century Fox. 1999.

Reality Bites. Dir. Ben Stiller. Perfs. Winona Ryder, Ethan Hawke, Ben Stiller. 1994. DVD. Universal Home Video. 2004.

Reservoir Dogs. Dir. Quentin Tarantino. Perfs. Harvey Keitel, Tim Roth, Michael Madsen. 1992. DVD. Lionsgate. 2003.

Retorno a Aztlán. Dir. Juan Mora Catlett. Perfs. Rodrigo Puebla, Amado Sumaya, Rafael Cortés. 1991. VHS. Volcán Producciones. 1992.

Revolución. Dirs. Diego Luna, Gael García Bernal, Mariana Chenillo, Fernando Eimbcke, Amat Escalante, Carlos Reygadas, Rodrigo Plá, Rodrigo García, Patricia Riggen, Gerardo Naranjo. 2010. DVD. Venevisión. 2011.

Río Escondido. Dir. Emilio Fernández. Perf. María Félix. 1948. DVD. Studio Latino. 2004.

Rojo amanecer. Dir. Jorge Fons. Perfs. Héctor Bonilla, María Rojo. 1989. DVD. Quality Films. 2009.

Rudo y cursi. Dir. Carlos Cuarón. Perfs. Gael García Bernal, Diego Luna. 2008. DVD. Universal Studios. 2008.

The Sacrifice. Dir. Andrei Tarkovsky. Perfs. Erland Josephson, Susan Fleetwood. 1986. DVD. Kino International. 2011.

Salón México. Dir. Emilio Fernández. Perfs. Marga López, Miguel Inclán. 1949. DVD. Alter Films, 2003.

Salón México. Dir. José Luis García Agraz. Perfs. María Rojo, Manuel Ojeda, Alberto Estrella. 1996. DVD. Quality Films. 2007.

Salvando al soldado Pérez. Dir. Beto Gómez. Perfs. Miguel Rodarte, Jesús Ochoa, Joaquín Cosío. 2011. DVD. Pantelion. 2012.

Sangre. Dir. Amat Escalante. Perfs. Cirilio Recio Dávila, Kenny Johnston. 2005. DVD. Videomax. 2006.

Santitos. Dir. Alejandro Springall. Perfs. Dolores Heredia, Alberto Estrella, Demián Bichir. 1999. DVD. NuVisión. 2007.

Say Anything. Dir. Cameron Crowe. Perfs. John Cusack, Ione Skye. 1989. DVD. 20th Century Fox. 2001.

Sex, Lies, and Videotape. Dir. Steven Soderbergh. Perfs. James Spader, Andie MacDowell, Laura San Giacomo. 1989. DVD. Columbia TriStar, 2004.

Sexo, pudor y lágrimas. Dir. Antonio Serrano. Perfs. Susana Zabaleta, Demián Bichir, Cecilia Suárez, Víctor Hugo Martín, Jorge Salinas, Mónica Dionne. 1998. DVD. 20th Century Fox. 2004.

Sin dejar huella. Dir. María Novaro. Perfs. Aitana Sánchez-Gijón, Tiaré Escanda. 2000. DVD. Venevisión. 2006.

Sin nombre. Dir. Cary Fukunaga. Perfs. Paulina Gaitán, Marco Antonio Aguirre. 2009. DVD. Universal Studios. 2009.

Sin remitente. Dir. Carlos Carrera. Perfs. Fernando Torres Laphame, Tiaré Escanda, Luis Felipe Tovar. 1995. DVD. Oxxo. 2004.

Sin ton ni Sonia. Dir. Carlos Sama. Perfs. Juan Manuel Bernal, Mariana Gajá, Cecilia Suárez. 2003. DVD. Columbia Pictures. 2003.

Sleepless in Seattle. Dir. Nora Ephron. Perfs. Tom Hanks, Meg Ryan. 1993. DVD. Columbia TriStar. 2003.

Sobrenatural. Dir. Daniel Gruener. Perfs. Susana Zabaleta, Alejandro Tommasi. 1996. DVD. Quality Films. 2007.

Sólo con tu pareja. Dir. Alfonso Cuarón. Perfs. Daniel Giménez Cacho, Claudia Ramírez. 1991. DVD. The Criterion Collection. 2006.

Sólo quiero caminar. Dir. Agustín Díaz Yanes. Perfs. Diego Luna, Victoria Abril. 2008. DVD. Maya Entertainment. 2010.

Somos lo que hay. Dir. Jorge Michel Grau. Perfs. Francisco Barreiro, Alan Chávez, Paulina Gaitán. 2010. DVD. IFC Films. 2011.

Spam: Una cadena de terror. Dir. Carlos Sariñana. Perfs. Sebastián Sariñana, Gloria Navarro. 2008. DVD. ZC Entertainment. 2010.

Stellet Licht/Luz silenciosa. Dir. Carlos Reygadas. Perfs. Cornelio Wall, Miriam Toews, Maria Pankratz. 2007. DVD. Palisades Tartan. 2008.

Su alteza serenísima. Dir. Felipe Cazals. Perfs. Alejandro Parodi, Ana Bertha Espín, Pedro Armendáriz. 2000. DVD. Desert Mountain Media. 2004.

Sultanes del sur. Dir. Alejandro Lozano. Perfs. Tony Dalton, Silverio Palacios, Ana de la Reguera. 2007. DVD. Warner Brothers Mexico. 2007.

Temporada de patos. Dir. Fernando Eimbcke. Perfs. Enrique Arreola, Diego Cataño. 2004. DVD. Warner Brothers. 2006.

Te presento a Laura. Dir. Fez Noriega. Perfs. Martha Higareda, Kuno Becker. 2010. DVD. Distrimax, 2011.

The Three Burials of Melquiades Estrada. Dir. Tommy Lee Jones. Perfs. Tommy Lee Jones, Barry Pepper. 2005. DVD. Sony Pictures. 2006.

Titanic. Dir. James Cameron. Perfs. Leonardo DiCaprio, Kate Winslet. 1997. DVD. Paramount. 1999.

Tizoc: Amor indio. Dir. Ismael Rodríguez. Perfs. Pedro Infante, María Félix. 1957. DVD. Laguna Films, 2006.

Tlatelolco: Verano de 68. Dir. Carlos Bolado. Perfs. Christian Vázquez, Cassandra Ciangherotti. 2013. Theatrical release. Corazón Films. 2013.

Trilogía de Pepe el Toro. Dir. Ismael Rodríguez. Perf. Pedro Infante. 1948–1953. DVD. Warner Home Video. 2009.

Todo el poder. Dir. Fernando Sariñana. Perfs. Demián Bichir, Cecilia Suárez, Luis Felipe Tovar. 2000. DVD. 20th Century Fox/Venevisión, 2003.

Tú te lo pierdes. Dir. Salim Nayar. Perfs. Paty Pereira, Alec Von, Lolita Cortés, Fernando Luján. 2005. DVD. Sfera Films. 2005.

Una familia de tantas. Dir. Alejandro Galindo. Perfs. Fernando Soler, David Silva, Martha Roth. 1949. DVD. Videomax. 2008.

Una película de huevos. Dirs. Gustavo and Rodolfo Riva Palacio. 2006. DVD. Huevocartoon Producciones. 2007.

Uncle Boonmee Who Can Recall His Past Lives. Dir. Apichatpong Weerasethakul. Perfs. Thanapat Saisaymar, Jenjira Pongpas, Sakda Kaeuwbuadee. 2010. DVD. Strand. 2011.

Un dulce olor a muerte. Dir. Gabriel Retes. Perfs. Diego Luna, Laila Saab. 1999. DVD. Studio Latino. 2005.

Un hilito de sangre. Dir. Erwin Neumaier. Perfs. Diego Luna, Jorge Martínez de Hoyos. 1995. DVD. Alterfilms. 2008.

Un mundo maravilloso. Dir. Luis Estrada. Perfs. Damián Alcázar, Cecilia Suárez. 2006. DVD. 20th Century Fox. 2006.

Vaho. Dir. Alejandro Gerber Bicecci. Perfs. Aldo Estuardo, Francisco Godínez, Roberto Mares. 2009. DVD. The Global Film Initiative. 2011.

Viernes de Ánimas: El camino de las flores. Dir. Raúl Pérez Gámez. Perfs. Irán Castillo, Claudio Lafarga, Pedro Rodman. 2011. DVD. Quality Films. 2012.

Vivir mata. Dir. Nicolás Echevarría. Perfs. Susana Zabaleta, Daniel Giménez Cacho. 2002. DVD. 20th Century Fox. 2004.

Volverte a ver. Dir. Gustavo Adrián Garzón. Perfs. Alfonso Herrera, Ximera Herrera. 2008. DVD. Videocine. 2009.

Voy a explotar. Dir. Gerardo Naranjo. Perfs. Juan Pablo de Santiago, María Deschamps, Demián Bichir. 2009. DVD. IFC Films. 2010.

When Harry Met Sally. Dir. Rob Reiner. Perfs. Meg Ryan, Billy Crystal. 1989. DVD. MGM Home Entertainment. 2001.

Y tu mamá también. Dir. Alfonso Cuarón. Perfs. Gael García Bernal, Maribel Verdú, Diego Luna. 2001. DVD. IFC Films/MGM Home Entertainment. 2005.

BOOKS AND ARTICLES

Abbott, Stacey, and Deborah Jermyn. *Falling in Love Again: Romantic Comedy in Contemporary Cinema.* London: I. B. Tauris, 2009.

Abrams, Jerold J. "A Homespun Murder Story: Film Noir and the Problem of Modernity in *Fargo.*" In *The Philosophy of the Coen Brothers.* Ed. Mark T. Conard. Lexington: University Press of Kentucky, 2009.

Acevedo-Muñoz, Ernesto R. *Buñuel and Mexico: The Crisis of National Cinema.* Berkeley: University of California Press, 2003.

———. "Sex, Class and Mexico in Alfonso Cuarón's *Y tu mamá también.*" *Film and History* 34.1 (2004): 39–48.

Acland, Charles R. *Screen Traffic: Movies, Multiplexes and Global Culture*. Durham, NC: Duke University Press, 2005.

Adler-Lomnitz, Larissa, Rodrigo Salazar-Elena, and Ilya Adler. *Symbolism and Ritual in a One-Party Regime*. Tucson: University of Arizona Press, 2010.

Agamben, Giorgio. *Homo Sacer: Sovereign Power and Bare Life*. Trans. Daniel Heller-Roazen. Stanford, CA: Stanford University Press, 1998.

Aguilar, Gonzalo. *Other Worlds: New Argentine Film*. New York: Palgrave Macmillan, 2008.

Aguilar Camín, Héctor. *La guerra de Galio*. Mexico City: Cal y Arena, 1992.

Al-Nemi, Hassan. "The Dramatization of Fiction: Najib Mahfuz's Novels into Films." Diss., Indiana University, 1995.

Al-Rifal, Hammam. "El machismo árabe frente al machismo mexicano en una novela y una película." *Ixquic: Revista hispánica internacional de análisis y creación* 6 (2005): 47–65.

Alcocer, Rudyard. "Going in Circles: Spanish American Identity and the Circular Motif in Nicolás Echevarría's *Cabeza de Vaca*." *Literature/Film Quarterly* 36 (2008): 250–58.

Aldama, Frederick Luis. *Mex-Ciné: Mexican Filmmaking, Production and Consumption in the Twenty-First Century*. Ann Arbor: University of Michigan Press, 2013.

Allegretto-Diiulio, Pamela. *Naguib Mahfouz: A Western and Eastern Cage of Female Entrapment*. Youngstown, NY: Cambria, 2007.

Alvaray, Luisela. "Imagi(ni)ng Indigenous Spaces: Self and Other Converge in Latin America." *Film and History* 34.2 (2004): 58–64.

Amado, Ana. *La imagen justa: Cine argentino y política*. Buenos Aires: Colihue, 2009.

Amago, Samuel. "Ethics, Aesthetics and the Future in Alfonso Cuarón's *Children of Men*." *Discourse* 32.2 (2010): 212–35.

Amaya, Héctor. "*Amores perros* and Racialised Masculinities in Contemporary Mexico." *New Cinemas: Journal of Contemporary Film* 5.3 (2007): 201–16.

Amaya, Héctor, and Laura Senio Blair. "Bridges between the Divide: The Female Body in *Y tu mamá también* and *Machuca*." *Studies in Hispanic Cinemas* 4.1 (2007): 47–62.

Amiot, Julie. "Carlos Reygadas, el cine mexicano y la crítica: ¿Una bonita historia?" *Cinémas d'Amérique Latine* 14 (2006): 154–65.

Arredondo, Isabel. "By Popular Demand: I Will See *Danzón* until I Can't Stand It Anymore." *Journal of Communication Inquiry* 23.2 (1999): 183–96.

———. "María Novaro and the Making of *Lola* and *Danzón*." *Women's Studies Quarterly* 30.1–2 (2002): 196–212.

———. *Palabra de mujer: Historia oral de las directoras de cine mexicano (1988–1994)*. Madrid: Iberoamericana Vervuert/Universidad Autónoma de Aguascalientes, 2001.

Aviña, Rafael. *Una mirada insólita: Temas y géneros del cine mexicano*. Mexico City: Conaculta/Océano, 2004.

Avritzer, Leonardo. "Civil Society in Latin America in the Twentieth-First Century: Between Democratic Deepening, Social Fragmentation, and State Crisis." In Feinberg, Waisman, and Zamosc 35–58.

Ayala Blanco, Jorge. *La condición del cine mexicano*. Mexico City: Posada, 1986.

———. *La disolvencia del cine mexicano*. Mexico City: Grijalbo, 1991.

———. *La eficacia del cine mexicano: Entre lo viejo y lo nuevo*. Mexico City: Grijalbo, 1994.
———. *La fugacidad del cine mexicano*. Mexico City: Océano, 2001.
———. *La grandeza del cine mexicano*. Mexico City: Océano, 2004.
———. *La herética del cine mexicano*. Mexico City: Océano, 2006.
Azcona, María del Mar. *The Multi-Protagonist Film*. London: Blackwell, 2010.
Azcona, María del Mar, and Celestino Deleyto. *Generic Attractions: New Essays on Film Genre Criticism*. Paris: Michel Houdiard, 2010.
Babb, Sarah. *Managing Mexico: Economists from Nationalism to Neoliberalism*. Princeton, NJ: Princeton University Press, 2001.
Baer, Hester, and Ryan Long. "Transnational Cinema and the Mexican State in Alfonso Cuarón's *Y tu mamá también*." *South Central Review* 21.3 (2004): 150–68.
Bartra, Roger. *Blood, Ink, and Culture: Miseries and Splendors of the Post-Mexican Condition*. Trans. Mark A. Healey. Durham, NC: Duke University Press, 2002. Originally published as *La sangre y la tinta*, 1999.
———. *The Cage of Melancholy: Identity and Metamorphosis in the Mexican Character*. Trans. Christopher J. Hall. New Brunswick, NJ: Rutgers University Press, 1992. Originally published as *La jaula de la melancolia*, 1987.
Barrueto, Jorge J. *Primitivismo, racismo y misoginismo en el cine latinoamericano/ Primitivism, Racism and Misogyny in Latin American Cinema*. Lewiston, NY: Edwin Mellen, 2008.
Baumann, Shyon. *Hollywood Highbrow: From Entertainment to Art*. Princeton, NJ: Princeton University Press, 2007.
Beard, Michael, and Adnan Haydar, eds. *Naguib Mahfouz: From Regional Fame to Global Recognition*. Syracuse, NY: Syracuse University Press, 1993.
Beckman, Karen. *Crash: Cinema and the Politics of Speed and Stasis*. Durham, NC: Duke University Press, 2010.
Benavides, O. Hugo. *Drugs, Thugs and Divas: Telenovelas and Narco-Dramas in Latin America*. Austin: University of Texas Press, 2008.
Benet, Vicente. "Principio y fin/Beginning and End." In Elena and Díaz López 211–20.
Benítez-Galbraith, Jacqueline, Elizabeth Irvin, and Craig S. Galbraith. "Gender Images and the Evolution of Work Roles in Mexican Film: A Plot Content Study of Pre- and Post-NAFTA Periods." *Hispanic Research Journal* 12.2 (2011): 167–83.
Benjamin, Walter. *Selected Writings:* Vol. 4, *1938–1940*. Ed. Howard Eiland and Michael W. Jennings. Cambridge, MA: Harvard University Press, 2003.
Berman, Sabina. *Puro teatro*. Mexico City: Fondo de Cultura Económica, 2004.
Bermúdez Barrios, Nayibe. "*Miroslava* by Alejandro Pelayo: Negotiated Adaptation and the (Trans)National Gendered Subject." In *Relocating Identities in Latin American Cultures*. Ed. Elizabeth Montes Garcés. Calgary: University of Calgary Press, 2007. 133–66.
Berra, John. *Declarations of Independence: American Cinema and the Partiality of Independent Production*. Bristol, UK: Intellect, 2008.
Berrueco García, Adriana. *Nuevo régimen jurídico del cine mexicano*. Mexico City: Instituto de Investigaciones Jurídicas/Universidad Nacional Autónoma de México, 2009.

Biskind, Peter. *Down and Dirty Pictures: Miramax, Sundance and the Rise of Independent Film*. New York: Simon and Schuster, 2004.

Blake, Linnie. *The Wounds of Nations: Horror Cinema, Historical Trauma and National Identity*. Manchester, UK: Manchester University Press, 2008.

Bogue, Ronald. *Deleuze on Cinema*. London: Routledge, 2003.

Bordwell, David. *The Films of Carl-Theodor Dreyer*. Berkeley: University of California Press, 1981.

Borreye, Orla Juliette. "The Significance of the Queer and the Dog in Alejandro González Iñarritu's *Amores perros* (2000): A Masculinity at War." *Wide Screen* 1.1 (2009): 1–9.

Bourdieu, Pierre. *The Social Structures of the Economy*. Trans. Chris Turner. Cambridge: Polity, 2005.

Boym, Svetlana. *The Future of Nostalgia*. New York: Basic Books, 2001.

Brinks, Ellen. "'Nobody's Children': Gothic Representation and Traumatic History in *The Devil's Backbone*." *JAC: A Journal of Composition Theory* 24.2 (2004): 291–312.

Buffington, Robert. "La 'Dancing' Mexicana: Danzón and the Transformation of Intimacy in Post-Revolutionary Mexico City." *Journal of Latin American Cultural Studies* 14.1 (2005): 87–108.

Caballero, Rufo. *Un pez que huye: Cine latinoamericano, 1991–2003; Un análisis estético de la producción*. Havana: Argos, 2007.

Cabeza de Vaca, Álvar Núñez. *Naufragios*. Madrid: Cátedra, 1996.

Cameron, Allan. "Contingency, Order, and the Modular Narrative: *21 Grams* and *Irreversible*." *Velvet Light Trap* 58 (2006): 65–78.

Campbell, Jan. *Film and Cinema Spectatorship*. New York: Polity, 2005.

Campesino, Juan. *La historia como ironía: Ibargüengoitia como historiador*. Guanajuato, Mexico: Universidad de Guanajuato, 2005.

Campos-Brito, Rosa. "Prostitutas, locas y vestidas: Un coqueteo subversivo en *Danzón* de María Novaro." In Igler and Stauder 123–36.

Carr, Barry. *Marxism and Communism in Twentieth-Century Mexico*. Lincoln: University of Nebraska Press, 1992.

Carroll, Rachel, ed. *Adaptation in Contemporary Culture: Textual Infidelities*. London: Continuum, 2009.

Cartmell, Deborah, and Imelda Whelehan, eds. *Adaptations: From Text to Screen, Screen to Text*. London: Routledge, 1999.

———, eds. *The Cambridge Companion to Literature on Screen*. Cambridge: Cambridge University Press, 2007.

Castañeda, Jorge G. *The Mexican Shock: Its Meaning for the United States*. New York: New Press, 1995.

———. *Utopia Unarmed: The Latin American Left and the Cold War*. New York: Knopf, 1993.

Castells, Manuel. *The Information Age: Economy, Society and Culture*. 3 vols. Oxford: Wiley-Blackwell, 1996–1998.

Castillo Berthier, Héctor. "My Generation: Rock and *La Banda*'s Forced Survival Opposite the Mexican State." In Pacini Hernández, Fernández L'Hoeste, and Zolov 241–60.

Castro Ricalde, Maricruz. "Historia y humor en *Entre Pancho Villa y una mujer desnuda*." *Archives Ouvertes*. 30 June 2010. hal.archives-ouvertes.fr.

Caterine, Darryl V. "Border Saints: *Santitos* (1999)." In *Catholics in the Movies*. Ed. Colleen McDannell. Oxford: Oxford University Press, 2008. 277–98.

Centeno, Miguel Ángel. *Democracy within Reason: Technocratic Revolution in Mexico*. University Park: Pennsylvania State University Press, 1997.

Cerrato, Rafael, Juan Miguel Perea, and Juan Carlos Rentero. *En la frontera con Iñarritu*. Madrid: Ediciones JC, 2007.

Chalaby, Jean K. *Transnational Television Worldwide: Towards a New Media Order*. London: I. B. Tauris, 2005.

Chaudhary, Zahid. "Humanity Adrift: Race, Materiality and Allegory in Alfonso Cuarón's *Children of Men*." *Camera Oscura* 24.3 (2009): 73–109.

Chávez, Daniel. "De faunos hispánicos y monstros en inglés: La imaginación orgánica en el cine de Guillermo del Toro." In Juan Carlos Vargas 371–408.

———. "The Eagle and the Serpent on the Screen: The State as a Spectacle in Mexican Cinema." *Latin American Research Review* 45.3 (2010): 115–41.

Chopra-Gant, Mike. *Cinema and History: The Telling of Stories*. London: Wallflower, 2008.

Cohen, Jean, and Andrew Arato. *Civil Society and Political Theory*. Cambridge, MA: Massachusetts Institute of Technology Press, 1994.

Connelly, Caryn. "Tanto de aquí como de allá: New Representation of the Illegal Immigrant Experience in *La misma luna* (2007) and *7 soles* (2009)." *Cincinnati Romance Review* 32 (2011): 13–30.

Copertari, Gabriela. *Desintegración y justicia en el cine argentino contemporáneo*. Suffolk, UK: Tamesis, 2009.

Crofts, Stephen. "Reconceptualizing National Cinema/s." In *Film and Nationalism*. Ed. Alan Williams. New Brunswick, NJ: Rutgers University Press, 2002. 25–51.

Crónica de la publicidad en México, 1901–2001. Mexico City: Asociación Mexicana de Agencias de Publicidad, 2002.

Couto Pereira, Helena Bonito. "Um crime em duas versões: *Padre Amaro* no cinema." *Comunicação e sociedade* 42 (2004): 95–105.

Cunneen, Joseph. *Robert Bresson: A Spiritual Style in Film*. London: Continuum, 2003.

DasGupta, Sayantani. "(Re)Conceiving the Surrogate: Maternity, Race and Reproductive Technologies in Alfonso Cuarón's *Children of Men*." In *Gender Scripts in Medicine and Narrative*. Ed. Marcelline Block and Angela Laflen. Newcastle upon Tyne, UK: Cambridge Scholars Publishing, 2010. 178–213.

Davies, Ann. "The Beautiful and the Monstrous Masculine: The Male Body and Horror in *El espinazo del diablo* (Guillermo del Toro 2001)." *Studies in Hispanic Cinemas* 3.3 (2007): 135–47.

———. "Guillermo del Toro's *Cronos*: The Vampire as Embodied Heterotopia." *Quarterly Review of Film and Video* 25 (2008): 395–403.

Davies, Laurence. "Guillermo del Toro's *Cronos*, or the Pleasures of Impurity." In *Gothic Science Fiction, 1980–2010*. Ed. Sara Wasson and Emily Alder. Liverpool, UK: Liverpool University Press, 2011. 87–101.

Dawson, Alexander S. *First World Dreams: Mexico since 1989*. London: Zed, 2006.

Day, Stuart. *Staging Politics in Mexico: The Road to Neoliberalism*. Lewisburg, PA: Bucknell University Press, 2004.

de la Garza, Armida. *Mexico on Film: National Identity and International Relations.* Bury St. Edmunds, UK: Arena Books, 2006.

de la Mora, Sergio. *Cinemachismo: Masculinities and Sexuality in Mexican Film.* Austin: University of Texas Press, 2006.

———. "'Tus pinches leyes yo me las paso por los huevos': Isela Vega and Mexican Dirty Movies." In Ruétalo and Tierney 245–58.

Deleuze, Gilles. *Cinema 1: The Movement-Image.* Trans. Hugh Tomlinson and Barbara Habberjam. Minneapolis: University of Minnesota Press, 1986.

———. *Cinema 2: The Time-Image.* Trans. Hugh Tomlinson and Robert Galeta. Minneapolis: University of Minnesota Press, 1989.

Deleyto, Celestino. *The Secret Life of Romantic Comedy.* Manchester, UK: Manchester University Press, 2009.

Deleyto, Celestino, and María del Mar Azcona. *Alejandro González Iñarritu.* Urbana: University of Illinois Press, 2010.

del Río, Joel, and María Caridad Cumaná. *Latitudes del margen.* Havana: Instituto Cubano del Arte e Industria Cinematográficos, 2008.

del Toro, Guillermo. *Alfred Hitchcock.* Guadalajara: Universidad de Guadalajara, 1990.

———. *El laberinto del fauno.* Madrid: Ocho y Medio, 2006.

de Luca, Tiago. "Carnal Spirituality: The Films of Carlos Reygadas." *Senses of Cinema* 55 (2010). sensesofcinema.com.

———. "Realism of the Senses: A Tendency in Contemporary World Cinema." In Nagib, Perriam, and Dudrah 183–206.

Derry, Charles. *Dark Dreams 2.0: A Psychological History of the Modern Horror Film from the 1950s to the 21st Century.* Jefferson, NC: McFarland, 2009.

Dever, Susan. *Celluloid Nationalism and Other Melodramas: From Revolutionary Mexico to fin de siglo Mexamérica.* Albany: State University of New York Press, 2003.

Díaz López, Marina. "¿Dónde están los hombres? Crisis de la masculinidad mexicana en *Y tu mamá también*." In Igler and Stauder 137–53.

Díaz Mendiburo, Aaraón. *Los hijos homoeróticos de Jaime Humberto Hermosillo.* Mexico City: Plaza y Valdés, 2004.

Dillon, Steven. *The Solaris Effect: Art and Artifice in Contemporary American Film.* Austin: University of Texas Press, 2006.

Dixon, Wheeler Winston, and Gwendolyn Audrey Foster. *21st-Century Hollywood: Movies in the Era of Transformation.* New Brunswick, NJ: Rutgers University Press, 2011.

D'Lugo, Marvin. "*Amores perros.*" In Elena and Díaz López 221–30.

———. "Authorship, Identification and the New Identity of Latin American Cinema." In *Rethinking Third Cinema.* Ed. Anthony Guneratne and Wimal Dissanayake. London: Routledge, 2003. 103–25.

———. "Luis Alcoriza; or, A Certain Antimelodramatic Tendency in Mexican Cinema." In Sadlier 110–29.

———. "Transnational Film Authors and the State of Latin American Cinema." In Wexman 112–30.

Domínguez, Jorge I., and Alejandro Poiré, eds. *Towards Mexico's Democratization: Parties, Campaigns, Elections and Public Opinion.* London: Routledge, 1999.

Donapetry, María. *Imagin/nación: La feminización de la nación en el cine español y latino-americano*. Madrid: Fundamentos, 2006.

Doremus, Anne T. *Culture, Politics, and National Identity in Mexican Literature and Film, 1929–1952*. New York: Peter Lang, 2000.

Drum, Jean, and Dale D. Drum. *My Only Great Passion: The Life and Films of Carl Th. Dreyer*. Lanham, MD: Scarecrow Press, 2000.

Duno-Gottberg, Luis, ed. *Miradas al margen: Cine y subalternidad en América Latina*. Caracas: Fundación Cinemateca Nacional, 2008.

Ďuričová, Nataša, and Kathleen Newman, eds. *World Cinemas, Transnational Perspectives*. London: Routledge, 2010.

Eça de Queirós, José María. *O crime do padre Amaro*. Lisbon: Libros do Brasil, 2000.

Egan, Linda. *Carlos Monsiváis: Culture and Chronicle in Contemporary Mexico*. Tucson: University of Arizona Press, 2001.

Ehrenberg, John. *Civil Society: The Critical History of an Idea*. New York: New York University Press, 1999.

Elasmar, Michael G. *The Impact of International Television: A Paradigm Shift*. Malwah, NJ: Lawrence Erlbaum Associates, 2003.

Elena, Alberto, and Marina Díaz López. *The Cinema of Latin America*. London: Wallflower, 2003.

Epplin, Craig. "Sacrifice and Recognition in Carlos Reygadas' *Japón*." *Mexican Studies/Estudios mexicanos* 28.2 (2012): 287–305.

Erro-Peralta, Nora. "Del objeto al sujeto: La representación de la mujer en tres películas mexicanas: *El secreto de Romelia, Danzón* y *Entre Pancho Villa y una mujer desnuda*." In Duno-Gottberg 71–93.

Esquivel, Laura. *Como agua para chocolate: Novela de entregas mensuales con recetas, amores y remedios caseros*. Mexico City: Planeta, 1990.

Evans, Peter William, and Celestino Deleyto, eds. *Terms of Endearment: Hollywood Romantic Comedy of the 1980s and 1990s*. Edinburgh: Edinburgh University Press, 1998.

Ezra, Elizabeth. "Transnational Cinema, Transgeneric Cinema." In Azcona and Deleyto 29–40.

Feinberg, Richard, Carlos H. Waisman, and León Zamosc, eds. *Civil Society and Democracy in Latin America*. New York: Palgrave Macmillan, 2006.

Fernández, Alvaro. "Carlos Reygadas: El lento estilo del espectáculo." In Juan Carlos Vargas 409–27.

Fernández F., José Antonio. *Historias personales: Entrevistas con publicistas, directores y creativos*. Mexico City: Creatividad en Imagen, 2000.

Fernández L'Hoeste, Héctor D. "Breves apuntes sobre las obsesiones de Guillermo del Toro." *Cuadernos de investigación de la Cinemateca Nacional de Venezuela* 8 (2002): 43–51.

Figuereido, Monica. "*El cimen del padre Amaro:* Du livre au film, un 'crime' qui a traversé les siècles." *Excavatio: Nouvelle revue Emile Zolá et le naturalisme international* 21.1–2 (2006): 273–83.

Finnegan, Nuala. "At Boiling Point: *Like Water for Chocolate* and the Boundaries of Mexican Identity." *Bulletin of Latin American Research* 18.3 (1999): 311–26.

———. "'So What's Mexico Really Like?': Framing the Local, Negotiating the Global in Alfonso Cuarón's *Y tu mama también.*" In *Contemporary Latin American Cinema: Breaking into the Global Market.* Ed. Deborah Shaw. Lanham, MD: Rowman and Littlefield, 2007. 29–50.

Fischer, Lucy. *Cinematernity: Film, Motherhood, Genre.* Princeton, NJ: Princeton University Press, 1996.

Flibbert, Andrew J. *Commerce in Culture: States and Markets in the World Film Trade.* New York: Palgrave Macmillan, 2007.

Florida, Richard. *The Rise of the Creative Class . . . And How It's Transforming Work, Leisure, Community and Everyday Life.* New York: Basic Books, 2002.

Fojas, Camila. *Border Bandits: Hollywood on the Southern Frontier.* Austin: University of Texas Press, 2008.

Foltz, Jonathan. "Betraying Oneself: *Silent Light* and the World of Emotion." *Screen* 52.2 (2011): 151–72.

Foster, David William. *Mexico City in Contemporary Mexican Cinema.* Austin: University of Texas Press, 2002.

Foucault, Michel. *The Foucault Reader.* Ed. Paul Rabinow. New York: Vintage, 1984.

Forcinito, Ana. "El cine posterior al TLCAN y violencia de género: Resignificaciones culturales de la transición mexicana." In *Estudios sobre cultura, género y violencia contra las mujeres.* Ed. Roberto Castro and Irene Casique. Mexico City: Universidad Nacional Autónoma de México, 2008. 197–228.

Franco, Jean. *Critical Passions: Selected Essays.* Ed. Mary Louis Pratt and Katherine Newman. Durham, NC: Duke University Press, 1999.

———. *Plotting Women: Gender and Representation in Mexico.* New York: Columbia University Press, 1989.

Frith, Simon. *Performing Rites: On the Value of Popular Music.* Cambridge, MA: Harvard University Press, 1996.

Gallo, Rubén. "Tlatelolco: Mexico City's Urban Dystopia." In *Noir Urbanisms: Dystopic Images of the Modern City.* Ed. Gyan Prakash. Princeton, NJ: Princeton University Press, 2010. 53–72.

Galt, Rosalind, and Karl Schoonover, eds. *Global Art Cinema: New Theories and Histories.* Oxford: Oxford University Press, 2010.

Game, Jérôme, ed. *Images des corps/corps des images au cinéma.* Lyon, France: École Normale Supérior, 2010.

———. "Images sans organs/récit sans télos: Carlos Reygadas et Gus Van Sant." In Game, *Images des corps* 149–70.

García Canclini, Néstor. *Consumers and Citizens: Globalization and Multicultural Conflicts.* Trans. George Yúdice. Minneapolis: University of Minnesota Press, 2001.

———, ed. *Los nuevos espectadores: Cine, television y video en México.* Mexico City: Conaculta/IMCINE, 1994.

Gaudreault, André. *Du Littéraire au Filmique: Système du récit.* Paris: Méridiens Klincksieck, 1989.

George, Rosemary Marangoly. "British Imperialism and US Multiculturalism: The Americanization of Burnett's *A Little Princess.*" *Children's Literature* 37: 137–64.

Gilbert, Dennis. *Mexico's Middle Class in the Neoliberal Era.* Tucson: University of Arizona Press, 2007.

Gomery, Douglas. *Shared Pleasures: A History of Movie Presentation in the United States.* Madison: University of Wisconsin Press, 1992.

Gómez Campos, Rubí de María. *El sentido de sí: Un ensayo sobre el feminismo y la filosofía de la cultura en México.* Mexico City: Siglo XXI/Instituto Michoacano de la Mujer, 2004.

González Vargas, Carla. *Rutas del cine mexicano, 1990–2006.* Mexico City: Conaculta/IMCINE/Landucci, 2006.

Gordon, Richard. *Cannibalizing the Colony: Cinematic Adaptations of Colonial Literature in Mexico and Brazil.* West Lafayette, IN: Purdue University Press, 2009.

Goss, Brian Michael. *Global Auteurs: Politics in the Films of Almodóvar, von Trier, and Winterbottom.* New York: Peter Lang, 2009.

Greene, Doyle. *Mexploitation Cinema: A Critical History of Mexican Vampire, Wrestler, Ape-man and Similar Films, 1957–1977.* Jefferson, NC: McFarland, 2005.

Guerrero, Javier. "Sexualidades ocultas, cuerpos enterrados: Carlos Reygadas y sus lecturas secretas de *Pedro Páramo.*" In Duno-Gottberg 93–118.

Gutiérrez, Carlos, ed. *Cinema Tropical Presents: The 10 Best Latin American Films of the Decade (2000–2009).* New York: Jorge Pinto Books, 2010.

———. "*Y tu crítica también:* The Development of Mexican Film Studies at Home and Abroad." In *The Sage Handbook of Film Studies.* Ed. James Donald and Michael Renov. London: Sage, 2008. 101–11.

Gutiérrez, Laura G. *Performing Mexicanidad: Vendidas y Cabareteras on the Transnational Stage.* Austin: University of Texas Press, 2010.

Gutmann, Matthew. *The Romance of Democracy: Compliant Defiance in Contemporary Mexico.* Berkeley: University of California Press, 2002.

Haber, Stephen, et al. *Mexico since 1980.* New York: Cambridge University Press, 2008.

Haddu, Miriam. *Contemporary Mexican Cinema, 1989–1999: History, Space, and Identity.* Lewiston, NY: Edwin Mellen, 2007.

———. "Historiography Goes to the Movies: The Case of Jorge Fons' *Rojo Amanecer.*" In Rix and Rodríguez-Saona 131–44.

———. "Love on the Run. Re-Mapping the Postmetropolis in Alfonso Cuarón's *Sólo con tu pareja.*" *Framework* 46.2 (2005): 71–89.

Hairston, Andrea. "Stories Are More Important than Facts: Imagination as Resistance in Guillermo del Toro's *Pan's Labyrinth.*" In *Narrative Power: Encounters, Celebrations, Struggles.* Ed. L. Timmel Duchamp. Seattle: Aqueduct, 2010. 137–51.

Hanley, Jane. "The Walls Fall Down: Fantasy and Power in *El laberinto del fauno.*" *Studies in Hispanic Cinema* 4.1 (2007): 35–45.

Hardcastle, Anne. "Ghosts of the Past and Present: Hauntology and the Spanish Civil War in Guillermo del Toro's *The Devil's Backbone.*" *Journal of the Fantastic in the Arts* 15.2 (2005): 119–31.

Hart, Patricia. "Visual Strategies in Gabriel Retes' Film *El bulto.*" In *Cine Lit II: Essays on Hispanic Film and Fiction.* Ed. George Cabello-Castellet, Jaume Martí-Olivella, and Guy H. Wood. Corvallis: Portland State University/Oregon State University/Reed College, 1995. 29–38.

Harvey, David. *A Brief History of Neoliberalism.* Oxford: Oxford University Press, 2005.

Haydar, Adnan, and Michael Beard. "Mapping the World of Naguib Mahfouz." In Beard and Haydar 1–9.

Herlinghaus, Hermann. *Violence without Guilt: Ethical Narratives from the Global South.* New York: Palgrave Macmillan, 2009.

Hernández Hernández, Óscar Misael, and Luisa Álvarez Cervantes, coords. *Sociedad y cultura en* El infierno: *Ensayos sobre una película mexicana.* Mexico City: Miguel Ángel Porrúa, 2012.

Herrera-Sobek, María. "Border Aesthetics: The Politics of Mexican Immigration in Film and Art." *Western Humanities Review* 60.2 (2006): 60–71.

Hershfield, Joanne. "Assimilation and Identification in Nicolás Echeverría's *Cabeza de Vaca.*" *Wide Angle* 16.3 (1995): 6–24.

———. "Women's Cinema and Contemporary Allegories of Violence in Mexico." *Discourse* 32.2 (2010): 170–85.

Hershfield, Joanne, and David R. Maciel, eds. *Mexico's Cinema: A Century of Film and Filmmakers.* Lanham, MD: SR Books, 2005.

Higgins, Ceri. *Gabriel Figueroa: Nuevas perspectivas.* Mexico City: Consejo Nacional para la Cultura y las Artes, 2008.

Hind, Emily. "Estado de excepción y feminicidio: *Backyard/El traspatio* (2009) de Carlos Carrera y Sabina Berman." *Colorado Review of Hispanic Studies* 8 (2010): 27–42.

———. "Pita Amor, Sabina Berman and Antonio Serrano: Camp in DF." *Hispanic Issues On Line* 3.1 (2008): 136–61.

———. "Post-NAFTA Mexican Cinema, 1998–2002." *Studies in Latin American Popular Culture* 23 (2004): 95–111.

———. "*Provincia* in Recent Mexican Cinema, 1989–2004." *Discourse* 26.1–2 (2004): 26–45.

Hinojosa Córdova, Lucía. *El cine mexicano: De lo global a lo local.* Mexico City: Trillas, 2003.

Hughes, Sallie. *Newsrooms in Conflict: Journalism and the Democratization of Mexico.* Pittsburgh: University of Pittsburgh Press, 2006.

Hughes-Warrington, Marnie. *History Goes to the Movies: Studying History in Film.* London: Routledge, 2007.

Ibarra, Jesús. *Los Bracho: Tres generaciones de cine mexicano.* Mexico City: UNAM, 2006.

Igler, Susanne, and Thomas Stauder, eds. *Negociando identidades, traspasando fronteras: Tendencias en la literatura y el cine mexicanos en torno al nuevo milenio.* Madrid: Iberoamericana, 2008.

Iglesias, Norma. "Gazes and Cinematic Readings of Gender: *Danzón* and its Relationship to its Audience." *Discourse* 26.1–2 (2004): 173–93.

Illouz, Eva. *Cold Intimacies: The Making of Emotional Capitalism.* London: Polity, 2007.

———. *Consuming the Romantic Utopia: Love and the Cultural Contradictions of Capitalism.* Berkeley: University of California Press, 1997.

IMCINE. *Anuario estadístico del cine mexicano 2011.* Mexico City: IMCINE, 2012.

Irwin, Robert McKee. *Mexican Masculinities.* Minneapolis: University of Minnesota Press, 2003.

Johnson, Michael K. "Not Telling the Story the Way It Happened: Alfonso Cuarón's *Great Expectations.*" *Literature/Film Quarterly* 33.1 (2005): 62–77.

Johnson, William. "Between Daylight and Darkness: *Forever* and *Silent Light*." *Film Quarterly* 61.3 (2008): 18–23.
Kantaris, Geoffrey. "Cinema and *Urbanías:* Translocal Identities in Contemporary Mexican Film." *Bulletin of Latin American Research* 25.4 (2006): 517–27.
———. "Cyborgs, Cities, and Celluloid: Memory Machines in Two Latin American Cyborg Films." In *Latin American Cyberculture and Cyberliterature*. Ed. Claire Taylor and Thea Pittman. Liverpool: Liverpool University Press, 2007. 50–69.
———. "Lola/Lolo: Filming Gender and Violence in the Mexican City." In *Cities in Transition: The Moving Image and the Modern Metropolis*. Ed. Andrew Webber and Emma Wilson. London: Wallflower, 2008. 163–75.
Kapur, Jyotsna, and Keith B. Wagner, eds. *Neoliberalism and Global Cinema: Capital, Culture and Marxist Critique*. London: Routledge, 2011.
Kilbourn, Russell J. A. *Cinema, Memory, Modernity: The Representation of Memory from Art Film to Transnational Cinema*. London: Routledge, 2010.
King, Geoff. *American Independent Cinema*. Bloomington: Indiana University Press, 2005.
———. *Indiewood, USA: Where Hollywood Meets Independent Cinema*. London: I. B. Tauris, 2009.
———. *New Hollywood Cinema: An Introduction*. New York: Columbia University Press, 2002.
———. "Weighing Up the Qualities of Independence: *21 Grams* in Focus." *Film Studies* 5 (2004): 80–91.
King, John, Ana M. López, and Manuel Alvarado, eds. *Mediating Two Worlds: Cinematic Encounters in the Americas*. London: British Film Institute, 1993.
Klosterman, Chuck. *Sex, Drugs and Cocoa Puffs: A Low Culture Manifesto*. New York: Scribner, 2003.
Knight, Alan. "The Modern Mexican State: Theory and Practice." In *The Other Mirror: Grand Theory through the Lens of Latin America*. Ed. Miguel Ángel Centeno and Fernando López-Alves. Princeton, NJ: Princeton University Press, 2001. 177–218.
Kraniauskas, John. "*Amores perros* y la mercantilización del arte (bienes, tumba, trabajo)." *Revista de crítica cultural* 33 (2006): 13–20.
———. "*Cronos* and the Political Economy of Vampirism: Notes on a Historical Constellation." In *Cannibalism and the Colonial World*. Ed. Francis Barker, Peter Hulme, and Margaret Iversen. Cambridge: Cambridge University Press, 1998. 142–57.
Kroeber, Karl. *Make Believe in Film and Fiction: Visual vs. Verbal Storytelling*. New York: Palgrave Macmillan, 2006.
Kroll, Juli A. "The Cinergetic, Experimental Melodrama: Feminism and Neo-Machista National Consciousness in Mexican Film." *Studies in Latin American Popular Culture* 26 (2007): 27–46.
Krutnik, Frank. "Conforming Passions?: Contemporary Romantic Comedy." In Neale 130–48.
———. "Love Lies: Romantic Fabrication in Contemporary Romantic Comedy." In Evans and Deleyto 15–37.
Kun, Josh. "Esperando La Última Ola/Waiting for the Last Wave: Manu Chao and the Music of Globalization." In Pacini Hernández, Fernández L'Hoeste, and Zolov 332–46.

Labanyi, Jo. "Memory and Modernity in Democratic Spain: The Difficulty of Coming to Terms with the Spanish Civil War." *Poetics Today* 28.1 (2007): 89–116.

Lahr-Vivaz, Elena. "Unconsummated Fictions and Virile Voiceovers: Desire and Nation in *Y tu mamá también*." *Revista de estudios hispánicos* 40.1 (2006): 78–101.

Lamas, Marta. *Feminismo: Transmisiones y retransmisiones.* Mexico City: Taurus, 2006.

Landy, Marcia. *British Genres: Cinema and Society, 1930–1960.* Princeton, NJ: Princeton University Press, 1991.

———. *Cinematic Uses of the Past.* Minneapolis: University of Minnesota Press, 1996.

Lara Chávez, Hugo. *Una ciudad inventada por el cine.* Mexico City: Conaculta, 2006.

Lawall, Sarah. "Naguib Mahfouz and the Nobel Prize: Reciprocal Expectations." In Beard and Haydar 21–27.

Lázaro-Reboll, Antonio. "The Transnational Reception of *El espinazo del Diablo* (Guillermo del Toro 2001)." *Hispanic Research Journal* 8.1 (2007): 29–51.

Leitch, Thomas. *Film Adaptation and its Discontents: From* Gone with the Wind *to* The Passion of the Christ. Baltimore: Johns Hopkins University Press, 2007.

León-Portilla, Miguel, ed. *Raíces indígenas, presencia hispánica.* Mexico City: El Colegio Nacional, 1993.

Lévi, Heather. *The World of Lucha Libre. Secrets, Revelations and Mexican National Identity.* Durham, NC: Duke University Press, 2008.

Lewis, Vek. "When 'Macho' Bodies Fail: Spectacles of Corporaleity and the Limits of the Homosocial/sexual in Mexican Cinema." In *Mysterious Skins: Male Bodies in Contemporary Cinema.* Ed. Santiago Fouz-Hernández. London: I. B. Tauris, 2009. 177–92.

Lim, Bliss Cua. *Translating Time: Cinema, the Fantastic and Temporal Critique.* Durham, NC: Duke University Press, 2009.

Linhard, Tabea. *Fearless Women in the Mexican Revolution and the Spanish Civil War.* Columbia: University of Missouri Press, 2005.

———. "Unheard Confessions and Transatlantic Connections: *Y tu mamá también* and *Nadie hablará de nosotras cuando hayamos muerto*." *Studies in Hispanic Cinemas* 5.1–2 (2008): 43–56.

Lomnitz, Claudio. "Narrating the Neoliberal Moment: History, Journalism, Historicity." *Public Culture* 20.1 (2008): 39–56.

Long, Ryan F. "Sex, Lies and Mariachis." DVD insert for *Sólo con tu pareja* 2–9.

Luhr, William G., ed. *The Coen Brothers'* Fargo. Cambridge: Cambridge University Press, 2004.

Luna, Ilana. "*Batalla en el cielo:* The Unfinished Struggle for Economic and Social Independence." Address to the 30th International Congress of the Latin American Studies Association, San Francisco, 26 May 2012.

Maciel, David R. "Cinema and the State in Contemporary Mexico, 1970–1999." In Hershfield and Maciel 197–232.

MacLaird, Misha. *Aesthetics and Politics in the Mexican Film Industry.* New York: Palgrave Macmillan, 2013.

———. "*Y tu mamá también* (Mexico 2001)." In Carlos Gutiérrez, *Cinema Tropical Presents* 47–53.

Magnarelli, Sharon. *Home Is Where the (He)art Is: The Family Romance in Late Twentieth-Century Mexican and Argentine Theater.* Lewisburg, PA: Bucknell University Press, 2008.

Martin, Michael T., ed. *New Latin American Cinema.* 2 vols. Detroit: Wayne State University Press, 1997.

Martin, Sean. *Andrei Tarkovsky.* Herts, UK: Kamera, 2011.

Martin-Barbero, Jesús. "The City between Fear and the Media." In Rotker 25–33.

———. *Oficio de cartógrafo: Travesías latinoamericanas de la comunicación en la cultura.* Santiago, Chile: Fondo de Cultura Económica, 2002.

Martínez, Gabriela. *Latin American Communications: Telefónica's Conquest.* Lanham, MD: Lexington, 2008.

Martínez, Raciel D. *Cine mexicano y multiculturalismo.* Xalapa, Mexico: Gobierno del Estado de Veracruz, 2009.

Martínez, Victoria. "*Como agua para chocolate:* A Recipe for Neoliberalism." *Chasqui* 33.1 (2004): 28–41.

Martin-Jones, David. *Deleuze, Cinema and National Identity: Narrative Time in National Contexts.* Edinburgh: University of Edinburgh Press, 2006.

Maslin, Janet. "Emotions So Strong You Can Taste Them." *New York Times.* 17 February 1993. *nytimes.com*.

Mazziotti, Nora. *La industria de la telenovela: La producción de ficción en América Latina.* Buenos Aires: Paidós, 1996.

McAnany, Emile G., and Kenton T. Wilkinson. *Mass Media and Free Trade:* NAFTA *and the Cultural Industries.* Austin: University of Texas Press, 1996.

McFarlane, Brian. "Reading Film and Literature." In Cartmell and Whelehan, *Cambridge Companion* 15–28.

McGowan, Todd. "The Contingency of Connection: The Path to Politicization in *Babel.*" *Discourse* 30.3 (2008): 401–18.

———. *Out of Time: Desire in Atemporal Cinema.* Minneapolis: University of Minnesota Press, 2011.

Medin, Tzvi. *El sexenio alemanista.* Mexico City: Era, 1990.

Medina, Manuel F. "La ciudad como espacio público y privado en *Sólo con tu pareja* y *Vivir mata.*" In Igler and Stauder 245–60.

Medrano Platas, Alejandro. *Quince directores del cine mexicano.* Mexico City: Plaza y Valdés, 2008.

Meléndez, Priscilla. "Marx, Villa, Calles, Guzmán . . . Fantasmas y modernidad en *Entre Villa y una mujer desnuda.*" *Hispanic Review* 72.4 (2004): 523–46.

Menne, Jeff. "A Mexican *Nouvelle Vague:* The Logic of New Waves under Globalization." *Cinema Journal* 47.1 (2007): 70–92.

Middlebrook, Kevin J, ed. *Dilemmas of Political Change in Mexico.* London: Institute of Latin American Studies; San Diego: Center of U.S./Mexican Studies, 2004.

Millán, Márgara. *Derivas de un cine en femenino.* Mexico City: Universidad Nacional Autónoma de México/Miguel Ángel Porrúa, 1999.

———. "Le corps-récit: Julián Hernández et Carlos Reygadas." In Game, *Images des corps* 241–52.

Miller, Marilyn Grace. *The Rise and Fall of the Cosmic Race: The Cult of Mestizaje in Latin America*. Austin: University of Texas Press, 2004.

Miller, Toby. "National Cinema Abroad: The New International Division of Cultural Labor, From Production to Viewing." In Ďuričová and Newman 136–59.

Miller, Toby, et al. *Global Hollywood 2*. London: British Film Institute, 2005.

Mills, Brett. *The Sitcom*. Edinburgh: Edinburgh University Press, 2009.

Monsiváis, Carlos. *Aires de familia: Cultura y sociedad en América Latina*. Barcelona: Anagrama, 2001.

———. "All the People Came and Did Not Fit Onto the Screen: Notes on the Cinema Audience in Mexico." In Paranaguá, *Mexican Cinema* 145–51.

———. *Entrada Libre: Crónicas de una sociedad que se organiza*. Mexico City: Era. 1987.

———. *Escenas de pudor y liviandad*. Mexico City: Grijalbo, 1988.

Monsiváis, Carlos, and Carlos Bonfil. *A través del espejo: El cine mexicano y su público*. Mexico City: El Milagro/IMCINE, 1994.

Mora, Carl J. *Mexican Cinema: Reflections of a Society, 1896–2004*. 3rd ed. Jefferson, NC: McFarland, 2005.

Moraña, Mabel, and Ignacio M. Sánchez Prado, comps. *El arte de la ironía: Carlos Monsiváis ante la crítica*. Mexico City: Era/UNAM, 2007.

Moreiras, Alberto. "Ethics and Politics in Héctor Aguilar Camín's *Morir en el Golfo* and *La guerra de Galio*." *South Central Review* 21.3 (2004): 70–84.

Mottram, James. *The Sundance Kids: How the Mavericks Took Back Hollywood*. New York: Faber and Faber, 2006.

Moya, Ana, and Gemma López. "'I'm a Wild Success': Postmodern Dickens/Victorian Cuarón." *Dickens Quarterly* 25.3 (2008): 172–89.

Mudrovcic, María Elena. "Cultura nacionalista *vs.* cultura nacional: Carlos Monsiváis ante la sociedad de masas." In Moraña and Sánchez Prado 124–36.

Murphy, Patrick D. "Television and Cultural Politics in Mexico: Some Notes on Televisa, the State and Transnational Culture." *Howard Journal of Communications* 6.4 (1995): 250–61.

Nagib, Lúcia. *World Cinema and the Ethics of Realism*. London: Continuum, 2011.

Nagib, Lúcia, Chris Perriam, and Rajinder Dudrah, eds. *Theorizing World Cinema*. London: I. B. Tauris, 2012.

Neale, Steve, ed. *Genre and Contemporary Hollywood*. London: British Film Institute, 2002.

Newman, Michael Z. "Character and Complexity in American Independent Cinema: *21 Grams* and *Passion Fish*." *Film Criticism* 31.1–2 (2006): 89–106.

———. *Indie: An American Film Culture*. New York: Columbia University Press, 2011.

Niebylski, Dianna. "Heartburn, Humor and Hyperbole in *Like Water for Chocolate*." In *Performing Gender and Comedy: Theories, Texts and Contexts*. Ed. Shannon Hengen. Amsterdam: Gordon and Breach, 1998. 179–97.

Niessen, Niels. "Miraculous Realism: Spinoza, Deleuze and Carlos Reygadas's *Stellet Licht*." *Discourse* 33.1 (2011): 27–54.

Noble, Andrea. *Mexican National Cinema*. London: Routledge, 2005.

Noriega, Chon A., ed. *Visible Nations: Latin American Cinema and Video*. Minneapolis: University of Minnesota, 2000.

Núñez Cabeza de Vaca, Álvar. *Naufragios*. Madrid: Cátedra, 1996.
O'Brien, Brad. "Fulcanelli as a Vampiric Frankenstein and Jesus as His Vampiric Monster: The Frankenstein and Dracula Myths in Guillermo del Toro's *Cronos*." In *Monstrous Adaptations: Generic and Thematic Mutations in Horror Film*. Ed. Richard J. Hand and Jay McRoy. Manchester, UK: Manchester University Press, 2007. 172–80.
O'Malley, Ilene V. *The Myth of the Revolution: Hero Cults and the Institutionalization of the Mexican State, 1920–1940*. Westport, CT: Greenwood, 1986.
Oropesa, Salvador. "Proxemics, Homogeneization and Diversity in Mexico's Road Movies." *Hispanic Issues On Line* 3.1 (2008): 92–112.
Pacini Hernández, Deborah, Héctor Fernández L'Hoeste, and Eric Zolov. *Rockin' Las Americas: The Global Politics of Rock in Latin/o America*. Pittsburgh: University of Pittsburgh Press, 2004.
Page, Joanna. *Crisis and Capitalism in Contemporary Argentine Cinema*. Durham, NC: Duke University Press, 2009.
Paranaguá, Paulo Antonio. *Arturo Ripstein: La espiral de la identidad*. Madrid: Cátedra, 1997.
———, ed. *Mexican Cinema*. Trans. Ana M. López. London: British Film Institute; Mexico City: IMCINE, 1995.
Parra, Max. *Writing Pancho Villa's Revolution: Rebels in the Literary Imagination of Mexico*. Austin: University of Texas Press, 2005.
Pastor, Beatriz. *El segundo descubrimiento: La Conquista de América narrada por sus coetáneos (1492–1589)*. Barcelona: Edhasa, 2008.
Pelayo, Alejandro. *La generación de la crisis*. Mexico City: IMCINE, 2012.
Pellicer, Juan. *Tríptico cinematográfico: El discurso narrativo y su montaje*. Mexico City: Siglo XXI, 2010.
Pérez Turrent, Tomás. "Crises and Renovations (1965–91)." In Paranaguá, *Mexican Cinema* 94–115.
Pick, Zuzana M. *The New Latin American Cinema: A Continental Project*. Austin: University of Texas Press, 1993.
Poblete, Juan. "New National Cinemas in a Transnational Age." *Discourse* 26.1–2 (2004): 214–34.
Podalsky, Laura. *The Politics of Affect and Emotion in Contemporary Latin American Cinema: Argentina, Brazil, Cuba and Mexico*. New York: Palgrave Macmillan, 2011.
Porras Ferreyra, Jaime. "El cine como instrumento de reinterpretación histórica en periodos de transición democrática." *Revista de Ciencias Sociales* 122 (2008): 89–101.
Potvin, Claudine. "*Como agua para chocolate*: ¿Parodia o cliché?" *Revista canadiense de estudios hispánicos* 20.1 (1995).
Power, Marcus, and Andrew Crampton, ed. *Cinema and Popular Geo-Politics*. London: Routledge, 2007.
Premios internacionales del cine mexicano, 1938–2008. Mexico City: Cineteca Nacional, 2009.
Preston, Julia, and Samuel Dillon. *Opening Mexico: The Making of a Democracy*. New York: Farrar, Straus and Giroux, 2004.
Price, Brian L. "Heterotemporal *Mise-en-scène* in the Films of Luis Estrada." *Arizona Journal of Hispanic Cultural Studies* 16 (2012): 259–74.

Quiroga, José. "(Queer) Boleros of a Tropical Night." *Journal of Latin American Cultural Studies* 3.1–2 (1994): 199–214.

———. *Understanding Octavio Paz.* Columbia: University of South Carolina Press, 1999.

Ramanathan, Geeta. *Feminist Auteurs: Reading Women's Films.* London: Wallflower, 2006.

Ramírez Berg, Charles. *Cinema of Solitude: A Critical Study of Mexican Film, 1967–1983.* Austin: University of Texas Press, 1992.

———. *Latino Images in Film: Stereotypes, Subversion and Resistance.* Austin: University of Texas Press, 2002.

Rangel, Liz Consuelo. "*La ley de herodes* (1999) vs. *Río Escondido* (1947): La desmitificación del triunfo de la Revolución Mexicana." *Divergencias: Revista de estudios lingüísticos y literarios* 4.1 (2006): 61–69.

Rashkin, Elissa J. *Women Filmmakers in Mexico: The Country of Which We Dream.* Austin: University of Texas Press, 2001.

Reber, Dierdra. "Love as Politics: *Amores Perros* and the Emotional Aesthetics of Neoliberalism." *Journal of Latin American Cultural Studies* 19.3 (2010): 279–98.

Reguillo, Rossana. "The Social Construction of Fear: Urban Narratives and Practices." In Rotker 187–206.

Restrepo, Luis Fernando. "Primitive Bodies in Latin American Cinema: Nicolás Echevarría's *Cabeza de Vaca*." In *Primitivism and Identity in Latin America: Essays on Art, Literature and Culture.* Ed. Erik Camayd-Freixas and José Eduardo González. Tucson: University of Arizona Press, 2000. 189–208.

Revolución 10.10. Mexico City: Random House Mondadori/IMCINE/Reservoir Books, 2010.

Ribas, Alberto. "'El pinche acentito ese': Deseo trasatlántico y exotismo satírico en el cine mexicano del cambio de milenio; *Amores perros, Y tu mamá también, Sin dejar huella*." *Hispanic Research Journal* 10.5 (2009): 457–81.

Riener, Deborah L., and John V. Sweeney. "The Effects of NAFTA on Mexico's Private Sector and Foreign Trade and Investment." In *Mexico's Private Sector: Recent History, Future Challenges.* Ed. Riordan Roett. Boulder, CO: Lynne Rienner, 1998. 161–88.

Ríos-Soto, Marilyn. "The Gaze as Mechanism of Self-Knowledge in the Mexican Novel and Film *Santitos:* The Outsider as Observer and Object of Desire." In *The Image of the Outsider in Literature, Media and Society.* Ed. Will Wright and Steven Kaplan. Pueblo, CO: Society of the Interdisciplinary Study of Social Imagery/University of Southern Colorado, 2002. 106–9.

Rix, Rob, and Roberto Rodríguez-Saona, eds. *Changing Reels: Latin American Cinema against the Odds.* Leeds: Trinity and All Saints University College, 1997.

Robles, Óscar. *Identidades maternacionales en el cine de María Novaro.* New York: Peter Lang, 2005.

Rodríguez Cruz, Olga. *El 68 en el cine mexicano.* Puebla: Universidad Iberoamericana-Golfo Centro/BUAP/Delegación Coyoacán/Instituto Tlaxcalteca de Cultura, 2000.

Rodríguez-Hernández, Raúl, and Claudia Schaefer. "*Cronos* and the Man of Science: Madness, Monstrosity, Mexico." *Revista de Estudios Hispánicos* 33.1 (1999): 85–109.

Rogers, V. Daniel. "Cabronas, palabrotas y otras amenazas a la nación: La Diana cazadora y *Entre Villa y una mujer desnuda*." In *Sediciosas seducciones: Sexo, poder y palabras en el teatro de Sabina Berman.* Comp. Jacqueline Bixler. Mexico City: Escenología, 2004. 151–60.

Rojo, Juan J. "La memoria como 'espectro' en *Rojo amanecer* de Jorge Fons." *Arizona Journal of Hispanic Cultural Studies* 14 (2010): 49–65.

Rosas Mantecón, Ana. "Auge, ocaso y renacimiento de la exhibición de cine en la Ciudad de México (1930–2000)." *Alteridades* 20 (2000): 107–16.

———. "New Processes of Urban Segregation: The Reorganization of Film Exhibition in Mexico City." *Television and New Media* 4.1 (2003): 9–23.

Rose, James. *Studying* The Devil's Backbone. Leighton Buzzard, UK: Auteur, 2009.

Rosenbaum, Jonathan. *Movies as Politics.* Berkeley: University of California Press, 1997.

Ross, Miriam. "The Film Festival as Producer: Latin American Films and Rotterdam's Hubert Bals Fund." *Screen* 52.2 (2011): 261–67.

———. *South American Cinematic Culture.* Newcastle upon Tyne, UK: Cambridge Scholars Publishing, 2010.

Rotker, Susana, ed. *Citizens of Fear: Urban Violence in Latin America.* New Brunswick, NJ: Rutgers University Press, 2002.

Rowlandson, William. "The Journey into the Text: Reading Rulfo in Carlos Reygadas's 2002 Feature Film *Japón.*" *Modern Language Review* 101 (2006): 1025–34.

Ruétalo, Victoria, and Dolores Tierney, eds. *Latsploitation, Exploitation Cinemas, and Latin America.* London: Routledge. 2009.

Ruffinelli, Jorge. *América Latina en 130 películas.* Santiago, Chile: Uqbar, 2010.

Sá, Lúcia. *Life in the Megalopolis: Mexico City and São Paulo.* London: Routledge, 2007.

Saavedra Luna, Isis. *Entre la ficción y la realidad: Fin de la industria cinematográfica mexicana, 1989–1994.* Mexico City: Universidad Autónoma Metropolitana, 2007.

Sabbadini, Andrea. "'Not Something Destroyed but Something That Is Still Alive': *Amores Perros* at the Intersection of Rescue Fantasies." *International Journal of Psychoanalysis* 84.3 (2003): 755–64.

Sadlier, Darlene J., ed. *Latin American Melodrama: Passion, Pathos and Entertainment.* Urbana: University of Illinois Press, 2009.

Saldaña Portillo, María Josefina. "In the Shadow of NAFTA: *Y tu mamá también* Revisits the National Allegory of Mexican Sovereignty." *American Quarterly* 57.3 (2005): 751–77.

Sánchez, Fernando Fabio. *Artful Assassins: Murder as Art in Modern Mexico.* Nashville: Vanderbilt University Press, 2010.

Sánchez, Francisco. *El cine nuevo del nuevo siglo (y otras nostalgias).* Mexico City: Juan Pablos/Instituto Zacatecano de Cultura, 2008.

———. *Luz en la oscurdad: Crónia del cine mexicano, 1896–2002.* Mexico City: Juan Pablos/Consejo Nacional para la Cultura y las Artes, 2002.

———. *Océano de películas.* Mexico City: Juan Pablos/Consejo Nacional para la Cultura y las Artes, 1999.

Sánchez Noriega, José Luis. *De la literatura al cine: Teoría y análisis de la adaptación.* Buenos Aires: Paidós, 2000.

Sánchez Prado, Ignacio M. "*Amores Perros:* Exotic Violence and Neoliberal Fear." *Journal of Latin American Cultural Studies* 15.1 (2006): 39–57.

———. "Carlos Monsiváis: Crónica, nación y liberalismo." In Moraña and Sánchez Prado 300–36.

———. "Claiming Liberalism: Enrique Krauze, *Vuelta, Letras Libres* and the Reconfigurations of the Mexican Intellectual Class." *Mexican Studies/Estudios Mexicanos* 26.1 (2010): 47–78.

———. "Monstruos neoliberales: Capitalismo y terror en *Cronos* y *Somos lo que hay.*" In *El cine de horror en Latinoamérica y el Caribe*. Ed. Rossana Díaz Zambrana and Patricia Tomé. San Juan, PR: Isla Negra, 2012. 47–64.

———. *Naciones intelectuales: Las fundaciones de la modernidad literaria mexicana (1917–1959)*. Purdue Studies in Romance Literatures 47. West Lafayette, IN: Purdue University Press, 2009.

———. "The Pre-Columbian Past as a Project: Miguel León Portilla and Hispanism." In *Ideologies of Hispanism*. Ed. Mabel Moraña. Hispanic Issues 30. Nashville: Vanderbilt University Press, 2005, 40–61.

Sánchez-Ruiz, Enrique. "Globalization, Cultural Industries and Free Trade: The Mexican Audiovisual Sector in the NAFTA Age." In *Continental Order? Integrating North America and Cybercapitalism*. Ed. Vincent Mosco and Dan Schiller. Lanham, MD: Rowman and Littlefield, 2001.

Sandoval, Adriana. *De la literatura al cine: Versiones fílmicas de novelas mexicanas*. Mexico City: Universidad Nacional Autónoma de México, 2005.

Schaefer, Claudia. *Bored to Distraction: Cinema of Excess in End-of-the-Century Mexico and Spain*. Albany: State University of New York Press, 2003.

Schlesinger, Philip. "On National Identity: Some Conceptions and Misconceptions Criticized." In *Nationalism: Critical Concepts in Political Science, Volume 1*. Ed. John Hutchinson and Anthony D. Smith. London: Routledge, 2000. 69–111.

Schrader, Paul. *Transcendental Style in Film: Ozu, Bresson, Dreyer*. Berkeley: University of California Press, 1972.

Schulz-Cruz, Bernard. *Imágenes gay en el cine mexicano: Tres décadas de joterío, 1970–1999*. Mexico City: Fontamara, 2008.

Segre, Erica. "'La desnacionalización de la pantalla': Mexican Cinema in the 1990s." In Rix and Rodríguez-Saona 33–59.

Serna, Enrique. *Las caricaturas me hacen llorar*. Mexico City: Joaquín Mortiz, 1996.

Sharrett, Christopher. "*Fargo* or the Blank Frontier." In Luhr 92–108.

Shary, Timothy. *Generation Multiplex: The Image of Youth in Contemporary American Cinema*. Austin: University of Texas Press, 2002.

Shaw, Deborah. "*Babel* and the Global Hollywood Gaze." *Situations* 4.1 (2011): 11–31.

———. *Contemporary Cinema of Latin America: 10 Key Films*. London: Continuum, 2003.

———. "The Figure of the Absent Father in Recent Latin American Films." *Studies in Hispanic Cinemas* 1.2 (2004): 85–101.

———. *The Three Amigos: The Transnational Filmmaking of Guillermo del Toro, Alejandro González Iñarritu and Alfonso Cuarón*. Manchester, UK: Manchester University Press, 2013.

———. "(Trans)National Images and Cinematic Spaces: The Cases of Alfonso Cuarón's *Y tu mamá también* (2001) and Carlos Reygadas' *Japón* (2002)." *Iberoamericana* 44 (2011): 117–31.

Shaw, Deborah, and Brigitte Roller. "*Como agua para chocolate:* Some of the Reasons for Its Success." *Journal of Latin American Cultural Studies* 3.1–2 (1994): 82–92.

Shklovsky, Viktor. *Theory of Prose.* Trans. Benjamin Sher. Normal, IL: Dalkey Archive Press, 2001.

Shumway, David R. *Modern Love: Romance, Intimacy and the Marriage Crisis.* New York: New York University Press, 2003.

Sinclair, John. "International Television Channels in the Latin American Audiovisual Space." In Chalaby 196–215.

———. *Latin American Television: A Global View.* Oxford: Oxford University Press, 1999.

———. "Neither West nor Third World: The Mexican Television Industry within the NWICO Debate." *Media, Culture and Society* 12 (1990): 343–60.

Sinnigen, John H. "*Cómo agua para chocolate:* Feminine Space, Postmodern Cultural Politics, National Allegory." *CIEFL Bulletin* 7.1–2 (1995): 111–31.

Sisk, Christina L. "Entre el Cha Cha Chá y el Estado: El Cine Nacional Mexicano y sus Arquetipos." *A contracorriente* 8.3 (2011): 163–82.

———. *Mexico, Nation in Transit: Contemporary Representations of Mexican Migration to the United States.* Tucson: University of Arizona Press, 2011.

Smith, Paul Julian. *Amores Perros.* London: British Film Institute, 2003.

———. "Transatlantic Traffic in Recent Mexican Films." *Journal of Latin American Cultural Studies* 12.3 (2003): 389–400.

———. "Transnational Cinemas: The Cases of Mexico, Argentina and Brazil." In Nagib, Perriam, and Dudrah 63–77.

Solomianski, Alejandro. "Significado estructura, historia y tercer mundo en *Amores perros.*" *A contracorriente* 3.3 (2006): 17–36.

Sommer, Doris. *Foundational Fictions: The National Romances of Latin America.* Berkeley: University of California Press, 1991.

Steinberg, Samuel. "Re-Cinema: Hauntology of 1968." *Discourse* 33.1 (2011): 3–26.

Sterritt, David. "*Fargo* in Context: The Middle of Nowhere?" In Luhr 10–32.

Stewart, Michael. "Irresistible Death: *21 Grams* as Melodrama." *Cinema Journal* 47.1 (2007): 49–69.

Stilwell, Robynn J. "Music, Ritual and Genre in Edward Burns' Indie Romantic Comedies." In Abbott and Jermyn 25–38.

Straubhaar, Joseph D., and Luiz G. Duarte. "Adapting US Transnational Television Channels to a Complex World: From Cultural Imperialism to Localization to Hybridization." In Chalaby 216–53.

Stock, Anne Marie. "Authentically Mexican? *Mi Querido Tom Mix* and *Cronos* Reframe Critical Questions." In Hershfield and Maciel 267–92.

———, ed. *Framing Latin American Cinema.* Hispanic Issues 15. Minneapolis: University of Minnesota Press, 1997.

Suárez, Juana. "Dominado y dominador: Aspectos de la representación de género en *Cabeza de Vaca.*" *Romance Languages Annual* 10 (1999): 836–42.

———. "Feminine Desire and Homoerotic Representation in Two Latin American Films: *Danzón* and *La Bella del Alhambra.*" In *Chicano/Latino Homoerotic Identities.* Ed. David William Foster. New York: Garland, 1999. 113–24.

Templeton, Alice. "The Confessing Animal in *sex, lies, and videotape.*" *Journal of Film and Video* 50.2 (1998): 15–25.

Tenenbaum, Barbara. "Why Tita Didn't Marry the Doctor, or Mexican History in *Like Water for Chocolate*." In *Based on a True Story: Latin American History at the Movies*. Ed. Donald F. Stevens. Wilmington, DE: SR Books, 1997. 157–72.

Thormann, Janet. "Other Pasts: Family Romances of *Pan's Labyrinth*." *Psychoanalysis, Culture and Society* 13 (2008): 175–87.

Throsby, David. *Economics and Culture*. Cambridge: Cambridge University Press, 2001.

Tierney, Dolores. "Alejandro González Iñarritu: Director without Borders." *New Cinemas: Journal of Contemporary Film* 7.2 (2009): 101–17.

———. *Emilio Fernández: Pictures at the Margins*. Manchester, UK: Manchester University Press, 2007.

———. "Silver Sling-backs and Mexican Melodrama: *Salón México* and *Danzón*." *Screen* 38.4 (1997): 360–71.

Toledo, Fernando. "Ritual, culpa y amor cortés en *Batalla en el cielo* de Carlos Reygadas." *Tiresias* 4 (2010): 101–14.

Tompkins, Cynthia. "A Deleuzian Approach to Carlos Reygadas' *Japón* and *Batalla en el cielo*." *Hispanic Journal* 29.1 (2008): 155–69.

———. *A Deleuzian Approach to Carlos Reygadas's Stellet Licht [Silent Light] (2008)*. Latin American and Iberian Institute Research Paper Series 51. Albuquerque: University of New Mexico, 2010.

Treviño, Jesús Salvador. "The New Mexican Cinema." *Film Quarterly* 32.3 (1979): 26–37.

Trouillot, Michel-Rolph. *Silencing the Past: Power and the Production of History*. Boston: Beacon, 1995.

Turan, Kenneth. *From Sundance to Sarajevo: Film Festivals and the World They Made*. Berkeley: University of California Press, 2002.

Udden, James. "Child of the Long Take: Alfonso Cuarón's Film Aesthetics in the Shadow of Globalization." *Style* 43.1 (2009): 26–44.

Uribe, Álvaro. *Expediente del atentado*. Mexico City: Tusquets, 2007.

Valdés, Mario J. "Hermenéutica de la representación fílmica de la mujer: *La Regenta, ¿Qué he hecho yo para merecer esto?* y *Danzón*." *Revista canadiense de estudios hispánicos* 20.1 (1995): 69–80.

Van Delden, Maarten. "Conjunciones y disyunciones: La rivalidad entre *Vuelta y Nexos*." In *El laberinto de la solidaridad: Cultura y política en México (1910–2000)*. Ed. Kristine Vanden Berghe and Maarten Van Delden. Foro Hispánico 22. Amsterdam: Rodopi, 2002. 105–19.

Vargas, Juan Carlos, coord. *Tendencias del cine iberoamericano del nuevo milenio: Argentina, Brasil, España y México*. Guadalajara: Universidad de Guadalajara/Patronato del Festival Internacional de Cine de Guadalajara, 2011.

Vargas, Margarita. "Sexual and Political Disillusion in *Y tu mamá también*." In *Coming of Age on Film: Stories of Transformation in World Cinema*. Ed. Anne Hardcastle, Roberta Morosini, and Kendall Tarte. Newcastle upon Tyne, UK: Cambridge Scholars Publishing, 2009. 68–80.

Vega, Sara, et al. *Historia de un gran amor: Relaciones cinematográficas entre Cuba y México 1897–2005*. Guadalajara: Universidad de Guadalajara/Instituto Cubano de Arte e Industria Cinematográficos/Cinemateca de Cuba, 2007.

Velazco, Salvador. "Cineastas mexicanos en Hollywood: La (im)posible integración." In Juan Carlos Vargas, *Tendencias* 189–206.

———. "*Rojo amanecer* y *La ley de Herodes:* Cine politico de la transición mexicana." *Hispanic Research Journal* 6.1 (2005): 67–80.

Waddell, Terrie. *Wild/Lives: Trickster, Place and Liminality on Screen.* London: Routledge, 2010.

Wahl, Jan. *Carl Theodor Dreyer and* Ordet: *My Summer with the Danish Filmmaker.* Lexington: University Press of Kentucky, 2012.

Waldron, John V. "The Discreet Charm of *Los de abajo:* Screening Class in Mexican Cinema." Address to the 30th International Congress of the Latin American Studies Association, San Francisco, CA, 26 May 2012.

———. "Introduction: Culture Monopolies and Mexican Cinema; A Way Out?" *Discourse* 26.1–2 (2004): 5–25.

———. "La risa política en la producción fílmica de Estada y Buñuel." Address to the 38th Annual Juan Bruce Novoa Mexican Conference, Irvine, CA, 28 April 2012.

Walter, Krista. "Filming the Conquest: *Cabeza de Vaca* and the Spectacle of History." *Literature/Film Quarterly* 30 (2002): 140–45.

Wayne, Mike. *Political Film: The Dialectics of Third Cinema.* London: Pluto, 2001.

Wehling, Susan. "Typewriters, Guns and Roses: Shifting the Balance of Power in Sabina Berman's *Entre Villa y una mujer desnuda.*" *Letras femeninas* 25.1–2 (1998): 69–79.

Welsh, James M., and Peter Lev. *The Literature/Film Reader: Issues of Adaptation.* Lanham, MD: Scarecrow, 2007.

Wexman, Virginia Wright, ed. *Film and Authorship.* New Brunswick, NJ: Rutgers University Press, 2003.

Williams, Linda. *Screening Sex.* Durham, NC: Duke University Press, 2008.

Wilt, David E. *The Mexican Filmography, 1916 through 2001.* Jefferson, NC: McFarland, 2004.

Wolf, Sergio. *Cine/Literatura: Ritos de pasaje.* Buenos Aires: Paidós, 2001.

Worrell, M. S. "Sexual Awakenings and the Malignant Fictions of Masculinity in Alfonso Cuarón's *Y tu mamá también.*" In *Sex and the Citizen: Interrogating the Caribbean.* Ed. Faith Smith. Charlottesville: University of Virginia Press, 2011. 157–67.

Wu, Harmony. "Consuming Tacos and Enchiladas: Gender and Nation in *Como agua para chocolate.*" In Noriega 174–92.

Yehya, Naief. "*Silent Light* (Mexico 2007): Carlos Reygadas's Meditation on Love and Ritual." In Carlos Gutiérrez, *Cinema Tropical Presents* 19–26.

Zaniello, Tom. *The Cinema of Globalization: A Guide to Films about the New Economic Order.* Ithaca: ILR/Cornell University Press, 2007.

Zavarzadeh, Mas'ud. *Seeing Films Politically.* Albany: State University of New York Press, 1991.

Zolov, Eric. *Refried Elvis: The Rise of Mexican Counterculture.* Berkeley: University of California Press, 1999.

Zunzunegui, Santos. "Between History and Dream: Víctor Erice's *El espíritu de la colmena.*" In *Modes of Representation in Spanish Cinema.* Ed. Jenaro Talens and Santos Zunzunegui. Minneapolis: University of Minnesota Press, 1998. 128–54.

Index

7 mujeres, 1 homosexual y Carlos (Bueno Camacho), 100
11:14 (Marcks), 179
21 Grams (González Iñarritu), 179–81, 184
1492: The Conquest of Paradise (Scott), 38, 230n19
2033 (Laresgoiti), 223–24

Abel (Luna), 218
Aguilar Camín, Héctor, 113, 135, 238n7
Aguilera, Pedro, 202
Aguirre: The Wrath of God (Herzog), 41
Alazraki, Gary, 247n4
    See also *Nosotros los nobles*
Alcoriza, Luis, 4, 13–19, 43, 48, 65, 108, 123, 176
    See also *Mecánica nacional*
Aldama, Frederick Louis, 227n5
Allá en el rancho grande (de Fuentes), 54
Allen, Woody, 67–68, 86, 98, 149, 197, 294n7
    See also *Annie Hall; Hannah and Her Sisters; Mighty Aphrodite*
Alonso, Lisandro, 196, 198, 201–2, 245n43
    See also *Liverpool*
Alta tensión (de Anda), 76, 234n12
Altman, Robert, 180
Alucarda, la hija de las tinieblas (López Moctezuma), 162
Amarte duele (Sariñana, F.), 240n27
Ámbar (Estrada), 149
Ambulante, 211, 218, 247n3
American visa (Valdivia), 238n14
Amor letra por letra (Reyes), 100
Amor Xtremo (Cartas), 237n33

Amores perros (González Iñarritu), 70, 156, 159–60, 171–82, 184–87, 190, 193, 207–8, 243n22–25
Anderson, Paul Thomas, 180, 246n54
Ángel de fuego (Rotberg), 123
Annie Hall (Allen), 68
Año bisiesto (Rowe), 245n47
Anoche soñé contigo (Sistach), 123, 234n6
Arau, Alfonso, 8, 11, 15–33, 39, 65, 110, 168, 188
    See also *Calzonzin inspector; Chido Guan; Como agua para chocolate; Mojado power*
Argos Cine, 92–93, 101
Arráncame la vida (Sneider), 59–60, 233n41, 239n18
Arredondo, Isabel, 36, 122
Arriaga, Guillermo, 243n23
    See also, *21 Grams; Amores perros; Babel; Burning Plain, The; El búfalo de la noche; Three Burials of Melquiades Estrada, The*
art cinema, 156–65, 179, 194–208, 241n3, 245n38, 246n49, 246n54
Así es la suerte (de Llaca), 120
A.T.M.: A toda máquina (Rodríguez, I.), 234n5
Athié, Francisco, 117, 242n18
    See also *Fibra óptica; Lolo*
Ave María (Rossoff), 27
Aviña, Rafael, 3, 144, 237n1
Awakenings (Marshall, P.), 111
Ayala Blanco, Jorge, 4, 34–36, 55, 59, 68, 69, 85, 87, 90–93, 99, 102, 107, 132, 175, 176, 232n33, 236n23, 239n25, 240n26
Azcona, María del Mar, 174, 180–82

Babel (González Iñarritu), 155–56, 180–81, 184, 241n2
Backyard / El traspatio (Carrera), 132, 219–20, 239n18, 248n12
Bajo California (Bolado), 199
Bandidos (Estrada), 149, 242n11
Barton Fink (Coen Brothers), 150
Bartra, Roger, 11–14, 23–26, 121
    See also imaginary networks of political power; post–Mexican condition
Batalla en el cielo (Reygadas), 202–7, 244n37, 246n49–50
Becker, Wolfgang, 111
    See also *Goodbye Lenin!*
Bend It like Beckham (Chadha), 194
Berman, Sabina, 85, 123–33, 144, 219, 233n3, 237n33, 238n13, 239n15–18
    See also *Entre Pancho Villa y una mujer desnuda*
Better Life, A (Weltz), 221
Bichir, Demián, 58, 84, 136–37, 213, 221, 235n20
    See also *Better Life, A*; *Bridge, The*; *Cilantro y perejil*; *Hidalgo, la historia más grande jamás contada*; *Pruebas de amor*; *Santitos*; *Sexo, pudor y lágrimas*; *Todo el poder*
Bienvenido/Welcome (Retes), 86–87, 116
Bienvenido/Welcome 2 (Retes), 236n24
Bigelow, Kathryn, 216
    See also *Hurt Locker, The*
Bissner, Joaquín, 101
    See also *Mosquita muerta*
Biutiful (González Iñarritu), 181, 193, 208
Blackout (Rigoberto Castañeda), 223
Blade 2 (del Toro), 171
Blancarte, Óscar, 233n38
    See also *Entre la tarde y la noche*
Bolado, Carlos, 169, 215–16
    See also *Bajo California*; *Colosio: el asesinato*; *Tlatelolco: verano de 68*
Bourdieu, Pierre, 7
Boym, Svetlana, 27–36
Boytler, Arcady, 26, 50, 229n8
Breillat, Catherine, 203
Bresson, Robert, 196, 198, 202, 244n38
Bridge, The (TV series), 221

Brown Bunny, The (Gallo), 204
Bueno, Juan Andrés, 236n28
    See also *Como tú me has deseado*
Bueno Camacho, René, 100
    See also, *7 mujeres, 1 homosexual y Carlos*
Buñuel, Luis, 13–16, 48–49, 123–25, 176–77, 228n9
    See also *Los olvidados*
Burning Plain, The (Arriaga), 243n23
Burns, Edward, 180, 234n7

Cabeza de Vaca (Echevarría, N.), 30, 37–41, 45, 47, 99, 229n14, 231n22–24, 234n11
Caetano, Adrián, 126
cage of melancholy, 11–12, 27
Calzonzin inspector (Arau), 17, 19
Canana Films, 207, 218, 222, 224–25
Canoa (Cazals), 105, 237n1
Cansada de besar sapos (Colón), 8, 70, 103–4
Capadocia (TV series), 225
Cardona, René, 19, 234n5
    See also *Escápate conmigo*; *La risa en vacaciones*
Carrera, Carlos, 8, 50–53, 59, 73, 76, 92–93, 110, 132, 188, 196–97, 199, 210–11, 219, 232n32–33, 235n15, 239n18, 246n48
    See also *Backyard / El traspatio*; *El crimen del padre Amaro*; *La vida conyugal*; *Sin remitente*
Carro, Nelson, 68–69
Cartas, Chava, 237n33
    See also *Amor Xtremo*
Casa de mi padre (Piedmont), 222
Castañeda, Rigoberto, 223, 241n9
    See also *Blackout*; *Kilómetro 31*
Cazals, Felipe, 13, 19, 23, 39, 65, 105, 116, 144, 151, 159–60, 176, 212–13, 229n11
    See also *Canoa*; *Chicogrande*; *Digna, hasta el último aliento*; *Su alteza serenísima*
Central do Brasil (Salles), 126
Centro de Capacitación Cinematográfica (CCC), 9
Centro Universitario de Estudios Cinematográficos (CUEC), 9
Cha Cha Cha Films, 193

Chadha, Gurinder, 194
  See also *Bend It like Beckham*
Chávez, Daniel, 146, 148, 164
Chenillo, Mariana, 224–25
  See also *Revolución*
Chicogrande (Cazals), 212, 214
Chido Guan (Arau), 18–19
Children of Heaven (Majidi), 178
Children of Men (Cuarón, A.), 155–56, 194–95
Chiles Xalapeños (Prada), 59
Christopher Columbus: The Discovery (Glen), 38, 230n19
Cidade de Deus (Meirelles), 126, 178
Cilantro y perejil (Montero), 75, 84–88, 92, 126–27, 131–32, 137, 143, 236n22
Cine Bella Época (Cine Lido), 2–3
Cine Continental, 3
Cine Ópera, 1–6
cinema of solitude (Ramírez Berg), 10–17, 42–47, 105–16, 159–68
Cinemark, 79–81, 131, 197, 209, 235n16
Cinemex, 80, 92, 197, 209–10, 235n16, 247n1
Cinépolis (Organización Ramírez), 80, 197, 209–11
Cineteca Nacional, 28, 196–98, 202, 244n36
citizenship of fear (Rotker), 133–44, 152, 174, 225
civil society, 93, 105, 134–44, 153, 175
Coen Brothers (Joel and Ethan), 150, 161, 178–79, 241n5
  See also *Barton Fink*; *Fargo*
Colón, Jorge, 8–103
  See also *Cansada de besar sapos*
Colosio: el asesinato (Bolado), 215–16
Como agua para chocolate (Arau), 3, 8, 14–33, 39, 50, 58, 60, 65, 68, 70, 78, 168, 188, 234n11, 237n30
Compañía Operadora de Teatros, S.A. (COTSA), 1, 3, 79, 80, 111, 131
Como tú me has deseado (Bueno), 236n28
Conejo en la luna (Ramírez Suárez), 151
Corazón de melón (Vélez), 237n30
Corazón marchito (Lucatero), 100
Cortés, Busi, 122, 124
  See also *El secreto de Romelia*
Costa, Pedro, 196
Crash (Figgis), 180
creative class (Florida), 86, 89–104, 120, 125, 128, 134, 137–38, 141–42, 173, 190–91, 194, 236n21
Cría cuervos (Saura), 169
Cronenberg, David, 167
  See also *Fly, The*
Cronos (del Toro), 3, 13, 30, 156, 161–71, 223, 227n8, 229n14, 234n11, 241n9
Crouching Tiger, Hidden Dragon (Lee), 179
Crowe, Cameron, 94
  See also *Say Anything*
Cuarón, Alfonso, 8, 11, 13, 24, 30, 68–78, 100–102, 110, 114, 120, 123, 127, 137, 143, 149, 153, 155–66, 182–95, 199, 208–9, 218, 227n8, 235n20, 236n23, 237n31, 244n28, 246n54
  See also *Children of Men*; *Gravity*; *Great Expectations*; *Harry Potter and the Prisoner of Azkaban*; *Little Princess, A*; *Sólo con tu pareja*; *Y tu mamá también*
Cuarón, Carlos, 193
  See also *Rudo y cursi*
Cuentos de hadas para dormir cocodrilos (Ortiz), 233n38

Danzón (Novaro), 3, 14, 22, 25, 30–37, 49–50, 53–54, 57, 59, 65, 72, 76, 109, 112, 116, 122, 162, 167, 230n15, 234n11, 248n11
Demasiado amor (Rimoch), 231n27
de Alba, Luis, 18
de Anda, Rodolfo, 76
  See also *Alta tensión*
de Fuentes, Fernando, 54, 159
  See also *Allá en el rancho grande*
de la Garza, Armida, 69, 71
de la Mora, Sergio, 22, 44, 231n27, 240n28
de la Reguera, Ana, 101–2, 204, 218–19, 225, 239n18, 248n12
  See also *Backyard / El traspatio*; *Capadocia*; *Ladies' Night*; *Por la libre*
de la Riva, José Antonio, 85, 229n15
  See also *Elisa antes del fin del mundo*; *Pueblo de madera*

de Lara, Maricarmen, 151
  See also *En el país de no pasa nada*
de Llaca, Juan Carlos, 101, 110, 117–21, 128, 150, 178–79
  See also *Así es la suerte*; *En el aire*; *Por la libre*
de Luca, Tiago, 201–4
  See also realism of the senses
de Oliveira, Manoel, 197
Déficit (García Bernal), 218
del Toro, Guillermo, 8, 11, 13, 30, 153–72, 181, 184, 193, 195, 208, 223, 240n1, 241n9, 242n15, 244n27
  See also *Blade 2*; *Cronos*; *El espinazo del diablo*; *El laberinto del fauno*; *Hellboy*; *Hellboy 2*; *Mimic*; *Pacific Rim*
Deleuze, Gilles, 22, 199, 228n6, 245n44
Deleyto, Celestino, 71–74, 91, 127, 130, 174, 181–82, 244n29
Desiertos mares (García Agraz, J.), 29–30, 53, 55
Desnudos (Gómez Vadillo), 236n26
Deutsch, Howard, 94
  See also *Pretty in Pink*
Díaz Yanes, Agustín, 183, 243n25
  See also *Nadie hablará de nosotras cuando hayamos muerto*; *Sólo quiero caminar*
Digna, hasta el último aliento (Cazals), 151
Divina confusión (Garcini), 100
Don Gato y su pandilla (Mar), 211
Doña Herlinda y su hijo (Hermosillo), 162
Dos crímenes (Sneider), 54–60, 81, 233n39
D'Lugo, Marvin, 4, 43, 159, 177
Dreyer, Carl Theodor, 196, 202, 207
  See also *Ordet*
Drama/Mex (Naranjo), 188, 218, 241n6
Dumont, Bruno, 197–98

Echeverría, Luis, 13–14, 214
Echevarría, Nicolás, 30, 37–41, 97–103
  See also *Cabeza de Vaca*; *Vivir mata*
Efectos secundarios (López), 100
Eimbcke, Fernando, 207, 224, 245n43, 246n48
  See also *Lake Tahoe*; *Revolución*; *Temporada de patos*
El anzuelo (Rimoch), 76, 78, 85

El atentado (Fons), 213–14
El búfalo de la noche (Hernández Aldana), 237n23
El bulto (Retes), 110–21, 128, 141, 146, 162, 171, 178, 234n11, 236n24
El callejón de los milagros (Fons), 47–51, 116, 126–27, 185, 188, 213–14, 247n7
El cielo dividido (Hernández, J.), 203
El coronel no tiene quien le escriba (Ripstein), 46
El crimen del padre Amaro (Carrera), 8, 47, 50–55, 60, 80, 102, 172, 188, 196, 211–12, 232n33, 239n18, 245n40
El efecto tequila (Serment), 153–54
El espinazo del diablo (del Toro), 169–71, 242n17, 244n27
El espíritu de la colmena (Erice), 169
El evangelio de las maravillas (Ripstein), 232n33
El infierno (Estrada), 153–54, 215–16, 240n37, 242n11
El jardín del edén (Novaro), 35, 123
El laberinto del fauno (del Toro), 155–56, 170–71
El lugar sin límites (Ripstein), 27, 42, 46
El pantera (TV series), 225
El secreto de Romelia (Cortés), 122
El tigre de Santa Julia (Gamboa), 57–58
Elisa antes del fin del mundo (de la Riva), 85
emotional capitalism (Illouz), 88–97
En el aire (de Llaca), 110, 117–20, 128, 172, 178
En el país de no pasa nada (de Lara), 151
En medio de la nada (Rodríguez, H.), 117
Entre la tarde y la noche (Blancarte), 233n38
Entre Pancho Villa y una mujer desnuda (Berman and Tardan), 85, 121–33, 137, 143, 185, 219, 233n3, 237n33, 238n13
Ephron, Nora, 68
  See also *Sleepless in Seattle*
Eréndira Ikukinari (Mora Catlett), 229n12
Erice, Víctor, 169, 242n15
  See also *El espíritu de la colmena*
Escalante, Amat, 196, 198, 202–3, 218, 225, 246n48
  See also *Los bastardos*; *Revolución*; *Sangre*

Escápate conmigo (Cardona), 234n5
Esmeralda, de noche vienes (Hermosillo), 67, 233n4
Esquivel, Laura, 15–25
Estas ruinas que ves (Pastor), 233n39
Estrada, Luis, 133, 144–54, 176, 178, 214–15, 233n41, 240n32, 240n34, 241n5, 242n11, 248n4
See also *Ámbar*; *Bandidos*; *El infierno*; *La ley de Herodes*; *Un mundo maravilloso*

Fargo (Coen Brothers), 150–51, 241n5
Fentanes, Óscar, 19
See also *Picoso pero sabroso*
Fernández, Emilio "El Indio", 26, 50, 148–49, 159, 181, 200, 245n41
See also *Río escondido*; *Salón México*
Fernández, Raúl, 19
See also *Lola la trailera*
festivals, 78, 156, 158–60, 178, 195–97, 203, 208, 211, 217, 236n24, 246n52
Fibra óptica (Athié), 117, 124
Figgis, Mike, 180
See also *Crash*
Figueroa, Gabriel, 200, 207, 245n41
Fly, The (Cronenberg), 167, 242n13
Flores Torres, Ángel, 237n31
See also *Piedras verdes*
Florida, Richard, 236n21
See also creative class
Fondo de Producción Cinematográfica de Calidad (FOPROCINE), 77, 92, 110
Fons, Jorge, 47–50, 105–6, 116, 148–49, 213–14, 232n30
See also *El atentado*; *El callejón de los milagros*; *Rojo amanecer*
For Greater Glory (Wright), 224
Foster, David William, 45, 85, 90–93, 127, 171, 240n35, 246n51
Four Weddings and a Funeral (Newell), 234n8
Franco, Jean, 122
Franco, Michel, 208
Fraude 2006 (Mandoki), 151, 240n36
From Prada to Nada (Gracia), 222
Fukunaga, Cary, 218
See also *Sin nombre*

Galindo, Alejandro, 1
See also *Una familia de tantas*
Galindo, Pedro, 19
See also *Pelo suelto*
Gallo, Vincent, 204
See also *Brown Bunny, The*
Gamboa, Alejandro, 57–58
See also *El tigre de Santa Julia*
García, Rodrigo, 193, 224
See also *Mother and Child*
García Agraz, Carlos, 229n9, 241n11
See also *Mi querido Tom Mix*
García Agraz, Jose Luis, 11, 26–27, 29–31, 85
See also *Desiertos mares*; *Nocaut*; *Salón México*
García Bernal, Gael, 51, 157, 172, 182, 193, 198, 204, 207, 211, 222, 224, 225
See also *Amores perros*; *Casa de mi padre*; *Déficit*; *El crimen del Padre Amaro*; *Revolución*; *Rudo y cursi*; *Y tu mama también*
García Canclini, Néstor, 69–78, 82, 95, 135–36, 139, 173
Garcini, Salvador, 100
See also *Divina confusión*
Garzón, Gustavo Adrían, 100
See also *Volverte a ver*
Gaviria, Víctor, 126
Gerber Bicecci, Alejandro, 247n5
See also *Vaho*
Gertrudis Bocanegra (Medina), 27, 39
Giménez Cacho, Daniel, 60, 68, 97, 120, 153, 186, 198, 214, 215, 238n14, 241n9
See also *American visa*; *Arráncame la vida*; *Cronos*; *El atentado*; *El infierno*; *En el aire*; *Sólo con tu pareja*; *Somos lo que hay*; *Vivir mata*; *Y tu mamá también*
Girl in Progress (Riggen), 222
Glen, John, 38
See also *Christopher Columbus: The Discovery*
global auteur (Goss), 155–59
global cinema, 155–208
Go for It (Marron), 222
Goal! Trilogy (various directors), 194

Golden Age (*Época de Oro*), 5, 10–18, 25–28, 31, 36, 42–44, 50, 54, 59, 62–63, 70–78, 94, 159, 168, 176, 181, 200, 220, 229n6, 231n27, 241n2
Gómez, Beto, 216
See also *Salvando al soldado Pérez*
Gómez Vadillo, Enrique, 236n26
See also *Desnudos*
González Iñarritu, Alejandro, 8, 149, 153, 155–60, 171–81, 184, 188, 190, 193, 195, 199, 208, 218, 240n1, 241n2
See also *21 Grams*; *Amores perros*; *Babel*; *Biutiful*
Goodbye Lenin! (Becker), 111
Goss, Brian Michael, 158
See also global auteur
Gracia, Ángel, 222
See also *From Prada to Nada*
Grau, Jorge Michel, 223, 241n9
See also *Somos lo que hay*
Gravity (Cuarón, A.), 195, 208
Great Expectations (Cuarón, A.), 184, 244n28
Greene, Doyle, 73, 229n13, 242n10
Gruener, Daniel, 127
See also *Sobrenatural*
Gutiérrez, José Luis, 224
See also *Marcelino, pan y vino*

Haddu, Miriam, 74, 85, 91, 105, 113–14, 230n20
Hannah and Her Sisters (Allen), 68
Harry Potter and the Prisoner of Azkaban (Cuarón, A.), 161, 194, 209
Harvey, David, 7, 227n4
Hayek, Salma, 46, 48, 157
See also *El callejón de los milagros*; *El coronel no tiene quien le escriba*
Hellboy (del Toro), 171, 184
Hellboy 2 (del Toro), 171
Hermosillo, Jaime Humberto, 64–67, 76–78, 87, 90, 116, 123, 149, 159, 162, 233n2–4, 241n5
See also *Doña Herlinda y su hijo*; *Esmeralda de noche vienes*; *La tarea*; *La tarea prohibida*
Hernández, Héctor, 194
See also *Los pajarracos*

Hernández, Julián, 196, 202–3, 245n46, 246n48
See also *El cielo dividido*; *Mil nubes de paz cercan el cielo amor, jamás dejarás de ser amor*
Hernández, Roberto, 117
See also *Presunto culpable*
Hernández Aldana, Jorge, 237n23
See also *El búfalo de la noche*
Herzog, Werner, 41
See also *Aguirre: The Wrath of God*
Hidalgo, la historia más grande jamás contada (Serrano), 213, 214
Higareda, Marta, 204, 218, 222
See also *Amarte duele*; *Te presento a Laura*
Hind, Emily, 54, 58, 96, 236n27, 244n31, 245n40, 248n12
Hinojosa Córdova, Lucila, 80–81, 136
Huerta, Ángel Mario, 237n29
See also *Inspiración*
Hurt Locker, The (Bigelow), 216

Ibarra, Epigmenio, 92
Illouz, Eva, 88, 91, 95, 99
See also emotional capitalism
imaginary networks of political power (Bartra), 11–14, 23, 121
Infante, Pedro, 18, 49, 67, 234n5
Inspiración (Huerta), 237n29
Instituto Mexicano de Cinematografía (IMCINE), 28, 40, 84, 92–93, 110, 127, 145, 173, 195, 210, 214, 244n35
Irwin, Robert McKee, 121
Isaac, Alberto, 126
See also *Mujeres insumisas*

Japón (Reygadas), 198–207, 244n37, 245n39, 246n49
Jonás y la ballena rosada (Valdivia), 127
Jones, Tommy Lee, 237n23
See also *Three Burials of Melquiades Estrada, The*
Joskowicz, Alfredo, 110
See also *Playa azul*

Kada Kien su karma (Serment), 153, 236n25
Kiarostami, Abbas, 196, 201
Kilbourn, Russell J. A., 118–19

Kilómetro 31 (Castañeda), 226, 241n9
Krauze, Enrique, 113, 135, 238n13
Krutnik, Frank, 67–68, 234n8

La ciudad al desnudo (Retes), 111
La ley de Herodes (Estrada), 133–35, 144–54, 175, 178, 186, 188, 233n41, 240n33, 241n5, 247n8
La misma luna (Riggen), 220–23
La mujer del puerto (Ripstein), 26–27, 37, 43, 45
La orilla de la tierra (Ortiz), 81, 127, 197, 199
La perdición de los hombres (Ripstein), 199
La reina de la noche (Ripstein), 28
La risa en vacaciones (Cardona), 19, 126
La tarea (Hermosillo), 64–68, 75–76, 87, 149, 162, 164, 233n3, 241n5
La tarea prohibida (Hermosillo), 233n4
La vida conyugal (Carrera), 76, 78, 235n15
Labios rojos (Lara), 222
Ladies' Night (Tagliavini), 70, 101–3, 225
Ladrón que roba a ladrón (Menéndez), 217
Lake Tahoe (Eimbcke), 245n43
Landy, Marcia, 39–41, 230n21, 231n23
Lara, Rafael, 222
    See also *Labios rojos*
Laresgoiti, Francisco, 223
    See also *2033*
Las buenas hierbas (Novaro), 120, 123
Leduc, Paul, 4, 159
Lee, Ang, 179
    See also *Crouching Tiger, Hidden Dragon*
Little Princess, A (Cuarón, A.), 184
Liverpool (Alonso), 245n43
Lola (Novaro), 35, 122, 242n18
Lola la trailera (Fernández, R.), 19, 248n9
Lolo (Athié), 242
Lomnitz, Claudio, 112–13, 240n33
López, Issa, 100
    See also *Efectos secundarios*
López Moctezuma, Juan, 162
    See also *Alucarda, la hija de las tinieblas*
López Portillo, José, 13, 214
Los bastardos (Escalante), 203
Los olvidados (Buñuel), 13, 49, 125
Los pajarracos (Hernández, H., and Rivera), 194
Los vuelcos del corazón (Valdez), 116–17

Lozano, Alejandro, 217
    See also *Sultanes del sur*
Lubezki, Emmanuel, 74, 84, 86, 114, 187
Lucatero, Eduardo, 100
    See also *Corazón marchito*
Lucía, Lucía (Serrano), 213
Luna, Diego, 157, 182, 193, 207, 211, 218, 222, 225
    See also *Abel; Rudo y cursi; Y tu mamá también*
Luz silenciosa (Reygadas). See *Stellet Licht*

Maciel, David, 3, 13, 105
MacLaird, Misha, 51–52, 77, 80, 85, 92–94, 145, 232n34, 240n32
Mad About You (TV series), 83–86
Mahfouz, Naguib, 42–50, 231n26, 232n30
Majidi, Majid, 178
    See also *Children of Heaven*
Mandoki, Luis, 151
    See also *Fraude 2006*
Mantarraya, 198, 202, 206–7, 245n43
Mar, Alberto, 211
    See also *Don Gato y su pandilla*
Marcelino, pan y vino (Gutiérrez), 224
Marcks, Greg, 179
    See also *11:14*
Marron, Carmen, 222
    See also *Go for It*
Marshall, Gary, 68
    See also *Pretty Woman*
Marshall, Penny, 111
    See also *Awakenings*
Martín-Barbero, Jesús, 142, 173–74, 177
Martin-Jones, David, 23, 26
Mazziotti, Nora, 78
Me quiero casar (Soler), 234n5
Mecánica nacional (Alcoriza), 13
Medem, Julio, 203
Medina, Ernesto, 27
    See also *Gertrudis Bocanegra*
Meirelles, Fernando, 126, 178
    See also *Cidade de Deus*
melodrama, 5, 16–17, 21, 26, 40–53, 62–67, 70, 75–78, 82–84, 88, 92–93, 106, 111, 115, 123, 168, 180–81, 187, 201, 220–24, 228n2, 231n27, 232n30, 235n14, 235n38, 236n26, 246n48

Méndez Esparza, Antonio, 208
Menéndez, Joe, 217
   See also *Ladrón que roba a ladrón*
Menne, Jeffrey, 8, 184
   See also Mexican *nouvelle vague*
Mexican film studies, 8–14, 226
Mexican *nouvelle vague* (Menne), 8, 184
Mexicanidad / Mexican self / Mexicanism, 4, 10–61, 73, 75, 77, 82, 97, 100, 104, 110, 126, 156–57, 171, 178, 188, 192, 199, 226
Mi querido Tom Mix (García Agraz, C.), 229n9, 242n11
Mighty Aphrodite (Allen), 100
Mil nubes de paz cercan el cielo amor, jamás dejarás de ser amor (Hernández, J.), 202–3
Mimic (del Toro), 171, 174, 184
Miravista, 101
Miroslava (Pelayo), 28, 229n11
Miss Bala (Naranjo), 208, 217–19, 223, 242n11
Mojado power (Arau), 18
Monsiváis, Carlos, 6, 12–14, 18, 26, 54, 62, 239n22
Montero, Rafael, 75, 84, 100, 235n20
   See also *Cilantro y perejil*
Mora, Carl, 4, 13, 14, 26, 28–29, 40–41, 85, 111
Mora Catlett, Juan, 28–29, 41, 229n12
   See also *Eréndira Ikukinari*; *Retorno a Aztlán*
Mosquita muerta (Bissner), 101
Mother and Child (Garcia), 193
Mujeres insumisas (Isaac), 126

Nadie hablará de nosotras cuando hayamos muerto (Díaz Yanes), 243n25
Naranjo, Gerardo, 207–8, 217–18, 221, 224–25, 237n33, 241n6, 242n11
   See also *Drama/Mex*; *Miss Bala*; *Revolución*; *Voy a explotar*
Nayar, Salim, 100
   See also *Tú te lo pierdes*
neoliberalism, 6–7, 33, 70–71, 81–83, 108–10, 112–13
Newell, Mike, 234n8
   See also *Four Weddings and a Funeral*

No eres tú, soy yo (Springall), 101, 153, 222
Noble, Andrea, 1, 4, 5, 18, 26, 50, 164, 190, 227n2, 244n26
Nocaut (García Agraz, J.), 27
Noriega, Fez, 100, 222
   See also *Te presento a Laura*
Nosotros los nobles (Alazraki), 247n4
Novaro, María, 11, 25, 31–37, 54–55, 92–93, 114, 117, 120, 122–26, 132, 218–19, 230n15, 233n37, 237n31, 238n12, 242n18
   See also *Danzón*; *El jardín del Edén*; *Esmeralda, de noche vienes*; *Las buenas hierbas*; *Lola*; *Sin dejar huella*
Novia que te vea (Schyfter), 122

Ordet (Dreyer), 202, 207, 246n53
Organización Ramírez, 111
   See also Cinépolis
Ortiz, Ignacio, 81, 127, 197, 199, 233n38
   See also *Cuentos de hadas para dormir cocodrilos*; *La orilla de la tierra*
Ozu, Yasujiro, 196, 202

Pacific Rim (del Toro), 208
Pantelion, 212, 221–22
   See also Televicine/Televisa
Pastor, Julián, 233n39
   See also *Estas ruinas que ves*
Pastorela (Portes), 194, 210–12, 221
Paz Octavio, 10–11, 227n6
Pelayo, Alejandro, 28, 229n11
   See also *Miroslava*
Pelo suelto (Galindo, P.), 19
Pereda, Nicolás, 208
Pérez Gámez, Raúl, 223
   See also *Viernes de Ánimas*
Pérez Turrent, Tomás, 2, 34
Perfume de violetas (Sistach), 219
Pick, Zuzana, 4
Picoso pero sabroso (Fentanes), 19
Piedmont, Matt, 222
   See also *Casa de mi padre*
Piedras verdes (Flores Torres), 237n31
Plá, Rodrigo, 224
   See also *Revolución*
Playa azul (Joskowicz), 110

Podalsky, Laura, 175–76, 181
Por la libre (de Llaca), 102, 120, 237n31
Portes, Emilio, 194, 210–12
　See also *Pastorela*
post–Mexican condition (Bartra), 24
Post Tenebras Lux (Reygadas), 160, 196
Prada, Fabrizio, 59
　See also *Chiles Xalapeños*
Presunto culpable (Hernández, R.), 152, 211, 215, 219, 223, 240n36, 247n2
Pretty in Pink (Deutsch), 94
Pretty Woman (Marshall, G.), 68
Principio y fin (Ripstein), 42–51, 231n27
Prior, Jorge, 235n20
　See also *Pruebas de amor*
privatization, 3, 6, 8, 28, 33–34, 62, 72, 75–104, 110–11, 173
Pruebas de amor (Prior), 235n20
Pueblo de madera (de la Riva), 229n15
Pulp Fiction (Tarantino), 93, 179

Ramírez, Arcelia, 20, 84
　See also *Cilantro y perejil*; *Como agua para chocolate*
Ramírez, Claudia, 68, 235n20
　See also *Pruebas de amor*; *Sólo con tu pareja*
Ramírez Berg, Charles, 10–14, 65, 227n6, 248n14
　See also cinema of solitude
Ramírez Suárez, Jorge, 151
　See also *Conejo en la luna*
realism of the senses, 201–2
Reality Bites (Stiller), 94, 96, 99
Reiner, Rob, 68
　See also *When Harry Met Sally*
Reservoir Dogs (Tarantino), 179
Retes, Gabriel, 86–87, 110–16, 125, 128, 144, 148–50, 176–79, 236n23–24, 238n5
　See also *Bienvenido/Welcome*; *Bienvenido/Welcome 2*; *El bulto*; *La ciudad al desnudo*; *Un dulce olor a muerte*
Retorno a Aztlán (Mora Catlett), 28–30, 38–41, 229n12
Revolución (Various directors), 224–25, 248n14

Reyes, Luis Eduardo, 100
　See also *Amor letra por letra*
Reygadas, Carlos, 8, 147, 153, 156–61, 195–208, 217–18, 224, 244n37, 245n38–47, 246n48–54
　See also *Batalla en el cielo*; *Japón*; *Post Tenebras Lux*; *Revolución*; *Stellet Licht / Luz silenciosa*
Riggen, Patricia, 157, 220–22, 224
　See also *Girl in Progress*; *La misma luna*; *Revolución*
Rimoch, Ernesto, 76, 231n27
　See also *Demasiado amor*; *El anzuelo*
Río escondido (Fernández, E.), 148–49
Ripstein, Arturo, 13, 16, 23–28, 42–53, 65, 110, 159–60, 195–99, 206, 229n8, 231n27, 232n30, 232n33
　See also *El coronel no tiene quien le escriba*; *El evangelio de las maravillas*; *El lugar sin límites*; *La mujer del puerto*; *La perdición de los hombres*; *La reina de la noche*; *Principio y fin*
Riva Palacio, Gabriel and Rodolfo, 211
　See also *Una película de huevos*
Rivera, Horacio, 194
　See also *Los pajarracos*
Rodríguez, Hugo, 117
　See also *En medio de la nada*
Rodríguez, Ismael, 18, 49, 176, 181, 234n5
　See also *A.T.M.: A toda máquina*; *Tizoc*
Rodríguez, Jesusa, 122, 238n11
Rodríguez-Hernández, Raúl, 163–66
Rojo amanecer (Fons), 105–8, 112, 126, 149
Rosas Mantecón, Ana, 81
Rosenbaum, Jonathan, 108
Rossoff, Eduardo, 27
　See also *Ave María*
Rotberg, Dana, 123–26
　See also *Ángel de fuego*
Rotker, Susana, 139
　See also citizenship of fear
Rowe, Michael, 245n47
　See also *Año bisiesto*
Rudo y cursi (Cuarón), 193–94

Saavedra Luna, Isis, 3
Sacrifice, The (Tarkovsky), 199–200

Salinas de Gortari, Carlos, 3, 7, 11, 14, 29, 92, 116, 122, 125, 133, 147, 237n29, 238n3
Salles, Walter, 126
See also *Central do Brasil*
Salón México (Fernández, E.), 26–27
Salón México (García Agraz, J.), 26–29, 31, 85
Salvando al soldado Pérez (Gómez)
Sama, Carlos, 100
See also *Sin ton ni Sonia*
Sánchez, Fernando Fabio, 178
Sánchez, Francisco, 90, 105, 152
Sánchez–Ruiz, Enrique, 234n13
Sangre (Escalante), 203
Santitos (Springall), 56–58, 188, 200
Sariñana, Carlos, 223
See also *Spam*
Sariñana, Fernando, 133–44, 153, 161, 174, 176, 225, 240n27, 241n8
See also *Amarte duele*; *Todo el poder*
Saura, Carlos, 169
See also *Cría cuervos*
Say Anything (Crowe), 94
Schaefer, Claudia, 31, 34, 164–66, 174–75, 230n16, 233n2
Schyfter, Guita, 122
See also *Novia que te vea*
Scott, Ridley, 38
See also *1492: The Conquest of Paradise*
Serment, León, 153–54, 235n25
See also *El efecto tequila*; *Kada kien su karma*
Serradilla, Ana, 103, 212, 218
See also *Cansada de besar sapos*; *Pastorela*
Serrano, Antonio, 88–97, 100, 133, 152, 174, 213, 236n26, 247n6
See also *Hidalgo, la historia más grande jamás contada*; *Lucía, Lucía*; *Sexo, pudor y lágrimas*
Sex, Lies, and Videotape (Soderbergh), 65–66, 233n2, 241n5
Sexo, pudor y lágrimas (Serrano), 88–103, 131, 137–38, 143–44, 152, 171, 174, 185–88, 198, 206, 213, 236n26, 237n29, 247n6
Shaw, Deborah, 15–16, 21, 24, 175, 187, 207, 228n1–3, 240n1, 243n22, 244n30
Shumway, David, 62–63, 76

Sin dejar huella (Novaro), 123, 219, 237n31
Sin nombre (Fukunaga), 218
Sin remitente (Carrera), 197, 246n48
Sin ton ni Sonia (Sama), 100
Sindicato de Trabajadores de la Industria Cinematográfica (STIC), 79
Sisk, Christina, 181, 244n35
Sistach, Maryse (Marisa), 123, 218–19
See also *Anoche soñé contigo*; *Perfume de violetas*
Sleepless in Seattle (Ephron), 68
Slim, Carlos, 92, 101, 117, 197
Smith, Paul Julian, 173, 184, 223, 245
Sneider, Roberto, 54–55, 59–60, 81, 233n39
See also *Arráncame la vida*; *Dos crímenes*
Sobrenatural (Gruener), 127
Soderbergh, Steven, 65–66, 149, 161, 179–80, 233n2, 241n5
See also *Sex, Lies, and Videotape*
Soler, Julián, 234n5
See also *Me quiero casar*
Sólo con tu pareja, 8, 13, 24, 30, 67–78, 83–88, 91, 98–103, 114, 120, 127, 132, 137, 143, 149, 158, 161, 162, 164, 167, 169, 173, 182–93, 206, 229n14
Sólo quiero caminar (Díaz Yanes), 243n25
Somos lo que hay (Grau), 223, 241n9
Soy tu fan (TV series), 225
Spam (Sariñana), 223
Springall, Alejandro, 56, 73, 101, 153, 222
See also *No eres tú, soy yo*; *Santitos*
Stellet Licht / Luz silenciosa (Reygadas), 207, 246n55
Stiller, Ben, 94
See also *Reality Bites*
Su alteza serenísima (Cazals), 39
Suárez, Cecilia, 89, 137, 152, 204
See also *Sexo, pudor y lágrimas*; *Todo el poder*; *Un mundo maravilloso*
Sultanes del sur (Lozano), 217
Syntek, Aleks, 93–96, 144, 236n27

Tabasco Films, 92–93, 101
Tagliavini, Gabriela, 101–3
See also *Ladies' Night*
Talancón, Ana Claudia, 51, 60, 101–2, 204, 225

See also *Arráncame la vida*; *El crimen del padre Amaro*; *Ladies' Night*; *Soy tu fan*
Tarantino, Quentin, 93, 149, 161, 179
   See also *Pulp Fiction*; *Reservoir Dogs*
Tardán, Isabel, 123–32, 219, 233n3, 237n33
   See also *Entre Pancho Villa y una mujer desnuda*
Tarkovsky, Andrei, 196, 199–200, 204
   See also *Sacrifice, The*
Tarr, Béla, 197, 201
Te presento a Laura (Noriega), 100, 104, 222
telenovelas, 18, 39, 44, 63, 78, 83, 85, 91–92, 124, 220–25, 235n14
Televicine/Televisa, 63, 67, 76–77, 84–86, 92–93, 96, 101, 111, 126, 131, 162, 212, 221, 225, 235n5, 235n19
   See also Pantelion; Videocine
Temporada de patos (Eimbcke), 246n48
Terrazas, Kyzza, 207
Third Cinema, 106–7, 140, 172
Three Burials of Melquiades Estrada, The (Jones), 243n23
Throsby, David, 196
Tierney, Dolores, 34, 149, 172–73, 180, 182, 245n41
Titán Producciones, 92–93
Tizoc (Rodriguez, I.), 18, 41
Tlatelolco: verano de 68 (Bolado), 216
Todo el poder (Sariñana, F.), 133–44, 148, 153, 174–75, 183, 196, 203, 225, 241n8
Trapero, Pablo, 127
Trevi, Gloria, 19
Tú te lo pierdes (Nayar), 100

Un dulce olor a muerte (Retes), 116
Un mundo maravilloso (Estrada), 152–53, 247n8
Una familia de tantas (Galindo, A.), 1, 5, 70
Una película de huevos (Riva Palacio), 211
Uncle Boonmee Recalls His Past Lives (Weerasethakul), 201

Vaho (Gerber Bicecci), 247n5
Valdelièvre, Christian, 92
Valdez, Mitl, 116
   See also *Los vuelcos del corazón*
Valdivia, Juan Carlos, 127, 238n14
   See also *American visa*; *Jonás y la ballena rosada*
Van Sant, Gus, 196, 201, 203, 245n44
Velazco, Salvador, 106, 148, 155
Vélez, Luis, 237n30
   See also *Corazón de melón*
Vergara, Jorge, 184, 244n27
Videocine, 101, 212
   See also Televicine/Televisa
Viernes de Ánimas (Pérez Gámez), 223
Villoro, Juan, 98–99
Vivir mata (Echevarría, N.), 97–100, 120, 236n28
Volverte a ver (Garzón), 100
Von Trier, Lars, 158, 197
Voy a explotar (Naranjo), 218, 241n6

Waldron, John, 165–66, 168, 247–48
Wayne, Mike, 106–7
Weerasethakul, Apitchapong, 198, 201
   See also *Uncle Boonmee Recalls His Past Lives*
Weltz, Chris, 221
   See also *Better Life, A*
When Harry Met Sally (Reiner), 68
Wright, Dean, 224
   See also *For Greater Glory*

Y tu mamá tambien (Cuarón, A.), 156, 159, 161, 182–95, 237n31, 244n28, 244n32

Zabé, Alexis, 207
Zavarzadeh, Mas'ud, 108–9
Zeta Producciones, 156

www.ingramcontent.com/pod-product-compliance
Lightning Source LLC
Chambersburg PA
CBHW081542300426
44116CB00015B/2724